First cut the throat of the Ter
it bleed, then plunge them in scalding
until the outside skin will c
Bib them until the meat wil
ff the feet then pen and pick
ff Here is nothing in the entra
up in pieces about an inch long
stew with the meat. Put all
the Gall, which be careful to
without breaking. Then put all
after picking from the
into a stew-pa
it was bril——
Table

Shrewsberry Cake

3 pints of flour and one of sugar
large spoonfuls of butter and 3
beat light and 3 spoonfuls of ro
H——flour and su

To make Cherry Bounce
2/3 Morells 1/3 of Black fill up
with Peach Brandy and half Spir
or West India rum let it stand 4
or 6 months, then draw of the
liquor to each gallon add one quart
of Syrup, to every p? put a pint
water put one quart to each
gallon of cherry bounce put
into the syrup whole boiling a
few cloves whip up. Whites of a
few eggs to clarify it let it boil
and 15 minutes

Mrs Galloway

To make Punch Ice
of 3 Lemons to 3

Maryland's Way

As Told by a Collection of Traditional Receipts
Selected from
Three Centuries of Maryland Cooking
With 145 Illustrations of
The Maryland Scene Which Inspired It

To My FAVORITE Aunts
FOR ALWAYS BEING SO
SUPPORTIVE . . . I'M
BRINGING A LITTLE BIT
OF MARYLAND TO YOUR
KITCHEN . . . ENJOY
Love ALWAYS
                    Jerry 5/20/94

TO

THE GENERATIONS OF MARYLAND COOKS

WHO

SINCE 1634

HAVE BLENDED THE FRUITS

OF

BAY, FIELD AND FOREST

INTO

MARYLAND'S WAY

The Hammond Harwood House
Annapolis, Maryland
1774

THE HAMMOND-HARWOOD HOUSE COOK BOOK

Mrs. Lewis R. Andrews
Mrs. J. Reaney Kelly

Published by

THE HAMMOND-HARWOOD HOUSE ASSOCIATION
Annapolis, Maryland • 1963

The Hammond-Harwood House Association, a non-profit, volunteer organization, incorporated in 1938 under the laws of the State of Maryland, administers the affairs of the museum, which is open to the public every day except Mondays and Christmas Day.

The proceeds from the sale of this book will further the preservation of Maryland's finest architectural heritage for the enjoyment and education of future generations of Americans.

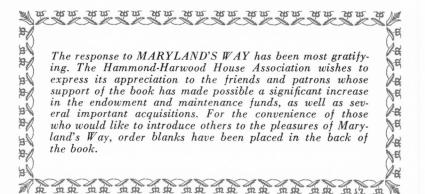

The response to MARYLAND'S WAY has been most gratifying. The Hammond-Harwood House Association wishes to express its appreciation to the friends and patrons whose support of the book has made possible a significant increase in the endowment and maintenance funds, as well as several important acquisitions. For the convenience of those who would like to introduce others to the pleasures of Maryland's Way, order blanks have been placed in the back of the book.

THIRTEENTH PRINTING

Table of Contents

William Buckland

The Preface

The Hammond-Harwood House stands as a witness for the Golden Age of Annapolis. It was designed and built in 1774 for Matthias Hammond by the brilliant colonial architect, William Buckland. The dream of a gifted architect, encouraged by a sensitive and discerning client, became a masterpiece of sophisticated beauty. The house has been designated a National Historic Landmark because of its distinction and authenticity.

The story of the preservation of the house and its opening to the public as a Maryland museum of exceptional interest and quality is one of timely and dedicated effort on the part of organizations and private citizens. St. John's College purchased the house when it was offered at auction in 1926, thus ensuring its preservation. Important restoration work was done, and the house was opened as a museum for the ensuing five years.

The Depression made it necessary to close the house and it was once more shuttered and unused. In 1938 the Federated Garden Clubs of Maryland, under the Presidency of Mrs. Harry R. Slack, were given permission to rent the house for a nominal sum. The shutters were opened and the sunlight streamed in. The cordial reception again given the old house demonstrated beyond doubt that it was a distinctive landmark with a place in the affections of the public.

Friends of the house joined together and embarked on the great undertaking which resulted in the purchase, restoration and furnishing of the museum. The group incorporated under the laws of Maryland and became the Hammond-Harwood House Association. Through the energetic leadership and vision of Mrs. Miles White of Baltimore, the Association acquired by gift or purchase an outstanding collection of furnishings of the Eighteenth Century.

The Maryland House and Garden Pilgrimage has contributed faithfully and substantially to the maintenance of the house over the years. Many individuals have given generously of their time, money and effort to constantly improve the musuem and carry on its work. The object of all is to "educate the public with respect to the historical, architectural and social significance of the Hammond-Harwood House, Annapolis, Maryland, and the period in which the house was built."

It has been interesting to observe the impact of the beautiful house on those who visit it. Perhaps in this day of too little time and too many harassments, the spirit is refreshed and calmed by a return, however brief, to the quiet dignity of an era characterized by perfect proportion, sure taste, and painstaking and creative workmanship.

No less important than the drawing room, ball room and library to the life of the times were the fine appointments of the dining room and the savoury creations of the kitchen, heart and hub of the house. It is in the spirit of perpetuating the legendary renown of this important part of Maryland life that the Hammond-Harwood House Association deems it appropriate to present this book of traditional cooking with related illustrations and anecdotes.

THE HAMMOND-HARWOOD HOUSE ASSOCIATION

Maryland's Way

THIS book of Maryland receipts is like a new grand-child. It resembles everyone who ever belonged to the family. And so it should. Its progenitors were three score or more hand-written note books, each a testament to culinary prowess and a repository of family secrets. Collected and recorded by succeeding generations of Maryland families, carefully preserved and zealously guarded through the years, they are now generously offered for you to share.

They come from houses most of which still stand where they were built two centuries and more ago, probably close to a navigable river, at peace with the ebb and flow of tidal waters and of history.

For its other inherited characteristics, the book is indebted to those Marylanders of today who share the belief of their forbears that the preparation, enjoyment and sharing of food and drink is now, as in days gone by, the cornerstone of Maryland's Way.

Sometimes the old receipts were recorded with a flourish, a splash of great capital letters across the page. Sometimes they were traced in spidery wisps which lost themselves in the crinkles of the paper. But a steady theme was traceable through the worn and faded pages, concern for the pleasure and well-being of family and friends. "What is it like?", wonders the mistress as she enters the long coveted receipt in her precious book. "Will it please? Can it be made more to our taste?" Another step is taken in the evolution of a famous Maryland dish.

The receipts which occur over and over again in these early note-books form the basis of Maryland cooking. They are found on the Eastern Shore of the Bay or in Southern Maryland, in Annapolis, Baltimore or the Western Counties, wherever people met in friendliness and exchanged their favorite dishes. It is on these receipts that the Hammond-Harwood House Cook Book has placed the greatest emphasis.

Kitchen of The Hammond-Harwood House
M. E. Warren

The Soups, the Hot Breads, the unsurpassed Fish, Crabs, Oysters and Clams from the Chesapeake Bay, the famed Diamond Back Terrapin, the barn-yard Fowl, the Game with which the region abounds; the Country Cured Hams and farm grown Meats; a great variety of Vegetables, some known to the Indians before the first settlers came, others developed from seeds the colonists brought with them; the Pickles, Preserves and Catsups, so needed when winter wrapped the scattered houses in lonely isolation; Puddings, Pies and Sweets in profusion, and of course, the Festive Bowl.

Some receipts remain in their original form, still interesting and comprehensible. Many have been tested and brought up-to-date in modern kitchens. All have been tested by time, and all suggest a land blessed by nature and thoroughly enjoyed by man. Herbs and wines have always been used with a liberal hand, imparting a certain savor and sparkle to Maryland cooking.

You will find scattered through this book, just as they were found hidden between those brittle, musty pages, some strangely spelled words, some unlikely passages, some provocative phrases. They have been put there, dear Reader, to add leaven to the "sponge" and spice to your interest.

Will you wonder why it was that Nannie Pinkney's Pudding was called "Comical"? Did she bring it to the table a sodden, heavy failure, her face so full of rueful concern that everyone burst into laughter? Or did she stir her high-spirited gaiety into her pudding to whet the appetites of the dears she wished to please.

As you follow the fortunes of Spangle in ·the Cock Fight, the thought may well linger that the fate of the defeated and ignominious bird was somehow mixed up with Dumplins.

Then there are those recurrent, telling phrases; "From dear Mrs. Chase; to the lovely Mrs. Chase". What rare gifts of grace and charm were hers that work-a-day receipts should be dispatched with such affection?

Squirrel Soup, Josey's Dick's way. Here was a man undoubtedly as handy with a gun as with a ladle.

Why did Mrs. Loockerman write "occupying the North East Turret of my Castle"? Had she been ill? Was she slowly regaining her health in spite of having taken one of the fantastic, futile cures of the time?

Then there was that wonderful day on which Miss Nancy Chase started off on her annual round of visits. "June 9th 1822, I left Annapolis. Thursday, 13th, Left Emily's for Sally." How welcome Emily's outstretched arms must have been after the cramped hours in the swaying, dusty coach. Or did she sail across the Bay on this sparkling June day, now that the season was deemed propitious for young ladies to travel. Ahead beckoned a summer gay with gossipy visits, and the promise of romance hovered on the wind.

Stop for a moment to share the good fortune of the Mistress who penned in a round, complacent hand, "1815, April 18th. Then came Kitty to serve in my kitchen· at Four Dollars per month."

You will be astonished to come upon a significant entry: "On Monday 2nd May 1762, I was married to Miss Nancy Baldwin, daughter of Thomas and Agnes Baldwin by the Rev. Mr. Barclay, Sam'l Chase." Samuel Chase, Signer of the Declaration of Independence, Patriot, Supreme Court Justice. Strange company indeed for Hartshorn Jelly and Flummery. Let us hope he had written his receipt for a Happy Life. You can never tell *what* you might find in a Cook Book.

And so, dear Reader, as you leaf through these pages, you are invited to use your imagination, your resourcefulness, your generosity, your labor, and your unfailing good-will in providing a fare of infinite goodness and variety for the health and happiness of your family and your friends.

For, after all, these are the secret ingredients in Maryland's Way.

H. A.

Soups

Soups with Oysters

Take half a gallon of oysters opened new with their liquor and stew them; when half done take a piece of butter the bigness of a teacup and rub in with as much flour as will thicken them. Season with pepper, salt and mace. Just before you take them up add half a pint of cream.

MR. PACA'S OYSTER SOUP

Mr. Paca's way

Original receipt from Miss Ann Chase's Book, dated May 8, 1811. William Paca was one of Maryland's four Signers of The Declaration of Independence.

2 tablespoons butter, 2 tablespoons finely chopped celery, 1 tablespoon finely chopped onion, 1 quart freshly shucked salt water oysters, 1 quart milk, heated; 1 tablespoon Worcestershire sauce, 1 teaspoon salt, ⅛ teaspoon cayenne, butter, paprika.

OYSTER STEW

Melt butter, add celery and onion and cook until tender. Drain oysters, add to mixture and cook slowly until edges curl slightly. Add milk and Worcestershire sauce and heat until oysters are fully curled, being careful not to over-cook. Add salt and cayenne and serve at once, placing a small lump of butter in each bowl. Garnish with paprika.

Garnett Y. Clark
South River

Anne Arundel

Oyster Fleet in Annapolis Harbor
M. E. Warren

DREDGE BOAT OYSTER CHOWDER — 3 pieces bacon, 3 potatoes, 3 cups water, 1 pint oysters and liquor, salt and pepper.

Fry out bacon which has been cut in small pieces, add peeled and cubed potatoes and water. Simmer until potatoes just start to dissolve. Mash a few against side of pot to thicken juice a bit. Add oysters with their liquor and cook until curled. Season to taste with salt and pepper.

Carroll McTavish Elder
Tred Avon River   *Talbot*

OYSTER BISQUE — 1 small onion, 2 stalks celery, 3 tablespoons butter, 3 tablespoons flour, 1 quart rich milk, ½ teaspoon mace, salt, pepper, dash of Tabasco sauce, 1 pint oysters, paprika.

In top of double-boiler cook chopped onion and celery in butter until tender. Blend in flour, then gradually stir in milk, making a smooth, thin cream sauce; add mace, salt, pepper and Tabasco. Let this steep over hot water for ½ hour or more; then purée vegetables and cream sauce in blender or put through sieve. Return to double-boiler. Put oysters and their liquor in blender or chop fine; add to cream mixture in double-boiler about 15 minutes before serving time. Adjust seasoning, heat through, and serve with a dash of paprika on each cup.

Alice's way
Tulip Hill, West River   *Anne Arundel*

CREAM OF OYSTER SOUP, ARABY — 1 quart oysters, 1 tablespoon butter, 1 tablespoon flour, 4 cups light cream, 2 tablespoons whipped cream.

Chop and scald oysters in their liquor. Blend butter and flour and add slowly to cream heated in a double-boiler. Stir until it is thickened and smooth, then add oysters and their juice. Just before serving stir in the whipped cream.

Mrs. Frank Jack Fletcher
Araby   *Charles*

Soups with Crab

Clean the Crabs and put them in water. To two **MRS. PLATER'S**
dozen put one gallon of water, and let it boil **CRAB SOUP**
down to two quarts. Thicken the soup with the
fat of the Crabs, a piece of butter rolled in flour, half a pint of cream,
pepper and salt to your taste, a little parsley, a few slips of Bacon if
you like it.

Mrs. Plater of Sotterley
Original receipt from Miss Ann Chase's Book, 1811　　　　　*Annapolis*

3

SOUTH RIVER CLUB CRAB SOUP — 2 tablespoons butter, 1½ tablespoons flour, 2½ cups milk, 1 teaspoon salt, ¼ teaspoon black pepper, ⅛ teaspoon red pepper, 1 pound crab-meat, 1 cup cream, 2 hard-boiled eggs, sherry to taste (about a wine glass).

Melt butter and stir in flour; then the milk, salt, black and red pepper. Stir until well heated and thickened. Add crabmeat and cream. Heat well. Add eggs which have been pressed through a sieve, then the sherry.

Mrs. Benjamin Watkins, III
Davidsonville   Anne Arundel

CREAM OF CRAB SOUP — A small onion, finely chopped; 1 tablespoon butter, 1 cup strong chicken stock, 1 quart rich milk, 1 tablespoon parsley, finely chopped; ½ teaspoon celery salt, ½ teaspoon mace, dash of red pepper, pepper and salt to taste, 1 pound crab meat, flour to thicken slightly, ¼ cup sherry.

Cook onion in butter until transparent; add chicken stock and slowly pour in milk. Add all seasonings, except sherry. Stir in crab meat, cleaned of all shell, and simmer 15 minutes. Make a thin paste with about 2 tablespoons flour and a little water; stir into soup to thicken slightly. Before serving, remove from heat and stir in sherry.

Mrs. R. M. Phelps
Whitehall Creek   Anne Arundel

GUMBO SOUP WITH CRAB — 2 pounds veal knuckle, 2 cups tender okra, sliced; 2 cups tomatoes, peeled and chopped; 1 small onion, chopped; 1 long red pepper, 3 sprigs parsley, 1 teaspoon salt, 3 pints water, 1 pound crab meat, 2 slices bacon.

Simmer all ingredients (except crab meat and bacon) in a covered vessel, for 2 hours. Skim as needed. Remove veal bones, parsley and red pepper. Add crab meat to soup and cook a little longer. Serve in large soup plates and garnish with chopped crisp bacon.

Mrs. Virgil Maxcy's Receipt, 1820, adapted
Mrs. Francis Markoe Dugan   Baltimore

Soups with Clams

18 hard clams, 2 tablespoons butter, 2 tablespoons **GOVERNOR'S**
minced onion, 2 stalks celery, 2 tablespoons flour, **CLAM SOUP**
3 cups rich milk, 1 teaspoon salt, white pepper.

Scrub clams clean, then scald them open. This may be done by steaming
over a little water or by placing in a warm oven for a few minutes.
Remove clam meat from shells, saving the liquor. Chop meat into small
pieces; let liquor come to a boil; add chopped clams and stew for a few
minutes. In the meantime, melt butter in a saucepan, add onion and
diced celery and cook slowly until tender. Blend in flour, add the milk
and stir until smooth. Add clam mixture and seasoning. When hot serve
in soup plates and sprinkle parsley on top.

Adapted from a book of Richard S. Mercer—April 1835
Cedar Park, West River *Anne Arundel*

4 slices salt pork or bacon, 1 large onion, 4 cups **CLAM CHOWDER**
clam juice and water, 4 cups diced raw potatoes,
1 teaspoon salt, pepper, celery salt and thyme to your taste, 3 tablespoons flour, 2 tablespoons butter, 4 cups milk, 2 cups chopped clams.

Put diced pork or bacon in a kettle and fry gently until fat is rendered,
but not crisp. Add chopped onion and fry until transparent; add combined clam liquor, water and potatoes. Cook until potatoes are done
but not soft; add seasoning. In another pan, mix flour with melted
butter, and stir over gentle heat, adding milk gradually. Add clams to
potatoes, allow mixture to come to a boil and remove from heat. Add
hot milk mixture to clams and potatoes. Mix well and serve.

Mrs. W. K. DuPont's receipt
Mrs. Harry R. Slack's Book *Baltimore*

Soups with Seafoods

CHOWDER,
A SEA DISH
¼ cup butter, ¼ cup chopped onion, ½ cup chopped leeks, 2 cups chicken stock, 1 cup chopped celery, 3 chopped carrots, 1 teaspoon salt, ⅛ teaspoon pepper, 2 bay leaves, ¼ teaspoon thyme, 1 cup flaked rock or hard-head, ⅓ cup flour, 3 cups milk, 1 cup light cream, ½ pound crab meat, 1 cup minced clams, parsley.

Melt butter in heavy stew pan, add onion and leeks and sauté until tender. Add stock, celery, carrots, salt, pepper, bay leaves, thyme and fish. Simmer for 30 minutes. Mix flour with 1 cup of milk until smooth, then pour slowly into chowder, stirring constantly. Add remaining milk and cream. Cook slowly until thickened. Add crab meat and clams. Serve in soup bowls with sea biscuit or oyster crackers. Garnish with parsley.

Miss Fanny's Receipt Book
West River   Anne Arundel

_____

SHRIMP
BISQUE
1 pound raw shrimp, ½ cup chopped onion, ½ cup chopped celery with some leaves, 1 medium carrot, sliced; 2 cups water, ¼ cup brandy, ½ cup dry white wine, 2 cups light cream, 1 tablespoon butter, 1½ teaspoons salt, dash of Tabasco, dash of nutmeg.

Wash shrimp thoroughly; put in saucepan with onion, celery, carrot and water. Bring to a boil and simmer for half an hour. Drain, reserving stock. Peel shrimp, devein and cut in pieces; combine with vegetables and stock in blender; blend until very smooth. Return to saucepan; add wine and brandy, then gradually stir in the cream. Add butter, bit by bit and season to taste; heat gently. Garnish with chopped chives. May also be served chilled. Serves 6.

Gertrude Allison Brewster
Olney Inn   Montgomery

Setting Snapper Traps   A. Aubrey Bodine

1 5-6 pound turtle, 2 stalks celery, with leaves; 2 **SNAPPER**
medium carrots, 1 large onion, 2 bay leaves, 1 **TURTLE SOUP**
garlic clove, sprigs of thyme and parsley, salt and
pepper, 4 tablespoons butter, 2 tablespoons flour, ½ cup sherry, 2 or
3 hard-boiled eggs.

Cut off the head of the turtle; stand it inverted to drain. After it has
bled well, scrub with a stiff brush. Drop into a kettle of boiling water
to cover and cook until skin and top of shell come off easily. Discard
this water and cover turtle with fresh water. Add to it the celery, carrots,
onion, bay leaves, garlic, thyme, parsley, salt and pepper to taste.
Simmer gently for 2 hours, then strain, reserving broth. Remove shells
and skin and pick out meat, being careful not to break the gall which
is in the liver. Cut meat into small pieces and brown it in butter. Blend
in flour, then the strained stock and let simmer until meat is tender.
To serve, pour into a tureen with the sherry wine and garnish with
sliced eggs. If you prefer, a few slices of egg may decorate each plate
of soup and a decanter of wine be passed at the table.

Carroll McTavish Elder
Tred Avon River   *Talbot*

---

3 terrapins, 5 to 7 inches; ½ cup butter, 1 heaping **TERRAPIN SOUP**
tablespoon flour, 1 pint milk, salt and pepper, 6
hard-boiled eggs, ½ pint thick cream; sherry wine.

Boil terrapins and pick out meat; melt butter in good size sauce pan.
Remove from fire, and blend in flour; stir in milk gradually, and season
with salt and pepper. Chop egg whites and add with terrapin meat to
milk mixture; stir in mashed yolks of eggs. Return to stove and simmer
until thickened. Last, add cream, and sherry wine to your taste.

Mrs. J. Millard Tawes
Government House   *Annapolis*

Soups with Fowl

CHICKEN SOUP AND BOILED CHICKEN — Use a good sized chicken. To 2 quarts water add giblets, feet and neck. Boil slowly for an hour, then put in chicken, 2 stalks celery and celery leaves, salt. Turn occasionally and cook gently 1½ hours. Remove chicken and strain broth.

Mix 1 heaping tablespoon flour with enough milk to make it very thin and add to soup to thicken. Then break an egg into 1 heaping table-spoon flour, and mix until very smooth; thin with milk to consistency of cream. Stir gently into soup; this will form delicate threads of dumplings. Serve first the soup; then the boiled chicken with drawn butter, surrounded with fresh garden vegetables.

Original old Howard County farm receipt
Mrs. Frederick G. Richards, Ridout House   *Annapolis*

CHICKEN GUMBO SOUP — 1 spring chicken, 1 slice of ham, heaping table-spoon of lard, 1 or 2 large tomatoes, 1 tablespoon of flour, 1 quart of okra, a little boiled rice.

Cut chicken and ham into pieces, put into saucepan with hot lard. When fried, add tomatoes, peeled and cut-up, and flour. Just cover with water and simmer slowly 1 hour. Add cut-up okra, simmer another hour. Place a little boiled rice in each soup plate with gumbo.

Mrs. Truxtun Beale's Book, 1903
Decatur House   *Washington*

CLEAR DUCK SOUP — 4 or 5 wild duck carcasses, 1 bunch of celery cut up with some leaves, several sprigs parsley, 2 cloves garlic, 1 bay leaf, a generous pinch rosemary, salt, pepper, ½ cup sherry.

Cover the broken up carcasses with water, add other ingredients except sherry and boil gently 4 hours. Strain and add sherry. Bring to boil before serving.

Barham R. Gary
Duke of Gloucester Street   *Annapolis*

1 cooked turkey carcass, 1 large onion, handful **OLD FASHIONED**
of celery tops, 1 teaspoon salt, 3 sprigs fresh thyme **TURKEY SOUP**
or ½ teaspoon dried, 3 stalks celery, 2 large car-
rots, ½ cup cooked rice, 1 cup or more diced turkey meat, white pepper.

Cover broken up carcass with water. Add onion, cut in pieces; celery
tops, salt and thyme. Boil slowly for a long time; then strain broth
and add chopped celery and carrots. Cook, uncovered, until vegetables
are tender and stock has cooked down a bit. Thicken with butter rolled
in flour, add rice and turkey meat and heat through. Season to taste
with more salt, if needed, and pepper and send to the table.

Maria T. Allison's Book, 1860 *Baltimore*

---

1 young chicken, 1 carrot, 1 large onion, 1 stalk **CURRIED**
celery, 1 sprig parsley, 2 bay leaves, 1 tablespoon **CHICKEN SOUP**
salt, pepper, fresh or dried thyme, 4 tablespoons
flour, 1 rounded teaspoon curry powder, cooked rice, lemon quarters.

Place chicken, whole or cut up, in soup kettle with coarsely sliced carrot,
onion and celery. Add parsley, bay leaves, salt, a dash of pepper and a
pinch of thyme. Cover chicken with cold water and bring to a boil.
Simmer until broth is reduced to 6 or 7 cups and chicken is very tender.
Remove chicken and pull apart into medium-sized pieces, discarding
skin and bones. Strain broth and reheat. Blend flour and curry powder
with ½ cup of broth, making a smooth paste. Add to broth in pot and
stir until soup is thickened. Adjust seasoning to taste. If too spicy add
a little milk. Pour over chicken pieces and heat. Divide chicken and
soup into 6 soup dishes. Serve with hot boiled or steamed rice to be
spooned on top of soup. Squeeze lemon over all.

Mrs. C. Victor Barry
Atholl *Anne Arundel*

Soups with Meats

MRS. OGLE'S MOCK TURTLE SOUP

"To make calves head soup in imitation of Turtle soup from Mrs. Ogle's James who learned it in the West Indies."

1 calf's head, 2 quarts cold water, a bunch of sweet herbs (such as thyme, basil, sweet marjoram and rosemary), 2 leeks, 2 teaspoons salt, 2 tablespoons flour, 2 tablespoons butter, 1 egg, ¼ teaspoon mace, ⅛ teaspoon cloves (ground), ¼ teaspoon pepper, 1 pint white or red wine, 1 tablespoon dark brown sugar, yolks of hard-boiled eggs.

When the head is cleaned and cracked, put it in a large stewpan and cover it with water. Tie up the herbs with the leeks by winding the green stems around the herbs and put them with the head. Add salt and let it simmer till done (about 3 hours) and the meat leaves the bone easy. Then strain the soup, cut the meat into little squares and return it to the stew-pan with the soup. Brown the flour very dark, add to it the butter, egg and seasoning, then the wine and sugar. Add this thickened mixture by degrees to the soup and stir well. Just before you put the soup into the tureen, have ready the number of hard-boiled yolks of eggs that you may require, generally allowing one to each plate of soup.

Original receipt from Mrs. Murray's Bride's Book, 1858
Ivy Neck, Rhode River   *Anne Arundel*

LAMB SOUP COUNTRY STYLE

Remainder of meat and bone of roast lamb, 1 large onion, 1 green pepper, 1 stalk celery with leaves, 1 small bunch parsley, several lettuce leaves, 2 large tomatoes, peeled and cut-up, 1 pound tender okra, ½ pound shelled lima beans, salt to taste.

Cover lamb bone with 2 quarts of water and boil for 30 minutes; then add onion and pepper, chopped. Add the celery, parsley and lettuce tied together. Boil another ½ hour, then put in tomatoes, sliced okra and lima beans. Boil, covered, 30 minutes longer. Remove bone and leaves and correct seasoning. Cut meat from bone and return it to the soup.

Mrs. John F. Meigs
Southgate Avenue   *Annapolis*

1 ox-tail, 1 tablespoon butter or bacon grease, 2 **OXTAIL SOUP**
onions, 1 small slice lean ham, 1 clove garlic, 1
tablespoon flour, 2 quarts beef broth, 1 bunch savory herbs (parsley,
thyme, bay leaf, summer savory), 3 cloves, 2 carrots, 1 turnip, 1 leek,
2 or 3 stalks celery, salt, pepper and cayenne, sherry or port wine.

Cut up ox-tail, separating pieces at the joints; wash thoroughly and pat
dry. Melt butter or bacon grease in heavy soup kettle, add chopped
onions, then ox-tail. Cook slowly until it begins to brown, add ham,
diced fine, and minced garlic. Continue to brown carefully, then dredge
in flour. When well browned, add beef broth, full 2 quarts if you have
it,—or half stock, half water. Add the herbs and cloves; then the carrot,
turnip, leek and celery, all cut in small pieces. Cover tightly and simmer
gently for 4 hours, seasoning with salt, pepper and cayenne to taste.
When ready to serve, add wine to your taste.

Mrs. C. H. Steele's Book, 1870 *Annapolis*

Soups with Game

1 muskrat, rich milk, 3 hard-boiled eggs, 1 table- **MUSKRAT SOUP**
spoon dry mustard, 1 tablespoon flour, black and
cayenne pepper and salt.

Cover prepared muskrat (musk removed and thoroughly washed) with
water in a pot with cover, and cook slowly until tender, adding water
if needed. Cool and take meat from bones and cut in small pieces with
scissors (it is important to use scissors). Save the pot liquor and add
an equal quantity of rich milk. Mash egg yolks, add mustard and flour
and stir liquid into it. Season to taste with black and cayenne pepper
and salt. Chop egg whites and, with the meat, add to soup after it has
boiled. Serve very hot. Sherry may be added at the table or before.

Mrs. Clifton M. Miller
Swan Cove, Chester River *Kent*

Quarter your squirrels and stew them in salted **SQUIRREL SOUP**
water. After they are done add milk, mace, salt,
pepper and butter "to yr taste".

Josey's Dick's way, original receipt
The 1814 Account Book, Harwood Papers *Annapolis*

11

Soups with Vegetables

FRESH ASPARAGUS SOUP   1 bunch fresh, green asparagus (2 pounds), 4 cups rich beef or veal broth (preferably homemade, with a hint of salt pork flavor); ½ cup mixed onion and celery, chopped, with some celery leaves; pinch of thyme, 1 tablespoon butter, 1 tablespoon flour, 1 or more cups milk, ½ cup cream, salt and pepper.

Wash asparagus, break off and reserve small, green tips. Simmer these until tender in a little milk or broth. Cut up stalks and cook slowly in meat broth with chopped onion, celery, celery tops and thyme. When tender, mash through coarse strainer. Bring again to serving heat, and thicken with flour and butter rubbed together. At the last, stir in milk, cream and tender tips which have been heated together; adjust seasoning. If soup is too thick, thin with a little milk.

Mrs. B. C. Howard's receipt, 1877
Mrs. Eric Purdon, Arden   *Anne Arundel*

FRESH GARDEN CORN CHOWDER   8 large ears of fresh, young corn; 2 quarts of milk, 4 egg yolks, 4 tablespoons butter, 2 teaspoons salt, or to taste; 2 teaspoons sugar, white pepper, chives and paprika.

Trim off carefully all silk from the corn, then grate corn off the cob into a large cooking vessel; add milk and heat slowly. Beat egg yolks and work the soft butter into them; add a little of the hot corn and milk mixture to egg and butter, beating well; then stir this into the kettle. Add salt, sugar and a dash of pepper and bring all to a simmer. Serve in large soup plates or bowls and, if you like, garnish with chopped chives and paprika. Makes 8 generous servings.

Mrs. Murray's Bride's Book, 1858
Ivy Neck, Rhode River   *Anne Arundel*

Homewood

A. Aubrey Bodine

Peel and cut into strips, 3 or 4 medium sized **CUCUMBER**
cucumbers. Scrape out the seeds and dice strips. **SOUP**
Put 1 tablespoonful of butter in pan; add 1 tablespoonful of grated onion and 3 cups of chicken broth. Add cucumbers
and simmer until they are very soft and transparent. Rub mixture
through a sieve and season with salt and pepper; add 1 cup of hot
cream. Just before serving, add 2 slightly beaten egg yolks. Heat in
double-boiler for a few minutes. Serve at once, as too long heating
hardens the egg yolks. The soup may be served cold. Sliced cucumbers
or radishes make a nice garnish.

Mrs. Charles Carroll of Homewood, Baltimore
Mrs. Gerald J. Muth
Howard

---

1 country ham bone with a little meat left on it, **KENNETH**
1 pound navy beans, ½ red pepper pod (take out **DUKE'S**
seeds), 1 large onion, 2 cups stewed tomatoes, **BEAN SOUP**
several stalks celery, salt if needed.

Cover ham bone with water, add beans which have been soaked overnight, red pepper pod, sliced onion, tomatoes and celery. Simmer until
beans are soft. This soup is better the second day. It will thicken, so
dilution may be necessary.

Kenneth Duke
St. Mary's

Soups with Vegetables

MUSHROOM SOUP 1 pint mushrooms, 1⅓ cups consomme, 2 tablespoons butter, 2 tablespoons flour, 2 cups strong, home-made chicken stock; freshly ground black pepper, salt, 1 tablespoon or more dry French Vermouth or Sherry Wine.

Clean and brush mushrooms. Simmer stems in consomme until soft, then purée stems and liquid in blender or put through sieve. Chop mushroom caps fine and sauté in butter 5 minutes. Blend in flour; add chicken stock gradually, stirring until smooth. Combine with puréed stem mixture and simmer 10 or 15 minutes. Season with pepper to taste and salt, if needed. Stir in Vermouth or Sherry.

Tulip Hill Receipts
West River   *Anne Arundel*

OKRA AND TOMATO SOUP 1 piece beef shin (about 2 pounds), 2 onions, small bunch of parsley, 2 pounds young green okra, 3 pounds red-ripe tomatoes, 1 tablespoon chopped fresh basil, 2 tablespoons flour, 1 tablespoon butter, 1 table-spoon sugar, salt and pepper to season.

Put meat in enamel soup kettle, add diced onions and parsley. Cover with water (about three quarts), then cover pot loosely and simmer on low heat for three hours or more. Strain and return broth to the pot. Take meat from the bone, cut small enough for the tureen, and return to broth in pot. Wash okra, peel tomatoes and cut all in small pieces; add to pot with basil. Continue cooking 1 hour. Rub flour into soft butter and add to soup to slightly thicken; add sugar, salt and pepper. Pour into large tureen. Serves 12.

Mrs. Frederick W. Brune's Book, 1860   *Baltimore*

Boil a small quantity of meat of any sort with some cabbage, parsley, onion, allspice, pepper and salt; throw in a slice of lean bacon, or hung beef. When well boiled, cut and throw in a good quantity of tomatoes; boil it well, and thicken it with a lump of butter rolled in flour. Then strain the whole through a sieve and serve it up with toasted bread cut in squares. **TOMATO SOUP BELVIDERE**

Original receipt of Mrs. Virgil Maxcy, 1820
Mrs. Francis Markoe Dugan   *Baltimore*

---

1 quart red ripe tomatoes (cut in pieces), 2 onions, 1 stalk celery, 1 clove of garlic, small bunch of parsley, 2 cups of beef or vegetable stock, ¼ teaspoon allspice, 1 teaspoon salt, dash of pepper, 1 teaspoon sugar, 1 tablespoon butter, 1 tablespoon flour, 1 pint thin cream, 2 slices bread, dill. **TOMATO CREAM SOUP**

Boil gently the tomatoes, onions, celery, garlic and parsley in stock for about 1 hour. Then strain the whole through a sieve which is fine enough to remove tomato seeds. Return to stove and add seasoning. Thicken with butter rolled in flour, add cream and stir well. When heated, serve with toasted bread croutons and garnish with fresh chopped dill.

Sue Cheston Hacker's Book, 1897
Cumberstone   *Anne Arundel*

---

2 pounds green peas in pods, 4 cups chicken or veal stock, 1 medium onion, a small slice bacon or ham, several lettuce leaves, a few spinach leaves cut small (for color), a sprig of mint, salt, pepper, sugar, 1 cup cream, if desired. **GREEN PEAS SOUP**

In shelling peas, divide large and small, reserving ½ cup or more of the small peas. Put remaining peas on to cook in stock with the sliced onion, bacon or ham slice, lettuce, spinach and mint. Stew until peas are quite soft. Remove bacon or ham and mint sprig; then pulp peas and vegetables by pressing them through a coarse sieve or colander with the stock. Reheat soup over boiling water and add whole, small peas which have been cooked just tender in a little water or broth. Season soup with salt, pepper and a pinch of sugar to 'relish' properly. If you wish it, stir in the cream carefully just before serving.

Mrs. McBlair's way
Maria T. Allison's Book, 1860   *Baltimore*

SPRING ONION SOUP 2 cups cut-up small spring onions with tender green tops, 3 cups strong chicken stock, 3 tablespoons butter, 1 tablespoon flour, salt and white pepper to taste, 1½ cups cream.

Simmer onions in chicken stock for about 15 minutes or until soft. Melt butter, stir in flour, salt, pepper and cream. When smooth, add the onion and stock mixture, slowly, stirring until well blended and hot. Serve in cream soup cups. The green and yellow onion bits are garnish enough. Serves 6.

Mrs. J. Reaney Kelly
Conduit Street   *Annapolis*

POTATO SOUP 4 cups peeled, cubed potatoes; 1 cup sliced onion, ½ green pepper, 3 cups water, a ham bone (a bit of meat left on), 1 teaspoon celery salt, 1½ cups milk, ½ cup cream, dash of red pepper, black pepper, salt to taste, 3 tablespoons butter, parsley, paprika.
Boil potatoes, onion and diced green pepper in water with ham bone. When vegetables are very tender, remove ham bone and press all through a colander; add celery salt, heated milk, cream, seasoning and butter. When hot and blended serve with parsley leaf and dash of paprika on each serving.

Miss Adelaide Colhoun
Ivy Neck, Rhode River   *Anne Arundel*

COLD VEGETABLE CREAM 1 cup diced potatoes, ¼ cup minced scallions, 1 cup raw green peas, 2 cups chicken broth, ⅛ teaspoon celery salt, ⅛ teaspoon curry powder, ½ cup heavy cream.

The day before using, place the vegetables in the broth to cook and when it boils, cover and simmer until vegetables are soft. Cool, add celery salt and curry powder with salt to taste. Press through strainer to purée or run in blender until smooth. Add cream and chill.

Mrs. Harry R. Slack's Book
Bishop's Road   *Baltimore*

1 large beef shank with meat (3-4 pounds), 2   **MRS. WATKIN'S**
cups peeled, chopped ripe tomatoes; 2 large   **VEGETABLE**
onions, minced; 2 cups lima beans, 2 cups fresh   **SOUP**
corn, 2 cups chopped cabbage, 2 cups cubed po-
tatoes, 1 sliced turnip, 1 cubed carrot, 1 sprig each thyme and parsley
tied together, salt, black pepper, cracked red pepper, 1 tablespoon
brown sugar.

Wash a beef shank, break the bone and put in large pot of cold water.
Bring to boil and simmer for several hours; skim off grease and add
vegetables and seasonings. Cook another hour, then remove bone and
meat. Shred meat and return to pot. Serve in large soup plates for a
hearty, winter's day meal.

Mrs. Spencer Watkin's receipt
Up-to-Date Cook Book, 1897   *Montgomery*

---

1 bunch watercress, 1 small cucumber, 3 slices   **CLEAR**
Spanish onion (or 1 white onion), 3 cups chicken **WATERCRESS**
stock or broth, 1 curl lemon rind, pinch English   **SOUP**
mustard, salt and pepper.

Add raw vegetables which have been cut in pieces to stock and cook
until soft. Pour into blender or put through food mill or fine sieve to
purée. Add lemon rind, mustard, salt and pepper. Serves 4-6. May be
served hot or cold.

Mrs. Eliot H. Bryant
Shipwright Street   *Annapolis*

---

*Chilled soups were introduced into England by the French aristocrats
in 1789 and soon found their way to Maryland tables.*

Breads

Amos Mill, Harford County

A. Aubrey Bodine

Ivy Neck

Light Bread and Rolls

4½ pints flour (9 cups), 3 tablespoons salt, 4½ tablespoons sugar, 3 tablespoons lard, 2 packages dry yeast, 3¼ cups warm water.

IVY NECK LIGHT BREAD

Sift together flour, salt and sugar, then rub in lard. Dissolve yeast in 1 cup of the warm water, add to flour. Work into stiff dough with remaining water added gradually, and knead until smooth. Cover and put in a warm place to rise until double in bulk. This amount will make four loaves in bread pans, or the same dough can be made into rolls. After placing in greased pans, let rise again until light, and bake in a moderately hot oven (about 400°) until nice and brown. This bread freezes beautifully.

Miss Anne Cheston Murray
Ivy Neck, Rhode River

Anne Arundel

Some of the Ivy Neck light bread dough can be used for Generals, so called because the receipt was given to our family by a relative of George Washington and spoken of as "My cousin General Washington's favourite breakfast cakes."

GENERALS

Roll out dough until about ½ inch thick. Cut out Generals with a biscuit cutter. Place on warm, greased griddle, let rise until double in bulk. Bake on griddle over not too hot a fire; when brown turn and brown on other side.

Miss Anne Cheston Murray
Ivy Neck, Rhode River

Anne Arundel

Sippets are evenly cut oblongs of bread, delicately toasted. They may be served as dry toast or with broiled birds, oysters or soups.

SIPPETS

Up-To-Date Cook Book, 1897
St. John's Church

Montgomery

19

FRIED BREAD   Pinch off pieces of bread dough when it has risen once, and form into balls the size of a walnut. Let rise again until double in size. Then fry in about ¾ inch of lard melted and medium hot. Watch carefully as they burn easily. Turn them over and around until brown on all sides. Serve with butter. This fried dough has various names, Holy Pokes, Huff-Puffs, Baptist Bread, Fol-Dols, and Yankee Notions are a few.

Mrs. Sidney Sappington
Briar-Cliff-on-Severn   *Anne Arundel*

HOT ROLLS   2 tablespoons shortening, 2 tablespoons sugar, 3 teaspoons salt, 2 cups water, 1 yeast cake, ¼ cup tepid water, 6 cups flour (unsifted).

Put shortening, sugar and salt in a 2-quart bowl and pour 1 cup of boiling water over to dissolve; then add 1 cup cold water to cool mixture. Dissolve yeast cake in less than ¼ cup tepid water and add. Stir in flour, a little at a time, sifting as you add it. This will soon be more than can be handled with a spoon, so use your hand. It may take a little more flour or a little less, but it is important not to have the dough too stiff; more moist than dry. When flour has been thoroughly worked in, let dough stand in bowl with a plate over it. It should rise for about 4 hours. Knead down, make into rolls and let rise again in greased pans for about another 3 to 4 hours. Bake in a preheated 450° oven for 15 to 20 minutes. This makes about 2 dozen large rolls or 2½ dozen small rolls.

Mrs. Henry M. Murray
Cumberstone   *Anne Arundel*

JUBILEE ROLLS   ½ cup sugar (or ¼ cup, according to your taste), ¾ cup shortening, 1¼ cups hot water, 1 yeast cake, 4 tablespoons lukewarm water, 1 teaspoon sugar, 2 eggs, 5 cups unsifted flour, 2 teaspoons salt.

Stir together sugar and shortening; add hot water and allow to stand until tepid. Dissolve yeast in lukewarm water to which the teaspoon of sugar has been added. Add to first mixture, then add beaten eggs, flour and salt. Stir all together, cover and place in ice-box for at least 1½ hours before making into shapes. Allow another 2 hours or so for the rolls to become light. Brush tops with melted butter before baking. Bake in 350° oven for 15 to 20 minutes.

Mrs. Felix Johnson
Jubilee Farm, Potomac River   *St. Mary's*

POTATO ROLLS

2 yeast cakes, ¼ cup lukewarm water, 1 teaspoon sugar, 3 eggs, 2 cups sweet milk, 2 cups mashed potatoes, 1 cup shortening, ½ cup sugar, 3 teaspoons salt, about 8 cups flour.

Dissolve yeast in warm water with a teaspoon of sugar. Beat eggs until light and lemon colored, then add milk which has been scalded, mashed potatoes, shortening, sugar and salt. When mixture cools a little, add softened yeast. Work in sufficient flour to make a stiff batter (not too stiff), about 4 cups. Put in greased bowl and let rise until light, then add flour to make dough stiff, about 4 more cups. Let rise again, shape into rolls and place in greased pans. When rolls are double in size, bake 15 or 20 minutes in a 350° oven. Butter the tops before and after baking. Freeze well.

Tulip Hill Receipts
West River   *Anne Arundel*

SALT STICKS

1 cake yeast, 2 cups lukewarm water, 1 teaspoon salt, ½ cup sugar, 1 egg, 7 cups flour, 3 tablespoons melted shortening, 1 egg for brushing, caraway seeds and salt.

Dissolve yeast in warm water, add salt, sugar, well-beaten egg and 4 cups flour. Beat mixture well, then add melted shortening; beat again and add 3 cups flour. Cover and let rise to double its bulk. Punch down. This dough may be kept several days in refrigerator. Grease top and cover tightly. To shape salt sticks, make dough into smooth balls about 2 inches in diameter; let stand ½ hour; stretch each into a triangle and roll, pressing down point firmly; stretch ends; brush sticks with whole beaten egg. Sprinkle with caraway seeds and salt. Let rise again (double bulk). Bake in 425° oven. Makes about 4 dozen.

Mrs. W. J. Nolan   *Prince George's*

Muffins

BUTTERMILK MUFFINS

1 quart buttermilk, 2 eggs, 1 tablespoon sugar, 4 cups sifted flour, 2 tablespoons cornmeal, 1 teaspoon salt, 1 teaspoon soda.

Stir milk into eggs beaten with sugar; add flour, cornmeal, salt and soda which have been sifted together. Beat hard and bake in hot oven (400°) for about 20 minutes in greased muffin tins.

Matilda Chase's way, adapted
Miss Ann Chase's Book, 1811   *Annapolis*

CORNMEAL MUFFINS

1¼ cups cornmeal, sifted; ½ teaspoon salt, ¼ cup flour, ¼ teaspoon soda, 1½ teaspoons baking powder, 1 egg, 1 cup buttermilk, 2 tablespoons shortening.

Sift and mix dry ingredients. Beat egg slightly and add buttermilk and melted shortening. Add liquids to dry ingredients, mixing with folding motion, enough to moisten meal. Pour at once into hot muffin tins. Bake in 450° oven for 20 minutes. Makes 8 to 10 muffins. Note: If buttermilk is not available, use 1 cup sweet milk, with 1 tablespoon of either lemon juice or vinegar.

The Old Wye Mill   *Talbot*

The site of The Old Wye Mill was patented for mill purposes in 1664. It is said to be the oldest commercial enterprise on the Eastern Shore of Maryland still in operation. Since its beginning only seven families have owned and operated it, grinding meal with its slow-moving water-driven cool mill stones. The Mill belongs to the Society for the Preservation of Maryland Antiquities.

Frances Townley Chase Loockerman

Muffins

3 cups sifted flour, 1 teaspoon salt, 1 teaspoon **GOOD MORNING**
sugar, 1 tablespoon melted butter, ¼ cake yeast, 2 **MUFFINS**
eggs, 2 cups milk.

Make a sponge by mixing together the flour, salt, sugar, butter and
yeast (which has been dissolved in a little warm water); when blended
add well-beaten eggs and milk, which should be lukewarm. Set the
sponge to rise in a warm place over night. In the morning, do not stir,
but carefully place tablespoonfuls of the light dough into warm, well-
greased muffin tins. Let them stand on the hearth or in a warm
draftless place for ten minutes, until quite light, then bake in a brisk
oven, 400°, 15 to 20 minutes and serve hot for breakfast. These should
be light and flaky.

Adapted from
Mrs. F. T. Loockerman's Book, 1835
"Occupying the North East Turret of my Castle." *Annapolis*

⅓ cup butter, ¼ cup sugar, 1 egg, ¾ cup milk, 2 **BERRY MUFFINS**
teaspoons baking powder, 1½ cups flour, pinch of
salt, huckleberries.

Cream butter and sugar. Add egg slightly beaten, milk and dry ingredients sifted together. Fill greased tins half full with batter. Put in
1 teaspoon berries. Cover berries with 2 teaspoons batter. Berries will
never go to bottom. Bake in moderate oven about 20 minutes.

Mrs. Clifton B. Cates
South River *Anne Arundel*

LAPLANDERS   2 cups milk, 1 tablespoon butter, pinch of salt, 2 eggs, 2 cups flour.

Heat milk to nearly, but not quite, boiling. Stir in butter and salt. Beat yolks of eggs and stir them into milk. Stir milk gradually into flour, making a smooth batter, and lastly fold in egg whites, beaten stiff. Have gem pans hissing hot; pour in batter, and bake until brown, about 20 to 30 minutes in a quick oven.

Mrs. McBlair's receipt
Maria T. Allison's Book, 1860   *Baltimore*

POPOVERS   2 large eggs (or 3 small), 1½ cups flour, 1½ cups milk, 1 tablespoon melted butter, ½ teaspoon salt.

Beat eggs very light, add flour and milk alternately, beating hard, then melted butter and salt. Grease tins, place in hot oven until well heated, then remove and fill half full of batter. Bake in a quick oven (450°) for 20 minutes, then reduce heat to 350° for about 15 minutes. Very nice. Makes 12 muffins.

Wye House, September 18, 1904   *Talbot*

CRUMPETS   1 pint milk, 1 egg, 1 teaspoon salt, about 3 cups flour, 4 tablespoons butter, ½ cake yeast.

Scald milk and let stand until lukewarm; add beaten egg, then add salt and flour and beat vigorously. Add melted butter and yeast, softened in a little tepid water. Beat again, cover and stand in a warm place until very light. Grease muffin rings and place them on a hot griddle. Fill each ring half full of batter; it should not be too stiff. Bake until brown on one side, then turn and brown on the other. Take from fire and set aside. When ready to use, split and toast the crumpets. Butter them nicely, and serve quickly on a hot plate.

Hester Ann Harwood's Book, 1848
Hammond-Harwood House   *Annapolis*

Biscuits

2 cups flour, 2 teaspoons baking powder, 1 tea- **HOT BISCUITS**
spoon salt, 1 tablespoon sugar, ⅓ cup shortening,
½ cup milk (or enough to put dough together).

Sift dry ingredients into a bowl. Cut in shortening, then add milk and
mix well together. Roll dough, cut out biscuits and bake in 400° oven
until browned.

Mrs. Floyd Lankford
Hawthorne Ridge
                                                    Anne Arundel

---

4 cups flour, heaping; 2 tablespoons shortening, 1 **BUTTERMILK**
teaspoon baking powder, 1 teaspoon soda, 1 table- **BISCUITS**
spoon sugar, a little salt, 1 egg, 1 pint buttermilk.

Work flour and shortening together as for pie crust, then add baking
powder, soda, sugar, salt, beaten egg, and last of all, the buttermilk.
Roll out an inch thick, cut with biscuit cutter, and bake in a hot oven.

Mrs. Page Bowie
Bay Ridge Farm
                                                    Anne Arundel

---

2 cups flour, 3 teaspoons baking powder, ½ tea- **ROSEMARY**
spoon salt, ⅓ cup sugar, ⅓ cup shortening, ¼ **BISCUIT**
cup finely chopped rosemary leaves (use scissors),
1 cup milk.

Sift flour, baking powder, salt and sugar together. Cut in shortening and
add rosemary. If dried leaves are used, they should be first soaked in
hot milk until soft, and drained. Add milk and mix. Roll out dough to
½ inch thick, cut in blocks and bake in 375° oven until browned.

Mrs. James W. Webb
Scaffold Creek
                                                    Anne Arundel

Maryland Beaten Biscuits

4 cups flour, 1 tablespoon lard, ½ tablespoon salt,   **MISS JULIA'S**
water.   **BEATEN BISCUIT**

Mix flour, lard and salt; then add water to make a very stiff dough. Knead it with the hands until pliable and smooth. Continue to knead until it pops with every pressure of the hand. It takes 20 minutes to half an hour. When it pops this is the test of its lightness. Then make balls of the dough about the size of a small egg. Flatten them on the board with the rolling pin, prick them in the center with a fork and bake in a quick oven, 400°, for 20 minutes to ½ hour. When the edges are hard, they are done, otherwise do not take from the oven or they will be undone and unwholesome.

Miss Julia Loker   *St. Mary's*

---

7 cups flour, ¾ cup lard, ½ tablespoon salt, ½   **MARYLAND**
tablespoon sugar, ½ teaspoon baking powder, 1½   **BISCUITS**
cups water.

Mix ingredients together and beat dough with hammer for 30 minutes. Form into small biscuits and prick top with fork. Bake 20-25 minutes in 500° oven. There are various ways of beating biscuits. You may use a sad iron, flat of an axe, or the heel of your hand. You must beat until dough blisters and is smooth looking. Beat at least 30 minutes, and 45 minutes for company.

Mrs. Donald E. Jefferson   *Caroline*

---

4 cups flour, 2 teaspoons (scant) baking powder,   **VANDALUSIA**
½ teaspoon salt, 2 tablespoons lard, cold water or   **BISCUIT**
milk (about 1 to 1¼ cups).

Sift flour, baking powder and salt into a bowl. Mix in shortening, then add cold water or milk, enough to make a rather stiff dough. Work hard until it is smooth and supple. Roll out and cut out biscuits. Bake in a moderate oven (375°) until golden brown, about 25 minutes. The biscuits will be crispy outside and soft inside. This receipt makes about 2 dozen medium sized.

Mrs. George S. Radford
Carvel Hall   *Annapolis*

Biscuits

Miss Anne Murray, Wearing Heirloom Quaker Dress

THIN WAFER
BISCUITS
2 cups flour, 5 level tablespoons lard, 1½ teaspoons salt, ½ cup plus 2 tablespoons water.

Mix and knead well. Roll out very thin, cut with cake cutter and bake in hot oven, 450°, until a light golden color, about 7 to 10 minutes. Serve hot from the oven in a linen napkin.

Old Ivy Neck receipt
Miss Anne Cheston Murray   Anne Arundel

MOONSHINES
1 egg, 2 tablespoons lard, 2 tablespoons butter, ¼ cup milk, 2 cups flour, ½ teaspoon baking powder, ½ teaspoon salt, 1 egg white, sesame seeds.

Beat egg until light; melt shortening and add to milk. Sift flour with baking powder and salt, and add to egg alternately with milk and shortening. Work well and chill dough. Break off a small amount of dough at a time and roll thin as your finger nail. Sprinkle with a little dry flour as you work which will make them easier to handle and crisp. Cut out with biscuit cutter, brush with unbeaten egg white and sprinkle with sesame seeds. Bake quickly in a 400° oven from 8 to 10 minutes, watching carefully. Serve with soup or sherry.

Randall receipt
Mrs. F. F. Beirne   Baltimore

28

Corn Breads

1 cup corn meal, 1 cup cold water, 3 cups boiling water, 1½ teaspoons salt.   **FRIED MUSH**

Mix corn meal with cold water. Add to boiling, salted water. Cover, cook over boiling water for half an hour, stirring occasionally. Pour into shallow dish about ½-inch thick, and put aside in cold place to set. Cut mush into diamond shaped pieces or rounds (a cookie cutter may be used). Sprinkle lightly with flour and pan fry in a small amount of hot shortening until golden brown on both sides. An excellent garnish for a platter of Maryland Fried Chicken.

Judge Benjamin Watkins' family receipt
The Locusts   *Anne Arundel*

---

2 cups yellow or white corn meal, 1 cup flour, 3 teaspoons baking powder, scant teaspoon salt, 2 eggs, 2 cups milk.   **CORN BREAD ELIZABETH**

Sift together corn meal, flour, baking powder and salt. Beat eggs, add milk and then beat into corn meal mixture. Pour into greased baking pan and bake at 450° for about 15 minutes or until brown.

Mrs. Charles Greenwell
Foxes Point   *St. Mary's*

---

2 cups white waterground cornmeal, 3 cups boiling water, 1 teaspoon salt, 1 teaspoon bacon fat.   **SCRATCH BACKS**

Scald cornmeal with boiling water, add salt and bacon fat. The batter should be consistency which sticks to wooden spoon and raises points on top as you plop a spoonful on greased pan. Bake in 400° oven for 30 to 35 minutes. Then slip under broiler to brown rough top. Result is nutty, crusty outside and soft cooked meal inside. Serve hot with butter. These are particularly good served in place of bread with wild duck or game. It is a very old family receipt. 10 portions.

Mrs. Beverley C. Compton
Ruxton   *Baltimore*

HOE CAKE   2 cups white cornmeal, 1 cup boiling water, 3 tablespoons butter, 1 teaspoon salt, butter or bacon grease.

Wet cornmeal with boiling water and stir in butter and salt. Let cool. Add more boiling water if the consistency is too thick (perhaps another cup). Heat ¼ inch of butter or bacon grease in iron skillet. Spread cornmeal mixture about ⅜ of an inch thick. Cook on top of stove over medium flame until browned on the bottom—about 10 minutes. Then put under broiler until the top surface is browned. Cut in pie shape pieces and serve immediately.

Mrs. Byam K. Stevens
North West Point Farm   *Queen Anne's*

JOHNNY CAKE   1 egg, 1¼ cups sweet milk, ½ teaspoon salt, 1 cup coarse white corn meal, 2 tablespoons each butter and bacon grease.

Break egg into mixing bowl and beat light. Add milk and salt, then stir in corn meal and mix until thoroughly blended. Put butter and bacon grease in an 8 by 10 baking pan and let it melt while oven is heating. When melted, drain butter into batter, leaving enough in pan to grease it well. Stir up batter and pour into pan. Bake in a 400° oven for 45 minutes or until brown and crisp. Serves 4. If 2 pans are needed, double all ingredients except the egg, and one will suffice.

Miss Agnes Tilghman
Gross' Coate, Wye River   *Talbot*

CORN WAFERS   2 cups yellow corn meal, 1 cup boiling water, 1 teaspoon salt, 3 tablespoons butter.

Wet corn meal with boiling water to which salt has been added. Add butter and let cool. Then add enough boiling water to allow mixture just to pour off spoon—about ¾ of a cup. Drop generous teaspoonfuls of mixture far apart on well-buttered cookie sheet. Slap bottom of cookie sheet until mixture spreads. Brush with butter when half baked. Bake until well browned, 12 to 15 minutes, in a 375° oven. Serve hot. May be kept in canister and reheated when ready to serve.

Mrs. Byam K. Stevens
North West Point Farm   *Queen Anne's*

2 eggs, ½ cup flour, 1½ cups cornmeal, 4 tea- **ATHOLL**
spoons baking powder, 1 teaspoon salt, 1 cup milk, **CORN STICKS**
3 tablespoons butter.

Beat eggs very light. Sift flour, cornmeal, baking powder and salt together and add, alternately with milk, to beaten eggs. Add melted butter. Grease iron corn stick molds well and put in oven to become hot. Then drop in the batter to fill molds. Bake in a 425° oven for 20 or 25 minutes until brown. If the batter is more than enough for your number of molds, thin it with a little milk and have delicious corn griddle cakes for breakfast.

Miss Fanny's Receipt Book
West River
Anne Arundel

¼ teaspoon salt, ¼ teaspoon soda, 1 cup corn- **CORNMEAL**
meal, 4 tablespoons shortening, 1 cup buttermilk, **STICKS**
2 tablespoons white corn syrup.

Add salt and soda to the cornmeal. Add melted shortening and stir. Then stir in buttermilk and syrup. Pour into greased iron cornstick pan. Bake in hot oven for half an hour. Makes six sticks.

The Old Wye Mill
Talbot

---

1 cup corn meal, ⅓ cup flour, 2 tablespoons sugar, **SPIDER**
1 teaspoon salt, 2 teaspoons baking powder, 1 **CORN BREAD**
egg, 1 cup milk, ¼ cup butter, ¾ cup milk.

Sift dry ingredients together. Beat egg and add to 1 cup milk. Mix into corn meal mixture. Turn into hot spider or iron skillet in which butter has been melted, then pour the ¾ cup milk over batter. Do not stir. Bake at 350° for about 30 minutes.

Mrs. J. Reaney Kelly
Conduit Street
Annapolis

AUNTIE'S SPOON BREAD 1½ to 2 cups of milk, 1 cup cooked grits, 4 tablespoons butter, 1 cup waterground corn meal, 2 teaspoons baking powder, 1 teaspoon salt, 1 tablespoon sugar, 2 eggs.

Pour some milk over grits, add melted butter and stir well to remove all lumps. Add corn meal, baking powder, salt, sugar and well beaten eggs. Then thin batter with milk to consistency of thin pancake batter. Bake in well greased baking dish about 45 minutes in 375° oven, until brown and well set.

Mrs. Walton Hopkins
Maryland Avenue   *Annapolis*

SOUTHERN SPOON BREAD 1 cup waterground corn meal, 2 cups cold water, butter size of large egg, 1 scant teaspoon salt, 1 cup very rich milk or cream, 3 eggs.

Put corn meal and water in top of double-boiler over boiling water. Stir until meal is scalded and quite stiff. Stir butter into hot meal until melted, then salt and milk or cream. Beat eggs until very light. When meal mixture is cool, beat in the eggs. Bake in a well greased baking dish in 350° oven for about 45 minutes or until slightly browned and firm.

Mrs. E. Churchill Murray
West River   *Anne Arundel*

RIVERSIDE FARM BATTER BREAD 2 cups milk, 2 tablespoons butter, 2 eggs, 1 tablespoon sugar, 1 teaspoon salt, 1 tablespoon flour, ⅓ cup yellow corn meal, 1 cup cold boiled rice.

Heat milk and butter together. Beat eggs and mix in remaining ingredients; then stir milk slowly into mixture. Stir and cook over low heat (or in double boiler) until it thickens. Transfer to buttered baking dish and bake in 375° oven until it browns, about 40 minutes. This is an old Cecil County receipt.

Mrs. Dorsey Hines
Chester River   *Kent*

Griddle Cakes and Pancakes

½ cake of yeast, 2 cups buckwheat flour, ½ cup flour, ¼ teaspoon salt, 1 egg, well beaten; 2 tablespoons shortening, 1 large tablespoon molasses, ½ teaspoon soda, dissolved in a little milk.

OLD FASHIONED BUCKWHEAT CAKES

At night dissolve yeast cake in a little lukewarm water. Add to the buckwheat, flour and salt. Mix quite stiff with warm water. Let rise until morning. Add egg, melted shortening and molasses, then soda. To this add enough milk to make a rather stiff batter. Cook on hot griddle. Serves 3 or 4 people.

Mrs. Robert L. Burwell
Hanover Street

Annapolis

---

1 yeast cake, 2 cups warm water, 2 cups milk, 3 cups buckwheat flour, 1 cup flour, 1 teaspoon salt, ¼ teaspoon soda, milk, 2 tablespoons molasses.

SOUTH RIVER CLUB BUCKWHEAT CAKES

Dissolve yeast cake in 1 cup warm water. Add milk diluted with 1 cup warm water. Beat mixture well. Put buckwheat, flour and salt in a pitcher or bowl and pour liquids on flour, stirring all the while. Set to rise over night. It may be set outside in the cold. In the morning add soda dissolved in a little milk and the molasses to batter. Buckwheat cake batter should not be too thin. Bake on hot griddle, preferably a soapstone one.

Gertrude's way
South River Club

Anne Arundel

South River Club

BUTTERMILK GRIDDLE CAKES   2 cups flour, 1 teaspoon soda, 1 teaspoon salt, 1 egg, 1 cup cream, 2 cups buttermilk.

Sift flour with soda and salt. Beat egg well and add gradually to flour with cream and buttermilk, making a smooth, thin batter. Spoon onto hot, sparsely greased griddle and brown on both sides. A very delicate pancake.

Miss Adelaide Colhoun
Ivy Neck, Rhode River   *Anne Arundel*

CORN CAKES   2 eggs, 1½ cups milk, ¾ cup corn meal, 1 teaspoon salt, 1 tablespoon sugar, 2 teaspoons baking powder, 2 tablespoons melted butter.

Beat eggs well, then stir in milk. Mix dry ingredients and sift into milk mixture. Add melted butter and beat together. Makes a very thin batter. Bake on a hot well-greased griddle.

Mrs. Edwin Warfield, Jr.
Oakdale Farms   *Howard*

SHROVE TUESDAY 'PANNE' CAKES   4 eggs, 3 cups rich milk, ¼ teaspoon salt, 1 heaping cup sifted flour.

Beat eggs until very light. Add milk and salt, then flour and beat until smooth. The batter will be very thin. Have a medium-sized frying pan well greased with butter and lard mixed. Pour some batter into hot pan and shake or turn so that batter thinly covers the bottom. Cook quickly and turn to brown other side. Butter each cake as it is removed from pan and add sifted powdered sugar, if desired, or mixed cinnamon and sugar. Each cake may be rolled and placed on a hot dish in a warm oven until all are cooked; or they may be piled one on top of the other and, when all are made, cut in wedges —pie fashion—to be served.

In old inventories, a cooking pan was often spelled 'pann' or 'panne.'

Mrs. William P. C. Lippitt
Cumberstone   *Anne Arundel*

1 cup flour, 1 whole egg and 2 yolks, a pinch of salt, 2 cups milk, 3 tablespoons melted butter. If for dessert, add 2 tablespoons sugar and small glass of brandy or rum.

FRENCH PANCAKES

Put flour in mixing bowl and break egg into center; add 2 yolks and salt, also sugar, if used. Pour in a little milk and mix with a fork. (If brandy or rum is used, mix in at this time.) Add rest of milk and beat until smooth; add butter and beat. Cover batter and set aside for 2 hours (not in ice-box). It should be consistency of whipping cream. If too thick, add more milk. To cook, melt additional butter (about 3 tablespoons) and put in a cup or small pitcher. Heat a 6 inch skillet and pour in a little butter. Turn skillet so that butter covers bottom and sides. When hot, ladle just enough batter to cover the bottom. Cook and turn. Pancakes may be rolled with various fillings or, for dessert, served with a fruit sauce or powdered sugar and wine.

Mrs. Frank Jack Fletcher
Araby

Charles

Waffles

3 eggs, 2 cups sour milk, 2 cups flour, ¼ teaspoon salt, 1 teaspoon soda, 2 teaspoons baking powder, 6 tablespoons shortening.

WEST RIVER WAFFLES

Separate eggs and beat yolks until light. Then add 1 cup sour milk. Meanwhile, measure and sift together flour, salt, soda and baking powder; add yolk mixture and beat. Add another cup of sour milk and beat again, then add melted shortening. At the last, fold in egg whites, beaten stiff. The batter is then ready for use in the waffle iron. Serves 6.

"I very often use only 2 eggs, using a little more milk, in fact I seldom make any thing exactly by a receipt. As I tell Mr. Will, most things I make out of my head."

Mrs. William P. C. Lippitt
Cumberstone

Anne Arundel

Waffles

**LIZA'S
WAFFLE'S**   2 eggs, 1 cup buttermilk, ¼ cup butter, ¼ teaspoon salt, ½ tablespoon cornmeal, 1 tablespoon
brown sugar, 2 cups sifted flour, ½ rounded teaspoon soda, ¼ cup hot water.

Beat eggs slightly; add other ingredients except water and soda. Beat
until smooth, then add water with soda well dissolved in it. Bake on a
hot greased waffle iron until light brown. Makes 8 or 9 waffles.

Olney Inn   *Montgomery*

**CONFEDERATE
WAFFLES**   1 cup white corn meal, 2 cups boiling water, 4
tablespoons butter and bacon grease, 2 eggs, 1 cup
flour, ½ teaspoon salt, 3 teaspoons baking powder.
⅔ cup cold water or milk.

Mix meal into boiling water, making a smooth mush. While hot add
butter and bacon grease. Set aside to cool. Stir in beaten eggs, then
add flour sifted with salt and baking powder. Thin with about ⅔ cup
of cold water or milk, if too thick. Bake on hot waffle irons.

Mrs. Hubard's way
Mrs. Frederick W. Brune's Book, 1860   *Baltimore*

**SUPERIOR
RICE WAFFLES**   2 cups flour, ½ teaspoon salt, ½ teaspoon soda, 2
eggs, 2 cups buttermilk, ½ cup boiled rice, 1 tablespoon melted butter.

Sift flour, salt and soda together. Beat egg yolks and add to buttermilk.
Add rice to buttermilk, and butter. Combine buttermilk mixture with
dry ingredients; then fold in well beaten egg whites. Bake quickly in
waffle irons.

Up-To-Date Cook Book, 1897
St. John's Church   *Montgomery*

Sweet Buns

1 yeast cake, ¼ cup lukewarm water, ½ cup sugar, **CINNAMON**
1 teaspoon salt, ¾ cup scalded milk, 2 eggs, 4 cups **ROLLS**
sifted flour, ¼ cup butter or shortening.

Soften yeast in lukewarm water with ½ teaspoon sugar. Let stand 10
minutes. Add remaining sugar and salt to hot milk, stir and cool to
lukewarm. Add yeast to milk mixture and stir well. Add beaten eggs
and half of the flour and beat until smooth. Beat in melted and cooled
shortening, then add remaining flour and stir thoroughly. Turn out on
lightly floured board. Cover dough and let stand for 10 minutes before
kneading. Knead until smooth and elastic (about 10 minutes), using
not more than ¼ cup additional flour. Round up into smooth ball,
place in clean greased bowl, turn once to bring greased side to top.
Cover and let rise until double in bulk, about 2 hours. Knead down and
pinch off about one fourth and roll out on board. Sprinkle generously
with cinnamon, sugar and seeded raisins. Then roll as a jelly roll and
cut with sharp knife in 2-inch sections. Cover bottom of baking pans
with melted butter and brown sugar (pecan meats, if desired), and
put in rolls with cut side down. Let rise again until doubled, about 2
hours, and bake in a 350° oven until brown. Makes about a dozen and
a half rolls.

Mrs. Henry M. Murray
Cumberstone
Anne Arundel

½ cake yeast, 1 cup warm water, ½ cup sugar, ½ **GARRETT**
cup lard, 2 or 3 eggs, 1 teaspoon salt, flour, brown **COUNTY**
sugar, cinnamon. **AMISH BUN**

Dissolve yeast in warm water. Cream sugar and lard together, then add
beaten eggs, salt and yeast. Work in enough flour to make a nice, soft
dough. Let it rise 1 hour, knead it down and let rise again, about 1 hour.
Put in pie pans about 1 pound (1 pint) to a pan; let them rise 1½
hours. Glaze with cream and sprinkle heavy with brown sugar and
cinnamon. Bake 30 minutes at 350° or until nice and brown. Will make
3 nice size coffee cakes.

Amelia Yoder
Grantsville
Garrett

Paca House

Sweet Buns

MR. PACA'S RUSK

3 eggs, 1 cup milk, 2 tablespoons butter, 3 tablespoons sugar, 1 good teaspoon salt, 1 cake yeast, ¼ cup lukewarm water, 1 teaspoon sugar, about 6 cups flour.

Beat eggs until light, add scalded milk (cooled a little), butter, sugar and salt. When mixture is tepid, add yeast (which has been dissolved in warm water with a teaspoon of sugar). Beat gradually into this 2 cups flour. Beat until all lumps are out and batter is nice and smooth. Let rise until bubbly, then add remaining flour, about 4 cups. Work well; rusks must be well kneaded and very light before being baked. Put in lightly greased bowl in warm place and let rise until double in bulk. Make into cakes about 5 or 6 inches in diameter, and 1 inch thick. Put on greased cookie sheet or in pie pans; let rise until double in size. Gently brush with milk or cream and sprinkle with sugar. Bake in a 325° oven for about 25 minutes or until nicely browned on top. Makes 5 rusks. When fresh they are delicious cut in slices ½ inch thick, buttered and toasted a light golden brown. Stale rusks may be sliced and dried in a slow oven until a fine golden color.

Mr. Paca's receipt, revised
Miss Ann Chase's Book, 1811   *Annapolis*

When making light bread, take about 1 pound   **RAISIN**
(1 pint) of the dough after it has risen once and   **COFFEE CAKE**
mix with it 1 beaten egg, 4 tablespoons melted
butter, 2 tablespoons sugar, 1 teaspoon cinnamon, ¼ cup floured raisins
and about 1 tablespoon finely slivered candied orange peel.

Knead until well mixed; put in a buttered ring pan and sprinkle
raisins, sugar and cinnamon over the top. Let it rise until light and
bake in 350° oven about 20 minutes.

Mrs. Mott's way, adapted
Maria T. Allison's Book, 1860   *Baltimore*

½ cup butter, 1 cup sugar, 3 eggs, beaten sep-   **COFFEE CAKE**
arately; 3 cups flour, 3 teaspoons baking powder,
½ teaspoon salt, 1 cup milk, little lemon extract and nutmeg.

Cream butter and sugar, mix in egg yolks, flour sifted with baking
powder and salt, and milk, alternately; then lemon extract and nutmeg.
Fold in stiffly beaten egg whites last. Pour into buttered shallow pans
and sprinkle over the top: ½ cup sugar mixed with 2 teaspoons cinnamon, pieces of butter and chopped nuts. Bake in 375° oven for 25
minutes. When cool, cut in squares.

Elizabeth R. Lloyd's Book, 1889   *Annapolis*

1¼ cups butter (or ½ butter and ½ lard), 1½   **ELEANOR**
cups sugar, 4 eggs, 4 cups sifted flour, 2 heaping   **CALVERT'S**
teaspoons baking powder, pinch of salt, 1½ cups   **SALLY LUNN**
milk.

Cream butter and half of sugar until very light. Beat eggs and remaining sugar, also very light. Combine with creamed butter and sugar.
Sift flour, baking powder and salt together, then add to butter and egg
mixture, alternately with milk as you would in mixing cake. Bake in
greased tube cake pan for an hour in 375° oven. Eaten hot for lunch
or supper with butter. Half this amount may be baked in a 10 by 10
oven dish for 35 minutes or until brown and cut into squares making
9 large servings.

Rev. Daniel Randall Magruder, great, great grandson of
Eleanor Calvert of Mt. Airy   *Prince George's*

Chesapeake Bay Shell-Fish

Deal Island, Somerset County   A. Aubrey Bodine

Oysters

**OYSTERS
MARYLAND**

1 pint select oysters, 8 toast points, 4 thin slices cooked Maryland country-cured ham, 2 cups cream sauce, chopped parsley.

Heat oysters in their own liquor until plump. Place toast points in flat oven dish; over this put thin slices of ham. Place oysters on ham, cover with hot cream sauce and place in moderate oven (350°) until bubbly and hot. Sprinkle with chopped parsley and serve.

Olney Inn   *Montgomery*

1 quart oysters, 2 cups coarse cracker crumbs, salt, **SCALLOPED**
pepper, ¼ pound butter, ½ cup cream. **OYSTERS**

Drain oysters and pick over for shells, rinsing in oyster liquor. Strain and
reserve the liquor. Butter a shallow oven dish; cover the bottom with a
layer of cracker crumbs, then a layer of oysters. Sprinkle over salt and
pepper and dot with butter. Repeat with a second layer. Pour oyster
liquor and cream over all, covering with cracker crumbs and butter.
Bake in a moderate oven (350°) for about 25 minutes.

Maudie Lee's way
Atholl
Anne Arundel

---

2 tablespoons chopped celery, ½ cup oyster liquor, **MISS KATE'S**
1 quart large oysters, drained; 1 cup grated bread **BAKED OYSTERS**
crumbs, 1 teaspoon salt, ⅛ teaspoon pepper, ⅛
teaspoon paprika, 4 tablespoons butter, ½ cup sherry.

Simmer celery in oyster liquor until tender. In the meantime, using
a large flat earthen baking dish, place a layer of oysters on the bottom,
then a layer of bread crumbs seasoned with salt, pepper and paprika.
Dot with small lumps of butter. Pour half of the celery and oyster
liquor over this, then repeat with another layer of oysters, seasoned
bread crumbs, butter and oyster liquor with celery. Pour sherry wine
over all. Bake in a hot oven until well heated (about 15 minutes).
Serve in the baking dish.

Miss Kate M. Thomas' Prize Receipt
The Baltimore Sun, 1911
Baltimore

---

1 quart oysters, 1 pint milk, 1 tablespoon butter, **CREAMED**
2 tablespoons flour, salt and cayenne pepper to **OYSTERS**
taste, chopped parsley, good sherry.

Put oysters into a double-boiler on a hot fire. When the gills curl take
out and put into a strainer for ten minutes. Put on the milk and soon
as it comes to a boil add the butter and flour which must be creamed
together, then salt and pepper and parsley. Add oysters and let all boil
for 5 minutes. Just as you are ready to serve add sherry. Serve in a
covered dish and have it very hot.

Mrs. J. P. McComas' receipt
St. Anne's Rectory
Annapolis

Widehall

Oysters

WIDEHALL OYSTERS   Large fat oysters, crisp crackers, melted butter, salt. Quantities according to your company.

Allow five or six oysters to a serving. Drain off liquor. Use hand crushed crumbs from crisp crackers. Do not crush them too fine. Use a shallow oven dish in which oysters may be served. Place oysters in the dish, close together but not on top of each other. One layer only. Sprinkle cracker crumbs generously over the oysters and pour melted butter over crumbs. Sprinkle on a little salt. Place in broiler until brown on top which should not take over 10 or 15 minutes. Serve at once.

Mrs. Wilbur W. Hubbard
Widehall, Chester River   *Kent*

Get the required number of oyster shells, five or **OYSTERS**
six on a plate. Have oysters well drained before **AU GRATIN**
putting in shells and heat over a pan of hot water.

Put in a saucepan 2 tablespoons butter, 2 tablespoons chopped parsley,
¼ of an onion, chopped, and 1 section garlic, minced. Cook until onion
is soft. Add 2 tablespoons flour and cream enough to make quite a
stiff sauce. Add a heaping handful of grated Swiss cheese, paprika and
salt to taste. Put sauce over oysters in shells, sprinkle with more grated
Swiss cheese and bake in very hot oven until brown.

Mrs. W. G. Fay
Mulberry Fields, Potomac River *St. Mary's*

Flaky pastry sufficient to line large pie pan and **OYSTER 'PYE'**
for top crust.

Line large pie pan (which can be sent to the table) with pie paste.
Cut a pastry circle which will form lid so that it will exactly fit over
pie when baked. Bake separately on a cookie sheet. The crusts must
be baked before pie is filled as "the oysters will be too much done if
they are cooked in the pye."

Oyster filling: 1 quart oysters, 1 small onion, chopped fine; 1 stalk
celery, scraped and chopped fine; 2 tablespoons butter, 2 tablespoons
flour, 1 cup oyster liquor, 1 cup thin cream, ½ teaspoon mace, a little
nutmeg and freshly ground pepper, a few drops hot sauce or a pinch
of cayenne.

Make a "body" in double boiler by cooking onion and celery in butter
until soft, then stirring in flour and seasonings; add oyster liquor and
let "body" steep over hot water to blend seasonings. Gradually add
cream which must not be cooked too long as it may curdle. Add oysters
to sauce about 5 minutes or so before serving and let them plump and
heat through only until edges curl.

When pastry is baked, fill with oysters and sauce, put on lid, and
send to table warm.

Adapted from Miss Leslie, 1837
Mrs. John F. Meigs' copy *Annapolis*

Chinese Chippendale Staircase at Sotterley

Maryland House and Garden Pilgrimage

Dining Room at Sotterley

Maryland House and Garden Pilgrimage

Take a quart of large oysters, parboil them in their   **SOTTERLEY**
liquor, a little bread grated, an onion and savoury   **OYSTER 'PYE'**
spices. When the Pye is baked, take out the onion
from the oysters, pour them in the Pye, lay on butter and close it
with your Paste.

Mrs. Plater's way
Miss Ann Chase's Book, 1811   *Annapolis*

---

1 dozen baked tart shells (use shallow oval or   **OYSTER BOATS**
boat-shaped tins if possible); 2 pints salt water
oysters, 3 or 4 hard-boiled eggs (yolks), 4 tablespoons butter, bread
crumbs, not too finely crumbled; mace, nutmeg, freshly ground pepper.

Choose 24 fat oysters to broil. Chop remainder coarsely and put in
stewpan with half their liquor. Let come to a boil and thicken with
grated egg yolks. Enrich with pieces of butter rolled in bread crumbs,
and season to taste with a little mace, nutmeg and ground pepper. A
pinch of salt may be needed. Broil the 24 oysters. Partly fill pastry
boats with chopped oyster mixture and place two broiled oysters on
each one. Sprinkle with a little finely cut parsley, if desired. Serve
immediately. A good first course.

Tulip Hill Receipts
West River   *Anne Arundel*

To mock roast shucked oysters, take a heavy   **MOCK ROAST**
skillet, lay your oysters flat out in the pan until   **OYSTERS**
you have the bottom of the pan covered. Then,
as they begin to make juice in the pan, pour it off or take it out with
a spoon. Keep turning oysters over and over until browned a little;
then have some melted butter in a hot serving dish, with pepper and
salt to suit taste. Lift the oysters from pan into butter sauce and send
to the table hot. This may be a little trouble to the cook, but the
persons who eat the oysters never get through talking about them.

Mr. J. D. Mallory
The Baltimore Sun, 1890   *Baltimore*

Oysters

STEAMED OYSTERS, BALTIMORE STYLE 1 quart counts or select salt water oysters, butter, salt and pepper.

Wash oysters in their own liquor, and drain. Put them in a shallow pan and place in a steamer over boiling water; cover and steam until they are plump with the edges ruffled, but no longer. Place in a heated dish with butter, pepper and salt. Serve immediately.

White House Cook Book, 1887
Contee, Rhode River   *Anne Arundel*

CHESTERTOWN DEVILED OYSTERS 2 tablespoons butter, 2 tablespoons flour, ½ cup milk, ¼ cup cream, ⅛ teaspoon mustard, ½ teaspoon Worcestershire sauce, ½ teaspoon salt, ⅛ teaspoon nutmeg, 1 pint oysters, 1 egg yolk, buttered crumbs.

Melt butter; add flour, milk, cream and seasoning. Add oysters which have been brought to a boil in their own liquor, drained and chopped. Simmer 2 minutes, and add beaten egg yolk. Put in baking dish, cover with buttered crumbs, and bake about 15 minutes.

Mrs. S. Scott Beck
Chestertown   *Kent*

Skipjack Fleet in Chesapeake Bay

1 pint salt water oysters, ¼ pound butter, ½ cup bread crumbs. **BROILED OYSTERS**

Drain oysters, dip in melted butter, roll in bread crumbs and lay on baking sheet. Put under preheated broiler and broil until brown, turn, and brown the other side. Serve with lemon wedges. Serves 6.

Mrs. Finley France
Ridout Creek *Anne Arundel*

---

1 pint oysters cut up fine, ¼ pound butter, melted; 1 cup cracker crumbs, 5 eggs beaten light, 1 green pepper cut up fine, 1 grated onion, ¼ cup chopped parsley, 1 teaspoon salt, ¼ teaspoon pepper, 2 teaspoons Worcestershire sauce. **DEVILED OYSTERS**

Mix oysters, butter and crumbs, leaving enough butter and crumbs for top of dish. Add eggs, pepper, onion and seasonings. Put in baking dish and bake uncovered in 350° oven for 30 to 40 minutes.

Mrs. Kenneth H. Noble
Severn River *Anne Arundel*

A. Aubrey Bodine

MY FAVORITE 4 tablespoons butter, 6 tablespoons flour, 2 cups
OYSTERS chicken stock, 1 cup cream, salt and pepper, 2
egg yolks, 8 shallots or scallions, 3 tablespoons
butter, ½ cup dry white wine, ½ cup finely sliced mushrooms, 2 pints
small oysters.

Melt butter and stir in flour, cooking a few minutes to blend. Add hot
chicken stock and stir until smooth and thickened. Stir in heated cream
slowly. Blend and add seasoning. Let sauce simmer at least 5 minutes
longer over low heat. Beat yolks, whisk in ¾ cup or so of hot sauce;
stir like mad. Add this to remaining sauce and set aside. Now slice
shallots or scallions very thin and cook in the 3 tablespoons butter until
soft and yellow, over medium heat. Add wine and mushrooms, cooking slowly until wine has almost evaporated. Stir this into sauce you
have set aside. Add oysters which have been poached in their own
liquor and very well drained. Heat gently, stirring until yolks thicken
sauce and all is very hot, but do not let it boil after adding yolks. Serve
in timbale cases or patty shells.

Miss Grace's Receipt Book
Tenthouse Creek   *Anne Arundel*

OYSTERS 2 dozen Chincoteague or Ocean Cove oysters,
BAKED IN scrubbed, opened and drained in colander, saving
HALF SHELLS liquor and deepest half of shell; thick cream sauce
with fresh ground nutmeg; 10 or 12 large shrimp,
shelled and deveined; 2 medium size raw clams, shelled and with liquor;
freshly ground black pepper, a sprig or so of parsley, and Parmesan
cheese. Variation: Sauterne wine may be substituted for milk in cream
sauce.

Prepare the oysters; make a thick cream sauce of butter, milk (or wine),
flour and a pinch of freshly ground nutmeg. Place in blender or food
chopper, add shrimp, clams, clam liquor and seasoning. Blend, slowly
adding oyster juice to make of a medium consistency. Place a spoonful
of sauce on oyster shell, next an oyster, and cover completely with
Parmesan cheese. Pop in a preheated very hot oven until the oyster
edges curl, then under broiler for a few seconds to brown the cheese
lightly. Serve immediately or oysters will continue to cook in sauce and
get too well done.

Edwin B. Perry   *Baltimore*

Blakeford

Oysters

2 quarts of oysters, 2 tablespoons flour, ¼ pound butter, cream, salt and pepper, 2½ pounds mushrooms, 3 red Pimento peppers, 1 dessert-spoon Worcestershire sauce, 3 tablespoons sherry.

OYSTERS 'CLARENCE'

Drain oysters well, reserving liquor. Make a smooth sauce of butter, flour, oyster liquor and cream. Brown oysters in butter and season to taste with salt and pepper. Broil the sliced mushrooms in butter, separately from the oysters. Mix mushrooms and oysters together in the sauce and keep hot in a double-boiler until ready to serve. Add Pimentos, cut in strips, Worcestershire and sherry, just before serving. Serves 10 to 12 persons.

Mrs. Clarence W. Miles
Blakeford, Chester River

Queen Anne's

Mulberry Fields   Maryland House and Garden Pilgrimage

Oysters

FRICASSEED   1 quart of oysters, 1 heaping tablespoon butter,
OYSTERS   1 heaping tablespoon flour, 1⅓ cups milk, small
                        pinch celery salt, cayenne pepper and salt to taste,
                        yolks of 2 eggs, 1 tablespoon chopped parsley.

Heat oysters in their liquor until the gills curl, then drain them. Melt
butter in a pan; add flour and mix until smooth, then add milk gradually. Stir until it boils. Add oysters and half a cup of the liquor, celery
salt, cayenne and salt. Again stir until the boiling point is reached.
Remove from fire and add the egg yolks, beaten light. Then stir in the
parsley. Serve at once with toast points or in patty shells.

Mrs. W. G. Fay
Mulberry Fields, Potomac River   *St. Mary's*

Mix up whole egg; dip oyster in egg and roll in **OYSTERS,** fine bread crumbs into which paprika and red **DEEP FRIED** pepper have been mixed. Do not roll heavily, just a thin coating of bread crumbs. Fry in deep, hot fat. Put oysters on brown paper to absorb grease, and place them in an open oven to keep warm. Serve on heated platter.

Women's Auxiliary, Christ Church
West River
                                                    Anne Arundel

---

Drain and dry nice big oysters, sprinkle with salt **OYSTERS, FRIED** and pepper, dip in partially beaten egg and roll **IN BUTTER** in home-made bread crumbs, not too finely crumbled. Cook in a frying pan with a generous amount of butter, but not nearly enough to cover them. Fry on one side and brown, turn and brown the other side and serve.

J. Harrison Colhoun
Windsor
                                                    Anne Arundel

---

25 nice fat oysters, 2 tablespoons flour, 1 table- **OYSTER** spoon butter, ½ cup oyster liquor, ½ cup milk, **CROQUETTES** 2 egg yolks, ½ cup soft bread crumbs, 3 shakes cayenne, salt to taste.

Drain oysters, saving liquor. Wash oysters and place them in a hot saucepan; stir over fire until they actually boil. Drain, saving liquor again, and adding this to first. Chop oysters fine. Blend flour and butter in saucepan, add oyster liquor and milk; stir over heat until thick and smooth. Take from fire, add egg yolks, slightly beaten, the oysters, bread crumbs and all the seasoning. Put back on fire and stir until mixture reaches boiling point. Turn out on platter to cool and when cold, mold into croquettes. Roll in beaten egg, bread or cracker crumbs and cook in deep fat. Serves 6 or 8.

Mrs. William T. Murray
Peach Hill
                                                    Anne Arundel

OYSTER FRITTERS   ½ cup flour, sifted; 2 teaspoons baking powder, salt and pepper, 2 eggs, 1 pint of large select oysters.

Mix dry ingredients and sift them into the beaten eggs. Beat into a smooth batter. Drop oysters, one at a time, into batter and then in hot fat in a small saucepan or skillet. Quick and easy! Serves 4.

Elizabeth W. Englar
Gibson Island   *Anne Arundel*

SPICED OYSTERS   1 gallon select oysters, ½ teaspoon whole cloves, 1 teaspoon whole allspice, 1 teaspoon black pepper, 1 stick mace (broken in small pieces), 4 tablespoons vinegar.

Drain oysters. Let oyster liquor come to a boil, skim; add to boiling liquor the cloves, allspice, pepper and mace. Put oysters in; when nearly done add vinegar. Let oysters cook until edges are well curled. Serve very cold as appetizers.

Margaret T. Slingluff
Melford Farms   *Prince George's*

MYRTLE GROVE PICKLED OYSTERS   To pickle 100 oysters, drain the liquor from the oysters, and put to them a tablespoonful of salt and a teacup of vinegar. Let them simmer ten minutes, taking off the scum as it rises. Then take out the oysters and put to the liquor a tablespoonful of whole black pepper, a teaspoonful each of mace and cloves; let it boil five minutes, skim and pour over the oysters.

Miss M. C. Goldsborough
Myrtle Grove, Miles River   *Talbot*

Crab

Take out the meat and clean it from the Skin. **MR. PACA'S**
Put it into a Stew-pan with half a pint of white **WAY TO**
wine, a little nutmeg, pepper and salt, over a **DRESS CRABS**
slow fire,—throw in a few crumbs of bread, beat
up one yolk of an egg with one spoonful of vinegar, then shake the
Sauce pan round a minute, and serve it upon a plate.

Miss Ann Chase's Book, 1811   *Annapolis*

¼ cup sweet butter, 4 medium mushrooms **CREAMED**
(sliced), 1 tablespoon chopped shallots, 2 ripe **LUMP CRAB**
tomatoes (peeled and diced), 1 pound fresh back-
fin crabmeat, 1 cup heavy cream, 1 teaspoon chopped mixed herbs
(chives, chervil and parsley), 2 tablespoons brandy, salt and pepper.

Melt butter in skillet, add mushrooms and cook 3 minutes. Add shallots
and tomatoes and cook 3 minutes longer, then add crabmeat. Season
and heat thoroughly. Add cream, stir carefully to keep lumps whole,
and boil 1 minute. Add herbs, brandy and seasoning to taste. Serve
immediately. Serves 5.

Mrs. Hortense Brook's Prize Receipt
Mischanton Contest   *Baltimore*

¼ pound butter, 2 tablespoons flour, 2 cups milk, **CRAB FLAKE**
1 pound lump crab meat, 1 teaspoon salt, 1 pinch **MARYLAND**
cayenne pepper, 1 cup cream, 1 glass sherry wine
(½ cup).

Melt half the butter in saucepan. Add flour and make cream sauce with
the heated milk; set aside to keep it hot. Heat rest of butter in a saucepan, add crabmeat and fry a little. Try not to break up lumps. Add
salt, pepper, cream sauce and cream. Let boil for 2 or 3 minutes, then
add sherry wine, mix well, but do not boil. Serve very hot from chafing
dish with toast.

Mrs. William Preston Lane
Hagerstown   *Washington*

3 tablespoons butter, 1½ tablespoons minced **CRAB ROYAL**
onion, 2 tablespoons minced green pepper, 2 table-
spoons flour, 1 teaspoon salt, 2 cups light cream, dash nutmeg, ¼ teaspoon dry mustard, 2 well beaten egg yolks, 3 cups flaked crab meat,
small mushroom caps, sautéed in butter; minced parsley.

Melt butter, add onion and green pepper and cook lightly. Blend
in flour and salt, add cream gradually, stirring until mixture is smooth.
Season with nutmeg and mustard, stir in egg yolks and crab meat, cook
a few minutes longer and remove from heat. Serve in individual dishes
and garnish with mushrooms and parsley. A delicious luncheon dish.

Mrs. George W. Mitchell
Ruxton   *Baltimore*

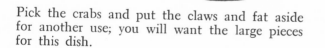

Pick the crabs and put the claws and fat aside   **MISS FANNIE'S**
for another use; you will want the large pieces   **PICKED CRABS**
for this dish.

¼ pound butter, salt, black and red pepper, nutmeg, 1 pound lump
crab meat, 1 tablespoon brandy, parsley.

Melt butter in heavy saucepan, add salt and peppers to your taste with
a generous grating of nutmeg. Then add crab meat, mixing gently
so as not to break lumps. When thoroughly heated (do not brown)
sprinkle over brandy and chopped parsley. Serve in individual dishes
with plenty of the butter sauce or on hot toast points spooning the
butter over.

*"This was written by Miss Fannie Chase, not by me. That of course is
a sufficient apology for it." Poor Miss Fannie!*

Adapted from The 1814 Account Book
Harwood Papers   *Annapolis*

Crab Floats, Crisfield
A. Aubrey Bodine

Crab

Packing Soft Shell Crabs   M. E. Warren

SOFT SHELL CRABS Clean crabs, removing eyes and sandbag, the 'dead men's fingers' under the points, and the 'apron' on lower back shell. Dry well, salt and pepper them, and sprinkle lightly with flour. Fry in deep hot fat. They will brown quickly. Dry out on brown or absorbent paper. Serve with lemon wedges or tartar sauce. (See Sauces for Fish.)

Mrs. Harry W. Hill
Prince George Street   *Annapolis*

SOFT CRABS, FRIED OR BROILED To *fry*, dry crabs thoroughly. Season lightly with salt and pepper. Fry in hot liquefied butter to a rich brown and serve on platter garnished with parsley butter and quarters of lemon. (Half butter, half shortening adds crispness.) Cooking hint:—To keep soft shell crabs from popping when frying, puncture legs and claws with sharp fork.

To *broil*, choose large crabs, dip in melted butter, season with a little salt and pepper, and arrange on gridiron. Broil until delicate brown, turning from side to side every few minutes. Arrange on rounds of toast, pour over a little hot melted butter flavored with a few drops lemon juice and chopped parsley.

Mrs. Page Bowie
Bay Ridge Farm   *Anne Arundel*

1 pound crab meat, salt and pepper to taste, 1 **EASTERN SHORE**
egg, ¼ pound butter, 1 tablespoon lemon juice, **CRAB CAKES**
1 hard-boiled egg, 1 tablespoon Worcestershire
sauce, bread crumbs.

Put crab meat in a bowl and season to taste with salt and pepper. Add
slightly beaten egg, melted butter, lemon juice, cut up hard-boiled egg,
and Worcestershire sauce. Then add just enough soft bread crumbs to
make it into cakes (2 or 3 slices of bread). Fry the cakes a golden brown.
An old receipt of my grandmother's from the Eastern Shore of Maryland.

Mrs. William W. Paca
Weston *Anne Arundel*

---

2 pounds crab meat (1 pound white, 1 pound **OLD DURHAM**
claw), 2 cups bread crumbs, 2 eggs (beaten), **CHURCH**
2 or 3 dashes hot sauce, 2 tablespoons minced **CRAB CAKES**
onion, 4 to 5 tablespoons mayonnaise, 2 teaspoons
salt, ¼ teaspoon pepper, 1 teaspoon dry mustard, ¼ teaspoon paprika,
2 teaspoons lemon juice and pulp.

Mix in order given. These crab cakes freeze well. Note: In making large
quantities, never mix but 2 pounds at a time.

Ladies Mite Society of Old Durham Church,
Organized 1876, Ironsides *Charles*

---

1 pound backfin crab lump, 1 tablespoon flour, **RICH**
1 egg, ¼ cup thick cream, salt, black pepper and **CRAB CAKES**
cayenne to taste, ⅛ pound butter.

Dredge flour over crab and stir gently to coat. Beat egg, cream and
seasonings together, pour over crab and mix gently. Melt butter in thick
skillet, then drop large spoonfuls of crab in hot butter and brown.
Makes 8 cakes.

Mrs. John Baldwin Rich
Heir's Purchase, Severn River *Anne Arundel*

MARYLAND CRAB FLAKE CAKES

4 slices of bread, ½ cup olive oil, ¼ teaspoon mustard, ½ teaspoon salt, 1 dash paprika, 1 teaspoon Worcestershire sauce, 2 eggs, 1 tablespoon chopped parsley, 1 pound crab flakes (backfin lump), 1 pound claw meat.

Trim crusts from bread. Lay on flat tin or platter. Pour olive oil over them. Let stand 1 hour. Pull bread apart lightly with two forks. To the small bits of bread add seasonings, yolks of eggs and crab meat; mix lightly with fork, fold in stiffly beaten egg whites and shape into cakes. Brown in hot skillet just brushed with fat. Cakes will be light, fluffy, and of delicate flavor. This receipt has been handed down for five generations in the Garey family of Aberdeen, Maryland.

Helen Cassin Kinkaid's Book
Hanover Street   *Annapolis*

YARDLEY'S CRAB CAKES

1 pound lump crab meat, 1 egg, 2 slices bread, 1 tablespoon chopped parsley, 1 tablespoon prepared mustard, 1 teaspoon Worcestershire sauce salt and pepper.

Pull inside of bread into small pieces, soak well in beaten egg with mustard and seasonings; add crab meat (try not to break it). Form into cakes and cook until brown in very hot bacon fat. Makes 6 big cakes. Serves three or Yardley.

Yardley
The Baltimore Sun   *Baltimore*

CRAB LOAF

Take a sound loaf, cut off the top and scrape out all the crumb. Have the crabs picked and dressed with pepper, salt, some mustard, a few celery seed, and a good deal of butter. Mix some of the crumb with a little sweet cream with the crabs. Fill the loaf, put the top on, and put in the oven to crisp.

(This old receipt makes good picnic fare as it can be heated over a beach fire with the aid of foil.)

Luly Duncan's way
Mrs. Frederick W. Brune's Book, 1860   *Baltimore*

The Maryland Scene

A Sailing Regatta

Crab Feast Ashore

Beer   Coffee

Steamed Crabs
Crab Loaf

Corn Roasted in the Husks

Dressed Cucumbers   Sliced Tomatoes

Mustard Pickle   Salt Sticks

Watermelon

A. Aubrey Bodine   Tred Avon River Regatta

Crab

STEAMED CRABS 12 Crabs, preferably Blue, but if you have to choose between size and weight, always take the small heavy crab rather than the large light one. Put in large pot, having top ready to keep crabs from escaping. Into two or three cups of cider vinegar or flat beer stir a tablespoon of Old Bay seasoning,—or if you prefer, mix your own such as salt, pepper, celery salt, mustard, etc. Pour over the crabs quickly, clamp on lid tightly, turn on heat under crabs and leave room until they stop scrambling,—about a minute, if you are squeamish. Don't forget they would bite you hard if they could.

The crabs are done when they turn red or when the apron is loose. (It should take about twenty minutes to cook them.) Remove from fire to cool in pot. Spread newspapers, put on a bathing suit, collect some cold beer or dry ginger ale and pitch in. If you don't know how to eat hot steamed crabs, get someone to show you.

John Baldwin Rich
Heir's Purchase, Severn River   *Anne Arundel*

CRAB CUTLETS 2 tablespoons butter, 2 rounded tablespoons flour, 1 cup white stock, veal or chicken; ½ teaspoon onion juice, chopped parsley, salt and pepper, 1 pound crab meat (backfin), beaten egg, bread crumbs.

Melt butter and blend in flour. Gradually add white stock and onion juice, then parsley and seasonings to taste. Cook to thick sauce consistency, then fold in crab lumps and chill. Shape mixture into oval cutlets; dip in slightly beaten egg, then roll in fresh bread crumbs. Fry in deep fat until golden brown. Serve with sauce.

Sauce: 2 cups clear white stock, veal or chicken; ½ bay leaf, ¼ teaspoon celery seed, 2 tablespoons cider vinegar, or, if preferred, sherry wine; ¼ cup better, 2 tablespoons flour. Heat stock in saucepan with bay leaf, celery seed and vinegar or sherry. Simmer ten minutes, then strain. Melt butter, blend in flour, and add strained stock gradually, stirring until smooth and thickened. Enough for 8 cutlets.

Miss Mary L. McDaniel
Easton   *Talbot*

1 pound crab meat, 1 tablespoon butter, 2 table- **DEVILED CRABS**
spoons flour, 1 cup cream, 1 teaspoon salt, ½ tea-
spoon mustard, Worcestershire sauce, red pepper, 2 hard-boiled eggs.

Blend butter and flour over low heat, then add cream. Stir until thick.
Add seasoning, making 'hot' according to your taste. Fold in crab meat
and eggs chopped fine. Fill shells. Cover with buttered bread crumbs
and brown.

Mrs. S. Scott Beck
Chestertown
Kent

1½ cups bread crumbs, 1 cup milk, 1 dessert- **CRABTOWN**
spoon dry mustard, 1 teaspoon salt, 1 salt-spoon **DEVILED CRABS**
red pepper, 1 pound crab meat, 4 tablespoons
butter, 1 egg, 2 dessert-spoons vinegar.

Soak bread crumbs in milk. Add mustard, salt and red pepper to crab
meat, then melted butter and beaten egg. Mix with bread crumbs and
milk, and last, the vinegar. Put into crab shells or individual baking
shells and bake ¾ hour in medium oven (350°).

Mrs. Harry W. Hill
Prince George Street
Annapolis

Combine 1 fresh green pepper, seeds removed, **CRAB IMPERIAL,**
and 2 pieces of canned pimento, both finely diced; **CHESAPEAKE**
1 tablespoon dry English mustard; salt and pepper
to taste (approximately 1½ teaspoons salt and ½ teaspoon white pepper), 2 raw eggs, 1 cup mayonnaise.

Add 3 pounds deluxe backfin lump crab meat and blend all the ingredients together with the fingers, so that the lumps of crab meat are not
broken.
Then divide the mixture between 8 crab shells, heaping it in lightly.
Top with a light coating of mayonnaise and sprinkle with paprika.
Bake in a moderate oven (350°) for 15 minutes approximately. Serve
hot or cold.
The traditional Baltimore garnish is a creamy cole slaw, tomato slices
with crisp lettuce, French fried potatoes.

Chesapeake Restaurant
Baltimore

Crab

ST. MARY'S   1 quart crabmeat lumps, ½ teaspoon black pep-
IMPERIAL CRAB   per, dash red pepper, 1 teaspoon dry mustard, 1
                    teaspoon salt, 1 teaspoon chopped parsley, ½ cup
butter, 2 large tablespoons flour, 1½ cups cream, 2 eggs slightly beaten,
clean crab shells, bread crumbs, dots of butter.

Mix crabmeat with pepper, mustard, salt and parsley. Melt butter
in top of double-boiler and blend in flour. Gradually stir in cream and
beaten eggs. Cook sauce over hot water, stirring until smooth and
thickened. Do not allow to boil. Pour sauce over seasoned crabmeat;
mix, keeping lumps whole, and put in crab shells. Spread with crumbs,
dot with butter, and place under broiler to brown slightly. Serve when
heated. Do not overcook.

Kitty Lee Hurry   *St. Mary's*

BURNSIDE   1 pound crab meat, 1 cup bread crumbs, 4 table-
CRAB   spoons butter, 1 teaspoon dry mustard, 3 table-
                   spoons vinegar, salt and pepper.

Put layers of crab meat in buttered baking dish. Cover each layer with
crumbs and liberal dots of butter. Mix dry mustard with vinegar and
seasoning. Pour over and bake in brisk oven, 400°, until hot and
browned.

Mrs. O. Bowie Duckett
Little Burnside   *Annapolis*

CRABMEAT   1 pound crabmeat, 4 tablespoons butter, 1 tea-
BALLS   spoon salt, ⅛ teaspoon cayenne, ⅛ teaspoon
                   mace, ⅛ teaspoon nutmeg, 1 teaspoon mustard,
                   ½ cup soft bread crumbs, 2 egg yolks.

Flake crabmeat. Melt butter, add seasonings and bread crumbs. Mix
in crabmeat and beaten egg yolks. Put mixture in ice-box to harden. Roll
into small balls, dredge with flour and fry in deep boiling fat to a nice
brown. Use to garnish fish dishes or as appetizer.

Mrs. Timothy J. Keleher
College Avenue   *Annapolis*

4 tablespoons butter, 2 tablespoons flour. Put in **DECATUR HOUSE** pan and brown, then add 1 cup cream. Stir until **BAKED CRAB** thick. Add ½ teaspoon ground black pepper, ½ teaspoon dry mustard, ½ teaspoon salt, 2 tablespoons Sherry, 2 tablespoons Bourbon whiskey, dash Tabasco sauce, dash Worcestershire sauce, dash red pepper.

Put in the picked crab (1 pound backfin). Pour into buttered baking dish; cover with small bread cubes that have been stirred with butter in a pan, but not browned. Bake until nicely browned.

Mrs. Truxtun Beale's Book, 1903
Decatur House   *Washington*

Decatur House

Historic Decatur House, on La Fayette Square, was built in 1818 by the Naval hero, Stephen Decatur. At that time, the President's House and St. John's Church were the only buildings marking out the now famous Square in the rustic countryside which was originally Maryland soil. The popular Commodore, who had been born on the Eastern Shore of Maryland, and his young wife enjoyed little more than a year in their mansion in the Federal City when he was mortally wounded in a duel.

The house was subsequently occupied by the French Minister to the United States and, later, by the Russian Czar's diplomatic representative, Baron de Tuyll who was a known epicure. He delighted in American foods and was quoted as saying, "Washington, with its venison, wild turkey, canvasback ducks, oysters and terrapin, furnishes better viands than Paris—and needs only cooks." Over the succeeding years many prominent persons lived in Decatur House, among them, Henry Clay and Martin Van Buren, both of whom aspired to the Presidency. One failed and the other succeeded.

Soon after the close of the Civil War, Decatur House was purchased by General Edward F. Beale. His son, Truxtun, inherited the famous mansion and brought his bride there in 1903. The tradition of lavish entertainment and hospitality in the historic residence was carried on for more than half a century. Mrs. Truxtun Beale bequeathed Decatur House to the National Trust for Historic Preservation.

MAIDSTONE　　　1½ cups rich white sauce, ½ cup mayonnaise
BAKED CRAB　　　dressing, ½ cup sherry wine, 2 pounds freshly
picked Maryland crabmeat, 1 cup buttered bread
crumbs.

Combine the above ingredients in order given, except the bread crumbs.
Pour mixture into a deep buttered baking dish, cover with crumbs and
bake ½ hour in a hot oven. Serve from the baking dish. Serves 8.

Miss Louise Wilson
Possum Point, Mill Creek　　　　　　　　　　　　　*Anne Arundel*

CRAB MOUSSE　　　1 tablespoon gelatin, 3 tablespoons cold water,
¼ cup mayonnaise, 3 tablespoons lemon juice,
1 tablespoon each of chopped parsley and chives, 1 tablespoon prepared
mustard, 2 tablespoons chopped pimentoes, salt and pepper to taste,
2 cups back-fin crab meat, ¾ cup heavy cream, whipped.

Soften gelatin in cold water, then thoroughly dissolve over hot water.
Mix gelatin with mayonnaise and other ingredients except crab meat
and cream. When well mixed, fold in crab meat, then whipped cream.
Pour mixture into a buttered mold and chill until set. Unmold on
lettuce leaves, and decorate as desired. For individual salads, put in
small molds (½ cup each).

Mrs. Heath Conrad Moorman　　　　　　　　　　　*Washington*

CRAB SALAD　　　1 pound backfin crab meat, ⅔ cup mayonnaise,
½ teaspoon salt, ½ teaspoon ground black pep-
per, 1 tablespoon fresh lemon juice, 2 teaspoons well-drained capers.

Pick over crab meat very carefully; do not break up the lumps. In a
separate bowl, mix all ingredients with the mayonnaise. Pour dressing
over crab meat; do not stir but pour from one bowl into another two
or three times while chilling. Serve on Boston lettuce.

Mrs. John P. Curtis
College Avenue　　　　　　　　　　　　　　　　*Annapolis*

Clams

Place clams, scrubbed and cleansed of sand, in a **STEAMED**
large pan, with very little or no water. Cover **SOFT CLAMS**
tightly. Heat until bubbles are visible around top
clams, then cook with lid slightly off for 4 or 5 minutes, until clam
shells are open. Pour clam broth into soup bowls. Dip skinned clams
individually into broth, washing off any sand residue, and dip in melted
butter with which each person is provided.

Logan Morrill
Meredith Creek   *Anne Arundel*

Soft clams, milk, eggs, salt, cornmeal, wheat flour, **FRIED CLAMS**
fat for deep frying.

Beat up a thin batter of milk, egg and salt, the quantity depending on
the number of clams to be dipped. Mix cornmeal and wheat flour together thoroughly, in the proportion of 4 parts cornmeal to 1 part wheat
flour. Dip clams in salted egg and milk batter, then toss them in cornmeal and flour mixture. Shake off excess coating. Immerse in deep fat
heated to 370° for 1 minute only.

Hanks Seafood Company
Easton   *Talbot*

Open the clams and cut them up fine, saving the **CLAMS BAKED**
liquor. To twenty-five clams take a tablespoonful **IN THE SHELL**
of butter, work into it a dessertspoonful of flour,
put it on the fire with a little pepper and salt, and stew to the consistency of thick gruel, putting in a little of the liquor from the clams,
then put in the clams and stew until tender. Place it then in clam
shells nicely washed, and bake it, sprinkling over it a few bread crumbs.

Mrs. B. C. Howard's receipt, 1877
Mrs. Eric Purdon, Arden   *Anne Arundel*

Clam Diggers

A. Aubrey Bodine

2 cups shucked clams and liquor, 1 teaspoon **DEVILED**
lemon juice, 3 tablespoons butter, 2 tablespoons **CLAMS**
minced celery, 1½ tablespoons minced green
pepper, 1½ tablespoons minced onion, ½ cup cracker crumbs, ¼ teaspoon prepared mustard, pinch of red pepper, salt (if needed), 1 egg.

Drain clams and chop very fine. Add liquor and lemon juice and simmer
for 3 minutes. Melt butter, add celery, green pepper and onion, and
cook until tender. Add clams and cracker crumbs. Add seasonings to
beaten egg and stir into clam mixture. Bake in large clam shells in 350°
oven for 15 minutes. Serves 4.

Miss Fanny's Receipt Book
West River   *Anne Arundel*

---

2 dozen clams with their juice, 2 medium-sized **OVEN CLAM**
onions, ½ pound salt pork, 3 large potatoes, 3 **CHOWDER**
handfuls cracker crumbs, ½ teaspoon thyme,
black pepper and salt, milk.

Chop clams, not too fine; chop onions very fine. Cut pork and potatoes
into small dice. Put in a baking dish a layer of pork, one of potatoes,
one of clams and so on. Add some of the cracker crumbs, thyme, and
pepper and salt to taste. Cover these ingredients with clam liquor and
milk until liquid rises 1 inch above the chowder. Sprinkle with cracker
crumbs. Bake in a moderate oven until liquid has almost disappeared.

Miss Alice Thornton, 1875
Maryland Avenue   *Annapolis*

Clams

Maninose or Soft Clams   The Skipper Magazine

MANINOSE   2 dozen maninose or soft clams, 4 eggs, well
PATTIES   beaten; ½ cup flour, ½ teaspoon baking powder,
salt, pepper, cayenne and nutmeg to taste, 1 tablespoon parsley, finely chopped.

Wash clams in their own juice, drain, and discard necks, chopping the
remainder into small pieces. Beat eggs well and add flour, baking powder,
seasonings to taste and parsley. Beat until well mixed and stir in chopped
clams. Shape mixture into small cakes and fry slowly in a heavy skillet
until browned on both sides.

Clam Industry Receipt   *Talbot*

CLARA'S   18 hard clams, steamed; 2 boiled potatoes, 2 hard-
CLAM PIE   boiled eggs, cut up; salt, pepper and nutmeg,
pastry.

Grind clams and potatoes together, add eggs, salt, pepper and 3 or 4
dashes of nutmeg. Mix ½ hour ahead of cooking with a little clam juice
and let stand. Then put in deep baking dish and top with pie crust.
Bake ¾ of an hour in a 350° oven. Serve with cream sauce.

Sauce: 3 tablespoons butter, 3 tablespoons flour, 1½ cups milk, ½ cup
clam juice, 2 hard-boiled eggs. Melt butter in saucepan, stir in flour,
then milk and clam juice until smooth. Add chopped eggs. Serve in
small pitcher to pour over each serving of pie.

Mrs. Henry C. Edgar
Evergreen   *Anne Arundel*

Other Seafoods

1 cup shrimp (cooked and cut into small pieces), 1 cup crab meat, 1 cup bay scallops (cooked and cut into small pieces), 4 tablespoons butter, salt and pepper to taste, 2 cups cream sauce, buttered crumbs, grated Parmesan cheese.

BAKED SEAFOOD IN SHELLS

Combine shrimp, crab meat and scallops and sauté them in butter for a few minutes, stirring constantly. Then sprinkle with salt and pepper and stir in cream sauce. Divide mixture among 6 individual shells, sprinkle generously with buttered crumbs and cheese and bake in moderate oven (350°) for about 30 minutes. May be frozen and baked when needed.

Mrs. William W. Paca
Weston   Anne Arundel

Make a heavy cream sauce of 4 tablespoons butter, 4 tablespoons flour, ½ cup milk, 2 cups cream (scant). Season with salt and pepper and add 2 teaspoons Worcestershire sauce. If desired, add a small amount of onion juice.

SEA FOOD IN A CHAFING DISH

To the cream sauce add 1 pound cooked and cut-up mushrooms, 1 pound cooked and cut-up scallops, 1 pound of backfin crab meat, 2 cups of cooked and cut-up lobster meat. Mix carefully and add sherry wine to taste. Serve hot in chafing dish as a dip, or thin the sauce and serve with toast triangles or rice.

Mrs. Wade DeWeese
King George Street   Annapolis

⅓ cup chopped onion, 2 tablespoons butter, 1 or 2 cloves of garlic, 2 pounds cooked shrimp, 1 cup raw rice, 3 cups stewed tomatoes, 2 cups chicken stock, 1 bay leaf, 3 tablespoons chopped parsley, ¼ teaspoon cloves, ½ teaspoon marjoram, 1 teaspoon chili powder, 2 teaspoons salt, ⅛ teaspoon pepper, dash of cayenne.

BAKED SHRIMP AND RICE

Brown onion in butter with garlic which has been put through press. Mix with shrimp and add all other ingredients in a large baking dish. Cover tightly and bake for 1½ hours in 350° oven.

Miss Fanny's Receipt Book
West River   Anne Arundel

Church and State Circles, Annapolis   M. E. Warren

Shrimp

SIX BOY   1 onion finely chopped, ¼ cup butter, 2 table-
CURRIED   spoons curry powder, 6 tablespoons flour, 2½
SHRIMP   cups chicken broth, 1⅔ cups cream, 2 pounds
                     cooked shrimp, cooked rice.

Sauté onion in butter, add curry powder and blend. Stir in flour and
cook 2 or 3 minutes. Gradually add broth, stirring constantly until
thick and smooth. Stir in cream and check seasoning. Add shrimp and
heat thoroughly.

Serve over rice. As "boys" use chutney, French fried onions, chopped
bacon, crushed peanuts, fresh cocoanut and chopped egg. Serves 5 or 6.

Mary Alderson
Cruise Inn, State Circle   *Annapolis*

2 pounds large raw shrimp, 2 tablespoons chopped **FRICASSEED**
onion, 2 tablespoons chopped green pepper, 1 **SHRIMP**
tablespoon chopped celery, 4 tablespoons butter,
4 tablespoons flour, 1 cup chopped, peeled tomatoes; ¾ cup dry white
wine, 2 cups clam broth, 2 bay leaves, ½ teaspoon crushed garlic, 1 sprig
each of thyme and parsley, salt and pepper to taste.

Prepare shrimp by peeling and removing black vein; rinse well. Add
onion, green pepper and celery to melted butter and cook slowly until
soft but not brown. Mix in flour until smooth, adding tomatoes, then
wine, broth, shrimp and seasonings. Simmer 20 minutes. Remove
thyme, parsley and bay leaves. Serve on platter surrounded by fluffy
rice and garnished with parsley.

Mrs. James W. Webb
Scaffold Creek   *Anne Arundel*

---

2 pounds large shrimp, ¼ cup flour, ¼ cup olive **BROILED**
oil, ¼ cup butter, 1 cup drawn butter sauce, 2 **SHRIMP**
large cloves garlic, 4 tablespoons finely chopped
parsley.

Drop shrimp into boiling salted water. Boil 3 minutes, remove from
water, shell and devein. Dust with flour. Put olive oil and butter in flat
baking dish and heat under broiler until butter is melted. Place shrimp
in dish and broil under low heat about 8 minutes. Add garlic, which has
been put through garlic press, and parsley to drawn butter sauce. Pour
over shrimp and stir until all are coated. Return to broiler and broil
under high heat 2 or 3 minutes. Serve immediately. Serves 4 to 6.

Drawn butter sauce: Mix 2 tablespoons melted butter with 2 tablespoons flour, ¼ teaspoon pepper, ½ teaspoon salt, 1 teaspoon lemon
juice and 1 cup hot water. Simmer for 5 minutes, stirring constantly.

Mrs. J. Reaney Kelly
Conduit Street   *Annapolis*

Scallops

SHRIMP WITH 2 pounds large shrimp, cooked, shelled and de-
CHUTNEY SAUCE veined.

Sauce: 2 teaspoons curry powder, 3 or 4 tablespoons chutney, 1 tablespoon lemon juice, ¼ cup chili sauce, drained; 1 cup mayonnaise. Mix
all ingredients into the mayonnaise and blend well. Let ripen before
using. (Sliver mango in the chutney; dry mustard may be used instead
of curry if you prefer.)

Shrimp may be arranged on lettuce leaves in individual servers, with
sauce in centre; or they may be placed in a large glass bowl set in ice,
with sauce used as a dip.

Miss Grace's Receipt Book
Tenthouse Creek   *Anne Arundel*

TO FRY Cover the scallops with boiling water and let them
SCALLOPS stand 3 minutes; drain, and dry them with a towel.
Season with salt and pepper, dip first in beaten
egg, then in bread crumbs, and fry golden brown in boiling fat or oil.

Mrs. William H. Kirkpatrick
Parkhurst   *Anne Arundel*

MUSTARD 6 tablespoons butter, 2 tablespoons lemon juice,
SCALLOPS 2 tablespoons prepared mustard, salt and paprika
to taste, 1½ pounds scallops, 1 cup diced celery,
buttered toast rounds, parsley.

Melt 3 tablespoons butter, add lemon juice, mustard and seasonings.
Cook scallops and celery in boiling water to cover until scallops begin
to shrink. Drain thoroughly. Sauté in remaining butter for 3 minutes.
Add to hot sauce; serve on toast with a sprinkling of chopped parsley.

Professor John Reed
U. S. Naval Academy   *Annapolis*

2 pounds scallops, ½ pound mushrooms, 1 small **BAKED**
onion, 4 tablespoons butter, 3 tablespoons flour, **SCALLOPS**
2 cups rich milk, ½ cup or more of broth in which **AND**
scallops were cooked, salt and pepper to taste, ½ **MUSHROOMS**
cup sherry, ½ cup buttered bread crumbs.

Wash scallops and barely cover with water; bring to a simmer and cook
10 minutes. Drain, reserving liquid. Cool, then cut scallops in half.
Wash and slice mushrooms, chop onion, and sauté both in butter. Add
flour and blend until smooth; add milk and scallop liquid and season
well with salt and pepper. Add sherry and cook slowly until thickened.
Mix in scallops and turn into buttered oven dish. Cover with buttered
crumbs and bake in 350° oven for about 30 minutes.

Mrs. H. Gates Sickel
Hanover Street
Annapolis

---

1 tablespoon butter, 2 tablespoons flour, 1 cup **LOBSTER CHOPS**
light cream, yolks of 3 hard-boiled eggs, 1 table-
spoon chopped parsley, salt, pepper, a little freshly grated nutmeg, a
dash of cayenne, 2 cups boiled lobster meat, cut up rather fine.

Melt butter in a saucepan; when it bubbles add flour; cook but do not
brown; add cream slowly, stirring until smooth. Remove from fire and
add egg yolks mashed fine, the parsley, salt, pepper, nutmeg and cayenne
to suit your taste. Stir in lobster meat. When all is well mixed, spread
on a platter to cool. The chops will mold better if mixture is left for
some time to chill and harden. Mold mixture into the form of chops.
Dip them in egg, roll in fresh bread crumbs and immerse in hot fat
until fried to an amber color. After they are fried, insert a small claw in
the pointed end to represent chop bone and arrange on a hot platter
garnished with parsley.

Miss Adelaide's Century Book, 1900
Ivy Neck, Rhode River
Anne Arundel

SCALLOPED
LOBSTER
4 small (1¼ pounds) boiled lobsters, 2 table-spoons butter, 2 tablespoons flour, 1 cup chicken broth, salt, red pepper, paprika to taste, ½ cup cream, 2 egg yolks, ½ cup sherry wine, bread crumbs with butter.

Remove meat from cooked lobsters and cut into small pieces. Make a dressing of butter, flour, chicken broth and seasoning. Simmer a few minutes and then add cream and beaten egg yolks. Stir constantly until thick and smooth. Mix the lobster meat, while hot, in this dressing, then stir in the sherry wine. Put it in the shells, previously prepared; fill them up, and put crumbs over them with a little butter. Bake in 400° oven until brown. Makes 4 servings.

A 19th century receipt, Mrs. Howard's
Miss Nancy D. Mitchell   *Baltimore*

LOBSTER
MOUSSE
1 envelope unflavored gelatine, ¼ cup water, 3 tomatoes, peeled and diced; 3 hard-boiled eggs, chopped; 2 cups cooked lobster meat, 1 teaspoon salt, ¼ teaspoon white pepper, ½ teaspoon dry mustard, 1 cup heavy cream.

Dilute gelatine in water and melt thoroughly over hot water. Add diced tomatoes and chopped eggs to lobster meat and season with salt, pepper and mustard. Add melted gelatine and mix well. Fold whipped cream into the mixture. Rinse a suitable fish or lobster mold in cold water, and fill with lobster mixture. Chill for several hours and serve with Aurora Sauce. (See Sauces for Fish.)

Mrs. Clifton B. Cates
South River   *Anne Arundel*

LOBSTER
SALAD BOWL
3 cups picked out lobster meat, ½ cup mayon-naise, 2 tablespoons tomato catsup, 4 tablespoons brandy, 2 teaspoons finely chopped chives, 1 tea-spoon finely chopped parsley, juice of 1 lime, paprika, salt and pepper.

Mix all ingredients together, and place in a glass bowl set in cracked ice. Serve on crisp lettuce leaves.

Mrs. Frank Jack Fletcher
Araby   *Charles*

Chesapeake Bay Fish

A. Aubrey Bodine

Bay Harvest

BAKED SHAD
WITH ROE
Whole shad and roe, 1 tablespoon chopped parsley, 1 tablespoon grated onion, ½ cup soft bread crumbs, ¼ cup soft butter, salt and pepper, white wine.

Scald roe for 2 minutes. Drain, split and scrape out roe. Add parsley, onion, bread crumbs, a little butter and seasoning; blend, then stuff fish. Tie or skewer, put in shallow greased pan and sprinkle with seasoned flour. Bake 35 minutes in hot oven, basting frequently with butter. Add white wine to pan butter for basting. Garnish with lime or lemon.

Mrs. H. K. Rigg
Replica, Holly Beach Farm   *Anne Arundel*

CHARCOAL
BROILED SHAD
Charcoal fire, 1 grill, 1 shad, split and with backbone and fins removed, 6 slices of bacon.

Place split shad between leaves of grill overlapping thin portions. Lay 3 slices bacon on shad, close grill and turn over, open other side and lay on 3 more slices bacon. Close grill and wait for fire to burn down to red coals. Broil shad over charcoal coals for about 13 to 14 minutes, turning grill about every 10 seconds. If result looks black, try it anyhow, and you will be surprised to find how good it tastes. It is the same flavor enjoyed in olden times when shad was cooked on a plank in the open hearth. If it is *too* burned, you should have turned it more frequently.

Admiral Kenneth H. Noble
Severn River   *Anne Arundel*

PLANKED SHAD   A 3 or 3½ pound shad, hard-wood plank, salt and pepper, melted butter, mashed potatoes.

Clean and split shad. Put skin side down on buttered hard-wood plank of generous proportions, sprinkle with salt and pepper, and brush over with melted butter. Bake 25 minutes in hot oven, 400°, or broil, not too close to grill. Remove from oven, spread again with butter, and surround with creamy mashed potatoes arranged in mounds. Return to oven until potatoes are lightly browned. Garnish with parsley and lemon slices and serve on plank. Serves 6.

Maryland Inn   *Annapolis*

Shad Bush
Francis E. Engle

Shad Roe

TO POACH
SHAD ROE
Handle roe carefully, with membrane intact. Cover with boiling water. For each quart of water, add 1 tablespoon vinegar or lemon juice, ½ teaspoon salt. Lower heat and simmer until white and firm, from 5 to 20 minutes, depending on size. Drain, and cover with cold water. Cool, and drain again. Remove membrane or not, as desired. After this poaching, roes may be either broiled or fried and served with Herb Sauce for Roe. (See Sauces for Fish.)

Mrs. John LeMoyne Randall
Winchester-on-Severn   *Anne Arundel*

SHAD ROE,
BAY STYLE
Season shad roe to taste with salt and pepper. Sauté it in ample butter in a heavy skillet with a cover over it. Cook it very slowly to prevent the eggs from exploding. Turn carefully from time to time to preserve the shape. It will take about half an hour to cook through and brown. Serve very hot, garnished with parsley and lemon wedges and accompanied with a sauce-boat of browned butter.

Carroll McTavish Elder
Tred Avon River   *Talbot*

SHAD ROE,
BROILED
For one pair of shad roe, make a marinade as follows: 3 tablespoons olive oil, 4 teaspoons lemon juice, ½ small onion, thinly sliced, 2 teaspoons chopped parsley, salt and pepper to taste.

Let roe rest in marinade from 1 to 2 hours, basting frequently. Do not break the roe membrane. Place roe in shallow broiling pan about 4 inches from the heat. As they broil, baste roe with remaining marinade and some melted butter. Brown each side nicely, turning carefully but once. Garnish platter with watercress and serve with Lemon, Chive and Butter Sauce (page 213) or Hollandaise Sauce for Shad Roe (page 212). Serves 2.

Alice's way
Tulip Hill, West River   *Anne Arundel*

Tulip Hill

Shad Roe

4 pairs of shad roe, butter, ½ pound lump crab, 1 cup rich cream sauce, well seasoned with salt, pepper and a pinch of mace.

STUFFED SHAD ROE

Cook slowly in a generous amount of butter in a heavy skillet until roes are a rich brown on both sides and not at all dry. In the meantime carefully mix crab lumps in enough cream sauce to bind together, and heat through in top of double boiler. Split each half roe, taking care not to unhinge it. Stuff neatly with crab meat mixture. Reheat briefly in oven, so as to send to table very hot. Serve with browned butter, or accompanied with fresh Maryland asparagus and Hollandaise Sauce. (See Sauces for Vegetables.)

Tulip Hill Receipts
West River

Anne Arundel

Rock

BAKED STUFFED 3 to 5 pound rock fish, 4 tablespoons butter, 2
ROCK FISH slices of salt pork, diced; ½ cup chopped onion,
¼ cup chopped celery, ¼ cup chopped green
pepper, 1 cup fine bread crumbs, 1 teaspoon thyme, ¼ cup chopped
toasted almonds, 2 or 3 slices of bacon, pepper.

Melt butter, add pork, onion, celery and green pepper and cook until
tender. Combine other ingredients and add to mixture. Stuff fish securing with tooth-picks. Take a piece of aluminum foil sufficiently large
to contain fish, and lay it on the foil. Brush fish with melted butter
and lay 2 or 3 slices of bacon on it. Sprinkle with pepper, fold up foil
and close ends. Place on a baking sheet, and bake in a 400° oven for
30 minutes. Then open foil, and continue baking for 15 or 20 minutes,
basting once, until done. Test with a fork. Serves 4 to 6 according to
size of fish.

Mrs. Finley France
Ridout Creek *Anne Arundel*

STRIPED BASS 1 striped bass, 3 to 5 pounds; salt, pepper, 2 table-
STUFFED WITH spoons chopped onion, ¼ cup chopped celery,
CRABMEAT ½ cup butter, 2 cups soft bread crumbs, 1 cup
flaked crabmeat, 1 tablespoon chopped parsley, 1
cup milk, 1 large onion, sliced; parsley and lemon.

Wash the bass and sprinkle it inside and out with salt and pepper.
Sauté chopped onion and celery in ¼ cup of butter until lightly
browned. Mix together the sautéed vegetables, bread crumbs, crabmeat,
chopped parsley, salt and pepper. Stuff fish and secure with skewers,
or sew it together. Place fish in a shallow baking dish, and put milk and
sliced onion in the pan. Pour ¼ cup melted butter over fish. Bake uncovered in a moderate oven at 350° for about 45 minutes. Garnish top
of fish with thin slices of lemon dipped in chopped parsley. Serves 4 to 6.

Maryland Inn *Annapolis*

Francis E. Engle

Rock Fisherman

Rock

1 large rock fish, about 5 pounds; ½ pound mush-rooms, 1 cup strong chicken stock, butter, 4 table-spoons chopped parsley, salt and pepper.

**POACHED
ROCK FISH**

Fillet the rock and cut fillet into 3 inch pieces. Place it in an oven dish and dot well with butter. Sprinkle over it the mushrooms, lightly sautéed in butter, and add a generous cup of strong chicken broth, the parsley and seasoning. Poach gently in a moderate oven until fish flakes with a fork. Remove fish, keep warm, and reduce stock on top of stove. Thicken slightly with butter and flour. Reheat fish in the sauce and serve.

*Carroll McTavish Elder
Tred Avon River*

Talbot

Rock

TO DRESS ROCK　　1 rock fish, about 3 pounds; 1 small onion, sliced;
WITH SAUCE　　　a bay leaf, 3 cloves, 1 carrot, 1 stalk celery, 1
tablespoon vinegar, 1 teaspoon salt, 3 or 4 peppercorns.

Tie up the cleaned fish in cheesecloth. Place it in warm water to cover,
to which has been added the onion, bay leaf, cloves, carrot, celery, vinegar, salt and peppercorns. Let come to boil quickly, then turn down to
simmer, and cook gently about ten minutes to the pound. Lift fish out
of water carefully and place on serving platter before removing cheese-
cloth.

Egg Sauce: 1 pint rich white sauce, 2 or 3 tablespoons fish stock, ¼
cup capers, pinch of cayenne, 1 teaspoon or more lemon juice, salt and
pepper to taste, 3 hard-boiled eggs, sliced; paprika.

Add all ingredients to the pint of white sauce and pour it over fish.
Sprinkle lightly with paprika, and garnish platter with thin slices of
lemon and sprigs of parsley.

Thos. Middleton's way
Miss Ann Chase's Book, 1811　　　　　　　　　　　　*Annapolis*

ROCK FILLETS　　1½ pounds rock fillets, 1 cup fish stock. (See
WITH CRAB　　　Sauces for Fish.)

Arrange rock fillets on baking dish, pour fish stock over them, and bake
in a hot oven, 475°, for about 12 minutes. Lift fillets carefully and set
aside; strain stock in pan.

Crab base for fillets: 1 pound crab meat, 2 tablespoons melted butter,
2 or 3 tablespoons cream, salt, pepper, cayenne, nutmeg. Add melted
butter to crab meat, add cream and seasonings to taste. Heat over slow
fire and spread on bottom of hot serving dish. Arrange fillets on top and
pour over sauce.

Sauce: 2 tablespoons butter, 2 tablespoons flour, salt and pepper, ½
cup fish stock, ½ cup heated milk, ½ tablespoon grated Parmesan
cheese, 2 tablespoons cream, whipped a little. Melt butter, blend in
flour, add strained fish stock. Thicken over medium flame and add milk,
stirring until mixture bubbles. Add seasonings to taste. Stir in cheese
and simmer a few minutes until creamy. Fold in whipped cream and
pour over fillets. If an oven-proof serving dish is used, the sauce will
brown quickly and prettily under broiler.

Miss Grace's Receipt Book
Tenthouse Creek　　　　　　　　　　　　　　*Anne Arundel*

Smoking Rock Fish

Rock

SMOKED ROCK FISH

Clean fish leaving head on. Soak overnight in salt water. Hang on stick through gills and smoke for 6 hours, using mostly red oak.

Captain Charles Haas
Deep Creek off the Magothy

Anne Arundel

FISH FILLETS 'KINSHIP'

6 fillets cut from 3 good sized flounder or rock fish, 4 tablespoons butter, ½ cup blanched almonds, ½ pound fresh mushrooms, juice of ½ lemon, 1 tablespoon chopped parsley, salt, pepper, nutmeg, ½ glass dry white wine.

Lay cleaned and dried fillets in a buttered pan, and season them with salt and pepper. Chop or slice mushrooms thin, and sprinkle them with lemon juice. Chop or sliver blanched almonds. Make a mixture of the softened butter, mushrooms with lemon, almonds and parsley; season with salt, pepper and a little nutmeg. Add the white wine to pan. Spread butter mixture evenly and rather thickly over fillets. Bake in a 475° oven for 15 or 20 minutes.

Miss Grace's Receipt Book
Tenthouse Creek

Anne Arundel

83

BAKED FILLET
OF FLOUNDER
1½ pounds fillet of flounder, 2½ pounds spinach, cooked and chopped; 3½ tablespoons flour, 4½ tablespoons butter, 2 cups milk (part table cream), 1 tablespoon chopped onion, ¼ cup grated sharp cheese, 6 whole cooked shrimp.

Spread spinach on bottom of oven dish. Place fillets on spinach and sprinkle chopped onion over fish; season with salt and pepper. Over all spread cream sauce made with butter, flour and milk and seasoned to taste. Arrange shrimp along top, sprinkle on the grated cheese and bake for 20 minutes until lightly browned in a 400° oven.

Mrs. John Kavanagh
Ruxton   *Baltimore*

BAKED
BLUE FISH
1 large blue fish, 2 or 3 tablespoons butter, salt and pepper, 1 large tomato, chopped; 3 shallots, finely chopped; 1 tablespoon chopped parsley, ½ lemon, cut in paper-thin slices; ½ cup dry white wine.

Place cleaned fish in a buttered oven dish. Season inside and out with salt and pepper. Dot well with butter and sprinkle with chopped tomato, shallots and parsley. Arrange lemon slices over fish, pour on wine. Butter a piece of waxed paper and place over the fish. Bake in a 375° oven about 12 minutes to the pound or until fish flakes easily.

Mrs. John F. Meigs
Southgate Avenue   *Annapolis*

BROILED
BLUE FISH
Blue fish, lemon juice, salt and pepper, flour, butter.

Wash fish and remove scales and head. Split, clean and remove larger bones. Wipe fish and sprinkle with lemon juice, salt and pepper. Sprinkle skin side lightly with flour. Dot fish with butter and place on greased broiler, flesh side up, about 3 inches from flame. Baste with butter and lemon juice frequently to prevent drying out. When fish is firm and white, remove carefully to warm platter, and garnish with lemon wedges and parsley.

Annapolis Yacht Club
Spa Creek   *Annapolis*

Roe Herring

Dredge roes lightly in flour seasoned with salt and pepper. Cook in hot butter in a heavy skillet until golden brown on both sides and cooked through. Serve with lemon wedges.

FRESH HERRING ROE

Woodfield's
Galesville, West River

Anne Arundel

After washing 1 pound of herring roe, steam in very little water; put in colander and drain. Mash with a spoon and pick out little strings. To a little grated onion, add Worcestershire sauce, paprika, salt and pepper to taste. Mix with roe. Then stir in 2 tablespoons melted butter and 1 beaten egg. Very light sprinkle of flour. Roll in cakes. Fry in very little fat.

FISH ROE CAKES

Mrs. Edward Lloyd
Eight Bells, Oxford

Talbot

SMOKED ROE HERRING Get 50 to 100 nice plump roe herring in the Spring. Scale and wash well. Pack in a crock between layers of dry salt for 2 weeks. They make their own brine. Take out and rinse well. Hang up and let dry one day. Then smoke about 24 hours or until a nice brown. These may be wrapped and frozen. Freshen overnight in water before using.

Carroll McTavish Elder
Tred Avon River   *Talbot*

SALTING ROE HERRING One 3 gallon crock, 40 cleaned roe herring, leaving tails on and roes in; 1 box black pepper, 6 pounds salt, 2 lemons.

When herring have been cleaned, soak them in brine overnight. Drain the herring and get crock, pepper, salt, etc., ready.

Sprinkle each herring inside and out with salt and pepper. As each is so treated, place on its back in the crock. With proper overlapping you can pack 10 to 13 in each layer. Pour salt over each layer to fill interstices. Squeeze juice of half a lemon over each layer and also throw in the rind cut in small pieces. When all the herring have been packed, make up about a gallon of brine and pour into the crock (brine strong enough to float an egg), so that when bubbles cease to rise, the contents of the crock are covered with brine. Put cover on crock and store.

Admiral Kenneth H. Noble
Severn River   *Anne Arundel*

FRIED SALT ROE HERRING 1 salt roe herring, bacon grease, cornmeal.

Soak the salt roe herring over night in fresh water. Dry, remove back fin and tail, and sprinkle with cornmeal. Put bacon grease in frying pan (more than you would use to fry an egg), and when hot, place fish in pan and cover. Adjust heat so that grease does not smoke. Cook fish for about five minutes on each side, or until brown and crisp.

Admiral Kenneth H. Noble
Severn River   *Anne Arundel*

Select fresh hardheads or croakers, pan size, one for each person to be served. **CRISP FRIED HARDHEAD**

To pan fry: Clean, season with salt and pepper, dip in flour or cornmeal and cook in skillet, preferably a thick-bottomed iron one, in shallow hot fat.

"When frying fish the fire must be hot enough to bring the fat to such a degree of heat as to sear the surface and make it impervious to the fat, and at the same time seal in the rich juices. As soon as the fish is browned by this sudden application of heat, the fire may be lowered, that the process may be finished more slowly." (From on old manuscript.)

Pan size perch, trout or Norfolk spot may be cooked in this way.

To oven fry: Clean, dry, season with salt and pepper, dip in crumbs, beaten egg, crumbs, and let stand. Place on a well greased oven pan or cookie sheet, with fish well separated. Sprinkle with melted fat, or dot liberally with butter, and bake in a moderately hot oven, 425°, for about 12 minutes, or until crisp and golden.

Woodfield's
Galesville, West River

Anne Arundel

2 cups cooked fish, 2 tablespoons chopped green pepper, 1 tablespoon minced onion, 2 tablespoons butter, 1 cup soft bread crumbs, ½ teaspoon salt, pepper, ½ lemon rind, grated; 2 eggs, separated; ½ cup milk. **FISH LOAF**

Shred the fish. Sauté pepper and onion in butter and add to fish with crumbs, seasoning and lemon rind. Add beaten egg yolks and milk. Fold in stiffly beaten egg whites, pour into greased loaf pan or fish mold, and bake 1 hour in a moderate oven in pan of hot water. Serve with sauce.

Sauce: 1½ cups thin white sauce with 2 tablespoons grated sharp cheese and 1 tablespoon prepared mustard blended into it.

Professor John Reed
U. S. Naval Academy

Annapolis

STUFFED PORGIES OR HARDHEAD
6 porgies (or small hardhead), ½ cup butter, 1 bunch of green onions, a few crustless bread slices, picked in small pieces; ½ cup chopped parsley, 1 teaspoon dill, salt and pepper, 1 pound cooked shrimp, ½ pound lump crab, bacon strips.

The key to this dish is in the unusual preparation and cleaning of the fish. Scale. The head may be removed or left on, as you prefer. Make a cut down center of one side from gills to tail. With a small knife work meat back to both sides and remove back bone. Clean fish from inside pocket thus provided, without breaking skin, and cut out gills. Salt and pepper fish, then stuff pocket with the following:

Sauté green onions in butter until tender, add bread crumbs, parsley, dill and seasonings, mix thoroughly. (While cooking, if. not moist enough, add more butter.) Reserve a few whole shrimp for garnish. Cut the rest in small pieces and add to stuffing with the crab lumps. Mix gently. Stuff fish well and garnish top with bacon and whole shrimp, using tooth picks to hold in shape. Place fish on squares of aluminum foil in roasting pan and bake 15 minutes in moderately hot oven, or until fish flakes easily. Remove tooth picks and arrange fish on hot platter.

Carroll McTavish Elder
Tred Avon River   *Talbot*

FISH TIMBALE
1½ pounds rock or hardhead (weigh after it has been cleaned, boned and skinned); whites of 4 eggs, 1 teaspoon cornstarch, juice of 1 small onion, salt, pepper and nutmeg, freshly grated; 2 cups milk, 2 cups thin cream.

Grind raw fish in food chopper or blender until fine. Add egg whites, one at a time, and continue blending until you have a very smooth paste. Add cornstarch, diluted in a little milk, and onion juice; season to taste with salt, pepper and nutmeg. Gradually add cream and milk, beating until mixture is very creamy and smooth. Pour into a buttered mold and bake in a slow (325°) oven in pan of hot water until timbale is firm. This looks very nice baked in a fish mold. Serve hot with Oyster, Shrimp or Lobster Sauce. (See Sauces for Fish.)

Mrs. Harry R. Slack's Book
Bishop's Road   *Baltimore*

Use cooked flounder, hardhead or rock bass. Dis- **FISH IN**
solve 1 envelope gelatine as directed, but instead **ASPIC**
of water for the liquid, use fish stock (see Sauces
for Fish) and ½ pint white wine. Taste for seasoning. Pour a thick
layer of aspic in bottom of fish mold, and when it has hardened slightly,
arrange clusters of peeled seedless white grapes, alternating with mounds
of flaked fish. Pour rest of aspic over all and chill until well set. Unmold, garnish with watercress and serve with mayonnaise or Cold
Cucumber Sauce (see Sauces for Fish).

Receipts from Araby   *Charles*

Frogs' Legs

Allow 6 small pairs of frog legs or 3 very large **FRIED**
ones per serving. They must be very fresh. **FROG LEGS**

Wash frog legs thoroughly, and sprinkle liberally with lemon juice.
Let them become very chilled in refrigerator. Rinse and pat them dry.
Season lightly with salt and pepper. Dredge with flour and dip in beaten
egg, then roll in freshly made small bread crumbs. Shake off excess
crumbs and fry in butter until brown on both sides. Serve hot, garnished
with watercress.

Annapolis Yacht Club
Spa Creek   *Annapolis*

Frog legs, 12 pairs of desired size; 1 tablespoon **FROG LEGS**
chopped parsley, 1 tablespoon chopped onion, 4
tablespoons butter, a few peppercorns, salt, ½ cup white wine, a little
lemon juice.

Clean frog legs thoroughly; blanch 5 minutes in boiling water, no more,
as it toughens them. Wipe dry with towel, wrap frog legs in it and put
on ice. Sauté parsley and onion in 2 tablespoons butter with peppercorns until butter is well flavored. Strain butter and return to pan. Add
2 more tablespoons butter and fry frog legs until lightly browned. At
the last, season lightly, add white wine and a few drops of lemon juice
while completing frying. Heap frog legs on hot platter and pour sauce
from pan over all.

Mrs. Truxtun Beale's Book, 1903
Decatur House   *Washington*

Diamond Back Terrapins   A. Aubrey Bodine

Diamond Back Terrapin

TO PREPARE AND COOK DIAMOND BACK TERRAPIN
It is a question of choice whether the terrapin's head should be cut off, some claiming that it should be, that it may bleed, others that it should be put in the pot alive.. If the head is cut off, place the terrapin with the neck down for a few minutes so the blood can run from it.

Have two vessels of boiling water, put them in one and let them remain for five or six minutes, then take them out, and a flaky skin can be easily removed from all the exposed meat by rubbing with the fingers. This cannot be done after the terrapin has been cooked and the meat has become soft.

Put them now in the other pot of boiling water and boil until you can, with the forefinger and thumb, easily press through the foot. For a five inch terrapin this takes about one hour, for larger ones of course longer. But, by taking it out of the pot and testing in this way, a mistake cannot be made. The great success of the dish is this cooking, for unless this is properly done they are apt to be stringy or tough.

After the terrapins are done, take them from the pot and put in a vessel that will hold the liquor that runs from them. Remove the top shell; if it is inclined to stick, use a thin knife to run up between the shell and the meat. Some little tidbits are apt to adhere to the shell. Save them. Sometimes the sand bags adhere too; these are one of the few things about the terrapin you must throw away. After removing the upper shell you will find the sand bags or lungs, unless they have remained on the top shell, on top of the meat. Remove these with a fork; they are thin and leathery looking.

Carefully open the meat, find the liver, open it and remove the gall with as little of the liver attached as possible. Some epicures break one gall to six terrapins. All the rest of the meat is good except some of the intestines at the extremity. Do not pick the meat too fine. Save the liquor that has come from the terrapin in the vessel in which they were placed, and add to this enough liquor taken from the pot in which they were last boiled to use when they are put in the chafing dish. A great many people never think of this and use plain water to make the necessary liquor; this is not nearly so rich.

When ready to serve, put the meat in the chafing dish, and add the liquor that has been saved as above, as you prefer, in good quantity or enough to keep from burning. A good quantity is recommended for it is delicious. Before this, butter should have been used; indeed when first the terrapin is put in the chafing dish lumps of butter should be placed all over; then light the chafing dish, give a stir so the butter will melt, stir again, add more butter, add a little more butter; just before serving season with red pepper and salt, add a little more butter, and then just a little more butter.

The chafing dish is not to cook it, simply to make it piping hot, and as soon as it reaches that stage, serve on hot plates. Should any be present who wishes wine, let him add it after it is served. Never put wine in when cooking.

Maryland biscuit should be served with terrapin.

Commodore Rodger's way
Sion Hill Papers
                                                                Harford

Terrapin

TO COOK
TERRAPINS
Boil a few and pick them, cutting out the gall; reserve the eggs and put all to stew with ½ pint of Claret, rather more Madeira wine, a tea cup of Catsup—season with cayenne, black pepper, salt, mace, cloves, nutmeg, sweet marjoram, parsley and onion—put a large lump of butter into flour and put into them then stew all well together. Garnish with the eggs and sliced lemon.

Sam'l. Chase (one of Maryland's four Signers of the Declaration of Independence).
Miss Ann Chase's Book, 1811   *Annapolis*

"On Monday, 2nd. May 1762, I was married to Miss Nancy Baldwin, daughter of Thomas and Agnes Baldwin, by the Rev. Mr. Barclay. Sam'l. Chase."

A receipt for a happy life, found in Miss Ann's Book.

MARYLAND
CLUB TERRAPIN
Put Diamond Back Terrapins in cold water. Keep in until they wake up and swim around; then drop in boiling water and scald for 3 minutes. Rub off skin. Put to boil again from 45 to 60 minutes according to weight. We use 6½ to 7 inch terrapins. Break shell apart, being careful not to break gall which is attached to liver and must be cut away. Slice liver small; wash eggs and set aside. Cool and pick. Reduce broth to strong jelly and use enough to cover meat being served. Use ¾ pound sweet butter per quart of meat; season with salt and cayenne pepper. Heat terrapin meat with stock, butter and seasonings for 10 to 15 minutes; place eggs on top before serving. Add sherry to taste at table.

Maryland Club   *Baltimore*

TERRAPIN
IN CREAM
6 hard-boiled eggs, 8 tablespoons butter, 2 cups cream, ½ teaspoon salt, pepper, allspice, nutmeg, 2 cups cooked, picked terrapin meat; ½ cup sherry.

Force egg yolks through sieve, then cream them with butter. Scald cream over hot water, add seasonings, and beat in egg yolk and butter mixture. Add terrapin, sherry, and heat thoroughly.

Mrs. S. Scott Beck
Chestertown   *Kent*

Domestic Fowl

A. Aubrey Bodine

Preparing Maryland Fried Chicken

Chicken

MRS. VIRGIL MAXCY'S FRIED CHICKENS

Cut up the chickens, pepper and salt them. Dredge them well with flour on both sides and lay them on a sieve, each piece separately. Take a large tablespoonful of nice lard, and when it boils, throw in a good bunch of parsley and fry it quickly that it may be green though crisp; then take it out, to be put on the chickens when served up. Afterwards put in the chickens and fry them briskly a yellowish brown and lay them on the dish with the parsley over them. Take the lard out of the pan and put in it a piece of butter the size of a small egg, and as soon as it boils, dredge in a little flour, and the moment it browns add a teacup of milk and after shaking it round briskly in the pan for a minute, pour it over the chickens and serve them up hot. Care should be taken that the chickens should not be put into the lard until it boils, and that they be fried quickly and taken as soon as done out of the pan, or they may taste of the lard. The parsley should be fried before the chickens, as it gives an agreeable flavour to the lard. In order to have this dish in perfection, the chickens should be about two months old and very fat.

Original Old Maryland Receipt
Mrs. Virgil Maxcy, Tulip Hill, 1815
Mrs. Francis Markoe Dugan   *Baltimore*

SOUTHERN FRIED CHICKEN

1 large frying chicken, cut in serving pieces; salt, 1 cup flour, 1 teaspoon baking powder, ½ teaspoon salt, vegetable oil.

Rub salt over chicken pieces and let drain, then dry well. Mix flour, baking powder and salt in a paper bag. Shake a few pieces of chicken at a time in flour mixture to coat. Fry quickly in deep hot vegetable oil until tender and golden brown. Serve immediately.

Women's Auxiliary, St. James Parish
Tracy's Landing   *Anne Arundel*

Sudley

Chicken

1 young frying chicken, 1 cup flour, ½ teaspoon salt, ¼ teaspoon pepper, fat for frying, butter, 1 cup milk. **MARYLAND FRIED CHICKEN**

Cut up chicken into serving pieces. Sift flour and mix with salt and pepper. Dredge chicken pieces well on both sides with seasoned flour. Have about ½ inch of hot fat in a large frying pan. Put chicken in and cover pan for 5 to 7 minutes. Uncover and turn chicken when underside is a rich, golden brown. Cover again for the same length of time, then remove top and finish browning chicken. Reduce heat, remove excess fat from pan, add a very little water, cover again and steam until tender, juicy and done through to bone. This will take about 10 to 20 minutes longer, depending on size of pieces. Take chicken out and arrange on hot serving platter. To make cream gravy, pour off most of fat, leaving the brown crumbs. Put a small lump of butter in pan and scrape up all crusty brown bits. Add a little seasoned flour and blend until smooth. Pour in gradually a cup of rich milk and stir until creamy and thickened. Test seasoning. Strain through a coarse sieve, if necessary. Gravy may be served over chicken or in a sauce boat. Fried Mush is a nice accompaniment, surrounding chicken on platter.

Elsie's way
Mrs. William F. Kelly, Sudley   *Anne Arundel*

CHICKEN WITH OYSTERS   1 tender chicken cut in quarters, 3 tablespoons butter, ½ cup milk, 1 pint oysters, 1 cup cream, salt and pepper.

Brown chicken slowly in butter. Place in baking dish and pour milk over it. Bake, covered, for ½ hour in a 375° oven. Then add oysters and cream, salt and pepper, and bake a little longer until heated through and oysters puff and frill. When done, remove chicken to platter, thicken sauce with flour rolled in butter and pour over chicken to serve.

Adapted from a 200 year old receipt
Miss Fanny's Receipt Book   *Anne Arundel*

A WHITE FRICASSEE   Take a very white delicate looking chicken, clean it perfectly and dry it in a clean cloth. Set on a stewpan with equal proportions of Milk and Water, put in the chicken well seasoned with salt and pepper, and stew it over a gentle Fire till it is thoroughly tender. Cut the chicken in pieces and strip off the skin. Set on another stewpan and put in it half a pint of chicken essence, the same quantity of cream and a piece of butter about the size of an egg mixed with a little flour. Boil the cream and butter and put the chicken into it. Add about four blades of mace just before taking up, finely powdered.

A BROWN FRICASSEE   Rub the Crumb of a Loaf to pieces then grate a little nutmeg and bruise a blade of mace,—rub this in the Crumb, and season it with salt and pepper. Cut a Chicken to Pieces and skin them and rub them over with the Yolk of an egg, and Roll them bit by bit in the seasoned crumbs. Set on a Saucepan with some butter,—when it is melted put in the chicken. Let the fire be brisk and fry the pieces brown,—stir them frequently to prevent them sticking to the pan. When they are brown drain off the butter and pour in a pint or more of strong chicken Broth, a large glass of red wine, and three spoonfuls of Mushrooms, pickled or fresh as you have them. Let these be well heated together and then put in a piece of butter rolled in flour. When it is melted and the sauce is thick send it up.

Two old Maryland Receipts labeled "the best Fricassees that ever was—the lovely Mrs. Chase's."
Miss Ann Chase's Book, 1811   *Annapolis*

Chase Lloyd House

Don Swann

6 chicken breasts, several celery stalks and leaves, 1 large onion, sliced; 1 clove garlic, pinch of rosemary, salt and pepper.

CHICKEN IN BATTER

Poach chicken breasts in very little water with celery, onion and 1 cut clove of garlic, seasoning with salt, pepper and rosemary when half done. When tender, lift breasts from pan and let cool; remove skin and carefully bone them. Dip in West River Waffle Batter (see Breads) and fry in deep fat (375°) until golden brown. Arrange on hot platter, garnish with watercress and serve immediately with Lemon Sauce. (See Sauces for Fowl.)

Mrs. James W. Webb
Scaffold Creek

Anne Arundel

STEWED CHICKEN WITH DUMPLINGS

1 large stewing chicken, celery tops, 1 onion, 1 bay leaf, pinch of powdered thyme, salt and pepper, 3 tablespoons flour, 3 tablespoons butter.

Cut chicken in serving pieces and place in a heavy stew pan. Barely cover with water, add celery tops, cut up onion, bay leaf, thyme, salt and pepper. Bring to a boil slowly but do not let it boil. Cover and simmer until tender. Remove chicken and keep it hot. Strain broth, return to stew pot and thicken with flour mixed with softened butter. Bring to boil and when bubbling add dumplings.

Light Dumplings: 1 cup flour, ½ teaspoon salt, 1 teaspoon baking powder, a pinch of soda, 1 tablespoon melted butter, ⅜ to ½ cup milk (sufficient to make soft dough).

Combine ingredients and drop by spoonfuls into the hot liquid. Cover tightly, boil gently for 20 minutes exactly, without lifting lid. Serve at once with chicken and gravy.

Mrs. McBlair's way
Maria T. Allison's Book, 1860   *Baltimore*

GENIE'S SMOTHERED CHICKEN

1 young chicken, cut up; salt and pepper, ½ cup (generous) of half cooking fat and butter, chicken giblets, 3 cups water, a few celery tops and onion slices, 3 tablespoons flour, 1 cup chopped mushrooms, minced parsley.

Season pieces of chicken well, and brown them in a big frying pan in the mixture of fat (bacon fat is good) and butter. While chicken browns, (it will take about 10 or 15 minutes), simmer giblets together with neck, back and wing tips in water with celery tops, onion slices and light seasoning. The giblet stock is used to make the gravy. When chicken is crisp and brown, take it off the fire and put it in a shallow baking pan. Add flour to fat in pan, brown it and pour in slowly the giblet stock, stirring with concentration so there won't be a sign of a lump. Add a trifle more water if you think you are skimping on gravy. When it has thickened, add chopped giblets. Taste for seasoning, then pour this gravy over chicken. Add mushrooms, if you would like a Senator's dish. Let chicken cook in a slow oven until meat is very tender and sauce rich and thickened. Serve this fine bird with a good splattering of minced parsley.

A very old receipt, long used at Olney Inn   *Montgomery*

8 whole breasts of squab chicken, boned (not too large). *Stuffing:* ¼ cup butter, ¼ cup chopped onion, 4 cups crustless bread, in small dice; 2 tablespoons chopped parsley, ½ cup chopped celery, ½ teaspoon salt, ½ teaspoon paprika, pinch of nutmeg, 1 pint oysters, drained, and coarsely cut up; milk.

BREAST OF SQUAB CHICKEN WITH OYSTERS

Melt butter; sauté onion in it until tender. Add the combined ingredients, toss thoroughly and moisten lightly with part milk and part oyster liquor.

Season each chicken breast and stuff with ⅓ to ½ cup dressing. Fold over the two sides, then the ends, securing with skewers or stout thread, as you would a package. Place in roasting pan, leaving a little space between birds, and rub breasts with softened butter. Roast in a moderate oven for ½ hour, or until done, basting occasionally with a little stock and melted butter. A few minutes under broiler flame at the end will brown tops nicely. Remove skewers or thread and serve at once with oyster sauce. (See Sauces for Fowl.) Serves 8.

Mrs. Carleton Mitchell
Sharpe's Point, Whitehall Bay

Anne Arundel

---

1 roasting chicken, 4 tablespoons butter, 8 baby carrots, whole (or 12 small pieces of carrot); 1 dozen tiny onions, ¾ cup chicken stock, salt and pepper, 1 dozen small, whole mushrooms; 1 wine glass dry white wine.

CHICKEN AND VEGETABLES WITH WHITE WINE

Melt butter in oven dish which can be covered. Tie up chicken and brown in butter, turning all around. Brown carrots and onions slowly in same butter, adding more if needed, then add stock and season all with salt and pepper. Cook in fairly hot oven (425°) for 25 minutes with top on. Baste occasionally with butter and stock. Add mushrooms and cook until chicken is tender, about 25 minutes. Lift chicken out and cut into serving pieces; take out vegetables with slotted spoon. To juice in baking dish add white wine. Let come to boil, replace chicken and vegetables, garnish with a little chopped parsley, and serve. Serves 4.

Mrs. Edwin N. Broyles
Bedford Place

Baltimore

CHICKEN WITH SHERRY WINE — 1 cut-up frying chicken, salt, pepper, flour, 4 tablespoons butter, 1 cup mushrooms, 1 cup cream, ½ cup sherry.

Season chicken pieces with salt and pepper and roll in flour. Brown well in butter. When nearly done add sliced mushrooms and cook ten minutes. Remove chicken and mushrooms to an oven dish and to sauce in pan add cream and mix well. Pour over chicken and cook slowly in oven (covered) until tender. Add sherry, warm and serve.

Mrs. Levin Campbell
Duke of Gloucester Street   *Annapolis*

CHICKEN TERRAPIN — 4 tablespoons butter, 2 tablespoons flour, 1 cup cream, ¼ teaspoon mace, 1 teaspoon salt, red and black pepper to taste, 3 hard-cooked eggs, ½ cup sherry, 1 quart diced cold chicken, (light and dark meat).

Melt butter in a saucepan over low heat. Blend in flour and gradually stir in cream, mace, salt and pepper, stirring constantly. Chop egg white fine and add to sauce. Mash yolks in a cup and mix with a little of the sauce; return to pan. Stir in sherry gradually. Add chicken and heat well. Serve at once on crisp toast. Serves 6.

Mrs. Morris K. Barroll
Byford Court, Chester River   *Kent*

AROMATIC BROILED CHICKEN — 1 3-pound frying chicken, cut up; 1 teaspoon salt, ¼ teaspoon pepper, 2 teaspoons paprika, ¼ teaspoon ground ginger, ¼ teaspoon rosemary or marjoram, ¼ cup sherry, 4 to 6 tablespoons butter.

Mix paprika, salt and pepper. Rub on chicken, then place chicken in broiling pan. Combine ginger, rosemary, melted butter and sherry, plus ⅛ cup water, and pour over chicken. Bake in moderate oven (375°) for 20 minutes or longer. When nearly tender, place on broiler rack, baste well with pan juices, and broil for about 10 minutes, or until both sides are browned.

Mrs. R. M. Phelps
Whitehall Creek   *Anne Arundel*

½ cup wild rice, 1 heart celery, 2 onions, 2 baby broilers, salt and pepper, 1 tablespoon chopped parsley, 3 tablespoons butter, 1 carrot, 1 chicken bouillon cube, 1 tablespoon brandy, watercress.

BABY BROILERS WITH WILD RICE STUFFING

Wash rice and cook in boiling salted water until tender but not mushy. Drain well, add celery chopped with one of the onions, salt, pepper and parsley. Stuff birds with this and skewer or sew up. Melt butter in a heavy roasting pan. Slice carrot and other onion fine and brown lightly in butter. Add birds and brown them carefully by rolling over and over. When they are a delicate brown, add bouillon cube dissolved in water, or a little very strong stock. Season and cover tightly. Cook slowly in the oven for ½ hour. Remove juice and pour brandy over chickens and light it. Reduce juice by simmering slowly on top of stove. Pour reduced juice over birds and serve. Garnish with watercress. Cornish Rock Hen or Squab may be dressed in this way.

Receipts from Araby

Charles

One 3 to 3½ pound frying chicken, flour, salt, pepper, butter or shortening, ½ pound mushrooms, 2 cups heavy cream, slices of Maryland country ham.

CHICKEN WITH MARYLAND HAM

Cut chicken in pieces. Sprinkle with flour, salt and pepper. Fry golden brown in butter or shortening. Remove chicken from fat. Drain slightly. Place in two-quart baking dish. Cover with sautéed mushrooms and cream. Bake in slow oven (325°) 40 to 45 minutes. Place pieces of chicken on hot slices of ham and spoon over cream sauce and mushrooms.

Mrs. William Preston Lane
Hagerstown

Washington

BRUNSWICK STEW — 1 large chicken, 6 cups fresh lima beans, 6 cups corn cut from the cob, 4 cups peeled and sliced tomatoes, salt and pepper to taste, liberal amount of butter, flour.

Simmer chicken until tender in enough water to cover. Remove bones and put meat back into the broth. Add beans, corn, tomatoes, salt and pepper. Cover and cook very slowly until thick enough to eat with a fork, stirring frequently to prevent burning. Add butter, cut in small pieces and rolled in flour. Stir constantly over the fire for a few minutes more.

Mrs. John Shallcross
Glyndon   *Baltimore*

TO CURRY A CHICKEN IN THE EAST INDIAN MANNER — One 5 pound fowl, ½ cup butter, 1 medium onion, 1 clove garlic, 1 stalk of celery, a small bay leaf, ¼ teaspoon dry mustard, 1 green apple, ¼ pound raw chopped ham, 2 tablespoons flour, ½ teaspoon powdered mace, 2 teaspoons curry powder, 2 cups chicken broth, ½ cup cocoanut milk, 1 cup cream.

Cook fowl in a savory broth until tender; cut in pieces as you wish to serve them, with or without bones. Place in saucepan. *Prepare curry as follows:* Melt butter in a heavy skillet, and in it cook the chopped onion, minced garlic and diced celery, the bayleaf, mustard, apple and ham for about 8 minutes, turning carefully. Add the flour, mace and curry powder and cook 4 minutes more. Add chicken broth, made stronger by reducing stock in which chicken was cooked. Add cocoanut milk (a good substitute may be made by pouring a cup of boiling water over 1 cup freshly grated cocoanut). Bring to a boil and let simmer very slowly for about an hour. Strain; carefully stir in cream, and test for seasoning. Pour over chicken pieces in saucepan and let cook for 10 minutes or until thoroughly hot. Serve with rice. Curry should be accompanied by these condiments: Chutney, grated cocoanut, chopped hard-boiled eggs, crisply fried chopped bacon, chopped almonds or peanuts, finely chopped spring onions.

Adapted from Mrs. McBlair's receipt
Maria T. Allison's Book, 1860   *Baltimore*

1 tablespoon butter, 2 tablespoons dried bread crumbs, ½ cup strong flavorful chicken stock, 2 cups cooked, ground chicken meat; 2 eggs, nutmeg, salt, pepper to taste.

HOT CHICKEN MOUSSE

Put butter in frying pan to melt, add crumbs and stock, stir until it boils. Take from fire and add chicken, eggs (slightly beaten) and seasoning. Fill mould and bake in a pan of hot water about an hour in a slow oven. Serve with sauce. Will serve six.

Sauce: 2 tablespoons butter, 2 tablespoons flour, 1 cup strong stock, 1 cup cream, 2 egg yolks, ½ teaspoon salt, pepper, 2 tablespoons finely cut parsley.

Melt butter and add flour; mix until smooth, then add stock and cream, stirring until it boils. Take from fire and add well beaten egg yolks, seasoning and parsley.

Mrs. Wade DeWeese
King George Street

Annapolis

---

1 young chicken or tender fowl, 1 onion, some celery tops and sprigs of parsley, thyme and rosemary, 3 eggs, 2 cups milk, 1 cup flour, ½ teaspoon salt, ¼ cup melted butter.

CHICKEN PUDDING

Cut up chicken and put pieces in a kettle with just enough water to cover well. Add sliced onion, celery tops and herbs. Stew gently and when almost tender season with salt and pepper and remove from heat. Take chicken from broth and remove skin and large bones. Place meat in a pudding dish or iron skillet. Pour over it ½ cup of broth. This makes a brown crust around the pudding. Beat eggs until light, add the milk, flour, salt and butter. It is well not to have batter too stiff. Pour over the chicken and bake in a 375° oven until set and brown—about one hour. While pudding is baking let broth cook down a bit to improve its strength. Make a gravy with the broth by adding butter rolled in flour to thicken. Add salt, pepper and chopped parsley.

Judy Tabb's way
Mrs. Frederick W. Brune's Book, 1860

Baltimore

CHICKEN
CUSTARD
1½ cups of chicken stock, free from grease. Scrape onion, and add with salt and pepper and 5 eggs, well beaten, to stock. Pour into baking cups and cook in a pan of water in oven until firm in center. Let stand a few minutes to shrink. Turn out each on a slice of toast, cover with parsley cream sauce, made with part chicken stock and part rich milk, and paprika.

From my grandmother's cook-book which came from Beverley near Pocomoke on the Eastern Shore. The house was in our family from 1669 until 1929.

Mrs. John W. Avirett II
Cock's Crow *Baltimore*

CHICKEN
POT PIE
1 plump, tender stewing chicken; 1 stalk celery, 1 onion, parsley, ½ teaspoon celery seed, yolks of 2 or 3 hard-cooked eggs, 1 tablespoon butter, 1 tablespoon flour, ¾ cup cream, pastry sufficient to line deep baking dish and make top cover, salt and pepper.

Cut up chicken and put in pot with just enough water to cover. Add celery, diced; onion, thinly sliced; parsley, chopped fine; celery seed, salt and pepper. Simmer until tender; an hour at least, or longer, if necessary. When done remove pieces of chicken from broth; take meat from bones, leaving it in as nice serving pieces as possible; discard skin and gristle. Line baking dish with pastry and arrange pieces of chicken in it. Stir into broth (about 2 cups) in which chicken cooked, the butter and flour rubbed together and the cream. Cook and stir until it thickens. Add yolks of hard-cooked eggs mashed smooth to make gravy a rich yellow. Pour over chicken and cover with pastry top. Crimp edges together and make a few vents to let out steam. Bake in a hot oven (425°) for 10 or 15 minutes; reduce heat and continue 25 to 30 minutes until pie is done. A few small onions, tiny new potatoes and carrot slices may be added if desired, but the plain chicken in rich yellow gravy is the old-fashioned way.

Mrs. Morris Hacker's
Up-to-Date Cook Book, 1897 *Anne Arundel*

4 very large broiler legs, including second joint; 2 medium onions, 2 tablespoons butter, 6 slices bread, ⅛ teaspoon thyme, 2 teaspoons sage, salt and pepper, chicken stock.

STUFFED CHICKEN LEGS

Make a cut the entire length of chicken leg on inside edge and carefully remove bone. Be very careful not to cut hole in skin over knee joint. Mince onion and sauté in butter. Add to the bread, picked fine; add the seasonings. Mix and stuff legs; sew them up with a needle and thread and brown in butter in frying pan on top of stove. Place browned chicken legs in an oven dish, and cover bottom of dish with about ⅓ inch chicken stock. Cover and bake in moderate oven until well done. Thicken pan juices with a little flour rubbed with butter. Remove thread before serving. Serves 4.

Carroll McTavish Elder
Tred Avon River

Talbot

---

1 chicken (4 pounds), 1 pint milk, 1 heaping tablespoon flour, ½ cup butter, 1 teaspoon minced onion, grating of nutmeg, 2 teaspoons chopped parsley, salt and pepper to taste, breadcrumbs, 1 egg.

AUGUSTINE'S CHICKEN CROQUETTES

Stew chicken and mince fine or grind the meat, making about 4 cups. Make cream sauce with the milk, flour, butter and seasonings, cooking until quite thick. Add the chicken meat and set aside to cool. Make into cone-shape croquettes. Roll in breadcrumbs, then in beaten egg, then again in breadcrumbs and fry a golden brown in very hot fat (butter and lard). Makes 12 croquettes.

Augustine, born a slave on a southern Maryland manor, became a famous caterer.

Miss Annie C. Claytor
Warrington, Harwood

Anne Arundel

Chicken

BARBECUED CHICKEN   3 broilers or frying chickens (about 2½ pounds each), vinegar, red and black pepper, salt, 1 cup butter, flour.

Split chickens down the back. Place in flat roasting pan, skin side down. Sprinkle vinegar over chickens. Season with red and black pepper and salt; pour one cup melted butter over all. Sprinkle with flour, lightly. Turn chickens twice during baking time; baste frequently. Bake in 325° oven, ¾ to one hour. Basting is the secret of well barbecued, moist chicken. If pan seems dry at intervals add small quantities of water. This is an excellent company dish as it can be prepared in advance, set aside in roasting pan, covered, of course, and heated again just before serving.

Mrs. Ralph H. Blackistone   *St. Mary's*

CHICKEN PANCAKES   ½ pound mushrooms, 3 tablespoons butter, onion juice, 2 white onions, 1 cup finely ground chicken, 1 cup cream, salt, pepper, cream sauce, Parmesan cheese.

Sauté mushrooms, which have been peeled and chopped fine, in 1 tablespoon butter to which has been added a little onion juice. Brown sliced onions in 2 tablespoons butter, then remove onions with slotted spoon and discard. Sprinkle chicken with flour and stir it into onion seasoned butter. Add mushrooms and cook gently a minute or two without browning. Add cream, salt and pepper to taste, and cook for a minute or two longer. Spread the chicken on French pancakes (see Breads) and roll up. Place them neatly in an oven dish, cover with cream sauce, sprinkle with cheese and bake in the oven until brown.

Receipts from Araby   *Charles*

12 chicken livers (about ½ pound), 2 tablespoons butter, 2 tablespoons chopped onion, ¼ pound mushrooms, 2 tablespoons flour, ½ cup chicken stock, ½ cup dry red wine, ½ teaspoon each chopped fresh thyme and parsley.

CHICKEN LIVERS WITH RED WINE

Cut chicken livers in two. Melt butter, sauté chopped onions and sliced mushrooms, then add chicken livers and sauté for about 3 minutes. Stir in flour, then slowly add chicken stock and wine, stirring until smooth. Add thyme and parsley and simmer gently for 10 minutes, stirring now and then. Add salt and pepper to taste. Serve hot on toast or rice. Serves 4.

Mrs. J. Reaney Kelly
Conduit Street

Annapolis

¼ pound chicken livers (about 6), 2 tablespoons butter, salt and red pepper to taste, 1 tablespoon sherry or brandy, 1 tablespoon grated onion, 3 ounces cream cheese, 1 teaspoon gelatin, 1 cup beef consomme.

CHICKEN LIVER PATÉ IN ASPIC

Cut livers in half and remove any fat or membrane. Cook gently in butter in a heavy saucepan, covered, so that they do not brown. When thoroughly done pour into a dish, including butter and liquid which has formed in pan. Chop livers, or put through sieve or ricer. Mash with a fork with salt, red pepper, sherry or brandy and grated onion to form a paste. Then mix thoroughly with softened cream cheese. Soften gelatin in a little cold water. Bring ½ cup of consomme to a boil, pour over gelatin and when dissolved, add remaining ½ cup. Coat bottom of a chilled mold with some of the consomme and place it in refrigerator to harden. Then fill mold with paté mixture. Keep cold and, with a knife, make a space around the mold. Fill in with rest of the aspic. Put back into refrigerator to harden. Serve turned out on a plate and decorate with watercress or parsley. If larger mold is wanted, double the quantity and use a ring mold. Fill center of the mold with crisp chilled watercress.

Amelia Pinkney D. Lurman

Harford

SMOKED
CHICKEN
1 tablespoon each of dried celery, sage, black pepper, parsley, thyme, marjoram, bay leaves, ¾ tablespoon sweet basil, ½ tablespoon each of coriander and cardamon, 4 pounds salt, 5 large roasting chickens.

Simmer all seasonings for 5 minutes in 5 gallons of water. Place chickens in large crock and, when cool, pour the liquid over them. Leave a 5 to 6 pound fowl in for 8 days. Rinse off in water and hang up to dry for one day. Smoke them mildly for 2 days; they may then be frozen. Bake chickens in a moderate oven 1 to 1½ hours. Slice thinly when cold. Delicious for parties. It usually is the first thing to disappear from the table.

Carroll McTavish Elder
Tred Avon River   *Talbot*

CHICKEN
SALAD
1 large stewing chicken, 1 bunch celery, salt, cayenne pepper, mayonnaise dressing, hard-boiled eggs, capers.

Cover chicken with water, add some celery tops and stew slowly until done. Let cool in broth. Remove chicken and disjoint, removing all meat from bones. Cut up white meat in fairly large pieces and dice dark meat in small pieces. Mix together. Cut into very small pieces half as much celery as you have chicken meat. Mix with chicken and strew salt and cayenne over all, then add mayonnaise, lifting and mixing. Use plenty of mayonnaise to coat every piece of chicken and celery. Place salad in a large bowl on lettuce leaves and garnish with sliced hard-boiled egg and capers.

Mrs. E. Churchill Murray
West River   *Anne Arundel*

The Maryland Scene

**Maryland House and Garden Pilgrimage
Church Luncheon**

Charles County

Old Durham Church Crab Cakes   Maryland Baked Ham

Potato Salad   Cole Slaw

Hot Biscuits

Fresh Strawberry Tarts or Rhubarb Pie

Tea   Coffee

Queen Anne's County

Chicken Salad, garnished with Tomato and
Hard-boiled Egg

Hot Buttered Asparagus

Rolls   Maryland Beaten Biscuit

Crabapple Jelly   Bread and Butter Pickle

Lemon Tarts

Old Maryland Churches

Christt Church, Charles   Maryland House and Garden Pilgrimage

A. Aubrey Bodine   St. James, Anne Arundel

Old Wye Church, Queen Anne's

Maryland House and Garden Pilgrimage

A. Aubrey Bodine

Trinity Church, Dorchester

111

**MARBLED
CHICKEN
IN JELLY**
1 stewing chicken, 1 medium onion, 1 bay leaf, 3 whole cloves, 1 blade of mace, peppercorns, ½ pound cooked ham or tongue, 1 or more stalks celery, 2 hard-cooked eggs, salt, red and black pepper, 1½ tablespoons gelatine, wine-glass of dry white wine.

Cut up chicken and put in kettle with sliced onion, bay leaf, cloves, mace and peppercorns. Barely cover with slightly salted water and simmer slowly until chicken is very tender (about 1½ hours if chicken is young). When done, remove from pot, take all meat from bones, rejecting skin and gristle, and separate white and dark meat. Put bones and skin back into kettle and simmer an hour longer, increasing strength of stock. Cut white meat, dark meat, and ham or tongue into small pieces in three separate piles. Cut celery into small dice. Slice eggs and arrange in the bottom of a square or oblong mold. Then make a layer of dark chicken meat, one of diced celery, one of white meat and one of ham or tongue. This will be the center layer; finish up with white meat, celery and dark meat.

Strain stock and test for seasoning, adding more salt, black and red pepper if needed. Chill stock thoroughly, so that all grease can be removed. Meantime, dissolve gelatine in ½ cup stock. Reheat 2½ cups stock to boiling and thoroughly dissolve gelatine in it. Add wine, and pour over meat in mold, being sure it reaches bottom and permeates all layers. Press down firmly, and when cool, place in ice-box for several hours. When thoroughly jelled, turn out on platter and garnish with lettuce leaves, water cress, and light colored celery tops. Serve with mayonnaise.

Mrs. Caton's, Feb. 21, 1877
A Private Journal   *Baltimore*

**PRESSED
CHICKEN**
1 stewing chicken, 1 medium onion, 2 stalks celery and tops, salt, pepper.

Stew cut up chicken gently in just enough water to cover. Add sliced onion and celery with tops to the pot. When nearly tender, season well with salt and pepper. Let it stew down until water is nearly boiled out and meat drops easily from the bones. Remove bones and gristle; chop meat rather coarsely, then turn it back into the stew kettle where broth was left (after straining and skimming off all fat) and let it heat through again. Turn it into a square mold, placing a platter on the top, and a heavy weight on the platter. This, if properly prepared, will turn out like a mold of jelly and may be sliced in smooth, even slices. Success depends upon not having too much water; it will not jell if too weak or if the water is allowed to boil away while cooking. It is a good way to cook old fowls.

White House Cook Book, 1887
Contee, Rhode River

Anne Arundel

---

6 chicken breasts, salt and pepper, 1 stalk celery, 1 small onion, small piece bay leaf, 2 sprigs parsley, 1 cup water, ½ cup white wine, paté de foie gras.

PLEASANT VALLEY CHICKEN

Season chicken breasts on both sides with salt and pepper and place in shallow oven dish. Dice celery and onion, break up parsley, and scatter over chicken. Add water, bay leaf and wine to pan, close tightly with a cover or foil, and poach chicken in a moderate oven for about half an hour, basting occasionally. When tender, lift chicken from pan, let cool, and carefully remove skin and bone, leaving each breast in one whole piece. Strain chicken essence from pan, remove any fat, and reserve for sauce. Spread chicken breasts with paté and chill.

The Sauce: 2 tablespoons butter, 3 tablespoons flour, 1 cup chicken stock, ⅓ cup cream, 1 teaspoon gelatine soaked in 1 tablespoon broth, 1 egg yolk, salt and pepper to taste.

Melt butter, add flour and stir until well blended. Add stock slowly and stir until smooth. Gradually add cream. Add gelatine which has been dissolved in broth; melt and mix it thoroughly in hot sauce. Remove from fire and stir in beaten egg yolk. Season to taste. When sauce is cool and beginning to stiffen, cover each piece of chicken with a thick coating. Decorate with truffles cut in fancy shapes and tarragon leaves. Glaze with aspic jelly of chicken if desired.

Harvey S. Ladew
Pleasant Valley, My Lady's Manor

Harford

Turkey

ALL HALLOWS THANKSGIVING TURKEY

Choose a fresh young Tom Turkey (we use them weighing 20 to 25 pounds). Make a strong turkey broth by simmering giblets and neck in water to cover.

The stuffing: 1 large loaf bread, 1 cup chopped celery, ½ cup onions, chopped; ½ cup butter, 2 teaspoons salt, 1 teaspoon black pepper, 1 teaspoon sage or poultry seasoning.

Break loaf into crumbs. Simmer celery and onions in butter until tender and golden. Mix crumbs, salt, pepper, and sage. Add butter, onion and celery mixture; blend well. Moisten with turkey broth, enough to dampen, but not make stuffing soggy (possibly 2 cups). Stuff turkey.

Rub stuffed bird lightly with salt and black pepper; dust with flour. Place in a roaster. Cover turkey well with aluminum foil (this saves frequent basting and prevents over-browning before turkey is done). Cook in hot oven (450°) for 20 minutes. Reduce heat to 350° and complete roasting. Allow 20 minutes per pound but be sure leg bone may be easily moved back and forth and away from body before taking turkey from oven. Foil may be removed to finish browning, but is usually not necessary with a large fat turkey.

All Hallows Parish
Davidsonville   *Anne Arundel*

The Maryland Scene

Thanksgiving Dinner
at
All Hallows Church

More than seventy years ago the ladies of All Hallows Parish, Davidsonville, served a Thanksgiving Dinner which, continuing through the years, has become a tradition to the people of the Parish and surrounding communities.

The menu has changed little. Home-raised food is prepared by good country cooks who, carefully and skilfully, follow the receipts of their mothers and grandmothers. The turkeys must be freshly killed and come from a nearby farm. The hams must be at least one year old and cured in the Maryland way. The Chesapeake Bay oysters are cooked by an old receipt.

Oyster Stew

Turkey   Dressing   Gravy

Old Country Ham

Mashed Potatoes   Green Limas

Candied Sweet Potatoes   Sauerkraut

Cranberries   Celery   Relish

Rolls   Coffee

White Potato, Pumpkin, Apple and Mince Pies

Cake   Ice Cream

Turkey

CHESTNUT STUFFING FOR TURKEY

For a 10 pound turkey: 1 pound chestnuts, ¼ cup chicken fat, ¼ cup butter, 2 cups chopped celery, ¼ cup chopped onions, 2 tablespoons chopped parsley, 1 egg, 6 cups bread crumbs, 2 teaspoons salt, ¼ teaspoon pepper.

Drop chestnuts into boiling water and cook for about 20 minutes. Remove shells and brown skins while hot, then mash or put chestnuts through a potato ricer. Melt chicken fat and butter; add celery, onion and parsley to cook a few minutes. Mix with the beaten egg, bread crumbs, chestnuts, salt and pepper. Stir until thoroughly mixed and stuff turkey which has been wiped dry inside and lightly sprinkled with salt.

Mrs. Dorsey's receipt, 1855
Loockerman Book, Hammond-Harwood House *Annapolis*

OYSTER STUFFING FOR TURKEY

¾ cup butter, 4 tablespoons chopped onion, 1½ cups chopped celery, 4 tablespoons chopped parsley, 1 pint oysters, 6 cups crustless, diced white bread; 1 teaspoon dried basil leaves, ¼ teaspoon nutmeg, 1½ teaspoons salt, 1 teaspoon paprika, about 1 cup milk and oyster liquor.

Melt butter, add onion, celery and parsley and sauté a few minutes. Then add drained, chopped oysters (or they may be left whole) to heat. Combine with bread and seasonings and moisten dressing slightly with milk and oyster liquor.

Maryland Cook Book, 1892
Mrs. Franklin B. Spriggs *Anne Arundel*

CORNMEAL TURKEY STUFFING

4 cups crumbled muffins or cornbread, 2 slices crumbled toast. To these add 1 cup chopped celery, 1 cup chopped onion, salt and pepper to taste. Moisten with turkey stock.

The Old Wye Mill *Talbot*

2 cups shelled peanuts, 1½ cups toasted breadcrumbs, 2 tablespoons melted butter, 1 egg yolk,
turkey broth.

**PEANUT
DRESSING
FOR TURKEY**

Have peanuts crisply parched; grind them and add breadcrumbs, melted
butter and egg yolk. Add a little broth from cooking neck and giblets
of turkey. For a turkey of size, use double this amount.

Mrs. Truxtun Beale's Book, 1903
Decatur House   *Washington*

A young turkey of middling size, about 8 or 9
pounds.

**BOILED
TURKEY WITH
OYSTER SAUCE**

Stuff turkey with an oyster or a bread stuffing (it
can be boiled, unstuffed, if you choose). Sew up turkey in a cheese-
cloth and dredge it round with flour. Put it in a large covered boiler,
add hot water to cover and let it come to a boil. Simmer it over slow
and even heat, about 15 minutes to a pound, or until tender. Skim
from time to time. Add salt about half way through cooking. The skin
should be whole and very white. When you dish it, pour on a little
oyster sauce, and serve more sauce in a boat. (See Sauces for Fowl.)

Mrs. C. H. Steele's Book, 1870   *Annapolis*

Cut up the turkey very fine, cold roast or boiled
turkey, until you have two cups. Drain a pint
of nice oysters and save the liquor, about 1

**TURKEY WITH
OYSTERS**

cup. Put a layer of turkey and one of oysters alternately in a baking
dish. Season them between the layers by pouring a little sauce made
this way:

Melt 3 tablespoons butter and stir into it 3 tablespoons flour; add
oyster liquor and stir until smooth. Meanwhile heat 1 cup light cream
with a few slices of onion; when steeped a little, throw away onion and
slowly stir cream into sauce. Season to your taste with salt, pepper and
a little mace.

Strew crumbs of bread on the top of your dish with small pieces of
butter and bake it brown in a moderate oven.

Miss Cheston's Queen of the Kitchen, 1870
West River   *Anne Arundel*

OLIO   Make in the same way as chicken salad, except that turkey and ham is used instead of chicken and is chopped very fine.

Receipts from Waverly   *Queen Anne's*

PEACOCK OR   2¾ pounds chestnuts, lard, consomme, 2 pounds
ROYAL TURKEY   pork, a Peacock, butter, bacon.

Split chestnuts and cover them with hot lard before removing skins. Cook prepared chestnuts in consomme until soft. Grind pork fine and mix it with the soft chestnuts, broken into small pieces. Fill the Peacock with this mixture. Spread bird with soft butter and lay slices of bacon over it. Place a dampened cloth over all. Baste frequently while roasting. When nearly done, remove cloth and brown, then sprinkle with salt and pepper.

Peacock is similar to Wild Turkey. Both Wild and Domestic Turkey may be stuffed and roasted in this way.

A famous painting of a wedding feast shows a Peacock ready to serve in its plumage. Or, this royal bird may be served resting on some of its beautiful feathers,—a feast for great occasions only. This dish was served at our fiftieth wedding anniversary.

Mrs. Charles Kellogg
Langshaws   *Talbot*

Langshaws   John Moll

Goose

A 10-pound goose, salt, marjoram. *For stuffing:* 3 tablespoons butter, 3 tablespoons chopped onions, 4 cups potatoes (which have been diced and parboiled 5 minutes only), ½ pound sausage meat, pepper and salt.

ROAST GOOSE WITH POTATO AND SAUSAGE STUFFING

Clean goose inside and out, dry well, and rub inside with salt and a little marjoram. Rub outside with salt. Let stand to ripen while preparing stuffing. Sauté onions in butter, then add parboiled potatoes and sausage meat. Season with pepper, very little salt; mix well and stuff goose lightly. Prick goose all over and cook, breast down, on rack in covered roasting pan, with hot water to rack height only. The oven should be moderately hot, 375°. Cook one hour, then turn goose over and prick again, finishing cooking with cover off.

Throughout cooking, baste frequently with pan gravy and a little water, skimming off excess fat. Ten minutes before goose is done, baste with browned butter and turn heat up a little to crisp skin. Allow about 20 minutes to the pound. Serve with spiced crab apples, or apple sauce.

Revised from Hester Ann Harwood's Book
Hammond-Harwood House   *Annapolis*

The Frugal Housekeeper's Kitchen Companion, 1847, "dedicated to those American Housewives who are not ashamed of economy. A fat kitchen maketh a lean will."

Choose young goose, 8 to 10 pounds. Singe, clean, cut off neck at body, wash and dry. Rub inside with salt and outside with salt and pepper and a clove of garlic if liked. Prick skin well with sharp fork to let fat run out. Roast uncovered, adding 1 cup hot water after ½ hour of roasting. Allow 20 to 25 minutes per pound for total roasting. Cut cold goose in pieces for serving. Reheat in the following:

SALMI OF GOOSE

119

Goose

Salmi Sauce: Melt ¼ cup butter, add 1 tablespoon finely chopped onion and a stalk celery cut fine. Cook until butter is brown, stir in ¼ cup flour, and when well browned add 2 cups consomme, as much goose essence (without fat) as you need; bit of bay leaf, parsley, mace, 2 cloves, salt and pepper. Cook 5 minutes.

Strain, add goose, and when reheated, add claret wine until sauce has desired consistency and flavor, and a double handful of mushrooms which have been cut in quarters and browned in butter. Serve very hot with wild rice.

Gertrude Poney's way
Troth's Fortune, Choptank River   *Talbot*

GOOSE IN ASPIC   Put a quartered apple and a quartered onion in goose cavity. Rub goose with salt and pepper and roast in 450° oven until bird is well browned. Remove all fat from pan. Turn oven to 300° and add:

1 sliced onion, 1 sliced carrot, 3 large sprigs parsley, 2 stalks celery, 1 bay leaf, a little thyme and 1 quart of stock, half chicken, half consomme. Cover pan and continue basting often until bird is tender. (A very large goose, over 6 or 7 pounds, may need several hours and more stock.) Lift goose from roaster and strain liquid; cool both. Skim any remaining fat from liquid. To each pint liquid, add 1 tablespoon plain gelatin (dissolved in a little stock), and heat until thoroughly melted. Madeira to taste may be added to aspic if desired.

Skin goose and slice thinly as possible, thinner the better. While aspic is hot, arrange slices of goose in fairly deep platter with vegetables such as baby carrots, sliced olives, a little finely chopped celery, pimento pepper, peas or asparagus tips,—whatever adds to the attractiveness of the platter. Pour aspic on gradually so as not to disturb design. It is more easily served if one keeps individual portions in mind when arranging goose and vegetables. Put in refrigerator until set.

Mrs. Edward K. Klingelhofer
Loblolly   *Talbot*

Duck

1 or more ducks, foaming butter, 1 wine-glass white wine, 1 dozen small white onions, 1 dozen small white turnips, 3 tablespoons butter, 1 generous tablespoon sugar, 1 cup veal or chicken stock, salt and pepper, a bay leaf, 1 tablespoon chopped parsley, 1 carrot.

TO BAKE DUCKS, WOODYARD RECEIPT

Have ducks nicely picked, then brown quickly on all sides in a little foaming butter. Pour wine over duck, cover, and let it stew gently for a while. Then strew over it small onions and turnips which have been pared and shaped to a uniform size, then browned and caramelized in butter and sugar in an iron skillet. Add stock to vegetable pan juices and pour over duck. Season with salt and pepper, add the bay leaf, parsley and carrot, thinly sliced. Cover tightly and cook slowly for an hour or more until tender. When nearly done, lift the cover to brown. Serve duck on hot platter, circled with vegetables—the sauce, from which excess fat has been skimmed, in a separate boat. The old receipt said, "When they are nearly done, put some embers on top of the oven to brown them."

Mrs. Virgil Maxcy's Receipt, Tulip Hill, 1815
Mrs. Francis Markoe Dugan

Baltimore

Have 2 ducklings dressed and ready for roasting. Stuff with 3 cups of broken-up corn bread mixed with ¼ cup melted butter, 6 chopped spring onions (with part of the green ends) and seasoned with salt, pepper and a sprinkle of powdered sage. Rub salt lightly over ducks and roast in 350° oven for about 2½ hours or until very tender. After first hour pour off fat from pan. After second hour glaze with 1 cup of orange juice which has been mixed with 1 tablespoon flour. Pour over ducks and baste once or twice with pan drippings until done. A giblet gravy may be made by stewing the giblets and necks until tender. Strain liquid and chop giblets fine. Mix a little flour with pan drippings and stir in broth and giblets. Season to taste with salt and pepper.

ROAST DUCKLING

Mrs. Kent Mullikin
Spa Creek

Annapolis

St. Richard's Manor Maryland House and Garden Pilgrimage

Ducks

BRAISED 2 or 3 ducks, depending on size, 1 bunch soup
DUCKS herbs, a few celery tops, 1 or 2 leeks, 1 or 2
onions, salt and pepper, 3 strips bacon, 2 onions,
a little butter, 4 tablespoons flour, 1½ dozen small silver onions, 1
bunch young carrots, cut up.

Parboil ducks a short while, as meat is easier to separate from bones.
Remove all meat and put aside. For stock, put bones and skin back
in broth and add soup herbs, celery tops, leeks, onions and seasoning.
Simmer 1½ hours, reducing stock, then strain. Cut duck meat in nice
pieces and place in oven dish. Fry out bacon chopped up with onions
until golden brown. Dip out bacon and onion pieces and scatter over
duck. Add a little butter to bacon grease and brown flour in it. Add
stock to make enough gravy to cover duck pieces well. Cover, place in
oven and simmer ½ hour, then add silver onions and cut-up carrots.
Simmer until vegetables are done. Correct seasoning. Serve with rice.
8 servings.

Carroll McTavish Elder
Tred Avon River *Talbot*

Guinea Hen

4 tablespoons butter, guinea hen, salt, 1 medium onion, 1 cup light sour cream, white pepper, powdered mace.

GUINEA BAKED IN SOUR CREAM

Melt butter in oven dish. Be sure not to let butter brown. Put in guinea, trussed and tied, having put the liver back inside with some salt. Put in onion, cut in sixths. Cover dish and bake in moderate oven for 25 minutes, turning often. In the meantime heat sour cream in a small pan, adding a pinch of salt, some white pepper and mace. When guinea is ready, pour over it the hot cream. Cover dish and cook about 20 minutes longer. Baste well about three times. Serve in the dish in which it is cooked. (Rock Cornish Game Hen may be prepared in this way.)

Mrs. Maynard Barnes
St. Richard's Manor, Patuxent River

St. Mary's

¾ cup wild rice, 2 young guinea hens, salt and pepper, 2 tablespoons butter, 1 teaspoon flour, ½ teaspoon paprika, 1 cup or more sour cream, ½ cup white raisins.

BREAST OF GUINEA HEN

Wash rice carefully and add to 1 cup boiling salted water in top of double boiler. Bring to boil again and skim. Place over simmering hot water and let stand, covered, and steam until rice is done and fluffy. Cut breasts of guinea from bone with a sharp knife; season them with salt and pepper and cook them in butter in a heavy skillet until brown and tender, turning carefully. Remove from pan and keep warm. Stir into pan the flour, paprika and sour cream. Add raisins which have been steamed in a colander over boiling water to make them plump. Heat sauce well, stirring until smooth. Arrange breasts of guinea on low mounds of wild rice on serving platter and pour sauce over each.

Mrs. Frank Jack Fletcher
Araby

Charles

GUINEA HEN WITH BLACK WALNUT STUFFING ½ cup milk, 4 tablespoons butter, pinch of ground cloves, ½ teaspoon grated nutmeg, 1 small onion, 2 cups fine bread crumbs, ½ cup chopped black walnut meats, 1 young guinea hen, 2 cups chicken broth, 2 tablespoons chopped celery, 2 teaspoons chopped parsley, ½ cup white wine, 2 egg yolks, salt, cayenne.

Scald milk, add butter, cloves, nutmeg and onion, finely chopped. Pour over the bread crumbs and toss together lightly. Mix in the black walnut meats. Sprinkle salt and pepper inside guinea and stuff. Place in hot oven until well browned, then reduce heat to 375°, add chicken broth, celery and cover. Baste frequently. Should be done in 1½ hours. To juice in pan add parsley, wine and egg yolks; stir over low heat until thickened. Add salt and cayenne to taste. Serve in gravy boat. Cornish hen is very nice done in this way.

Miss Fanny's Receipt Book   *Anne Arundel*
West River

Squab

BONED SQUAB *How to bone a Squab:* Cut off neck and all but first joint of wings but keep the skin of the neck as long as possible. With a very sharp pointed knife (there are small boning knives made for the purpose) cut a straight line down the back beginning at the neck. Now begin to scrape and cut flesh from backbone right down to shoulder blade, being careful not to pierce skin. At leg and wing joints, cut through the joints. To keep an attractive shape, drumstick bones and wing pinions are left in. When all flesh is off the carcass, the flesh and skin are turned back again and stuffed.

Stuffing: Stuff birds with wild rice which has been cooked in beef bouillon. It is necessary to wash wild rice completely free of dirt, which will take about 17 or 18 rinsings.
Sew skin together carefully on the back of the bird, pressing squab so that it conforms to its original shape. Season with salt and pepper, brush lightly with melted butter, and roast at 350° until done.

Henry Powell Hopkins   *Baltimore*

City Dock, Annapolis, Md.

John Moll

4 squabs, ¼ pound butter, 4 tablespoons chopped **PANNED SQUAB**
onion, 3 cloves or pinch of powdered cloves, 3
blades of mace or ½ teaspoon powdered mace, 1 teaspoon salt, ¼
teaspoon pepper, 1 cup chicken broth, 3 tablespoons flour.

Split cleaned squabs down the back. Spread out in covered shallow
roasting pan. Do not let squabs over-lap. Combine melted butter with
chopped onion, cloves, mace, salt and pepper. Cook slowly until onion
is soft, then add chicken broth and pour over squabs in roasting pan.
Cover pan tightly and cook in moderately hot oven (375°). Baste with
pan juices. When almost tender, remove cover and let squabs get a
delicate brown. Keep them juicy by basting until ready to serve. Remove birds to a hot platter. Discard cloves and mace blades, if used,
from liquid in pan. Add flour, mixed with a little water, and stir until
smooth, making a gravy to be served over squab. Taste for seasoning.

Mrs. C. H. Steele's Book, 1870   *Annapolis*

Split squabs open through the backbone and lay   **BROILED**
them out flat in the broiler. Broil, not too close   **SQUAB**
to the flame, turning several times to cook evenly
without scorching. When tender, place them in a dripping pan, season
with salt and pepper, and butter them well. Cover and keep warm.
Make a toast for each squab, butter it and trim off crusts. Lay a squab
on each slice, place on warm platter, pour over each bird butter from
pan, and garnish with parsley. Very nice.

Mrs. Maurice Ogle
Severn River
                                                        Annapolis

125

Game Birds

Wild Duck

Ducks should be carefully picked, drawn, wiped **WILD DUCK**
clean or washed quickly in very little water. Stuff
with a tart raw apple, quartered, or a peeled onion, cut in halves.
Sprinkle with salt and pepper and cover breast with very thin slices of
salt pork or bacon; or, rub with butter, if preferred. Place breast side up
in a shallow roasting pan. Bake 20 to 30 minutes, according to size, in a
very hot oven (500°), basting every 5 minutes with fat from pan. Red
juice, not blood, should follow the carving knife. Serve with tart jelly
or sauce made by warming a glass of currant jelly in half as much port
wine.

Mrs. Philip G. Wilmer
Chestertown

Kent

Prepare ducks and roast them in a hot oven **BREAST OF**
(500°) for about 20 minutes. Remove from pan **WILD DUCK**
and, with a sharp knife, carve off the meat from
each breast in one whole nice serving piece. Have a heavy iron skillet
ready with some hot, foaming butter. Quickly sear the breasts on one
side, then the other, until the meat is neither too rare nor too well done,
but succulent. Place each breast on a piece of crustless bread which has
been previously fried in butter to a rich, golden crispness. Take the pan
juices, after removing excess fat, add any essence saved from carving,
and boil them up in the pan in which duck was seared. Add red wine
to your taste and pour some over each serving. Serve extra sauce in a
boat.

Carroll McTavish Elder
Tred Avon River

Talbot

Ashby

Wild Duck

ASHBY'S PRESSED WILD DUCK
Preheat oven to 450°. Place 3 large wild ducks over dripping pan in hot oven for 7½ minutes. Reduce temperature to 350° and cook for 15 minutes. Remove from oven. Carve off each breast in one piece and remove skin. Put carcass in duck press and get essence from it. Place duck breasts in chafing dish with duck sauce, essence from duck press and essence from inside duck. Do not use drippings from pan in sauce. Do not baste with fat in pan.

Wild Duck Sauce: 1 cup fine sherry, 1 cup red currant jelly. Add essence from press. Let stand in chafing dish covering breasts for 5 to 10 minutes. Serve. Use sauce on wild rice and breasts of duck.

Charles S. Todd
Ashby, Miles River   *Talbot*

Stuff 1 duck with dressing of 1 cup toasted bread **ROAST**
crumbs, 1 onion, chopped; 2 stalks celery, cut-up, **WILD DUCK**
and sautéed together in butter. Add salt and pep-
per to taste and 2 tablespoons brandy. Butter breasts of duck and add to
pan ½ cup good red wine and ¼ cup water. Cover and roast in 325°
oven for 2 hours, basting frequently with juices in pan. Serves 2.

Mrs. William Heintz
Bayfields *Anne Arundel*

Duck meat, 1 cup or more, finely chopped; 1 **WILD DUCK**
hard-boiled egg, 1 cup brown sauce, ¼ cup **CROQUETTES**
Claret, ¼ teaspoon each of thyme and marjoram,
salt and pepper.

Put left-over lean duck meat through fine blade of meat chopper.
Grind until consistency is smooth and fine. Chop hard-boiled egg and
mix with duck. Add enough brown sauce (browned flour and butter
with milk added) to make a paste. Moisten this paste still further with
a little Claret. Duck meat, being dry, absorbs more sauce than you
would think. Mix through it the powdered herbs and season it up well
to your taste. Shape and pan fry in a little butter. The left-over meat
of goose and other birds can be used in this way.

Old Receipt of Uncle Milton's
The Anchorage, Miles River
Mrs. Levin Campbell *Annapolis*

Wild ducks, liver paté. **SUMMER DUCK**

Aspic for one duck: 1½ cups strong beef bouillon, ¾ envelope plain
gelatine, sherry to taste.

Place one or more wild ducks (unstuffed) in a covered roasting pan.
Roast 2 hours in a moderate (325°) oven. Let cool and carve off each
breast in one piece and remove skin. Spread each breast with paté de
foie gras; domestic does excellently. Combine in a saucepan over low
heat the bouillon, gelatine and sherry. When blended, pour ¼ inch
of aspic in bottom of serving platter and chill to harden. Place duck
breasts side by side on aspic, decorate with thin slices of olives and
gently pour remaining aspic over them. Chill in ice-box. Each duck
serves 2. Domestic duck is also very good done in this way.

Mrs. Morgan B. Schiller
Wye House, Wye River *Talbot*

Sunrise Alert   A. Aubrey Bodine

Wild Duck

MALLARD OR WILD DUCK IN CLARET   2 large wild ducks, quartered; salt and pepper, butter, 4 red onions, sliced; 2 cups Claret wine, a pinch of marjoram or sage, if you like it.

Season quartered ducks with salt and pepper, and brown them in butter in an iron kettle. Add onions and sauté until clear. Add one cup of Claret, cover kettle and cook slowly, adding the other cup of wine as needed. Add a pinch of marjoram or sage if you like. Cook from 1½ to 2 hours. This dish is just as good reheated the next day.

Mrs. Frederic C. Thomas
Troth's Fortune, Choptank River   *Talbot*

Wild Goose

A wild goose, salt and freshly ground black pepper, seedless white grapes, tangerine or orange sections, bread crumbs, butter, dry white wine.

HONGA RIVER WILD GOOSE

Rub cavity with a little salt and lots of black pepper. Stuff with white seedless grapes, tangerine or orange sections, held together with bread crumbs which have been tossed in melted butter. Cook for 10 minutes in a hot oven, preheated to 550°, then reduce heat to 450° and continue cooking for 25 or 30 minutes, basting frequently with dry white wine. Use fresh wine for each basting, in all about 1 pint of wine. Never cook a goose over 35 minutes unless very large, then 40 minutes at most, as it toughens and dries out.

A specialty sometimes served at Honga River Gun Club or Hooper's Island sporting feasts.

Mrs. William Doeller
Church Creek

Dorchester

A young goose—never bother with an old one. (A fine young goose should be heavy for its size, the flesh of the breasts being firm and plump and the skin clear, the wings tender to the touch.) Celery stalk, olive oil, salt and pepper, red wine.

TO ROAST A WILD GOOSE

Salt and pepper goose inside and out. Put a stalk of celery in cavity. If lean, rub with olive oil. Roast for 50 minutes in a hot oven, 500°. Baste frequently with red wine. To carve, cut ¼ inch slices into breastbone all the way down each side, then loosen the whole side. It may all be put back again for serving. This way each slice has a piece of crisp skin and the various layers of meat.

Carroll McTavish Elder
Tred Avon River

Talbot

Wild Goose

CHESTER RIVER Rub wild goose with bacon grease, salt and pepper.
WILD GOOSE Place in roaster and cover with brown paper, tucking in well. Put top on roaster and cook 3 hours at 350° F. Do not uncover while roasting. Plan to serve immediately.

Mrs. Harry H. Deringer
Chestertown   Kent

COOKING A A young goose, about 4½ pounds dressed weight,
WILD GOOSE 2 stalks celery and ½ green pepper (or potato) for cavity.

Marinade: 1 cup tarragon vinegar, ½ cup sherry wine, ¼ cup peanut oil, 1 teaspoon ginger, salt and black pepper.

Let goose lie in marinade for ½ hour, turning several times. Stuff cavity with celery and green pepper or potato. Bake in 450° oven, breast down in marinade, covered container. Baste with marinade two or three times. Turn goose over for last 15 minutes and brown, open container. Bake 10 minutes per pound of goose (45 minutes for 4½ pound goose, dressed weight). This will give a medium rare meat. If you want a well-done bird, bake 11 minutes per pound.

Howard C. Eley   *Talbot*

GLEBE KITCHEN Prepare bird for roasting and rub inside and out
WILD GOOSE with garlic or onion, and season with salt and pepper. Some raw onions, celery and celery salt placed in the cavity is better suited to game birds than a stuffing.

Place bird breast side up on wire rack in roasting pan not over 2 inches deep, so that heat can circulate under bird. Keeping bird from touching juices in bottom of pan will prevent skin and flesh from cracking. Do not cover. This is the secret for deliciously moist and pink goose. Roast about 12 hours or overnight, with oven temperature at 165° and not over 200°, depending on size and age of bird. Do not baste. Bird is done when leg or large wing joint will twist easily.

Mrs. Carroll R. Harding
Glebe House   *Talbot*

Kitchen Hearth at Glebe House

Wild Goose

"In Glass's Book is a Yorkshire Christmas Pie which seems to be much like what used to be in my Family; but the Cooke is dead who made them, so that the method she used is lost.

MR. BORDLEY'S CHRISTMAS PIE

A *fat* Swan, however old, is fine; as is the whole Pie, when it has been frozen and thawed several Times, and is of sound standing. Our Materials were, a Swan, a Turkey or two, a Goose, 2 or 4 Pullets, 2 or 4 Ducks, sometimes Beef Steaks, etc. It is fortunate to have a cold Winter for freezing the Pie often, by which the old Swan, the Crust etc. are improved and made tender—the Crust short."

Mr. J. B. Bordley in the
Lloyd Papers, Maryland Historical Society

Baltimore

Pheasant

ROAST PHEASANT WITH ENGLISH BREAD SAUCE

Pheasant, butter, salt and pepper, thin pieces larding pork.

Sprinkle pheasant with salt and pepper, and rub well with butter. Cover breast and thighs with thin pieces larding pork and tie in place. (The pheasant is a dry bird, and must be well larded.) Roast in a moderate oven for about three quarters of an hour, or until bird is tender. Remove larding pork, skim fat from pan juices and strain to serve with pheasant. Accompany with English bread sauce (see Sauces for Fowl), and spiced gooseberries or currant jelly.

Mrs. Thomas Morton
Crab Creek   *Anne Arundel*

PHEASANT WITH CREAM AND HORSERADISH

2 pheasants, flour, salt and pepper, butter, 2 tablespoons brandy, ½ cup chicken stock, 1 bay leaf, 1 tablespoon minced onion, 1 tablespoon finely chopped celery, 2 cups cream, ⅓ cup horseradish.

Cut pheasants into serving pieces. Dredge in seasoned flour. Sauté in butter in a heavy skillet until golden brown. Place birds in large, preheated oven dish with a little butter. Warm and ignite brandy and pour over birds. Add chicken stock, bay leaf, onion and celery. Cover and cook in a quick oven (400°) for half an hour. Warm the cream separately after adding horseradish, which has been drained and washed very briefly to remove vinegar. (Fresh horseradish, grated, is preferable.) Add mixture to dish (birds should be about half covered), and cook, uncovered, basting frequently, for 20 to 30 minutes longer in a moderate oven until birds are thoroughly done. Sauce should be perfect for serving.

Willard G. Triest
Severn River   *Annapolis*

The Lord's Bounty

1 pheasant, 2 or more cups chopped, tart apples; butter, about ½ cup cream, 2 or 3 tablespoons of apple brandy.

PHEASANT WITH APPLES

Truss a pheasant whole, season it inside and out, and sauté it slowly in butter on all sides until it takes on a golden brown hue. Place it in an oven dish on a bed of rather tart apples which have been peeled, chopped and lightly sautéed in butter. Surround pheasant with more apples which have been similarly prepared. Baste with melted butter. Heat in oven for 10 minutes, then baste with thick fresh cream. Cover baking dish and roast in a quick oven for 25 minutes when the bird should be tender. Add brandy and serve in dish in which it was cooked.

Mrs. Lew Garrison Coit
The Lord's Bounty

Anne Arundel

Place the birds in a steamer, over a pot of boiling water, until tender. Have ready a saucepan of large fresh oysters, scalded just enough to make plump and seasoned with pepper-sauce, butter and a little salt. Rub the cavity of the birds with salt and pepper, fill with oysters and sew up. Broil until a light brown. Place on a hot dish and sift over them browned crackers. Add butter and pounded cracker to oyster liquor. Boil it up once and pour into the dish but not over the birds.

PHEASANT STUFFED WITH OYSTERS

Tucker Family receipt
Elizabeth W. Bond

Baltimore

135

Marina Hiatt

Quail or Partridge

READBOURNE
QUAIL
Wash and truss four quail; place them in a heavy frying pan and brown in about four tablespoons butter.

After they have browned, place them in an oven dish; make sauce by adding 3 tablespoons flour to remaining butter in frying pan and stir in slowly about 2 cups of chicken stock and ½ cup of sherry; blend well, add a little salt and pepper to taste; pour over the quail. Cover tightly and cook in a moderate oven about 1 hour. The birds are good and moist when cooked this way. Wild rice should be served with the quail.

Mrs. William Fahnestock, Jr.
Readbourne, Chester River   *Queen Anne's*

SOMETHING TO
KNOW ABOUT
GAME BIRDS
When a Quail, Dove or Pheasant has been frozen (this applies to Guinea and Squab as well), if when thawed it is allowed to soak in rich milk or cream·for 2 or 3 hours, the process will· make the bird very tender and bring back and heighten the original flavor.

Eleanor Addison Miles
Blakeford, Chester River   *Queen Anne's*

4 quail, salt, pepper, flour, ¼ cup butter, ¾ cup **QUAIL ON**
chicken stock, 6 mushrooms, sliced; 4 buttered **TRENCHERS**
toast slices or trenchers.

Sprinkle quail inside and out with salt, pepper and flour. Melt butter
in skillet; add quail and brown on all sides. Add stock and mushrooms.
Cover and cook over low heat 15 minutes or until birds are tender. Serve
on buttered toast or trenchers, which are cut from 2-inch thick slices of
French bread or half of a large roll. Scoop out center to make a cup
to hold bird; butter and toast trencher. Pour over sauce from pan.

Miss Fanny's Receipt Book
West River   *Anne Arundel*

Place partridges in salt and water an hour or two **TO BROIL**
before broiling. When taken out wipe dry and **PARTRIDGES**
rub all over with fresh butter, pepper and salt.
First broil under, or split side, on gridiron over right clear coals, turning
till upper side is fine, light brown. It must be cooked principally from
under side. When done rub well again with fresh butter, and if not
ready to serve immediately put in large, shallow tin bucket, which will
keep them hot, without making them dry and hard; when served sift
over them powdered crackers browned.

Mrs. Spencer Watkins' receipt, 1897   *Montgomery*

Quail, oysters, butter, bread crumbs, flour, salt **QUAIL STUFFED**
and pepper, thin slices salt pork or bacon. **WITH OYSTERS**

Clean quail thoroughly. Stuff by dipping oysters in melted butter, then
rolling in bread crumbs, and placing 2 or 3 in each bird. Dredge quail
with flour and smother with butter. Season with salt and pepper. Place
birds in roasting pan, lard the breasts with very thin slices of salt pork
or bacon, and bake until tender, about half an hour or so, basting well
with pan juices. Serve on beds of fine bread crumbs crisped and browned
in butter.

White House Cook Book, 1887
Contee, Rhode River   *Anne Arundel*

137

Hunting for Rail Birds   A. Aubrey Bodine

RAIL BIRDS   Rail birds, or any small bird such as Reed birds or
                   Ortolans, may be prepared in the same way as the
Quail Stuffed with Oysters; although one oyster will suffice for each bird.

Miss Leslie, 1837
Mrs. John F. Meigs' copy   *Annapolis*

Dove

RACHEL'S   Split doves down the back. Have some sweet but-
MOURNING   ter sizzling hot and put them in the pan to brown
DOVE   quickly. Then reduce the heat, add a little water
                   to the pan and salt and pepper. Cover and cook
slowly until done. Serve on toast and pour the gravy over all.

Mrs. Claude Handy
Duke of Gloucester Street   *Annapolis*

$\mathcal{G}ame$

Venison

TO ROAST VENISON

Rub the haunch or saddle of venison well with salt and pepper; pour over it a cup of water and set in a hot oven (425°). Roast 15 minutes to the pound, basting frequently with melted butter at first, then with the pan drippings. When done remove to a hot dish. Add two tablespoons of flour to fat in the pan, stir until brown; add two cups of good stock, stir constantly until it boils; take from fire, add one tablespoon of currant jelly and one of sherry, season with salt and pepper to taste. Serve in a boat. Currant jelly and water-cress should accompany this dish.

Senator Kenna on Venison
The Baltimore Sun, 1891

Baltimore

VENISON STEAKS, BROILED

Steaks are usually cut from the leg or haunch. As it requires but a very short time to broil them, and they should be served very hot, see that everything is ready before broiling. Heat the dish in which they are to be served; put in it a piece of butter the size of a walnut, a quarter-teaspoonful of salt, two tablespoonfuls of port wine, and a tablespoonful of currant jelly. Grease the bars of the gridiron with suet, lay the steaks on it, and broil over a clear, hot fire, turning almost constantly. If your steaks are a half-inch thick, eight minutes will broil them. Put them in the heated dish, and turn them in the mixture once or twice. Serve immediately on heated plates. The quantities given are for two steaks.

John Mercer, 1831
Cedar Park, West River

Anne Arundel

VENISON To one pint of olive oil grate four onions, and beat up in a dish. Get the skillet very hot, and put a little butter in it to keep it from sticking. Dip the venison steaks thoroughly in the olive oil and onions. Cook quickly and turn frequently, searing the steaks medium to well done according to how liked best.

If a venison roast, pour the olive oil and onions over the roast as you start to roast it. Baste thoroughly while cooking.

Woodmont Rod and Gun Club
Woodmont *Washington*

HUNTER'S 3 pounds venison meat, 3 tablespoons butter, 1 **VENISON** large onion, 1 bay leaf, 1 teaspoon minced thyme, 2 tablespoons flour, salt and pepper, 4 cups veal or beef stock, 1 lemon rind, grated; ½ cup red wine.

Cut up the meat into 2-inch square pieces. Brown slowly in melted butter, then add chopped onion, bay leaf and thyme. Cook a few minutes, stir in flour, salt and pepper; add 2 cups of warm stock and let simmer a while. Pour in remainder of stock and stew until meat is tender. Taste for seasoning, add lemon rind and wine and cook slowly a little longer until thick.

Lew G. Coit
The Lord's Bounty *Anne Arundel*

A PRETTY Cut a breast of venison in steaks. Make quarter of **DISH OF** a pound of butter hot, in a pan; rub the steaks **VENISON** over with a mixture of a little salt and pepper, dip them in wheat flour, or rolled crackers, and fry a rich brown. When both sides are done, take them up on a dish, and put a cover over. Dredge a heaping teaspoonful of flour into the butter in the pan, stir it with a spoon until it is brown, without burning; put to it a small teacup of boiling water, with a tablespoonful of currant jelly dissolved into it; stir it for a few minutes, then strain it over the meat and serve.

Mrs. James Cheston's Everyday Book, 1857
West River *Anne Arundel*

Rabbit

Dip joints of rabbit (which have been marinated **RABBIT** in oil for 2 hours) in milk and then roll in flour. **MARYLAND** Fry some pieces of salt pork and when drippings are very hot, put in rabbit, cover and put on back of stove to cook slowly. When brown on one side, turn and brown other, then remove to hot dish. Add to drippings 2 tablespoons flour. Stir until smooth, then slowly add 1 pint rich milk or cream; stir until it thickens, add 1 tablespoon finely chopped parsley, pour over rabbit and heat.

Mrs. Truxtun Beale's Book, 1903
Decatur House   *Washington*

---

1 rabbit, cut up; flour, salt and pepper, ¼ pound **BOUNTY HARE** butter, 1 small slice raw ham, fat removed; 5 or 6 small white onions, 1 clove minced garlic, 1 cup sliced mushrooms, 1 tablespoon chopped parsley, 1 bay leaf, crumbled; a touch of thyme, 1 cup good claret.

Dredge the pieces of rabbit in seasoned flour, and sear in hot butter. When turning golden, remove from pan and put in good sized earthenware oven dish. In same butter in browning pan cook lean ham, cut in small pieces, with onions, minced garlic and mushrooms until well mingled and lightly browned. Add to oven dish and sprinkle in the parsley, bay leaf and thyme. Now pour over all a cup of good claret (preferably the same to be served with dinner). Cover and bake in moderate oven until rabbit is tender. Thicken sauce further if necessary with a little flour. This is best made ahead of time and reheated, as flavor is improved.

Mrs. Lew Garrison Coit
The Lord's Bounty   *Anne Arundel*

Letter from Mr. Cecilius Calvert, Secretary of Maryland, residing in England, circa 1760 to His Excellency the Governor: "Captain Love having hinted to me of your desire of some English Hares he informs me you have a villa and grounds to keep them in. It gives me pleasure your being in such a situation, the recess of Happiness. I have ordered Hares to be got at Woodcote. The Steward has ketched four Brace. I shall have them augmented to more if I can and send them by Captain Love."

A Colonial Governor in Maryland 1753-1773 by Lady Edgar.

SAVORY FRIED RABBIT   Fry rabbit according to receipt for Maryland Fried Chicken (see Chicken). Instead of adding water for steaming, add about ½ cup of dry white wine and strew over 2 tablespoons fresh tarragon leaves, or 1 teaspoon dried tarragon, well powdered. When rabbit is tender, arrange pieces on heated platter and strain pan essence over them.

Mrs. James Cheston's Everyday Book, 1857
West River   *Anne Arundel*

Squirrel

SQUIRREL   Prepare and cut up in pieces as you would a rabbit. Dredge in flour well seasoned with salt and pepper. Brown in bacon fat. Add a little water, cover and steam for an hour or more until tender.

Josey's Dick's way
The 1814 Account Book, Harwood Papers   *Annapolis*

SQUIRREL BRUNSWICK STEW   2 squirrels (or 2 young chickens) cut up, 3 slices bacon, 1 onion, 1 quart peeled tomatoes, 2 ears corn, grated; 3 potatoes, 1 handful butter-beans, 1 pod red pepper, 1 tablespoon butter, 1 tablespoon bread crumbs.

Put squirrels, bacon and sliced onion on to boil in a gallon of water about 4 hours before dinner. Stew about 1 hour, then add other ingredients and stew until the bones of the squirrels can be readily removed. Then put in the bread crumbs and butter.

Galt family receipt
Elizabeth W. Bond   *Baltimore*

A. Aubrey Bodine

Home of the Muskrat

Muskrat

3 muskrats, cleaned, with musk removed, cut up and soaked in the following marinade over night.

MUSKRAT TRED AVON

The marinade: ¼ cup vinegar, 1 onion, finely chopped; 1 carrot, cut small; 1 stalk celery and leaves, cut fine; 1 clove garlic, minced; 2 cloves, 2 tablespoons chopped parsley, 1 large bay leaf, crumbled; 1 teaspoon pepper, 2 cups red wine.

Stir these ingredients together and simmer them for 20 minutes. When cool, add ¼ cup olive oil.

Drain muskrat, season pieces with salt and pepper, dip in flour and fry in hot fat until browned and tender. Take out meat, stir flour into juices left in pan and add enough strained marinade to make gravy. You may add a tablespoon of currant jelly to gravy before serving.

Carroll McTavish Elder
Tred Avon River

Talbot

Meats

Beef

A four-rib roast of beef, soy sauce, salt and black pepper, Bourbon whiskey.

RIB ROAST ON A SPIT

Rub roast thoroughly all over with the soy sauce, salt and pepper. Place it on the spit of your rotisserie. Insert thermometer. Cook until desired doneness as indicated by thermometer, basting every 15 minutes with sauce. When done, before removing from spit and turning off heat, splash generously with Bourbon which should ignite. Then remove from spit and serve at once.

The basting sauce: 6 tablespoons olive oil, 1 tablespoon cider vinegar, 1 tablespoon salt, 1 teaspoon black pepper, 1 tablespoon Worcestershire sauce, 6 dashes Tabasco sauce. An oven roast may also be basted with this sauce.

John Baldwin Rich
Heir's Purchase, Severn River

Anne Arundel

Have a prime rib roast of beef at room temperature. Rub the meat with salt and coarsely ground black pepper. With a sharp knife criss-cross the fat side and sprinkle with salt and pepper. Place in a roasting pan, resting on the bone ends, fat side up. Sear in preheated oven (450°) for 15 minutes, reduce heat to 300° and continue cooking, allowing 20 minutes to the pound of meat, (including the 15 minutes searing period) for medium rare beef. When done, remove to a heated platter and let stand for about 20 minutes before carving.

ROAST BEEF WITH YORKSHIRE PUDDING

Yorkshire Pudding: Turn up oven to 450° when meat is removed. Leave about ¼ inch of beef fat and drippings in the roasting pan and keep very hot. Sift 1 cup of flour with ½ teaspoon salt into a mixing bowl. Make a well in center of flour. Pour in 1 cup of milk and break 2 eggs into milk. Mix and beat vigorously for several minutes until batter is smooth and bubbly. Pour into sizzling hot fat in pan and bake for 15 minutes or until pudding has risen. Reduce heat to 350° and continue baking until crisp and golden (about 15 minutes longer). Cut in squares and place around roast to serve.

Mrs. Frederick G. Richards
Ridout House

Annapolis

FILLET OF BEEF

The fillet is the whole tenderloin of beef. Have butcher trim away all fat, then it may be larded or not, as you choose. If not larded, rub well with butter and season with salt and pepper. Pour in pan a cupful of stock or water, add salt and pepper and a bouquet of parsley. Bake in hot oven (450°) for 30 to 45 minutes; baste frequently. The fillet should be rare. The time for cooking is always uniform, for the weight is in the length, and not in the thickness of the meat. When done remove meat; strain the gravy, and skim off grease. Put into same pan a tablespoon each of butter and flour; stir until they are browned; then add slowly the gravy strained from pan; if not enough to give a cupful, add some stock. Stir until it boils; then add a cupful of sliced mushrooms and let them simmer for five minutes. A half cupful of Madeira or sherry may be used in place of mushrooms if preferred. Spread sauce on serving dish, and lay fillet on it. In carving, cut fillet diagonally in thick slices, and put a little gravy in center of each slice. Garnish with parsley.

Miss Adelaide's Century Book, 1900
Ivy Neck, Rhode River   *Anne Arundel*

MARYLAND PLANKED STEAK

Have a Porterhouse or Sirloin steak cut 1½ to 2 inches thick. Place about 3 inches from heat under preheated broiler set at high, and cook 7 to 8 minutes on each side for rare. Remove steak from broiler, brush with melted butter and season with plenty of salt and pepper. Have plank ready, brushed with oil and heated. Place steak on plank and quickly arrange seasonable Maryland vegetables around meat. These may be bundles of Asparagus, Baked Tomato Halves, Stuffed Bell Peppers or Broiled Stuffed Mushrooms (see Vegetables). Have mashed potatoes ready, prepared with a generous amount of butter, milk, seasoning and the beaten yolk of an egg. Pipe a border of potatoes around edge of plank and place in 350° oven for several minutes until potatoes brown slightly. Garnish with parsley and place plank on platter or tray to be served from the table.

Major James M. Petty
Shelburne House   *Anne Arundel*

A prime sirloin steak, 2 to 3 inches thick, prepared **SIRLOIN STEAK** mustard, salt, butter. **'JUBILEE'**

Spread steak with prepared mustard until you can hardly see meat. Pour salt liberally over each side of steak, using at least ½ pound. The mustard will make it cling to meat and salt crust seals in juices. Light off a charcoal fire and allow it to become very hot. Place steak in a wire broiler. Cook about 12 minutes on each side, turning frequently as steak catches fire. Do not be alarmed, as this is essential part of operation. It may be necessary to cut steak to determine when it is done. Outside should be burned, center should be red; do not overcook. Remove from fire, put a large pat of butter on each side, carve in ½ inch slices and serve. Keep steak warm in oven, as all hands will be back for seconds, and probably thirds!

Admiral Felix Johnson
Jubilee Farm, Potomac River *St. Mary's*

---

1 medium onion, chopped; beef drippings or but- **BEEFSTEAK** ter for browning, 1 pound top round steak, cut in **IN YORKSHIRE** ½-inch cubes; ¾ cup beef broth, ¼ cup tomato **PUDDING** juice, ½ teaspoon Worcestershire sauce, salt and pepper to taste, 1 tablespoon butter, 1 tablespoon flour, a few pieces of cooked tomato, Yorkshire Pudding batter. (See Roast Beef with Yorkshire Pudding.)

Cook onion in beef drippings or butter until clear; add steak cubes to pan and brown. Pour on broth and tomato juice; add Worcestershire sauce and season to taste. Cover pan and simmer gently until meat is tender. Thicken juices with butter rubbed in flour. Fold in a few nice pieces of drained, cooked tomato.

Cover bottom of square baking pan with melted butter or beef drippings. Put in hot oven and heat until it sizzles. Pour ½ the quantity of Yorkshire Pudding batter into pan, about ½-inch deep. Put in hot 450° oven and bake until puffed and set, about 15 minutes. Spread meat and gravy mixture on pudding, cover with remaining half of batter, and continue to cook in hot oven for another 10 to 15 minutes, reducing heat as the baking is accomplished. The outside should be crisp and golden brown, the inside soft.

Tulip Hill Receipts
West River *Anne Arundel*

Beef

STEAK AND KIDNEY PIE

2 veal or 6 lamb kidneys, 2 pounds top round steak, flour, 6 tablespoons butter, ½ cup onions, sliced very thin; ½ pound (2 cups sliced) mushrooms, 2 cups boiling water, 2 teaspoons salt, ¼ teaspoon pepper, 1 teaspoon crushed dried or chopped fresh rosemary, 1 cup red wine.

Soak kidneys in salted water one hour. Cut steak into 1-inch cubes, dredge in flour and brown in 3 tablespoons butter; add onions and cook until soft. Remove fat and membrane from kidneys, cut in slices and add with mushrooms and remaining 3 tablespoons butter to steak mixture. Stir and cook all together gently for a few minutes. Then add boiling water, salt, pepper and rosemary. Simmer until meat is tender. Add wine and thicken the gravy with flour mixed to a smooth paste with cold water. Pour all into a large baking dish and cover with a good, rich pastry. (See Pastry.) Bake in hot oven until brown.

Miss Fanny's Receipt Book
West River   *Anne Arundel*

STRAWBERRY HILL BEEF STEW

3½ pounds of a round of beef cut into walnut size cubes, all gristle removed; flour, ⅓ cup of leaf lard, tried suet, or other shortening; 1 clove garlic, minced; 1 large onion, coarsely chopped; 3 stalks of celery, coarsely chopped.

Shake cubes in paper bag with the flour until well coated. Brown them in the shortening in an iron kettle with the garlic, onion and celery. When well browned, add 2 cups stewed tomatoes, 3 cups rich beef stock, 1 cup chopped onions browned in a little butter, salt, coarse ground black pepper. Simmer slowly for one hour, stirring occasionally. Then add 6 carrots, fresh from the garden, cut into bite size pieces; 10 or 12 small whole white onions, 10 or 12 small peeled new potatoes, 1 large fresh tomato, cubed. Add a little water if necessary, and continue simmering for another hour. Then stir in 2 cups of shucked, freshly picked garden peas. Continue simmering for 20 to 30 minutes, and serve with a sprinkling of chopped parsley, warm crusty bread, and sound red Burgundy. This should serve 8 or 10 persons. It "warms over" very satisfactorily.

An old Maryland receipt for Beef Stew from the "Cooking Notes" of Alice Evans Peacock, which were passed down to her from Ann Bye Ellicott, her great-grandmother. Served on occasion at the New Providence Club in Annapolis.

Jack Peacock-Green
Dogwood Mooring, Whitehall Creek   *Anne Arundel*

A round steak about ⅓-inch thick, salt and pepper, carrots, celery stalks, bacon slices, bacon fat,
1 cup good stock, ½ cup red wine, flour.

**ROLLED BEEF
COLLOPS**

Cut steak into collops about 2 by 4 inches in size. Season with salt and
pepper and place on each collop a strip each of carrot, celery and bacon
cut the same length as meat. Roll up collops and tie them with thread.
Brown them in a little bacon fat in a heavy skillet. Pour stock and wine
over meat rolls and place a close fitting lid over pan. Let collops simmer for about 2 hours, adding a little more stock if needed. When meat
is tender, lift to serving dish and remove threads. Thicken gravy with
flour mixed to a smooth paste with a little cold water and test seasoning; then pour over collops and serve.

Mrs. C. H. Steele's Book, 1870

Annapolis

---

2 pounds round steak, salt and pepper, 8 small
white onions, 6 carrots cut in strips, ½ pound
mushrooms, sliced; 2 tablespoons butter, 1 cup

**SAVOURY
ROUND STEAK**

tomatoes, peeled and cut in pieces; 2 cups red wine (or 1 cup good
beef stock and 1 cup red wine), 1 clove garlic, thoroughly crushed; ¼
teaspoon each, chervil, marjoram, rosemary, and savoury; 1 tablespoon
butter, 1 tablespoon flour.

Cut steak in individual serving pieces of about ¼ pound. Season meat
with salt and pepper, and brown it with the onions, carrots and mushrooms in butter in an iron pot or Dutch oven. Pour off extra fat but
leave a nice brown sediment and pan juices for gravy. Add tomatoes
and just cover with red wine, or equal parts of meat stock and wine.
Add garlic and savoury herbs; cover and simmer very gently until meat
is thoroughly done, 2 to 3 hours. Thicken gravy a little with flour
rubbed into butter.

Receipts from Araby

Charles

Mince cold roast beef, fat and lean, very fine;
add chopped onion, pepper, salt, and a little good
gravy. Fill scallop shells two parts full, and fill

**'A NICE LITTLE
DISH OF BEEF'**

them up with potatoes mashed smooth with cream. Put a bit of butter
on the top, and set them in an oven to brown.

An original receipt, 1828
Ivy Neck papers

Anne Arundel

An 8 or 10 pound round of beef, 1 gallon water, 1 **SPICED BEEF**
teaspoon salt petre, ½ box mixed spices, 2 sticks
cinnamon, 1 dozen cloves, 1 cup sugar, 1 quart salt.

Boil ingredients (except beef) together for 10 minutes. When cold, put
round of beef in and let it remain for 2 weeks. Weight it down. Turn
over on end after first week. No harm will result if it remains in the
mixture longer. To cook, place beef in stout kettle with lid, cover with
liquid, half spice mixture and half water, and cook slowly 15 to 20 minutes to the pound or until thoroughly tender. Serve cold, carving in
very thin slices. I recommend serving with thin slices of home-made
white bread, although biscuits or rolls may be used.

Captain Walter D. Sharp
Hanover Street   *Annapolis*

The Maryland Scene

June Week—U. S. Naval Academy
Buffet Supper

Army and Navy Punch

Deviled Maryland Ham   Crabmeat Balls

Tiny Maryland Biscuits

Hot Chicken Mousse   Crabtown Deviled Crabs

Mattie's Baked Rice

Oven Creamed Mushrooms

Spiced Beef   Lobster Salad Bowl

Mixed Green Salad   Jubilee Rolls

Strawberry Ice Mould

Lemon Sherbet

Seven Seas Cake   Coffee

All are Receipts of Naval Officers and their wives.

Beef

BEEF	Marinate a fine Pot Roast for 24 hours in the fol-
POT ROAST	lowing marinade, and use the liquid freely and

often for basting roast. Cook in covered pot using
very low heat until meat is thoroughly tender.

Marinade for Beef Pot Roast: 1 cup salad oil, 1½ cups red wine, 1
clove cut garlic, 2 tablespoons chopped celery leaves, 2 tablespoons
coarsely chopped parsley, ½ tablespoon salt, ¼ teaspoon dried marjoram, ½ cup lemon juice, 1 teaspoon freshly ground pepper, 2 bay
leaves, 2 carrots and 1 onion, coarsely chopped.

Mrs. Truxtun Beale's Book, 1903
Decatur House   *Washington*

TO 'DOBE' A	3 to 4 pound round of beef, ¼ pound salt pork,
ROUND OF BEEF	1 teaspoon mixed sweet herbs (such as thyme,

marjoram, savoury), 1 tablespoon minced parsley,
1 clove garlic, crushed; pinch of cayenne, salt and pepper, 1 cup red
wine, 1 cup meat stock.

Cut salt pork in thin strips. Mix together herbs and seasonings and roll
pork strips in mixture. Make incisions in beef and insert pork strips.
Season beef with salt and pepper and place in heavy kettle with wine
and stock. Cover closely, and simmer until very tender, about 3 hours.
Lift out beef and strain stock.

For the 'Dobe': 2 pounds lean veal, 2 well-cleaned pigs' feet, salt and
pepper, 1 stalk celery with leaves, 2 sprigs parsley, 1 large onion, sliced;
1 cut clove garlic, 1 bay leaf, ¼ teaspoon thyme, ½ cup sherry.

Season veal and pigs' feet with salt and pepper and place in stew pan
with water to barely cover. Add ingredients except sherry and cook
slowly until meat falls from bones. Strain veal stock and combine with
beef stock; add sherry and chill until all fat may be removed. Mince
veal and pigs' feet, discarding all bones; combine minced meat with
stock. Place beef in a large mold or bowl and cover it with stock and
minced meat. Take care that jelly surrounds meat with a good thick
layer. It will form a most appetizing dish when cold, to be cut in thin
slices for serving. An excellent dish for a summer buffet.

Receipt from Old Mrs. Scott, February 14, 1851
Mrs. F. T. Loockerman's Book   *Annapolis*

A 3 to 4 pound pot roast, salt pork or bacon, **POT ROAST**
finely chopped parsley, 1 clove garlic, minced; 2 **WITH CIDER**
cups cider, 2 onions, chopped; ¼ teaspoon ginger,
3 cloves, ¼ teaspoon cinnamon, salt and pepper, flour, 2 tablespoons
butter or drippings.

Roll small strips of salt pork or bacon in chopped parsley and minced garlic, and lard pot roast with them. Combine the cider, chopped onion and spices, and let meat rest in it for several hours, turning occasionally. When ready to cook, remove meat from liquid, pat dry with paper towel, season with salt and pepper and dredge with flour. Melt butter or drippings in a heavy iron pot, and when it is hot, sear meat all over until it is well browned. Pour over it the cider mixture in which it was soaked, which should be about 2 cups. Cover pot closely, reduce heat, and simmer gently for 2 to 3 hours, until meat is very tender. Strain stock and thicken it with flour to make the sauce.

Mrs. C. H. Steele's Book, 1870   *Annapolis*

To Corn Beef: Put 2 or 3 quarts of water in a **CORNED BEEF**
large crock. Place whole egg or potato in water,
then pour in large-grained salt and stir until the egg or potato floats. This will probably take a whole box of salt. Remove egg or potato and put in pieces of beef—brisket or chuck is best. Put in cool place and cover. (If outdoors, weigh down lid—dogs and coons like corned beef, too.) Leave beef in brine for 3 to 6 days, depending on temperature (6 days if cold). If water seems a little thick, remove beef. The longer it is left in the brine (up to 6 days) the more "corned" it will be. This makes a slightly greyish but very tender corned beef. It will keep for several days, but not as long as the commercial grade which uses saltpeter. It can be frozen.

To Cook: Wash off beef; place in large pot, barely cover with water and add 1 chili pepper, leaves from several stalks of celery, 1 sliced onion, 1 teaspoon each of mace, clove and cinnamon and 1 bay leaf. Simmer for 3 hours. One hour before dinner add potatoes and carrots; one-half hour before dinner add whole onions; twenty minutes before dinner, add cabbage, cut in sections.

Mrs. R. M. Phelps
Whitehall Creek
                                        Anne Arundel

Beef

The *"corns" used in preserving beef in the 17th and 18th centuries were corns of gunpowder. The method of preserving beef for long sailing voyages, particularly on naval vessels, was to put a carcass of beef in a tub of sea water and add an appropriate amount of gunpowder which came in small pellets (corns) and contained an amount of saltpeter. Readers of 18th and early 19th century novels may remember a dish commonly served in that period called "powdered beef," which is "gunpowdered beef," not, as one might logically think, hash.*

DRIED BEEF, MARYLAND STYLE   ½ pound dried beef, 2 tablespoons butter, 1 tablespoon flour, 2 cups milk.

Shred beef and place in a frying pan, cover with cold water and gradually heat to scalding. Drain and return to stove, stirring and shaking beef in the pan to dry off all water. Add butter and cook until beef is slightly frizzled. Sprinkle over flour and stir well; add milk, stirring constantly. It will thicken quickly and should form a creamy dressing for the beef when done. Dust lightly with pepper and serve on hot toast. This amount will serve a family of six.

Note: Dried, smoked beef, such as found in the Lexington Market in Baltimore, should be scalded in this manner to remove some of the salt. Packaged chipped beef need not be first scalded. However, do not add salt to cream sauce.

Up-to-Date Cook Book, 1897
St. John's Church   *Montgomery*

SUNDAY MORNING KIDNEY STEW   2 beef kidneys, 4 tablespoons butter, 1 onion, chopped; ½ green pepper, chopped; 3 tablespoons flour, 2 quarts hot water, salt and pepper.

On Saturday afternoon soak kidneys one hour in cold, salt water, then cut in small pieces, removing gristle. Put butter in skillet, add onion, green pepper and flour and cook to a golden brown, stirring constantly. Slowly add hot water while stirring. When incorporated and smooth, add prepared kidney, and allow to simmer for 2½ to 3 hours, taking at least ½ hour to come to a boil, and adding more water as it thickens. Next morning season to taste and serve hot for breakfast. We also cook large quantities, as it freezes with great success.

Mrs. Charles McCurdy Mathias,
Court Square   *Frederick*

1 large fresh beef tongue, 1 bay leaf.

SPICED FRESH BEEF TONGUE

Cover tongue with salted water, add bay leaf, and simmer 3 hours or until tender. Let cool in liquor. Skin.

Make a sauce by mixing together these ingredients: ½ cup corn syrup, 1 cup mild vinegar (or half vinegar, half tongue stock), ½ cup raisins, 1 teaspoon whole cloves, 1 teaspoon ground cinnamon, 1 teaspoon ground allspice. Simmer tongue in sauce for ¾ hour, turning and basting frequently. To serve: slice, arrange on platter and spoon sauce over tongue.

Mrs. Lew Garrison Coit
The Lord's Bounty

Anne Arundel

---

1 large smoked beef tongue, 1 onion, sliced; 1 carrot, sliced; 1 stalk celery with leaves, a bay leaf, sprigs of parsley and thyme, a few whole cloves and peppercorns.

SMOKED TONGUE WITH PORT WINE SAUCE

Wash tongue thoroughly and set to soak overnight. Draw off water. Put in a large pan with enough water to cover and add the vegetables and seasonings. Bring to the boil and simmer slowly for 3 to 4 hours. Skin and serve hot with Port Wine Sauce. (See Sauces for Meats.)

Receipts from Araby

Charles

---

1 beef tongue, bay leaf, 1½ cups chicken broth, ½ cup dry white wine, 2 tablespoons gelatin, ½ cup cold water, watercress.

TONGUE IN WHITE WINE ASPIC

Simmer tongue in salted water to cover if tongue is fresh (unsalted, if smoked), with a bay leaf. When done, let it cool in water in which it was cooked, then remove and skin. Slice tongue diagonally and arrange slices slightly overlapping in two rows on a shallow, rectangular dish. Heat chicken broth and wine together. Soften gelatin in cold water and dissolve in the hot liquid. Taste for seasoning. Cool a little, then pour over tongue slices. Chill until firm, garnish with watercress and serve with Horse-radish Sauce. (See Sauces for Meats.)

Miss Fanny's Receipt Book
West River

Anne Arundel

Veal

MARINATED VEAL ROAST   A rolled, boned roast of veal, about 5 or 6 pounds; 2 slices lean bacon, cut up; 1 teaspoon marjoram, 1 teaspoon thyme, ½ teaspoon caraway seed, ¼ cup chopped parsley, 1 large onion, chopped; 1 minced clove of garlic, ½ cup olive oil, ½ cup lemon juice.

Make a marinade of all ingredients and let seasonings blend for half an hour, then pour over veal which has been placed in a shallow roasting pan. Cover with foil and marinate about 24 hours, turning occasionally. Roast in a slow, 300° oven for about 3 hours, uncovered. When tender, lift veal to hot platter and serve in its own juices.

Mrs. C. Victor Barry
Atholl   Anne Arundel

SAVOURY ROLLED ROAST VEAL   A nice piece of rump of veal, 3½ to 4 pounds, boned and rolled; garlic, parsley, onion, salt and pepper, butter, glass of white wine, 1 cup sour cream.

Rub inside of veal thoroughly with a clove of garlic, then sprinkle with chopped parsley and grated onion; season with salt and pepper and smear generously with butter. Roll veal, tie with string, and repeat the above procedure on the outside, being sure to have a good coating of butter. Put veal in an uncovered roasting pan with 2 tablespoons of butter, place in a hot oven and turn and sear meat until golden brown on all sides. Then reduce heat to moderate, pour wine into roasting pan, cover it and cook until meat is tender. Remove veal to a platter and keep hot while you gradually stir in a cup of sour cream to juices left in pan. Pour this sauce over the roast, or serve separately.

Receipts from Araby   *Charles*

6 veal loin chops (cut 1 inch thick), 3 tablespoons flour, 4 tablespoons butter, ½ cup dry white wine, ½ teaspoon dried basil, salt and pepper to taste, cooked asparagus to serve 6, 1 cup chicken broth, 1 cup sour cream, paprika.

VEAL LOIN CHOPS WITH ASPARAGUS

Dust chops with flour and reserve remaining flour to thicken sauce. Brown chops slowly on both sides in 3 tablespoons of butter in a heavy skillet. Then add the wine, basil, salt and pepper. Cover and cook over low heat for 30 minutes. Arrange chops, surrounded by hot asparagus, on a warm platter. Add 1 tablespoon of butter to sauce in pan and stir until butter is melted. Mix in flour; then add chicken broth, sour cream and paprika and blend well. If sauce is too thick, thin it with a little milk. Pour it over the chops and asparagus. Serves 6.

Mrs. J. Reaney Kelly
Conduit Street

Annapolis

---

6 veal collops or slices cut from the leg, nutmeg, cloves, mace, salt and freshly ground black pepper, flour.

VEAL COLLOPS WITH OYSTER FORCEMEAT

Lay collops on a wet 'bisquit' board and dust lightly with spices and seasoning. Dip in flour and pound with a wooden mallet until thin.

The force-meat: 1 or 2 veal collops, 6 or 8 oysters, 3 strips bacon, salt, pepper, nutmeg, mace, cloves, 1 tablespoon chopped parsley, a pinch of any other desired herb such as thyme or sage, but not too many. Grind together veal, oysters and bacon, sprinkle lightly with seasonings and mix in parsley and herbs. Spread force-meat on collops, roll up and tie securely.

To cook: 2 tablespoons butter, ½ cup strong meat broth, ½ cup white wine, 2 shallots cut fine, 1 clove garlic, minced; 1 anchovy, mashed; ½ pound fresh mushrooms, 1 tablespoon butter, 1 tablespoon flour.

Melt butter in skillet and fry rolled collops until brown. Place in covered oven dish and add broth which has been stirred into pan in which collops were browned. Pour over the white wine and add the shallots, garlic, anchovy and prepared mushrooms, sliced. Cover dish and cook in a moderate oven for about an hour. Remove top and add butter rolled in flour to thicken gravy.

Adapted from Mrs. Hannah Glasse's Art of Cookery, 1774
Mrs. Frank Jack Fletcher

Charles

Veal

VEAL BIRDS 1 to 1¼ pounds veal steak cut very thin, 1¼ cups
WITH soft bread crumbs, ½ cup chopped celery, 2 tea-
SOUR CREAM spoons chopped onion, ¼ teaspoon salt, pepper,
⅛ teaspoon sage, 5 tablespoons melted butter, salt
and pepper, flour, 1 cup boiling veal or chicken stock, 1 cup thick sour
cream.

Trim veal and cut in 6 portions. Combine crumbs, celery, onion, salt,
pepper, sage and 3 tablespoons butter and mix well. Put a spoonful
of dressing in center of each piece of veal. Roll up and tie with thread.
Sprinkle with salt and pepper and roll in flour. Brown in remaining
two tablespoons of butter, turning often. Add stock, cover tightly and
let simmer for an hour or more until tender. Turn from time to time
and add more liquid if necessary. Remove meat and cut off threads.
Mix a little flour with sour cream until smooth. Add to meat gravy
and cook, stirring constantly until it thickens. Season with salt and
pepper, add veal birds and heat through.

Mrs. Rorer's Receipt, adapted, 1885
Ivy Neck, Rhode River *Anne Arundel*

VEAL 3 pounds veal from the leg, ¼ pound lean pork,
BEWITCHED 1 cup bread crumbs, 3 teaspoons salt, 1 teaspoon
black pepper, ½ teaspoon cayenne pepper, a little
pinch cloves, 2 eggs.

Chop veal and pork very fine. Mix all other ingredients together with
the raw eggs, then work together with the meat. Place in a common
mould, shut it up tight and steam for two hours. Then put it in a
warm oven, leaving door open, and let it stay a short time to dry.
When cold turn out and cut in thin slices. It is much improved by covering it with aspic meat jelly.

Miss Agnes Tilghman
Gross' Coate, Wye River *Talbot*

Pastry for a top crust. 2 cups cooked lean veal, diced; 1 tablespoon diced salt pork, 1 chopped onion, 1 cup rich cream sauce, salt and pepper, pinch rosemary, 1 pint oysters. **VEAL AND OYSTER PIE**

Roll and cut pastry to fit top of baking dish. Bake crust in hot oven for 10 or 15 minutes while preparing veal and oysters. Sauté salt pork and onion; mix with veal in cream sauce; add seasonings to taste. Cook over hot water for about 20 minutes. Pour into baking dish and cover with a layer of oysters placed close together. Dot with butter and place in fairly hot oven until oysters puff and gills curl. Remove from oven, cover pie with baked top crust, and send to table.

Mrs. Thomas Morton
Crab Creek

Anne Arundel

---

3 pounds of breast of veal, 1 bay leaf, 1 onion, sliced; black pepper, salt, ½ pound calf's liver, 2 hard-boiled eggs, red pepper, a good dash of nutmeg, sherry to taste, about ½ cup. **MOCK TERRAPIN**

Boil the veal in enough water to cover well. Add bay leaf, onion, pepper and salt. Cook until meat will shred with a fork. Roll calf's liver in flour. Fry until no blood runs when stuck with a fork. Cut in pieces to imitate terrapin liver. Brown some flour and make a thin sauce with some of the stock. Add shredded veal, liver and hard-boiled egg yolks, to resemble terrapin eggs. Season with cayenne, nutmeg and sherry. Serves 6.

Amelia Pinkney D. Lurman

Harford

Take a young calf's liver which should weigh no more than 2½ to 3 pounds. Make small holes all through and lard by filling them with bits of **A BAKED CALF'S LIVER**
bacon and onion. Place in a roasting pan with flour, salt and pepper on top. Put strips of bacon across the liver. Add a little water or chicken broth to the pan, with a bay leaf, pinch of thyme and butter the size of a walnut. Bake in a moderate oven, 350°, for 1 hour or until tender, basting frequently. Slice very thin on a slant and serve with pan gravy, slightly thickened.

Mrs. Florence Fay Valiant
Carvel Hall

Annapolis

Veal

CALF'S LIVER
MARYLAND
2 tablespoons butter, 1 onion, chopped; 2 or 3 cloves, 1 small garlic bud, minced; 2 tablespoons finely chopped parsley, a pinch each of savory, marjoram and thyme; 1 pound calf's liver, 3 slices bacon, cayenne and black pepper, ¼ cup beef broth, salt, ¼ cup or more Madeira or sherry.

Brown onion lightly in butter with the cloves, garlic, parsley and herbs. Remove cloves. Prepare liver by removing any membranes and slicing into serving pieces; arrange in baking dish. Spread with onion mixture and place bacon strips over top. Sprinkle with peppers, and pour in broth. Cover and bake until tender. Do not let it cook too fast, or become dry. When ready to serve, add wine and a pinch of salt, if needed. Remove liver to hot platter and thicken gravy with a little flour mixed to a smooth paste with cold water. Let it bubble and spoon over liver slices. Sprinkle with additional finely cut parsley.

Fifty Years in a Maryland Kitchen, 1873
Miss Agnes Tilghman, Gross' Coate   *Talbot*

TO PREPARE
SWEETBREADS
Soak sweetbreads in cold water for an hour or more. Change water several times, so that all blood will be extracted, and leave the sweetbreads very white. Put them on the fire in cold water with a little vinegar or lemon juice. Simmer (not boil) for twenty minutes; then immerse them again in cold water. This is to parboil and blanch them. Remove all the pipes, strings, and fibers it is possible to do without breaking sweetbreads. If they are to be cooked whole, when half cold tie each one in a piece of cheese-cloth, drawing it tightly into an oval form, and place under a light weight until cold. They will then be smooth and a uniform shape.

Mrs. Hugh P. LeClair
Holly Hill   *Anne Arundel*

160

Francis E. Engle

Holly Hill

Veal

3 pairs sweetbreads, 2 tablespoons butter, 2 tablespoons flour, 2 cups cream, 1 cup mushrooms,
chopped very fine; ¼ teaspoon mace, salt, white
pepper, wine glass sherry.

**CREAMED
SWEETBREADS**

With a silver knife, cut sweetbreads (cleaned and parboiled) into
pieces. Melt butter and stir in flour until smooth, then the cream, stirring constantly until it bubbles. Add mushrooms and let simmer for 5
minutes. Add mace and season well to taste with salt and pepper. Stir
in wine and, when well blended, add the sweetbreads and cook slowly
for 5 minutes longer. May be served in patty shells or on thin sliced
Maryland ham.

Mrs. Hugh P. LeClair
Holly Hill

Anne Arundel

Veal

GLAZED
SWEETBREADS
1 veal knuckle, 3 pairs sweetbreads, 1 teaspoon sugar, 2 tablespoons butter, flour, salt and pepper, 1 tablespoon chopped parsley, ¼ teaspoon powdered thyme.

Boil a knuckle of veal the day before sweetbreads are to be used, so that the broth will jell. Prepare and parboil sweetbreads, keeping them whole. Brown them in sugar and softened butter mixed with a little flour. Stir in about a teacupful of veal jelly, salt and pepper to taste, parsley and thyme. Let them simmer slowly over low heat until glazed and ready to serve.

Mrs. C. H. Steele's Book, 1870   *Annapolis*

BAKED
CALF'S HEAD
1 calf's head, skinned and split; a few whole allspice, ½ teaspoon whole cloves, ¼ teaspoon celery seed, salt, black and red pepper, 1 cup sherry, buttered crumbs.

Allow cleaned head to stand in cold water for 1 hour to draw off blood. Then take it out, wash well, put into cold water and cook slowly until meat drops from bones; (remove brains and cook separately). Take meat from bones and chop fine with the skinned and chopped brains and tongue. Mix and moisten meat with a little of the stock in which it was cooked. Season with cloves, allspice, celery seed, salt, black and red pepper; add sherry. Place in baking dish and cover with buttered crumbs. Bake in moderate oven until a light brown. Garnish with slices of lemon and hard-boiled egg.

This is such a delicious and rich dish that it should be served with a green salad or green vegetable, rolls that are not too rich, white wine —and followed with fruit or a simple dessert.

Pinkney family receipt
Amelia Pinkney D. Lurman   *Harford*

Calf's brains, 1 egg, 1 teaspoon flour, ¼ teaspoon salt, ¼ teaspoon baking powder. (Double or treble ingredients according to your company.)

CALF'S BRAIN CAKES

Wash brains, remove membranes and soak 1 hour in cold water, then parboil them for 5 minutes in gently boiling salted water. Drain off water and rinse. Break egg into the brains and stir in flour, salt and baking powder. Mix and spoon out on hot griddle, brown, turn over and cook other side. Serve very hot. Some prefer more flour to make a thick cake but I do not, the thin, hot cakes being very palatable.

Captain Walter D. Sharp
Hanover Street   *Annapolis*

---

2 pounds lean veal, 1 veal knuckle, cracked; 2 onions and 2 carrots, sliced; 1 cup dry white wine, 1 teaspoon salt, a few peppercorns, 1 bay leaf, a few parsley sprigs, 1 teaspoon mixed dried sweet herbs (thyme, marjoram, summer savory), ¼ pound cooked ham, 2 hard-boiled eggs, rich pie pastry to cover dish. (See Pastry.)

VEAL AND HAM PIE, JELLIED

Put veal and veal knuckle in a kettle with onions and carrots. Pour wine over it, and add just enough water to cover well. Add the salt, peppercorns, bay leaf, parsley and sweet herbs. Simmer veal until tender, then strain stock. Reduce stock and increase strength by simmering a little longer. Cut veal into small pieces, the ham in thin slices. Arrange in a deep pie dish a layer of veal, a layer of ham, a layer of thin slices of egg, until the dish is full. Pour on seasoned stock, filling to the top, and cover with a crust of rich pastry. Make vent for steam to escape and bake until crust is nicely browned. Cool and refrigerate until served. There should be plenty of jellied stock in the pie which makes it a delicious dish for hot weather.

Mrs. James Cheston's Everyday Book, 1857
West River   *Anne Arundel*

Lamb

ROAST SADDLE OF LAMB OR MUTTON *"The best mutton", says Mayor Latrobe, "comes from Southdown sheep, and the finest South-down in the country, in my judgment, are in the Druid Hill Park flock. They have been carefully bred, the city of Baltimore having imported the rams from the flocks of Lord Wolsingham, the Prince of Wales and other noted breeders of Southdowns. I would suggest to the epicure to obtain a saddle of mutton from a three-year-old sheep bred from the Druid Hill flock; let it hang about a week in cold weather, then have it perfectly roasted, —cooked through but not overdone, using a marinade of sweet herbs. Have a good company around your table and dry champagne. For your favored guest, cut the slice down the back nearest the bone, and if he cannot enjoy this delicacy he must be hard to please."*

A saddle, or two-sided rack or loin of lamb or mutton, weighing 6 or 7 pounds. A marinade consisting of sweet marjoram, thyme, parsley, onion and garlic, all bruised and minced fine, oil and lemon juice; salt and pepper.

Make some incisions between the ribs and smooth the marinade in around the bone. The lamb may be left overnight to absorb the marinade. Roast on rack in open pan in moderately slow oven from 2½ to 3 hours. Baste occasionally with the marinade, season with salt and pepper, and turn smooth side up for last half hour to brown top.

To serve, cut along back bone on either side to loosen meat, then slice at right angles to bone, slipping knife underneath to free from rib bones.

Mayor Latrobe's way of serving Saddle of Mutton
The Baltimore Sun, 1891   *Baltimore*

Fred Thomas · *Troth's Fortune*

Lamb

LEG OF SPRING LAMB, BRAISED

Small leg of spring lamb, butter, 4 carrots, cut in pieces; 2 onions, quartered; 2 cloves garlic, a bunch of savory fresh herbs, or 1 teaspoon mixed dried ones; 1 cup meat or vegetable stock, ¼ cup Madeira, salt and pepper.

Brown lamb in foaming butter in heavy pot just large enough to contain it. Turn frequently so that it takes on a fine color on all sides. Remove meat from pot and brown vegetables in same butter. Replace lamb on top of vegetables and add stock and wine. Cover pot closely and cook very slowly, basting occasionally with its own liquor, and seasoning it with salt and pepper as soon as it begins to be tender. When cooked, strain pan juices, remove excess fat, and thicken gravy with flour. Serve lamb surrounded by little mounds of whole young carrots, new potatoes and fresh green peas, cooked separately according to your way.

Mrs. Frederic C. Thomas
Troth's Fortune, Choptank River · *Talbot*

Lamb

BROILED Have steaks cut 1 inch thick from leg of lamb or
LAMB STEAKS shoulder. Crush a clove of garlic into ½ cup olive
oil. Make a fagot of celery leaves with sprigs of
rosemary and parsley tied together. Brush the oil on steaks with the
fagot of herbs; put under the broiler and brush now and then while
meat is cooking and after turning. When done, season steaks with salt
and freshly ground black pepper.

Hester Ann Harwood's Book, 1847
Hammond-Harwood House *Annapolis*

LAMB CURRY 2 or 3 large sliced onions, 4 tablespoons butter, 3
cups raw lamb cut in inch cubes, ½ teaspoon
salt, ¼ teaspoon freshly ground pepper, pinch of thyme, pinch of
cloves, 2 tablespoons flour, juice and grated rind of ½ a lemon, ½ a
green pepper, cut in small pieces; ⅔ cup of currants, 2 large tart
apples, peeled and sliced thin; 2 teaspoons curry powder.

Cook onions in butter until soft and yellow. Add meat and sprinkle
with salt and pepper, thyme and cloves. Dust flour over meat, turn and
mix well, adding lemon and green pepper. Cover with a little water
and simmer until meat is half done. Add currants and apples and more
water if necessary, but it should not be soupy. When thoroughly cooked,
add curry powder, blend well and cook a little longer until it is incorporated, but do not over cook.

Receipts from Araby *Charles*

LAMB SHANKS 6 lamb shanks, no fat; flour, olive oil, 2 medium
onions, chopped; ½ pound mushrooms, 3 me-
dium sized potatoes, diced; 3 large carrots, inch lengths; 1 clove garlic,
minced; 1 cup chopped celery, ¼ cup chopped parsley, 1 apple, diced;
1 tablespoon horseradish, 1 tablespoon curry powder, 1 teaspoon Worcestershire sauce, 1 teaspoon salt, ½ teaspoon freshly ground pepper,
hot pepper to taste (either 1 long red pepper pod or 4 shakes of
cayenne or Tabasco); 1 cup red wine (Burgundy best); ¾ cup of
chicken broth.

Dredge lamb shanks in flour and brown in olive oil. Remove to oven dish. Sauté onions and mushrooms in same oil, then sprinkle over dish. Add all other ingredients, cover, and cook 2 hours at 300°. Serve with rice or hot biscuits.

Mrs. Beverley C. Compton
Ruxton

Baltimore

A SAVOURY LAMB PIE

3 or 4 pounds lean stewing lamb, salt and pepper to taste, the least quantity of ground mace, cloves and nutmeg (about ½ teaspoon together), 1 pair sweetbreads, 1 pint oysters, 2 tablespoons butter, 2 tablespoons flour, oyster liquor and lamb broth to make 2 cups, 1 egg yolk, ½ cup claret, baked pastry shell in deep dish with pastry lid.

Cut lamb in pieces, season with salt, pepper and spices; cover with water and stew until tender, reserving broth. Prepare sweetbreads (see Meats—Veal). Cut them in pieces and combine with lamb. Heat oysters in liquor until gills curl, then drain and add to lamb and sweetbreads, saving liquor. Make a drawn butter sauce with butter, flour and liquids. Season to taste. When smooth and thickened, mix in beaten egg yolk and wine.

Add the lamb, sweetbreads and oysters to the sauce and heat well. Pour into hot pastry shell, replace pastry lid and serve.

Fifty Years in a Maryland Kitchen, 1873
Miss Agnes Tilghman, Gross' Coate

Talbot

KIDNEY STEW, BREAKFAST STYLE

12 lamb kidneys, 1 veal kidney, 2 tablespoons butter, 3 to 4 large tablespoons finely chopped onion, 1 tablespoon flour, ¼ cup water, salt and pepper, ¼ cup claret.

Clean kidneys, cutting out all suet, and slice. Using large skillet, sauté onion in butter until golden. Sift over the flour and blend in. Add kidneys and water, cover tightly and stew for 15 or 20 minutes over low heat, turning frequently. Add water, if necessary, to make plenty of gravy. When almost tender, season to taste and add claret. Cook 3 minutes longer and serve very hot with Superior Rice Waffles (see Breads).

Willard G. Triest
Severn River

Anne Arundel

FOX-HUNTING

In colonial days, the gentlemen of a neighbourhood would foregather in season for fox-hunting, which is believed to have taken its first hold in America in Tidewater Maryland. One early devotee of the sport, Robert Brooke, sailed out of England in 1650 with his family, a large retinue of servants and his pack of hounds and in that year established himself on the Patuxent River.

A good instance of the popularity of the sport is found in George Washington's diary for March, 1773.

"28 Went with Mr. Dulaney and Mr. Digges, & ca., to dine with Mr. Benj. Dulaney at Mrs. French's.—

"29 Went a hunting with those Gentlemen. Found a Fox by Thos. Bailey's and had it killd by Our Dogs in half an hour.

"30 Went a hunting again—found Nothing.

The Maryland Scene

A Maryland Hunt Breakfast
for
Thanksgiving or New Year's Day

Maryland Rye Whiskey   Hot Apple Toddy

Steamed Oysters, Baltimore Style

Roast Suckling Pig   Old Maryland Baked Ham

Roast Turkey   Brunswick Stew

Sauerkraut   Big Hominy   Spoon Bread

Tomatoes Brown   Broccoli

Hot Rolls   Cornmeal Sticks

Spiced Crab Apples   Celery   Cranberry Sauce

Pumpkin and Mince Pies   Plum Pudding

Caramel Ice Cream   Little Sponge Cakes

Coffee   Fruit   Nuts

Pork

PORK LOIN ROAST, SOUTHERN WAY   A 4 or 5 pound center cut loin of pork, flour, salt and pepper, 2 medium onions, 1 carrot, 1 stalk of celery with leaves, sprigs of parsley, thyme or marjoram (or dried), 1 bay leaf, 1 cup boiling water or more, brown sugar.

Rub roast with salt and pepper and dust well with flour. Make a bed of chopped onions and carrot in an open roasting pan. Tie celery, parsley and herbs together and place them in pan to flavor basting juices. (A sprinkling of dried herbs will do if you do not have fresh ones.) Place pork loin, fat side up, on the bed of vegetables and pour 1 cup of boiling water into pan. Roast in moderate oven for 2½ hours or more, until pork is tender, basting often with juices in pan. Add more water if needed. For the last quarter hour of roasting, sprinkle top of loin with brown sugar, sufficient to make a nice glaze, and let it color in a fairly hot oven.

To make sauce, remove bunch of herbs and excess fat, and thicken drippings with flour. Leave vegetable bits in the gravy. Serve with apple sauce, sweet potato pone and one of the "Greens" such as kale, collards, or spinach.

Mrs. William H. Kirkpatrick
Parkhurst   *Anne Arundel*

BARBECUED PORK CHOPS   ¾ cup vinegar, ¾ cup tomato ketchup, 1½ cups water, 1 medium onion, chopped; 1 clove garlic, minced; 2 teaspoons salt, ½ teaspoon pepper, 1 tablespoon Worcestershire sauce, ¼ teaspoon Tabasco, 3 tablespoons brown sugar, 8 thick pork chops, 4 tablespoons butter.

Combine ingredients, except chops and butter. Simmer sauce for ½ hour, stirring occasionally. Brown chops on both sides in butter. Place in a shallow baking pan; pour sauce over chops and bake uncovered in a 350° oven for 1 hour, or until chops are tender, basting frequently. Barbecued chops may also be cooked over an outdoor grill and basted with the sauce.

Miss Fanny's Receipt Book
West River   *Anne Arundel*

Pork tenderloin, salt, pepper, dash of sugar, flour for dredging, 2 tablespoons drippings, ½ cup hot water.

PORK TENDERLOIN WITH SHERRY APPLE RINGS

Select tenderloin from each side of backbone of the pig. Scald with a dash of boiling water. Drain. Score each tenderloin lengthwise and then crosswise. Rub with salt, sprinkle with pepper and a dash of sugar. Roll in flour thoroughly. Place in pan in which drippings have been previously heated. As tenderloin is placed in pan, add hot water to it. Be careful not to let meat stick, adding more water from time to time and turning meat. The oven should be slow to moderate. When meat is a delicate brown and tender, place on hot platter, surrounded by Sherry Apple Rings. The juices in bottom of pan make a rich gravy.

Sherry Apple Rings:—4 small apples, 1 cup sugar, ¾ cup sherry, ¼ cup water, 1 teaspoon cinnamon (or 1 tablespoon red cinnamon drops), 2 tablespoons lemon juice.

Pare and core apples, then cut each into 4 rings. Combine sugar, ½ cup sherry, water and cinnamon (or drops), and simmer for 5 minutes. Add apple slices, cover and simmer until tender but firm. Remove from heat; add remaining ¼ cup sherry and lemon juice. Let rings cool in syrup. Remove and serve with roast goose, duck or pork. Reserve syrup for basting baked ham.

Maudie Lee's Way
Atholl

Anne Arundel

Pork chops cut ¾ inch thick, one per serving; salt and pepper, dredging flour, cooked wild rice, allowing ¼ cup per serving; onion slices, green pepper rings, cooked tomatoes and tomato juice, 1 tablespoon Worcestershire sauce.

PORK CHOPS WITH WILD RICE

Salt and pepper chops, and dredge lightly with flour. Brown them in a greased, hot skillet. Place large spoonful of rice in baking dish and on that place pork chop, then generous slice of onion, another spoonful of rice, then a ring of green pepper and spoon tomatoes in the pepper ring. Add Worcestershire sauce to sufficient tomato juice to moisten dish well, rinse skillet with that and pour over the chops and wild rice. Cook covered in a 350° oven for one hour or until chops are very tender.

Mrs. E. R. Henning
Little Flower Hill

Anne Arundel

Pork

PORK AND   1 fresh pork butt (any pork may be used), cut in
SAUERKRAUT   pieces. Allow ¾ pound of pork to 2 cups sauer-
                  kraut. Wash sauerkraut well. Fill the bottom of
a baking dish with sauerkraut and lay over it the pieces of pork. Season
with salt and pepper. Spread over pork a layer of cut-up onions (4
medium size), then cover well with sauerkraut. Add water enough to
fill two-thirds of the baking dish. Bake, covered, in a moderate oven
from 4 to 5 hours. Add water if sauerkraut becomes at all dry.

Mrs. Wade DeWeese
King George Street   *Annapolis*

TO ROAST   Put spare-rib (3 to 4 pounds) in a baking pan;
A SPARE-RIB   sprinkle lightly with pepper; add ½ teaspoon salt
                  to ½ cup boiling water, and pour in bottom of
pan. Chop a large onion and strew it over the spare-rib. Cover pan, and
roast in 350° oven for about 1½ hours, basting frequently. Fifteen
minutes before it is done, remove cover, dust spare-rib with ½ teaspoon
powdered sage, and finish browning. When nice and brown, make a
gravy and serve.

Gravy: Allow 2 tablespoons fat to remain in pan, add 2 tablespoons
flour and brown well; add a cup or more of boiling water and stir constantly until it boils. Add salt and pepper to taste, ½ teaspoon powdered
sage, and 1 tablespoon tomato catsup; strain, and serve in a boat.

Hester Ann Harwood's Book, 1848
Hammond-Harwood House   *Annapolis*

On dieting: *"The supposition too commonly entertained among young
ladies that living very delicately will add to their personal charms, is
exceedingly erroneous. A generous diet is, in most instances, absolutely
essential to the complexion; while a regimen ill-adapted to the con-
stitution, is frequently injurious to the beauty of the countenance, and
destructive to the symmetry of the form. The truth is, there is nothing
so beautiful in the human form, as nature adorned with health."*

From Hester Ann's "Frugal Housekeeper's Kitchen Companion."

A young pig, six to eight weeks old, prepared for **ROAST**
roasting. After washing with cold water, pat dry **SUCKLING PIG**
and salt inside and out. Weigh. Prop open mouth
with small block of wood. Stuff with any poultry dressing, preferably
one with onion or apple. Sew opening together, cover ears with cloth
dipped in melted butter, or aluminum foil. Rub pig with melted butter
and dredge with flour. Spread legs forward and back, so that pig will
lie flat. Roast in a 350° oven, 30 to 35 minutes to the pound, basting
frequently with butter or fat in pan. Remove covering on ears the last 30
minutes. When ready to serve, remove block from mouth and replace
with small red apple. Put cranberries in eyes, and a wreath of parsley or
boxwood around neck. Make a gravy with pan juices skimmed of fat.

Dr. Emily Wilson
Obligation
Anne Arundel

---

1 cup chopped apples, 2 slices bread, ½ small **STUFFED**
onion, chopped; 1 tablespoon brown sugar, ½ **BAKED**
teaspoon salt, ⅛ teaspoon pepper, 4 pounds spare- **SPARERIBS**
ribs, sage.

In a bowl mix the apples, bread (broken into small pieces), onion,
sugar, salt and pepper. Cut meat into two even sized pieces. Place one
piece on rack of roasting pan and spread dressing over it evenly and top
with the other piece. Tie together. Sprinkle sage, salt and coarsely ground
pepper over meat. Bake in a hot oven (475°) for 20 minutes, uncovered;
then reduce heat to 325°, cover and bake for 1 hour longer. To serve,
cut through the two pieces of meat with dressing between. Serves 4.

White House Cook Book, 1887
Contee, Rhode River
Anne Arundel

---

11 pounds unground pork, 2 tablespoons salt, 2 **WICOMICO**
tablespoons red pepper (freshly ground), 4 table- **PORK SAUSAGE**
spoons sage. Season pork well and then run it
through the grinder.

Mrs. H. Lay Phillips
Wicomico

Pork

IVY NECK   15 pounds pork meat (⅓ fat), 4 tablespoons salt,
SAUSAGE   4 tablespoons black pepper, ⅔ cup sage. (The
                      sage grown in the herb garden is far superior to
any other.) Meat should be ground fine and after salt, pepper and sage
are added, worked very thoroughly by hand.

Forbes Colhoun's way
Ivy Neck, Rhode River   *Anne Arundel*

TOAD-IN-   1 cup milk, 2 eggs, lightly beaten; 1 cup flour, ½
THE-HOLE   teaspoon salt, 1 pound country sausage meat or
                     link sausage.

Mix milk and eggs, then gradually combine with sifted flour and salt.
Beat with rotary beater until smooth and covered with bubbles, about
10 minutes. Let stand 1 hour. Heat oven to 450°. Shape sausage meat
into patties; cook patties or links until meat is rendered of its fat. Drain,
saving 2 tablespoons fat. Reheat fat in a shallow oven dish; arrange
patties or links in bottom of dish and place in oven until very hot. Pour
on batter and bake 30 to 40 minutes. Serve immediately in dish in which
it was baked.

Mrs. C. Victor Barry
Atholl   *Anne Arundel*

SCRAPPLE   Take one hog's head and liver. Cleave the head,
                     clean it and soak well. Boil it until the bones drop
out. Save liquor it is boiled in. Boil liver in separate water; crumble it
up fine while still warm; throw this water away. Chop meat from the
head very fine, put pot with liquor over the fire, stir in meat and buckwheat meal pretty thick, also a handful of Indian meal. Season it well
with pepper and salt, a little sage and sweet marjoram and let it boil
until it does not stick to the paddle, say a couple of hours. When nearly
done, stir in liver. When finished pour out in pans and set away. A very
tasty Scrapple.

Miss Emily H. Murray
Ivy Neck, Rhode River   *Anne Arundel*

Take the head, tongue, feet and any other pieces. **PORK CHEESE**
Boil them until meat drops from bones. Then put
all the meat into a large pan. Pick all bones out carefully, and all fat.
Pour liquor in a pan and let it stand all night. Next morning, scrape
off all fat from the surface. Chop meat up fine when it is warm. Season
with salt and pepper, and if you choose, herbs, sage and thyme. Put
meat and jelly together; let it come to a boil. Stir well and put into
moulds.

Mrs. Thompson's way
Maria T. Allison's Book, 1860

Baltimore

½ hog's head, 1 jowl, 2 livers, 3 large onions, salt, **LIVER PUDDING**
black pepper, sage.

Cook hog's head and jowl in salt water to cover until meat falls from
bones. In a separate pot cook livers in salt water to cover. Cut meat and
liver in small pieces and put through meat grinder, alternating with raw
cut-up onions to evenly distribute ingredients. Add more salt, if necessary; black pepper and sage to taste. Mix thoroughly. Put in large bowls
and cover with freshly rendered lard; store in cold place. When ready to
use, slice pudding in ½ inch slices and warm in frying pan. Delicious
served with hominy or hot cakes.

Old Spriggs' Farm Receipt
Magothy River

Anne Arundel

Soak pigs' feet, cleaned and scraped, in cold water **PIGS' FEET,**
2 or 3 hours; then wash and scrub well. Split feet **PLAIN AND**
and crack in 2 or 3 places. Put them into a stew- **PICKLED**
pan and just cover them with cold water; add to
the pot a sliced onion, 2 cut-up celery stalks with leaves, a bay leaf, salt
and pepper.

Place over a moderate fire and simmer until tender. Some of the pigs'
feet may be eaten hot with mashed potatoes and sauerkraut.

Pickle remaining pigs' feet as follows: Boil together for 1 minute a half-
pint of good cider vinegar, 3 blades of mace, 1 dozen whole cloves, and
a bay leaf. Pour the seasoned feet, with their broth, into an earthen
basin, and add the spiced vinegar while hot; then stand in a cold place.
They will be ready for use the next day.

Old Spriggs' Farm Receipt
Magothy River

Anne Arundel

Smoke House—Southern Maryland   Francis E. Engle

Maryland Country Ham

**REFLECTIONS
ON MARYLAND
COUNTRY HAM**

"The most exquisite peak in culinary art is conquered when you do right by a ham, for a ham, in the very nature of the process it has undergone since last it walked on its own feet, combines in its flavor the tang of smoky autumnal woods, the maternal softness of earthy fields delivered of their crop children, the wineyness of a late sun, the intimate kiss of fertilizing rain, and the bite of fire. You must slice it thin, too, almost as thin as this page you hold in your hands. The making of a ham dinner, like the making of a gentleman, starts a long, long time before the event."

W. B. Courtney from "Congress Eate It Up."

An Old Country Ham that has been cured, aged
and cooked as our Grandparents did it makes just
about perfect eating.

**SOUTHERN
MARYLAND
WAYS WITH
OLD HAM**

There are several ways to cure and cook a ham
which will bring it to its state of perfection. Some people cure ham in a
brine or 'pickle', others dry salt it, and each will defend his own way as
the best. But there are hazards in both methods.

It is surprising that a ham will absorb the seasoning faster in dry form
than it will in the brine. Therefore the weather plays a part in it, and
if it should get very warm while the ham is in brine, the liquid will sour
and spoil it.

On the other hand, in curing with dry seasoning, if the weather should
turn very cold and the ham should freeze, it will not take the cure, but
will spoil around the bone. A sugar-cured ham is juicier because the
sugar dissolves, forming a syrup which is absorbed by the ham, thus pre-
venting it from becoming dry and hard.

After a six weeks period of taking the cure, a ham must be hung
in the smoke house, and smoked very slowly with a green hickory or
apple wood fire which has been smothered with sawdust of the same
wood. It is best to smoke ham when the weather is damp and heavy and
it will take at least ten days (not consecutive ones) of smoking to bring
the color to a rich cherry red.

Then the ham must be rubbed with red pepper and a little borax or
wood ash, wrapped in paper, bagged, and hung up to age. The best age
for a ham is one year. After that it becomes drier and harder, and consequently tastes a little saltier. A ham will lose at least one fourth of its
weight in the first year.

The cooking of a ham is very important, as the best ham can be ruined
if not cooked properly. In the old days it was judged that a ham had
boiled enough when the small flat bone at the hock could be pulled
out. In our days of constant heat it is better to cook it by timing. When
the ham has been boiled and baked it should be allowed to get
thoroughly cold so that it can be sliced to advantage, in slices that are
paper thin.

Ellen Davidson Shepherd
Harwood

Anne Arundel

Country Ham

TO CURE A   Rub the Gammon with Molasses and put Salt
GAMMON   Petre, about half a teaspoonful, on the Knuckle
Bone and rub it well in. Moisten it with molasses
and water mixed, and Sprinkle it with Salt Petre, particularly under
the Bone; then cover and rub well with Salt.

Original receipt of Samuel Chase, Signer
Miss Ann Chase's Book, 1811   *Annapolis*

TO CURE HAMS   Have meat thoroughly cold and keep out of sun
while handling. As soon as cut up, rub with salt
for ten minutes, using as much salt as meat will absorb. Lay out hams
in meat house for three hours. Then use the following mixture and rub
each ham thoroughly for twenty minutes.

Amounts for six hams: 2½ pounds brown sugar, 2½ ounces saltpeter,
10 ounces black pepper. (Red pepper is used in the mixture by some
people in Southern Maryland.) It will take about a peck of salt for
eighteen hams, and after rubbing thoroughly as above, pack in sugar
barrel skin side down for six weeks. Remove, and hang up and smoke
about six times, then seal up in cloth sacks and make air-tight by
dipping in lime.

Mrs. J. Spence Howard
St. Mary's Manor   *St. Mary's*

MISS FANNY   Boil a ham two-thirds done. Draw the skin off
CHASE'S   and dress the top of the ham with cloves and
SPICED HAM   slips of lemon peel two inches long. Put it on a
baking dish with some of its juices, place it in an
oven and continue to cook it done, frequently basting it with one pint
of white wine, half a pound of brown sugar and a teaspoonful of
powdered mace. When all the gravy is cold, skim off the fat from
the gravy and decorate the ham with the good jelly. The ham may
be sliced and the thin slices arranged on the platter before garnishing
with the jelly if you like.

Miss Fanny Chase's original receipt
Miss Ann Chase's Book, 1811   *Annapolis*

TO COOK AN OLD HAM

Cover ham with cold water and soak for 24 hours. Remove and clean ham thoroughly and place in boiler with cut side down. Cover with cold water to which has been added 1 cup of vinegar. Bring to boil and reduce heat to simmer, allowing about 15 minutes per pound. Ham should be done but firm; do not over-cook, as baking is to follow.

Remove from stove and allow to cool in liquor it was cooked in. Then remove ham from boiler and peel off skin. Place in baking pan with fat side up, score fat with a knife, add 2 or 3 cups of liquid from boiler and bake in 350° oven for 1 hour, or until the fat begins to dry out and brown. Then stick with whole cloves, or sprinkle with powdered cloves and cover with ⅔ cup of brown sugar which has been moistened with 2 or 3 tablespoons of sherry wine or vinegar. Return to oven for 15 or 20 minutes until it is well browned and glazed.

Mrs. Isaac Shepherd
Harwood

Anne Arundel

SOUTHERN MARYLAND STUFFED HAM

One country cured 12 pound ham, 3 pounds kale, 3 pounds water cress (field cress), 2 pounds green cabbage, 1 bunch green celery, 1 hot red pepper, 6 tablespoons salt, 2 tablespoons black pepper, 2 tablespoons red pepper, 2 tablespoons mustard seed, 2 tablespoons celery seed, 2 teaspoons Tabasco sauce.

Choose a plump, thick ham, thin layer of fat. Parboil 20 minutes. Steam and remove all skin. Cut greens in small pieces (1 to 1½ inches). Chop celery and pepper fine. Blanch greens, celery and pepper in boiling water until limp. Drain well. Add seasonings and mix. Cool ham until comfortable to handle. Starting at butt end of ham, cut 3 lengthwise slits, 2 inches long, all the way through. Second row—2 slits. Third row—3 slits, so that one slit for stuffing does not split into another. The ham is now ready for stuffing. With the fingers, push the seasoned greens into slits first from the top, then from the under side till you feel every space is filled. The remaining greens are banked over the top of the ham.

For keeping ham in shape, use large square of clean cloth. Place ham, skin side up, on cloth, fold ends over tightly and secure with pin. Return to ham boiler and simmer 15 minutes to the pound. Let cool 2 hours in 'pot likker'. Chill in refrigerator over night in cloth.

Mrs. Edward J. Edelen
Mulberry Grove, Port Tobacco

Charles

Country Ham

MARYLAND HAM STEAKS WITH PAN GRAVY
2 slices Maryland ham, 2 tablespoons butter, 1 tablespoon flour, 1 teaspoon mustard, pinch cayenne, freshly ground pepper, 1 cup milk, parsley.

Cut slices of ham ½ an inch thick, lay them in hot water to cover for half an hour, or give them a scalding in a pan over the fire; then take them up, dry them, and brown them lightly on each side in 1 table-spoon of butter in a hot skillet. Add ½ cup hot water, cover pan tightly and simmer until ham is tender and water absorbed. Remove ham to hot platter and keep warm. Melt 1 tablespoon of butter in skillet, blend in flour, mustard and peppers; slowly add milk, stirring until sauce is smooth and thickened. Pour sauce over ham, sprinkle with fine parsley and serve. Good with fried tomatoes.

Mrs. James Cheston's Everyday Book, 1857
West River   *Anne Arundel*

LITTLE HAM PUDDINGS
1 small onion, 2 small stalks celery, 3 tablespoons butter, 3 tablespoons flour, 1 cup milk, 2 eggs, 1 or more cups of ground ham, ½ teaspoon paprika, ¼ teaspoon dry mustard, 1 teaspoon baking powder.

Chop onion and celery very fine and cook slowly in butter until soft but not brown. Blend in flour, add milk, and stir until smooth and thickened. Remove from fire and add beaten egg yolks; then stir in ham, paprika, mustard and baking powder. Add salt, if needed. Just before baking, fold in stiffly beaten egg whites. Pour into greased patty pans or muffin tins for individual servings. Bake in 350° oven about 30 minutes. Mushroom sauce enhances the puddings. (See Sauces for Meats.) Serves 4.

Adapted from Mrs. C. H. Steele's Book, 1870   *Annapolis*

Yolks of three eggs, 1½ cups stock or ham water,   **HAM MOUSSE**
2 tablespoons gelatin, dissolved in ½ cup of the
stock; 1½ cups ham, chopped very fine; pinch of powdered cloves,
paprika, salt and pepper to taste; 1 cup whipping cream, aspic jelly.

Cook beaten egg yolks and stock in double boiler, stirring until
thickened. Add softened gelatin to hot stock and mix in the ham.
Season to taste with cloves, paprika, salt and pepper. When cool,
fold in whipped cream. Cover bottom of mold with aspic, and when
it has jelled, pour in ham mousse before it is entirely stiff. Place in
refrigerator to set. Turn out on platter to serve and garnish with
parsley or watercress.

Mrs. Francis I. Gowen's receipt
Elizabeth R. Lloyd's Book, 1889   *Annapolis*

---

2 cups ground ham (leftover scraps, mostly lean),   **DEVILED HAM**
cream sauce made as follows:

1 cup cream (or cream and milk), 4 tablespoons butter, 1 tablespoon
flour, dash of red pepper, ½ tablespoon dry mustard. Blend and cook
until very thick, about 10 minutes. Add ham, mix thoroughly, put in
mould and chill. Deviled Ham may be turned out whole on a serving
dish (good for Sunday night supper), or used as a spread for crackers.

Priscilla's way
Windsor   *Anne Arundel*

---

2 cups chopped lean ham, 1 tablespoon butter,   **HAM TOAST**
2 beaten eggs, toast, pepper.   **FOR**
        BREAKFAST
Melt butter; lay in the ham. Season, and when
hot, stir in the eggs. Stir until they set slightly; then spread on slices
of toast and serve. Be careful not to let the egg harden too much. Cold
tongue may be used in this way.

Fifty Years in a Maryland Kitchen, 1873
Miss Agnes Tilghman, Gross' Coate   *Talbot*

Vegetables

Historic Annapolis, Inc.

ASPARAGUS   Tie asparagus stalks in bundles and stand them in a deep saucepan of boiling water (about half filled), with a spoonful of salt; cover and boil from 12 to 20 minutes. Take up the moment they are tender, to have the tips unbroken and preserve their color and flavor. Serve on a toast with heads inward; pour over them melted butter and add a grating of nutmeg if you like it. (Asparagus may also be served with Hollandaise or Lemon Sauce,— see Sauces for Vegetables.)

Hester Ann Harwood's Book, 1848
Hammond-Harwood House   *Annapolis*

182

12 French Pancakes (see Breads), 24 or more **ASPARAGUS** plump, cooked asparagus spears; 4 tablespoons **IN PANCAKES** flour, 4 tablespoons butter, 2 cups milk, 1 teaspoon paprika, 1 teaspoon dry mustard, 1 teaspoon salt, 1 cup cubed or shredded mild cheese.

Keep pancakes warm as they are made and, when finished, roll each one around 2 or 3 warm spears of asparagus which have been buttered and seasoned with salt and pepper. Place the rolls closely side by side on an oven dish which may be taken to the table, or on individual oven-proof plates. Make a sauce with additional ingredients by blending flour into melted butter over low heat; slowly stir in milk, then seasonings. When smooth, add cheese and stir until melted and well blended. Pour sauce over rolled pancakes and place under broiler to become brown and bubbly. Serves 4-6.

Mrs. J. Reaney Kelly
Conduit Street
Annapolis

The amount of asparagus and mushrooms de- **ASPARAGUS** pends on the number of people to be served. **WITH** Use only plump stalks. Allow 3 or 4 mushrooms **MUSHROOMS** per person.

Steam asparagus; do not boil to avoid breaking tips. Sauté mushroom caps in sweet butter. When done, drop into each heart a small quantity of finely chopped parsley.

Place asparagus on a large, hot platter; do not crowd it. Distribute mushrooms around asparagus. Over asparagus pour a rich cream sauce. Do not let sauce cover mushrooms. The stems of the mushrooms should be sautéed in butter, finely chopped and added to the heavy cream sauce. Season sauce with salt and white pepper. Can be lightly browned under broiler if platter is oven-proof.

Mrs. Sidney de la Rue
Chestertown
Kent

Vegetables

JERUSALEM   The Jerusalem Artichoke is a native of North
ARTICHOKES   America. It contains no starch.

Wash artichokes in cold water, scrape them, and drop immediately into cold water; let them soak an hour or so. Drain, cut in convenient pieces and put in saucepan. Cover with boiling water, salt it slightly, and add 1 tablespoon lemon juice or vinegar to each quart of water. This prevents graying. Cook artichokes slowly until tender, about 20 to 25 minutes. Watch carefully and do not over-cook, as they will easily harden again. Serve with Drawn Butter or Cream Sauce. (See Sauces for Vegetables.)

Mrs. Frederic C. Thomas
Troth's Fortune, Choptank River   *Talbot*

GREEN BEANS   2 pounds green beans, 4 sprigs fresh summer
WITH HERBS   savory (or 1 teaspoon dried), 4 tablespoons butter, 2 teaspoons chopped parsley, 2 teaspoons chopped basil, salt.

Prepare small young beans and drop them whole into enough boiling water to barely cover. Add a bouquet of summer savory, or the dried tied in a cloth bag. Cook about 15 minutes, uncovered, letting the water boil down. Add 2 tablespoons butter and continue to cook slowly until beans are tender. Drain, remove bouquet of savory, salt to taste and return to heat to evaporate for 2 minutes. Shake, place in serving dish and top with remaining butter to which finely chopped fresh parsley and basil have been added.

Large and not-so-young beans may be cooked in the same way by breaking into small pieces or slicing.

Miss Fanny's Receipt Book
West River   *Anne Arundel*

12 small white onions, 2 cups cooked fresh string
beans, 2 tablespoons butter, 2 tablespoons flour,
1 cup milk, 1 teaspoon salt, ½ teaspoon paprika,
1 tablespoon lemon juice, a little white pepper, buttered bread crumbs.

SCALLOPED STRING BEANS

Cook onions in boiling, salted water until tender, then drain and put
in a buttered baking dish with string beans. Melt butter, add flour
and stir in milk. Cook until thickened and season with salt, paprika,
lemon juice and pepper. Pour sauce over vegetables and cover with a
layer of buttered crumbs. Bake in a hot oven (400°) for 15 minutes
or until brown.

Mrs. Charles dePeyster Valk's Book
Duke of Gloucester Street

Annapolis

---

1 quart young limas, shelled; 1 tablespoon butter,
½ teaspoon salt, 2 tablespoons milk, 2 tablespoons cream.

FRESH LIMA BEANS

Cover washed beans with boiling salted water, and add butter. Simmer
them from 15 to 20 minutes, until nearly tender, then increase heat
and boil quickly until water has evaporated. Add milk and cream
and heat through.

Mrs. Francis F. Beirne
Ruxton

Baltimore

Shell young lima beans until you have a cup; cut
the kernels from ears of young corn until you have
an equal amount. Barely cover lima beans with
boiling, salted water, and cook until almost done; then add the kernels
of corn. Continue cooking until both are tender. Drain off water, shake
pan over low heat to dry a little and add butter, enough to coat the
beans and corn, and season well with salt and pepper.

SUCCOTASH, AN INDIAN DISH

Maryland Cook Book, 1892
Mrs. Franklin B. Spriggs

Anne Arundel

Silver Condiment Set, Hammond-Harwood House

Vegetables

NEW BEETS 2 bunches of small, new beets; ½ cup beet juice (water beets were boiled in), ½ cup brown sugar, ¼ cup vinegar, 2 teaspoons arrowroot powder, pinch of salt and pepper, 2 tablespoons butter.

Boil beets until tender. Add other ingredients, except butter, to beet juice. Cook the sauce in double boiler until slightly thick and add butter. When smooth and hot, pour over the skinned beets.

Mrs. Timothy J. Keleher
College Avenue   *Annapolis*

TO PICKLE Parboil some of the finest Red Beet Rootes in
BEETS water, then slip off skins and slice them thick. Put them into a Saucepan with some scraped Horseradish, some onions and shallots made very fine, Bay leaves, a little of the best vinegar, a little sugar, salt and pepper to your taste. Heat until all is incorporated. Serve cold.

Sophia Ridgely's way
Miss Ann Chase's Book, 1811   *Annapolis*

SPICED BEETS 2 bunches tender beets, ¼ cup vinegar, ½ cup sugar, ½ cup water, 1 teaspoon ground cinnamon, ¼ teaspoon ground allspice, ¼ teaspoon ground cloves, ½ teaspoon salt, 2 teaspoons lemon juice.

Cook beets in salted water until done; remove skins under cold water, slice. This should make about 1 or 1½ pints of sliced beets. To make dressing, mix ingredients and bring to a boil; add sliced beets and simmer about 8 minutes. Delicious either hot or cold.

Mrs. Francis E. Engle
Southwood Avenue   *Annapolis*

1 bunch broccoli, 2 tablespoons minced onion, 3 tablespoons butter, 1 teaspoon salt, pepper, ¼ teaspoon powdered marjoram, ½ teaspoon dry mustard, 3 tablespoons flour, 2½ cups milk, ½ cup grated parmesan cheese, paprika, 2 tablespoons additional cheese.

BROCCOLI BAKED WITH CHEESE SAUCE

Cook broccoli until almost tender; drain and arrange in shallow baking dish. Sauté onion in butter, blend in seasonings and flour, then stir in milk until smooth and thickened. Add cheese and stir until melted. Pour sauce over broccoli, sprinkle with paprika and additional cheese. Bake in 375° oven for about 20 minutes, or until browned.

Miss Fanny's Receipt Book
West River

Anne Arundel

---

1 quart Brussels sprouts, 3 tablespoons butter, ½ teaspoon crushed dill weed, salt and pepper.

BRUSSELS SPROUTS WITH DILL BUTTER

Wash and trim sprouts; cut a cross on stem end, for more uniform cooking. Put them into boiling, salted water, just enough to cover. Cook quickly until tender-crisp (about 10 minutes). Drain well. Melt butter, add dill, salt and pepper and sprouts. Turn them in the butter sauce to coat.

Mrs. James H. Murray
Popham's Creek

Anne Arundel

---

1 small, solid white head of cabbage; 1 tablespoon finely chopped celery, 2 eggs, 2 tablespoons sugar, ½ teaspoon salt, 1 teaspoon dry mustard, ¼ teaspoon pepper, ½ cup vinegar, 2 tablespoons butter, ½ cup cream.

COLD SLAW

Slice the cabbage very thin with a sharp knife or slicer. Add and mix in celery. Place eggs and sugar in a saucepan and beat with a spoon to combine. Add seasonings which have been mixed together. Stir well, add vinegar and butter. Place saucepan over slow heat and stir constantly until mixture thickens like a soft boiled custard. Remove from stove and chill. When cold, add cream, stir and pour over sliced cabbage. Serve ice-cold.

Katherine Gittings Monvid
Harwood

Anne Arundel

HOT SLAW 1 medium head cabbage, 1 cup milk, 1 small lump butter, 1 tablespoon meat fryings, 1 tablespoon flour, vinegar, sugar, salt and pepper to taste.

Cut cabbage not very fine. Add milk, butter and meat fryings. Let boil about 15 minutes, then add flour, vinegar, sugar, salt and pepper.

Family receipt of
Governor Lloyd Lowndes, Cumberland *Allegany*

CABBAGE 1 large green cabbage (Savoy is best).
PUDDING OR
STUFFED *For stuffing:* 1 tablespoon butter, small bunch
GREEN spring onions, cut fine; 1 clove garlic, minced;
CABBAGE 1 pound veal, ground; ½ pound or more lean pork, ground; 1 slice bread, crumbled; 1 tablespoon chopped parsley, ¼ teaspoon thyme, ¼ teaspoon marjoram, salt and pepper.

Melt butter in skillet, sauté onions and garlic lightly, then add ground meats, bread crumbs, parsley and seasonings and stir until blended.
Place cabbage on draining rack in sink and pour boiling water over it, a little at a time, carefully separating the leaves to open out cabbage head. Drain, then spoon stuffing between the leaves and over centre crown. Fold up outside leaves, closing cabbage in original form, and tie up with string.

For the Dutch oven: 2 tablespoons butter, 1 large onion, chopped; 2 or 3 carrots, sliced; 1 cup or more meat broth, 1 bay leaf, 1 teaspoon caraway seed, salt, flour.

Melt butter in Dutch oven, arrange onion and carrots in bottom of pot and place stuffed cabbage on them. Pour stock around cabbage and add bay leaf and caraway seed. Sprinkle cabbage lightly with salt. Cover kettle tightly and simmer over low fire for about 2½ hours. Remove cabbage to hot serving platter. Thicken sauce with flour and surround cabbage with vegetables and a little sauce. Serve the remainder in a tureen.

Sophia Ridgely's receipt, revised
Miss Ann Chase's Book, 1811 *Annapolis*

Boil a firm white cabbage 15 minutes, changing the water then for more from the boiling tea-kettle. When tender, drain and set aside until perfectly cold and chop fine. Mix 2 beaten eggs with a tablespoon of butter, pepper, salt and 3 tablespoons of rich milk or cream. Pour over cabbage and stir all well together. Bake in a buttered pudding dish until brown. Serve very hot. This dish resembles cauliflower and is very digestible and palatable.

LADIES' CABBAGE

White House Cook Book, 1887
Contee, Rhode River

Anne Arundel

---

1 medium head red cabbage, 2 tablespoons finely chopped onion, 3 tablespoons butter, 2 tart apples, pared, cored and sliced; 1 teaspoon salt, ¼ cup boiling water, 4 tablespoons red wine, 2 tablespoons brown sugar, or more to taste.

RED CABBAGE

Remove core and hard veins from sections of red cabbage, shred and put to soak in cold water. Sauté onion in butter for a few minutes and add drained cabbage. Cover and simmer for 15 minutes. Add apples, salt and boiling water to cabbage, stir, cover and simmer gently for an hour or more. If water is absorbed too early, add a little more. When cabbage is tender and water dissipated, add red wine and brown sugar and simmer until all is incorporated and thoroughly heated.

Mrs. James H. Murray
Popham's Creek

Anne Arundel

---

6 medium apples, 2 tablespoons brown sugar, 1 onion, 2 cups sauerkraut.

SAUERKRAUT BAKED WITH APPLES

Pare, core and slice apples; mix sugar through them (more may be needed if apples are very tart). Chop onion fine, mix with apples and sauerkraut, and put all in a buttered baking dish. Cover, and cook slowly 2 or 3 hours, the longer the better. Do not let it get dry, and stir occasionally. Uncover for last stage of baking. The apples must be the kind that will cook up soft. In a pinch, the same amount of applesauce can be used.

Mrs. Donald Ross
Easton

Talbot

ASHBY'S
MAGIC RING
1 pint whipping cream, 3 yolks of eggs, 1 cup cracker meal, ½ teaspoon salt, 3 whites of eggs, beaten stiff; 1 cup cooked carrots, mashed fine; 1 tablespoon butter, melted.

Whip cream, beat one egg yolk at a time and add to cream. Then add cracker meal, salt, whites of eggs beaten stiff and carrots. Mix all together and pour into large ring mold over melted butter. Set in pan of hot water and bake in hot oven 30 minutes. Serve with creamed crab in center of ring mold; or as vegetable course filled with tender green peas or baby lima beans.

Mrs. Charles S. Todd
Ashby, Miles River   *Talbot*

CARAMEL
CARROTS
Scrape and lay as many carrots as you need in cold water for ½ hour. Put them down in boiling, salted water and cook until barely tender. Drain them dry; cut larger carrots in long, thin strips; small summer carrots may be left whole. Put into the frying pan a large lump of butter and drippings. When very hot, add carrots; sprinkle with sugar, pepper and salt, and fry until edges are well browned. Sprinkle with chopped parsley or mint, to accompany veal or lamb.

Mrs. Blanchard Randall
Kenmore Road   *Baltimore*

BAKED
CAULIFLOWER
If the cauliflower is exceptionally perfect and fine, pick off the coarse outer leaves, wrap in a cheesecloth, cover and cook in boiling, salted water for about half an hour, but do not cook until it is sodden. Drain thoroughly and put into a deep dish, dredge thickly with grated parmesan cheese, then a thinner layer of stale breadcrumbs. On top drop a number of little pieces of butter the size of filberts. Cook in a brisk oven to a golden brown and serve hot. If the cauliflower is not perfect after cooking, break into flowerets, put them with the stems, broken in pieces, in a shallow baking dish, sprinkle with pepper, grated cheese, crumbs and melted butter, and bake.

Mrs. Charles dePeyster Valk's Book
Duke of Gloucester Street   *Annapolis*

1 large bunch of celery, 3 or more tablespoons
butter, flour, 1 cup rich meat stock, salt and
pepper.

**BRAISED
CELERY**

Cut prepared celery in 2-inch lengths; melt butter in a heavy skillet
and add celery. Cover tightly and simmer over low heat for ¾ hour
or until tender. Dredge with flour from sifter, cover with stock and
cook until thick. Use care when adding seasonings.

Mrs. William H. Kirkpatrick
Parkhurst

Anne Arundel

Fill a 2 quart saucepan about two thirds full
of chestnuts and barely cover with cold water.

CHESTNUTS

Bring to a boil and continue to boil until a fork can be stuck in shell.
Drain off water and as soon as chestnuts can be handled without burning your fingers, take a small sharp knife and remove hard shell and
inner brown skin (mean job).

Chestnuts may then be cut in small pieces for use in stuffing, or left
whole and cooked until tender in salted water, drained and put in
Bechamel sauce for use as a vegetable.

Teresa William's way
Mrs. J. B. Rich, Heir's Purchase

Anne Arundel

Gather chestnuts as they drop from the tree and
store in refrigerator until ready to use. Make a
criss-cross knife cut in shell of each chestnut and

**CYNTHIA'S
CHESTNUTS**

place on metal pan to roast at 450° in oven until shell starts to curl
and loosen, about six minutes. Remove and peel off outer shell, then
blanch nuts in scalding water a few minutes so that inner skin may
easily be removed. Put nuts through a medium grinder. Do not over-
cook nuts or they will be too soft for easy grinding. Ground nuts may
be stored in refrigerator or deep freeze. When ready to serve, place
ground chestnuts in double-boiler; add milk or cream, plenty of butter,
salt and black pepper to taste; heat and mix to pleasant consistency.

Mrs. Beverley C. Compton
Ruxton

Baltimore

CORN OFF THE COB Any fresh corn may be used, but the yellow, older corn at the end of the season is best. Cut and scrape the ridges and put loose corn in a deep, greased baking dish with plenty of butter, salt and black pepper mixed into it. Bake in a moderate oven (350°) until set and crusty brown on top. Addition of egg or milk spoils this dish.

Mrs. Beverley C. Compton　　　　　　　　　　　　　　　　*Baltimore*

FRIED CORN Select garden-fresh corn, husk and remove silk. With a sharp knife slice corn from cob. Place in a skillet and pour in a little water, barely enough to cover bottom of pan. Cover and simmer for 5 to 8 minutes. Remove cover, add butter, according to quantity of corn, salt and pepper. Let cook until butter is melted and liquid has evaporated. Cream may be added, if desired.

Mrs. Frederick G. Richards
Ridout House　　　　　　　　　　　　　　　　　　　　　　*Annapolis*

CORN PUDDING 2 eggs, 1 teaspoon salt, 1 tablespoon flour, 1 teaspoon sugar, 1 cup milk, 1 cup grated corn, butter.

Beat together the eggs, salt, flour and sugar; then add the milk and grated corn. Pour into a greased baking dish, placing small pieces of butter over the top. Bake in a 350° oven until it is consistency of thick custard, about 45 minutes. Serves 4 to 6.

Betty Worthington Briscoe
Old Field　　　　　　　　　　　　　　　　　　　　　　　*Calvert*

ARTIFICIAL OYSTERS 2 cups scraped corn, 2 eggs, ½ teaspoon salt, pinch of both cayenne and black pepper, 2 heaping tablespoons flour, 2 tablespoons butter.

Score corn and press out pulp. Beat eggs separately; add first the yolks, then the whites to corn, mixing gently. Add salt, pepper and flour, and blend. Put about 2 tablespoons of butter or shortening in a skillet. When hot, drop mixture by spoonfuls into it, shaping to resemble oysters. When brown on one side, turn and brown the other.

Aunt Ery's way, Harwood Papers　　　　　　　　　　　　*Annapolis*

1 cup scraped corn, 4 tablespoons thick cream, **CORN FRITTERS,**
2 tablespoons flour, ½ teaspoon baking powder, **IVY NECK**
½ teaspoon salt, 1 teaspoon sugar, dash of pepper.

Mix corn with other ingredients. The amount of flour depends on milkiness of corn. Fritters should not be thick. Use just enough flour to keep them together. Fry in hot deep fat.

Miss Adelaide Colhoun
Ivy Neck, Rhode River   *Anne Arundel*

Bury young cucumbers in ice for long enough to **DRESSED**
chill them thoroughly, or put them, unpeeled, **CUCUMBERS**
in a pan with ice and salt. At the latest moment
before using, peel cucumbers, leaving a touch of green, and slice as thin as possible. At the moment of serving, add a simple dressing of vinegar, salt and cayenne; sweet oil may be added, if liked. Cucumbers should never be allowed to stand and wilt in the dressing.

Mrs. Franklin B. Spriggs
Lilac Hill   *Anne Arundel*

---

4 cucumbers, salt, 4 slices of bacon, 1 tablespoon **WILTED**
sugar, freshly ground pepper, 1 tablespoon vine- **CUCUMBERS**
gar, 1 tablespoon flour.

Pare whole cucumbers and score sides lengthwise with a fork to flute edges, then slice into thin rounds. Spread slices on a large platter, sprinkle with salt and let stand for 30 minutes. Dice bacon and fry slowly, stirring often until crisp and brown. Drain salted cucumbers well and mix with bacon. Sprinkle with sugar, a few grindings of pepper, and add vinegar. Cover pan and simmer gently for about 20 minutes. Sprinkle cucumbers with flour, blend it in carefully, and cook a little longer. Good with Shad Roe or Fish.

Tulip Hill Receipts
West River   *Anne Arundel*

1815 April 18th "Then came Kitty to serve in my Kitchen @ Four Dollars per Month."

EGGPLANT FRIED IN BATTER

1 medium eggplant, garlic salt, 1 egg, 1 cup flour. ½ teaspoon salt, ⅛ teaspoon pepper, 1 cup milk.

Pare eggplant and cut in thin slices. Sprinkle each slice lightly with garlic salt, stack in little piles on a platter, and press under a weighted plate for ½ hour. Make a batter by beating the egg and stirring in the seasoned flour alternately with the milk. Beat until smooth and bubbly. Drain and dry eggplant, and dip each slice in batter. Fry brown and crisp in hot fat.

Alice's way
Tulip Hill, West River   *Anne Arundel*

GROSS' COATE EGGPLANT

1 eggplant, 3 tablespoons butter, 3 tablespoons thick rich cream, salt and pepper, bread crumbs, dots of butter.

Pare eggplant, cut in pieces and cook until tender in boiling salted water. Drain thoroughly, and mash with potato masher while still hot. Stir in butter and cream, and season to taste with salt and pepper. Put in baking dish, sprinkle with crumbs of bread, picked small, and dot with butter. Bake in a moderate oven until browned.

Miss Agnes Tilghman
Gross' Coate, Wye River   *Talbot*

"1849, Nov. 8, Thursday, left Baltimore in the Steamer Republic, newly built through the efforts of some energetic Baltimoreans who were anxious to extend the connection of their city with the South. The persons on board in whom we took most interest were Gen'l. Tench Tilghman with his wife, four children and two nurses."

A Private Journal, 1849

1 large eggplant, 4 tablespoons butter, ½ onion, chopped; 1½ cups bread crumbs, 1 tablespoon chopped parsley, salt and pepper.

BAKED STUFFED EGGPLANT

Wash eggplant, cut in half lengthwise, and remove meat, leaving a shell casing about ½ inch thick. Melt 2 tablespoons of the butter in a skillet and sauté onion until golden. Dice eggplant meat and mix it with 1 cup of the crumbs and the parsley. Add to onion in skillet and mix well together, seasoning with salt and pepper to taste. Pile eggplant mixture lightly in shells and set them in a greased baking dish. Cover the two halves with ½ cup bread crumbs and dot with 2 tablespoons butter. Add 2 or 3 tablespoons hot water to bottom of dish. Bake about 40 minutes in a moderate oven, 350°, or until eggplant is tender and top browned.

Mrs. A. C. Dick
Maiden Lot Farm, Chester River

Kent

Collards: A variety of cabbage which does not head, but the leaves are cooked and served as other cabbage, usually boiled with a piece of salt pork, or in 'pot liquor' (water in which ham was boiled).

'GREENS' COLLARDS, FIELD CRESS, KALE, POKE SALAD

Field Cress: Wash well, cut off root and cook as collards.

Kale: Clean, trim off root and heaviest part of leaf. Cook in boiling water until tender. Drain, chop coarsely, and season with butter, salt and pepper. Bacon fat may substitute for butter.

Poke Salad: Gather the first shoots of the pokeberry plant in the early Spring when they are but 6 or 8 inches tall. Wash thoroughly, leaving the stalk with leaves intact. Cover with cold water, bring to boil and cook about ½ hour until tender. Drain, season with salt and pepper and serve with melted butter or drawn butter sauce.

Old Spriggs' Farm
Magothy River

Anne Arundel

Vegetables

BAKED HOMINY GRITS 1 cup milk, 1 cup water, ½ cup hominy grits, 3 eggs, 1 teaspoon salt, 2 tablespoons butter.

Combine milk and water and scald over low heat. Stir in the grits and continue cooking, stirring until thick. Cool slightly. Beat egg yolks until light; add salt and melted butter. Add yolk mixture to grits and blend well. Beat egg whites until stiff and fold into grits. Turn into a buttered baking dish and bake at 325° for about 45 minutes.

Mrs. J. Reaney Kelly
Conduit Street   *Annapolis*

HOMINY PATTIES 3 cups of cold, boiled hominy grits; 2 tablespoons melted butter, 2 eggs, ½ teaspoon salt, milk, flour, grated cheese.

Add melted butter to hominy and mash fine. Add well-beaten eggs, salt and a little milk, as much as you find necessary to mold into small flat fritters, and flour lightly to aid in handling. Place these on a buttered pan, dust with grated cheese, and brown in the oven,—or you may fry them in hot fat on the stove.

Mrs. Harry R. Slack's Book
Bishop's Road   *Baltimore*

BIG HOMINY Wash 2 cups whole, cracked, hominy and soak in warm water overnight. In morning drain and place in double-boiler with 3 cups of water, adding more hot water as needed. Add 2 teaspoons of salt and let simmer all day. When water has cooked up and hominy is dry, add ½ cup table cream and ¼ pound butter. Then continue cooking for about 2 more hours. Stir well to mix before serving. Hominy cooked in this way will take all day and will make about 2 quarts. It is good for rewarming as long as it lasts.

Mrs. Amos Hutchins
Wardour   *Annapolis*

196

Select as many large, fresh mushrooms as you wish to serve. Sauté chopped stems in a small amount of butter and season to taste. Mix with enough seasoned bread crumbs to fill the caps, putting a small piece of butter on each. Place under broiler long enough to brown. Sausage or any other forcemeat may be added to the stem filling. **BROILED STUFFED MUSHROOMS**

Mrs. F. Marion Lazenby
Ferry Farms, Severn River

Anne Arundel

---

3 pounds fresh mushrooms, ¼ pound butter, 2 large onions, chopped; 2 tablespoons flour, 1 cup strong chicken stock, ½ cup Madeira wine, celery salt, salt and freshly ground black pepper, dash cayenne. **MUSHROOM PIE**

Sauté onions in butter until golden, after which cook mushrooms in same butter about 10 minutes. Place mushrooms and onions in shallow baking dish. Brown flour in 2 tablespoons of the butter, slowly add chicken stock and Madeira wine, stirring constantly until thickened and smooth. Season to taste. Pour sauce over mushrooms and cover with a rich pastry crust as you would a pie. Bake in a 375° oven for about ½ hour. Serves 12. Excellent accompaniment for Roast Beef.

Receipts from Glebe kitchen
Mrs. Carroll R. Harding

Talbot

---

1 pound fresh mushrooms, 2 tablespoons butter, 2 tablespoons flour, ½ cup chicken broth, ½ cup cream, salt and pepper, 2 tablespoons sherry wine. **OVEN CREAMED MUSHROOMS**

If mushrooms are large, cut in halves or quarters and lay on a buttered cookie sheet. Barely cover the bottom of the pan with water and place it in a warm oven (275°) for a half an hour. Then make a cream sauce with melted butter, flour, chicken broth and liquid from the pan in which the mushrooms were cooked. When smooth, add cream and then mushrooms, salt and pepper to taste and lastly, the sherry.

Mrs. Wade DeWeese
King George Street

Annapolis

197

ONION PIE 2 cups sliced onions, ½ cup butter, 6 eggs, separated; ½ cup heavy cream, salt, pepper, 1 cup white wine, pastry for deep pie plate.

Cook onion slowly in butter, covered, for 30 minutes, until soft and clear. Do not allow to brown. Remove from fire and cool. Stir in well-beaten egg yolks; add cream, salt and pepper to taste. Add wine gradually, stirring hard. Beat whites of eggs until stiff and fold into mixture. Line a deep pie plate with pastry and carefully pour in onion mixture, which must be at least 2½ inches deep. Bake for 30 minutes in a moderate (350°) oven.

Mrs. Frank Jack Fletcher
Araby   *Charles*

ONION CIRCLES 1 tablespoon olive oil, 3 tablespoons butter, 1 pound onions, freshly ground pepper, and salt.

Put the olive oil and butter in a deep pot and heat. Slice onions in circles and put in pot. Cover tightly. Cook, not very fast, until onions are creamy in color, translucent and limp. Put in a lot of freshly ground pepper just before they are done, but use salt sparingly. Pour onions into a serving dish and cover with sauce remaining in the pot.

Receipts from Araby   *Charles*

OYSTER PLANT Scrape thoroughly and lay in cold water imme-
OR SALSIFY diately, as contact with the air will turn it black. Cut in 2-inch lengths and cook in boiling, lightly salted water until tender. It is best to use a china-lined kettle for this. Dish the salsify and drain it quite dry; sprinkle a few drops of vinegar on every piece, and pour over it a rich Cream Sauce. Cooked salsify may also be mashed through the colander and made into cakes as directed for Parsnip Cakes.

Mrs. McBlair, Walnut Grove
Maria T. Allison's Book, 1860   *Baltimore*

6 or 8 sprigs of parsley, 1 tablespoon of shorten- **FRIED PARSLEY**
ing.
Pick off the delicate leaves and branches of very young parsley; wash
well, drain very dry, and put in a frying pan in which you have placed
a tablespoon of shortening and allowed to reach a medium hot state.
Fry slowly, drain, and use as an edible garnish.

Mrs. Henry C. Edgar
Evergreen   *Anne Arundel*

---

4 medium parsnips (1 pound), 2 tablespoons **PARSNIP CAKES**
butter, 1 teaspoon salt, dash of pepper, 2 tablespoons milk, 3 tablespoons flour, 2 tablespoons drippings.

Wash parsnips and cook in a little water until tender (about 30 minutes). Cool and peel, removing center core if tough and woody. Mash
thoroughly or force through chopper or ricer. Add butter, salt, pepper
and milk. Shape into 8 cakes, dip in flour and brown slowly in hot
drippings. Non-parsnip eaters eat these.

This is an old Baltimore receipt. Hopkinson Smith wrote about them
in his book "The Wood Fire in Number Three".

Miss Nellie Shackelford
The Anchorage, Miles River   *Talbot*

Large lettuce leaves, 2 cups shelled green peas, 12 **GREEN PEAS**
small spring onions, 3 tablespoons butter, ½ tea-   **WITH**
spoon salt.   **SPRING ONIONS**

Line a heavy saucepan with washed outer leaves of a head of lettuce.
Pour in the peas and white ends of spring onions (about 1 inch long).
Add 2 tablespoons of water, butter, and salt. Cover with more wet
lettuce leaves and close the saucepan tightly. Cook over low heat until
vegetables are tender, 15 to 20 minutes. Remove lettuce leaves and
serve peas and onions with sauce from the pan. Serves 4.

Mrs. Truxtun Beale's Book, 1903
Decatur House   *Washington*

SMOTHERED SWEET PEPPERS

Cut green peppers in 1-inch strips, removing seeds and stem end. Place in a heavy skillet with butter (or half butter and half olive oil). Season with salt and pepper, cover tightly and cook over low heat until tender, turning once. When done, remove to hot serving dish; add a little water to the pan and stir around in the browned butter. Pour over the peppers and serve.

Willie Hall's way
Miss Agnes Mayo   *Anne Arundel*

STUFFED BELL PEPPERS

6 green peppers, 4 ripe tomatoes, peeled and chopped; 1 onion, minced; 1 cup celery, chopped; 1 cup cooked rice or bread crumbs, salt, pepper, 1 teaspoon fresh, chopped oregano or basil; butter.

Cut off slice from stem end of peppers; remove seeds and inner membrane. Drop them into boiling, salted water to parboil for 5 minutes. Drain and stuff with other ingredients, well mixed together, placing a piece of butter on top of each. Place peppers in a buttered baking dish in a 350° oven for about 1 hour.

Mrs. Fred G. Boyce, Jr.
Greenway   *Baltimore*

SOUTHERN CREAMED POTATOES

4 medium potatoes, 1 cup thin cream (or half cream—half milk), salt and black ground pepper to taste, 2 tablespoons butter, 1 teaspoon chopped chives, 1 teaspoon chopped parsley.

Peel and cut potatoes into small cubes. Cover with cream in a saucepan, add salt and pepper and cook gently (not boiling) until potatoes are soft but not mushy. When done add butter and sprinkle with chives and parsley. Serves 4.

Mrs. Fred G. Boyce, Jr.
Greenway   *Baltimore*

A. Aubrey Bodine

Vegetables

½ cup flour, 1 teaspoon baking powder, ½ tea- **POTATO PUFFS**
spoon salt, 1 cup rich mashed potatoes, 1 egg, 1
teaspoon chopped parsley.

Sift flour, baking powder and salt; add to mashed potatoes, then add
lightly beaten egg and parsley. Drop small teaspoonfuls in deep hot fat
and brown. Have a bowl of cold water handy and dip spoon into it
before dipping potatoes. These may be frozen and reheated in oven.

Carroll McTavish Elder
Tred Avon River

Talbot

1¼ cups grated raw potatoes, 1 egg, 4 tablespoons **POTATO**
flour, 1 teaspoon baking powder, ½ teaspoon salt, **PANCAKES**
pepper, grated onion.

Peel and grate potatoes into a bowl of cold water to avoid discolora-
tion. Drain and dry well before using. Combine potato, well beaten
egg, flour, baking powder, salt, pepper and onion. Drop by tablespoonfuls into a frying pan with a little hot fat and cook until golden brown
on both sides.

Sion Hill Papers
Mrs. John F. Meigs

Annapolis

Vegetables

SWEET POTATO PONE ¼ cup butter, ½ cup sugar, 2 eggs, 2 cups grated sweet potato, grated rind of 1 orange or half a lemon, ½ teaspoon ginger, ½ teaspoon mace, dash of cinnamon, ½ cup milk.

Cream butter and sugar, add beaten eggs and sweet potato. Beat well. Add orange or lemon rind, spices and milk, and continue to beat. Pour into a well buttered oven dish and bake in a moderate oven for 1 hour. Good with roast duck or roast pork.

Mrs. Y. Kirkpatrick-Howat
Contee, Rhode River   *Anne Arundel*

OLNEY INN SWEET POTATOES 4 cups cooked, mashed sweet potatoes; ½ cup sherry, ¼ teaspoon salt, ½ cup sugar, ½ cup black walnuts, chopped; 2 eggs, beaten; ½ cup butter, melted.

Whip all ingredients together until light. Fold into buttered pan and bake in moderate oven until golden.

Gertrude Allison Brewster
Olney Inn   *Montgomery*

SWEET POTATOES AFLAME 6 long sweet potatoes of uniform size, 4 cooking apples, 1 jar preserved chestnuts, ¼ cup butter, sugar to taste, ½ cup rum.

Parboil potatoes, peel and cut across into circles about ⅜ inch thick. Peel, core and cut the apples across in rings. Fill a deep baking dish with a layer of sweet potatoes, then a layer of apple rings, then a layer of preserved chestnuts with a little of the syrup. Repeat until dish is filled, having a layer of potatoes on top, the circles fitted as closely as possible together. Melt butter and sugar, pour over dish and bake until brown. Heat rum, pour over dish just before serving and light.

Mrs. George Maurice Morris
The Lindens   *Washington*

Use left-over boiled rice for this. Put in a well buttered baking dish a layer of rice, a layer of raw tomatoes, peeled and sliced; sliced onions and green peppers, slivered thin. Continue until the dish is full. Make a cream sauce and pour over and through the dish, then cover the top with grated cheese and bake in a moderate oven for 30 minutes.

MATTIE'S BAKED RICE

Receipts from Araby   *Charles*

Melt about 6 tablespoons of butter for 2 cups of rice. Stir the sorted, dry rice in the butter until it becomes a golden brown, or darker if you prefer. Then pour 4 cups boiling water, to which 1½ teaspoons salt and ⅛ teaspoon pepper have been added, over the rice and stir until it is done,—not too soft, but puffed, and flaky.

BROWN RICE

Mrs. Harrison Tilghman
Foxley Hall   *Talbot*

---

1 large onion, ½ cup butter, 1½ cups long grain rice, 4 cups rich chicken broth, 1½ teaspoons mixed herbs, 1 cup chopped parsley.

SAVOURY RICE

Sauté finely chopped onion in melted butter until golden yellow. Add rice; cook and stir until rice turns golden. Add chicken broth, herbs, and ¾ of the parsley. Pour into baking dish, cover and bake in a 325° oven for about an hour, or until all liquid is absorbed and rice is soft. Sprinkle with remaining parsley to serve. This is also a delicious way to prepare wild rice, substituting ½ pound of fresh sliced mushrooms for the parsley.

Mrs. Richard E. Lankford
Richard's Gift, South River   *Anne Arundel*

---

1 cup of water to ¾ cup of wild rice, (1½ cups rice serves 8).

TO COOK WILD RICE

Wash rice carefully; add to boiling salted water in top of double-boiler Bring to boil again and skim. Place over simmering hot water and let stand, covered tightly, to steam until done and fluffy.

Mrs. Lew Garrison Coit
The Lord's Bounty   *Anne Arundel*

SPINACH STEWED WITH CREAM   Wash the spinach well in several waters, then steam it in a saucepan without water. Strain it from the liquor, but do not render it hard and dry by squeezing. Chop it, and beat it well with a spoon, taking care to have picked out all the fibres. Put it into a stewpan, with a piece of butter, pepper, and salt. You may add a few drops of onion juice and a little scraped horseradish, or grated nutmeg, if liked. Stir it well as it stews, adding by degrees as much cream as will make it the proper thickness. Garnish with triangles of fried toast.

A 19th century receipt, Mrs. Howard's
Miss Nancy D. Mitchell   *Baltimore*

SPINACH TIMBALES WITH EGG GARNISH   3 pounds spinach, ½ teaspoon salt, 2 tablespoons butter, pepper, ¼ cup cream, 3 hard-boiled eggs, white sauce.

Clean the spinach, washing it in several waters. Put it in a deep saucepan with 2 cups boiling water and salt. Boil rapidly for 10 minutes, then drain in a colander, and chop very fine. Drain again, pressing out all liquid. Add butter, pepper and cream. Pack tightly in individual buttered custard cups. Place these in a pan of hot water and bake 5 minutes in a hot oven. Turn out onto a heated serving platter. While timbales are in the oven chop whites of eggs fine and rub the yolks through a fine sieve. Keep separate. Add the chopped egg whites to the well-seasoned white sauce, pour around the timbales and garnish with powdered egg yolks.

Mrs. Charles dePeyster Valk's Book
Duke of Gloucester Street   *Annapolis*

A DISH OF SPRING VEGETABLES   1 small cauliflower, 1 bunch spring onions, 8 baby carrots, 8 small new potatoes, 1 cupful fresh peas, 2 cupfuls cream sauce, ½ cupful grated cheese.

Each vegetable should be nicely cooked in boiling salted water until tender, but firm. Separate cauliflower into flowerettes; cut spring onions into 2 or 3 inch lengths, showing green. Arrange the vegetables in a buttered oven dish, and pour over them the cream sauce. Sprinkle cheese over the top and brown in a moderate oven.

Katharine del Valle's Book
Cornhill Street   *Annapolis*

Cornhill Street, Annapolis   John Moll

Vegetables

3 acorn squash, 6 teaspoons butter, 6 teaspoons **BAKED**
brown sugar, 6 teaspoons Bourbon whiskey, 1 **ACORN SQUASH**
teaspoon salt, ¼ teaspoon nutmeg.

Remove seeds from halved squash. Place in lightly greased baking dish
and in each half put 1 teaspoon each of butter, sugar and Bourbon.
Sprinkle with salt and nutmeg. Cover and bake at 400° for about half
an hour or until tender. Serves 6.

Mrs. J. Reaney Kelly
Conduit Street   *Annapolis*

---

4 young cymlings, 2 tablespoons butter, 1 table- **CYMLINGS**
spoon chopped onion, salt and pepper, 2 tablespoons flour, 1 cup milk, 1 cup fine buttered bread crumbs.

Cut up cymlings and boil in salted water. When soft, strain and press
through colander. Add the butter, onion, and seasoning to taste, then
beat in flour which has been mixed until smooth with the milk. Spoon
mixture into an oven dish, cover with buttered crumbs and bake until
brown.

Mrs. Charles W. Williams
Welcome Here, Glyndon   *Baltimore*

SUMMER SQUASH

3 medium size squash, a little thick cream, 2 tablespoons butter, ½ teaspoon salt, 1 teaspoon nutmeg (less if you prefer).

Wash squash, cut in pieces and cook in boiling water until tender. Drain thoroughly, then rub through colander. Add cream, butter and seasonings; bring to a boil, and serve at once.

Mrs. Cecil F. Backus
Kirkland Farm   *Talbot*

SQUASH CAKES

2 medium size yellow or summer squash, 1 tablespoon sugar, 1 teaspoon salt, little pepper, 1 egg, ½ cup flour, ½ teaspoon baking powder.

Grate the squash with a medium grater, making about 2 cups. Add sugar, salt, pepper and egg. Mix well, causing mixture to become quite juicy. Add flour and baking powder. More or less flour may be needed to obtain proper consistency for dropping by tablespoons into frying pan with hot bacon grease or butter. Cook slowly to golden brown, turn cakes and brown other side. Cook about 20 minutes.

John Tayman
Old Phibbons Farm   *Anne Arundel*

ZUCCHINI STUFFED WITH TOMATOES

3 medium zucchini squash, 3 large tomatoes, 2 cups small buttered croutons, salt and pepper, 1 cup grated mild cheese.

Wash zucchini and simmer whole without peeling for 15 minutes or until just tender. Cut in half lengthwise and scoop out seeds. Let drain, then fill each half with peeled and chopped tomatoes which have been mixed with the croutons, salt and pepper. Cover with cheese and bake in hot oven (450°) about 20 minutes. Run under broiler to brown. Serves 6.

Mrs. Clifton B. Cates
South River   *Anne Arundel*

Maryland's Favorite Vegetable

A. Aubrey Bodine

Vegetables

Select firm ripe tomatoes. Cut off top and bottom and slice into ½ inch sections. Salt and pepper one side generously and dredge with flour. In iron skillet have about ¼ inch fat (half bacon grease, half butter) piping hot. Place seasoned side of tomato in fat and cook over medium flame until brown. Salt and pepper exposed side of tomato and on each slice sprinkle a scant teaspoon sugar and shake on enough flour to cover. Turn, lower heat and cook until brown and tender.

FRIED TOMATOES AND CREAM GRAVY

Remove tomatoes to hot platter, sift some flour into pan and blend thoroughly; add some rich milk, stirring constantly until gravy is brown and the right consistency. Pour around tomatoes and serve.

Mrs. Harry F. Ogden
Gibson Island

Anne Arundel

207

Dining Room at Blakeford   Maryland House and Garden Pilgrimage

Vegetables

FRIED GREEN TOMATOES   Take nice, solid green tomatoes and slice ½ inch thick. Dip in flour, salt and pepper on both sides. Fry in butter on top of stove until a good brown on one side. Place tomatoes in an oven dish, browned side down, and be sure that the dish is well filled with tomatoes. Put a little brown sugar on each tomato. Now put tomatoes in a very hot oven. Turn off bottom burner and leave on top one, placing tomatoes about 3 inches from top burner. Cook until dark brown.

Mrs. Clarence W. Miles
Blakeford, Chester River   *Queen Anne's*

TOMATOES BROWN   2 slices stale bread broken into crumbs, ½ onion, chopped; 4 cups cooked tomatoes or fresh ones, peeled and quartered; 1 cup brown sugar, salt and pepper to taste.

Bring all ingredients slowly to a boil, about 10 minutes; then simmer for 3 hours or more, stirring occasionally.

Mrs. Clarence W. Miles
Blakeford, Chester River   *Queen Anne's*

Peel as many tomatoes as desired and place in a
heavy baking pan. Sprinkle a little salt in each
tomato. Put in the oven (350°) for half an hour.
Then drain the liquid off. Add a dash of pepper

**BELLHAVEN
BAKED
TOMATOES**

and one large tablespoon sugar to each tomato. Put a small quantity of
very dry bread crumbs and a generous piece of butter on each tomato.
Bake two hours in a moderate oven (350°).

Miss Hannah W. Bell
Chestertown

Kent

---

4 medium tomatoes, 1 teaspoon salt, dash of
pepper, 1 tablespoon sugar, 3 tablespoons melted
butter, ¾ cup bread crumbs.

**BAKED TOMATO
HALVES**

Wash tomatoes and slice top off each. Cut in halves. Place on a baking
sheet and sprinkle with combined salt, pepper and sugar. Pour melted
butter over crumbs, toss, and top tomatoes with buttered crumbs. Pour
just enough water in pan for moisture during baking. Bake at 350°
until tender. Serve hot. May be topped with individual corn puddings
for variety.

Gertrude Allison Brewster
Olney Inn

Montgomery

---

6 red-ripe tomatoes, salt and pepper, brown sugar,
3 cups bread crumbs, 3 tablespoons butter.

TOMATO PIE

Scald tomatoes to remove the skins; cut each in two crosswise. Butter
a deep pie dish and place six halves on bottom. Season with salt and
pepper and sprinkle with sugar. Cover with crumbs and add a few bits
of butter. Repeat with a second layer and bake in a 350° oven for ½
hour.

Fifty Years in a Maryland Kitchen, 1873
Miss Agnes Tilghman, Gross' Coate

Talbot

CLARA'S TOMATOES AND OKRA

8 tomatoes, 1 large onion, 4 okra pods, 1 tablespoon sugar, salt and pepper to taste.

Slice vegetables and place in a shallow kettle on high heat until it starts to boil, then turn to medium. Cook along, turning over frequently until done. Serve at once or reheat in a baking dish topped with buttered crumbs.

Clara's way
Sion Hill Papers   *Harford*

Sion Hill

BROWNED TURNIPS

Peel and slice young white turnips or make into olive shapes. Blanch for a few minutes in boiling salted water and drain quite dry. Melt butter in a frying pan, and when smoking hot, lay in the turnips. When they begin to brown, sprinkle heavily with sugar, and season lightly with salt and pepper. Cook more slowly until well browned on both sides.

Maryland Cook Book, 1892
Mrs. Franklin B. Spriggs   *Anne Arundel*

Sauces

for

Fish, Fowl, Meats

and Vegetables

Sauces for Fish

6 tablespoons butter, 6 tablespoons flour, 2 cups **ANGEL SAUCE**
milk, ½ cup cream, ½ cup dry white wine, 2
tablespoons sherry, 1 tablespoon anchovy paste, ½ teaspoon Worcestershire sauce, 1 teaspoon salt, ½ teaspoon pepper, 2 tablespoons chopped
parsley.

Melt butter, blend in flour, add milk and all other ingredients, stirring
constantly. Bring the mixture up to the boil. This sauce may be used
in preparing any dish of fish filets or shell fish. It may be kept success-
fully in the ice box for several days and used as needed.

Mrs. Clyde Robinson
Anne Arundel

1½ cups mayonnaise, ⅓ cup heavy cream, **AURORA SAUCE**
whipped; ⅓ cup chili sauce, 2 teaspoons Wor-
cestershire sauce, 1 teaspoon lemon juice. Combine all ingredients and
serve well chilled.

Mrs. Harry R. Slack's Book
Bishop's Road
Baltimore

---

4 heaping tablespoons peeled and grated cucum- **COLD**
bers, 4 tablespoons olive oil, 1½ tablespoons **CUCUMBER**
vinegar, salt and cayenne. **SAUCE**

Stir ingredients well together and put on ice until wanted for use.

Mrs. De Courcy May
Elizabeth R. Lloyd's Book, 1889
Annapolis

EGG SAUCE 1 pint rich white sauce, 2 or 3 tablespoons fish stock, ¼ cup capers, pinch of cayenne, 1 teaspoon or more lemon juice, salt and pepper to taste, 3 hard-boiled eggs, sliced; paprika. Mix all ingredients with white sauce. Serve hot with boiled fish.

Thos. Middleton's way
Miss Ann Chase's Book, 1811   *Annapolis*

FISH STOCK Fish carcasses, including the heads; ¼ cup butter, 1 sliced onion, 1 sliced carrot, 1 stalk sliced celery, 6 peppercorns, 1 sprig thyme or ¼ teaspoon dried thyme, 3 sprigs parsley, 1 bay leaf, 1 or more cups water, ¼ cup dry white wine.

Melt butter in deep sauce-pan. Sauté onion, carrot and celery a few minutes. Add fish carcasses, all seasonings, water and wine. Bring slowly to a boil and simmer until stock is a little reduced and strong. Strain. Excellent for use in chowders or any fish dish.

Miss Grace's Receipt Book
Tenthouse Creek   *Anne Arundel*

HERB SAUCE 2 tablespoons butter, 2 teaspoons Tarragon vine-
FOR ROE gar, 1 teaspoon lemon juice, 1 teaspoon chopped chives and minced onion, ¼ teaspoon dried basil or chervil.

Heat butter in skillet until lightly browned, then mix in other ingredients. If frying roe, it can be done right in this mixture after seasoning it with salt and pepper.

Mrs. John Le Moyne Randall
Winchester-on-Severn   *Anne Arundel*

A HOLLANDAISE Make a drawn butter with ⅓ cup butter, 3 table-
FOR SHAD ROE spoons flour, ½ teaspoon salt, a pinch of pepper,
AND FISH 1½ cups hot water or fish stock.

Melt butter and stir in flour and seasonings. Pour on hot stock gradually and cook a few minutes, stirring constantly until smooth. When you have finished the drawn butter, take it from the fire and add gradually the beaten yolks of 2 eggs, the juice of half a lemon and a teaspoon of onion juice.

Aunt Sally Murray's Choice Receipts
Ivy Neck, Rhode River   *Anne Arundel*

Clarify ¼ pound butter. Grate rind of 1 lemon, **LEMON, CHIVE**
chop 3 tablespoons chives. Add rind, juice of **AND BUTTER**
lemon and chives to butter, heat and serve at **SAUCE**
once.

Tulip Hill Receipts
West River
Anne Arundel

---

2 cups cream sauce (made with half milk, half **LOBSTER SAUCE**
cream, and seasoned to taste with salt, pepper and
nutmeg); add 1 cup cooked lobster meat, cut in small pieces. Let steep
in double boiler 20 minutes, stirring occasionally. When ready to serve,
stir in ¼ cup Sherry wine. Serve with Fish Timbale.

Mrs. Harry R. Slack's Book
Bishop's Road
Baltimore

Stock for Cooking Shrimp: 1 tablespoon butter, **SHRIMP STOCK**
1 sprig parsley, cut up; 2 tablespoons each of **AND SAUCE**
minced celery, carrot and onion, 1 quart water,
1 tablespoon vinegar, ½ tablespoon salt, piece of bay leaf, ½ clove
garlic, 2 or 3 whole pepper berries, ½ cup white wine, a little fresh dill.

Cook butter, parsley, celery, carrot and onion for 3 minutes, then add
the other ingredients. Let broth come to boil slowly and simmer 10
minutes before adding shrimp. This amount will cook 2 pounds of
shrimp and makes a delicious sauce, strained, seasoned with curry and
thickened.

Mrs. Truxtun Beale's Book, 1903
Decatur House
Washington

---

1 cup mayonnaise, 1 teaspoon prepared mustard, **SAUCE TARTARE**
1 teaspoon chopped gherkin, 1 teaspoon chopped
Chervil herb, 1 teaspoon chopped fresh parsley, 1 teaspoon chopped
chives, 2 teaspoons chopped olives, 1 teaspoon chopped capers, 1 teaspoon onion juice, a dash of cayenne, Tarragon vinegar to taste.

Mix all ingredients together with the exception of the Tarragon vinegar. After well mixed together, add the vinegar slowly until the desired
tartness is reached, possibly a tablespoon or more.

Maryland Cook Book, 1892
Mrs. Franklin B. Spriggs
Anne Arundel

CHICKEN STOCK
FOR
MANY USES
5 or 6 chicken backs, 3 carrots, 3 stalks celery with leaves, 2 medium onions (all vegetables sliced), 1 bay leaf, salt to taste.

Barely cover chicken and vegetables with water. Add herb and light seasoning. Cook slowly until chicken meat is very tender. Remove chicken and bay leaf from pot and let stock cool. Purée stock with vegetables in blender until smooth. It is a perfect basic ingredient for soups, sauces and a variety of creamed dishes. It may be frozen in jars.

Alice's way
Tulip Hill, West River   *Anne Arundel*

DRY BREAD
SAUCE
2 tablespoons butter in pan, 1 cup finely rolled bread crumbs. Place in oven. Turn often with long spoon until golden brown; sprinkle a little salt and pepper. Serve separately, or on platter as 'nests' for partridges.

Mrs. Page Bowie
Bay Ridge Farm   *Anne Arundel*

ENGLISH BREAD
SAUCE
Put 2 cups rich milk in double boiler. Add 1 onion stuck with a few cloves, ¼ teaspoon mace, and half a bay leaf. Leave in 5 minutes and strain. Add ½ cup very fine white bread crumbs, 2 tablespoons butter, ½ teaspoon salt, dash of cayenne. Cook 5 minutes. Serve in sauce boat with Guinea Fowl, Chicken or Pheasant.

Mrs. Thomas Morton
Crab Creek   *Anne Arundel*

CHESTNUT
SAUCE
1 pint large chestnuts, 1 large tablespoon butter, 1 tablespoon flour, 2 cups chicken stock, salt and pepper.

Roast chestnuts; when done, peel them, mash fine. Melt butter and stir until a dark brown, then add the flour, mix well; add stock and chestnuts, stir continually until it boils; add salt and pepper. This is especially nice for roasted poultry.

Mrs. Rorer's receipt, 1885
Ivy Neck, Rhode River   *Anne Arundel*

4 cups cranberries, 2 cups boiling water, 1½ to **CRANBERRY**
2 cups sugar, according to taste. **SAUCE**

Bring sugar and water to a boil and let it boil about 5 minutes. Add
the cranberries, and let them boil in the syrup without stirring. When
all the skins have popped, the sauce will be ready, in 5 minutes or so.
Serve with Roast Turkey, Fowl and Pork.

Mrs. Austin McLanahan
Owings Mills
Baltimore

To 3 cups of seasoned white sauce made with **LEMON SAUCE**
rich milk, add the juice of 3 lemons and blend in
smoothly. Make the sauce a fine yellow color by blending in 2 or 3
well-beaten egg yolks, using brown country eggs, if possible. Good
with Fowl or Asparagus.

Mrs. James W. Webb
Scaffold Creek
Anne Arundel

---

1 pint oysters, ⅔ cup rich milk or cream, cayenne, **OYSTER SAUCE**
salt, 1 tablespoon flour, 2 tablespoons butter.

Heat oysters in own liquor until they begin to ruffle. Skim out oysters
into a warm dish, put into the liquor the cream and seasoning.
Thicken with flour and butter stirred to a paste, boil up and then add
oysters. For fish, boiled turkey, chickens.

Herman's receipt from Farmlands
Lloyd Papers, 1890
Annapolis

---

1 pint freshly shucked small oysters, 4 tablespoons **OYSTER SAUCE**
flour, 2 tablespoons butter or chicken fat, ½ cup **WITH WINE**
oyster liquor, ½ cup heavy cream, 1 tablespoon
lemon juice, salt, pepper, few drops brandy, ½ cup white wine.

Poach oysters until edges just curl. Drain from liquor and keep warm.
Blend flour with melted butter or chicken fat, add oyster liquor,
cream, very slowly; then lemon juice and seasonings. Add brandy and
white wine, very slowly, stirring like mad. Stir until smooth. Add
oysters, well drained. To be served with chicken or turkey.

Miss Grace's Receipt Book
Tenthouse Creek
Anne Arundel

Sauces for Meats and Game

APPLE JELLY   1 teaspoon dry mustard, ¼ teaspoon powdered
SAUCE FOR HAM   cloves, ¼ teaspoon cinnamon, 2 tablespoons vinegar, 1 8-ounce glass apple jelly.

In a double boiler mix mustard, cloves, cinnamon, with vinegar and jelly. Heat over slow heat until jelly is melted, stirring constantly. Serve hot with Baked Ham.

Mrs. Laws' receipt
Elizabeth R. Lloyd's Book, 1889   *Annapolis*

MADEIRA SAUCE   1 cup Sultana raisins, 1 cup ham liquor, or beef or
FOR HAM   vegetable stock; 1 tablespoon butter, 1 tablespoon flour, ¼ cup brown sugar, 2 tablespoons currant jelly, 1 tablespoon lemon juice, ¼ teaspoon dry mustard, pinch of ground cloves, ½ cup Madeira wine.

Soak raisins in ham liquor (or stock) to soften. Melt butter and brown a little but do not burn it. Stir in flour, then the liquid with raisins and stir until sauce is smooth. Add sugar, jelly, lemon juice, mustard and cloves and stir until blended. Add pepper and salt, if needed. Stir in wine and remove from heat. Serve over slices of baked ham.

Mrs. Rees' receipt
Elizabeth R. Lloyd's Book, 1889   *Annapolis*

GOOD FAMILY   12 medium-sized apples, 1 cup sugar, 1 cup water.
APPLE SAUCE   Pare, core and chop apples. Put them in a deep pudding dish, sprinkle sugar over them and add water. Place them in the oven and bake slowly 2 hours or more, until they are a deep red brown. Quite as nice as preserves for Pork, Roast Goose and Duck.

From Cousin H. Ridout, 1842
Loockerman Book, Hammond-Harwood House   *Annapolis*

216

1 cup tomato catsup, ½ cup butter, 2 tablespoons **MARYLAND**
Worcestershire sauce, 1 teaspoon salt, 1 teaspoon **BARBECUE**
chili powder, 2 dashes Tabasco sauce, 2 cups water, **SAUCE**
juice of 1 lemon.

Combine ingredients in a saucepan; bring to a boil and then simmer
for 10 minutes. Use for basting pork or fowl.

Mrs. James W. Webb
Scaffold Creek
Anne Arundel

---

4 tablespoons currant jelly, 1 wine glass Port wine, **PORT WINE**
1 finely chopped onion, 1 soup spoon each of **SAUCE**
orange and lemon juice, ½ teaspoon powdered
ginger, ½ teaspoon paprika, 1 tablespoon mixed orange and lemon
peel in very fine slivers.

Mix together all ingredients except orange and lemon peel. Heat to
boiling point and strain through fine sieve or cheesecloth. Add orange
and lemon slivers and simmer until tender. Serve hot with Tongue.

Receipts from Araby
Charles

---

1 pound mushrooms, 4 tablespoons butter, ½ tea- **MUSHROOM**
spoon salt, pepper, 1 teaspoon grated onion, ½ cup **WINE SAUCE**
dry red wine, 1 cup brown sauce.

Slice mushrooms across in rather thick slices and brown lightly in
butter. Add salt, pepper, onion and wine. Mix with brown sauce and
simmer for several minutes, stirring occasionally.

To make brown sauce: Mix 1 tablespoon melted butter with 1 tablespoon flour and stir over medium heat until smooth and very brown.
Add 1 cup beef stock (or consomme) and boil and stir for 5 minutes;
then simmer for 20 minutes.

Mrs. Fred G. Boyce, Jr.
Greenway
Baltimore

217

MUSTARD
CREAM SAUCE
2 tablespoons butter, 2 tablespoons flour, 1 cup rich milk, salt, pepper, 1 tablespoon prepared mustard, 1 teaspoon dry mustard.

Make a cream sauce by melting butter, blending in flour and stirring in milk gradually until sauce is smooth and thick. Remove from heat and add mustards. When cool, serve with cold meats.

Miss Fanny's Receipt Book
West River   *Anne Arundel*

ONION SAUCE   Pull some onions and boil them in plenty of water 1 hour. Put them to drain. Afterwards chop them fine and put in saucepan with a little flour sprinkled over them. Add a large piece of butter and cream to make as you like it. Set them over the fire, put a little salt and pepper, and when the butter is melted they will be sufficiently done. For veal or mutton.

Receipts from Waverly   *Queen Anne's*

TOMATO SAUCE   Stew 6 tomatoes ½ hour with 2 cloves, a sprig of parsley, a little sugar, a sprig of thyme, salt and pepper. Press this through a sieve. Put a little butter into a saucepan over the fire; when it bubbles add 1 tablespoon of flour. Mix and cook well; add the tomato pulp. Stir until smooth and 'consistent'. Some add one or two slices of onions at first. Meat stock is an improvement (3 or 4 tablespoons).

Receipts from Waverly   *Queen Anne's*

WINE SAUCE
FOR GAME
½ glass currant jelly, ½ glass water, 1 tablespoon butter, 1 teaspoon salt, juice of ½ lemon, pinch of cayenne, 3 cloves, ½ glass Port wine.

Simmer all together a few minutes, adding Port to strained sauce. A few spoonfuls of the gravy from the game may be added to it. This sauce is especially nice with Venison.

Senator Kenna on Venison
The Baltimore Sun, 1891   *Baltimore*

1 onion, chopped; 3 tablespoons butter, 1 table- **CURRANT JELLY**
spoon flour, 1 pint stock, 1 bay leaf, 1 celery top, **SAUCE FOR**
shredded; 2 tablespoons vinegar, ½ cup currant **VENISON OR**
jelly, salt and pepper. **WILD DUCK**

Cook onion in butter until it begins to color. Add flour and stir until
brown. Add stock, bay leaf, celery and vinegar, and simmer 20 minutes.
Strain and skim off fat. Add jelly and stir over slow fire until it is melted.
Season to taste.

Mrs. Francis F. Beirne
Ruxton *Baltimore*

Mix 2 tablespoons fresh grated or prepared horse- **HORSERADISH**
radish, well drained, with 1 cup of whipped sour **SAUCE**
cream. Add ⅛ teaspoon salt and ¼ cup mixed
chopped parsley and chives. Chill and serve with cold tongue or roast
beef.

Mrs. Wade DeWeese
King George Street *Annapolis*

Take fresh young spearmint leaves stripped from **MINT SAUCE**
the stems; wash and drain them, or dry on a cloth.
Chop very fine. Put in a sauce boat, and to 3 tablespoons mint put 2 of
white sugar. Mix and let it stand a few minutes. Then pour over it 6
tablespoons of good cider or white-wine vinegar. The sauce should be
made some time before it is to be used, so that the flavor of the mint
may be well extracted. For Roast Lamb.

Mrs. Gaylord Lee Clark
Margaret Meadows *Baltimore*

Wash a pint of small button mushrooms; remove **MUSHROOM**
the stems. Stew them slowly in veal stock, rich **SAUCE**
milk or cream; add an onion, chopped very fine
and season with pepper and salt. Thicken with a little butter rolled
in flour. Their flavor will be heightened by salting a few the night
before to extract the juice. For meat, fish or vegetables.

Kitty Worthington's receipt, 1839 *Anne Arundel*

Sauces for Vegetables

OLD-FASHIONED BOILED DRESSING
3 eggs, butter, 1 lump the size of an egg; 1 teaspoon salt, ½ saltspoon pepper, 2 saltspoons mustard, vinegar, 1 cup cream.

Beat eggs very light. Add butter, salt, pepper, mustard and a little strong vinegar. Stir over fire until it boils. Take off and add rich cream.

Bowie family receipt
Elizabeth W. Bond   *Baltimore*

DRAWN BUTTER SAUCE
3 tablespoons butter, 1 tablespoon flour, 1 cup boiling water, ½ teaspoon salt, dash of pepper, 1 teaspoon lemon juice.

Put 2 tablespoons of butter in the saucepan. When it bubbles, sprinkle and stir in flour. Stir until smooth, then add boiling water gradually, stirring all the while until it thickens. Add salt and pepper, the extra tablespoon of butter and lemon juice. Take from the fire and use immediately.

Miss Agnes Tilghman
Gross' Coate, Wye River   *Talbot*

CREAM PARSLEY SAUCE
2 tablespoons flour, 2 tablespoons melted butter, 1½ cups rich milk or light cream, salt and pepper, ¼ cup finely chopped parsley.

Stir flour in butter in a saucepan over low heat until well blended. Gradually add milk, stirring constantly until thickened. Add salt and pepper to taste and, just before serving, stir in the parsley. If a richer sauce is preferred, stir in 2 egg yolks, well beaten.

Maryland Cook Book, 1892
Mrs. Franklin B. Spriggs   *Anne Arundel*

*Sauceboat by
Wm. Faris,
Annapolis, 1770*

This receipt has been made many times, sometimes even a day or so before using. It can be put in an ice box or cool place and reheated and I have never known it to curdle.

**HOLLANDAISE
SAUCE,
MODERN WAY**

3 egg yolks, 2 tablespoons lemon juice, 1 spray parsley, ½ teaspoon salt, dash pepper, ½ cup butter (room temperature), ½ cup boiling water.

Place all ingredients except water in container and turn on blender. Remove cover, and with blender running, gradually pour in water. Run until contents are thoroughly blended, about 1 minute. Cook over hot water (in double boiler), stirring constantly, to consistency of a soft custard.

*J. Harrison Colhoun
Windsor*

Anne Arundel

½ cup butter, yolks of 2 eggs, juice of ½ lemon, 1 saltspoonful salt, a good pinch cayenne pepper, ½ cup boiling water.

**HOLLANDAISE
SAUCE, OLD
WAY**

Rub butter to a cream; add egg yolks, one at a time, and beat well; then add very slowly the lemon juice, salt and cayenne. About 5 minutes before serving add the boiling water; place the bowl in a pan of hot water and stir rapidly until the sauce thickens like custard.

*Miss Page
Maryland Cook Book, 1892*

Anne Arundel

Pastries and Pies

Pastry

PLAIN PIE PASTE

2¼ cups sifted flour, ¼ teaspoon baking powder, 1 teaspoon salt, ⅔ cup cold shortening, ⅓ cup ice water (about).

Sift flour, baking powder and salt together in a bowl. Cut in shortening until pieces are about size of peas. Add water, a small amount at a time, mixing lightly with a fork. Press into a ball, cover and chill. This will make pastry for a two-crust pie. Divide dough into 2 parts. Roll out to ⅛ inch thickness and line pie pan. Pour in desired filling and cover with top crust. For a pastry shell, use half amount, line pie pan, prick with fork and bake in 450° oven for approximately 10 minutes or until lightly browned. Keep pastry cold if you want it flaky. Roll out and up, not back and forth.

Aunt Sally Murray's Choice Receipts
Ivy Neck, Rhode River   Anne Arundel

PASTRY FOR TARTS

½ teaspoon baking powder, 1 scant teaspoon salt, 2½ cups sifted flour, ½ cup shortening, ½ cup butter, 6 to 8 tablespoons ice water.

Add baking powder and salt to flour. Cut in shortening until it looks like coarse corn meal. Stir in ice water with a fork, a little at a time, until all the flour is moistened and dough can be gathered into 2 balls; chill dough. Roll out each ball on a lightly floured board, handling as little as possible. Fit pastry into 2 large tart pans or 12 small tart shells; trim, leaving an overlap to be turned under and fluted or crimped for an attractive edge. Bake in a 450° oven for about 12 minutes or until a light golden color. Cool before filling. Half this quantity will make an average size pie.

Alice's way
Tulip Hill, West River   Anne Arundel

Pies

About 3 pounds tart apples, 1¼ cups sugar, ¼ cup water, salt, 1 tablespoon flour, pastry for a 2-crust pie, 1 tablespoon butter, ½ teaspoon cinnamon.

APPLE PIE

Pare and core apples and cut in eighths. Bring sugar and water with a pinch of salt to a boil. Drop in apples and simmer, covered, until just tender. Remove apples and thicken syrup with flour mixed with a little water; there should be about ⅓ cup. Cool the syrup. Mix pastry, roll out and line pie pan with paste, fill with apples and pour over the syrup, then dot with butter and sprinkle with cinnamon. Moisten edges of paste, cover with top pastry and crimp edges firmly. Slit in several places for steam to escape. Bake in hot oven, 450°, for 15 minutes, then reduce heat to 400° and continue baking for 25 minutes or until done.

Miss Fanny's Receipt Book
West River

Anne Arundel

---

1 cup apples, stewed and sifted; 1 cup sugar, ¼ cup butter, 1 wine glass whiskey, 1 cup cream, a little nutmeg, 3 eggs, beaten separately; whipped cream.

APPLE WHISKEY PIE

Beat hot apples with sugar and butter; when slightly cooled add whiskey, cream, nutmeg and egg yolks. Add whites last and more whiskey if you wish. Pour into pastry lined pie pan (no upper crust) and bake in hot oven, 425°, for 10 minutes to set crust. Reduce heat to 325° and bake 30 minutes longer. Decorate cooled pie with sweetened whipped cream.

Miss Annie Claytor
Warrington, Harwood

Anne Arundel

223

INGLESIDE
APPLE
CUSTARD PIE
½ pound butter, 1½ cups sugar, 4 eggs, 6 large tart apples, ½ to 1 teaspoon vanilla, a little freshly grated nutmeg.

Cream butter and sugar and stir in well beaten eggs. Add apples that have been peeled and chopped fine. If apples are not tart enough, sprinkle them with lemon juice. Add seasonings to taste. Pour into pastry lined pie tin and bake in a moderate oven until apples are done. No top crust is used. Do not be disconcerted by amount of butter called for. The pie is very rich but delicious, and smaller helpings suffice.

Mrs. Edmund P. Harrison
Cold Spring Lane   *Baltimore*

RIPE BERRY
PIES
Line your pie-pan with good crust, fill half full of berries, shake over them a tablespoonful of sifted flour (if very juicy), and as much sugar as is necessary to sweeten sufficiently, about a cupful. Dot with a few bits of butter, and fill up the crust to the top, making quite full, as berries will cook down. Cover with a top crust, or in lattice fashion. Bake about 40 minutes, the first 10 minutes at 450°, the remaining half hour at 350°. Huckleberry and blackberry pies are improved by putting into them a little ginger and cinnamon.

Bessie Finch's receipt
Elizabeth R. Lloyd's Book, 1889   *Annapolis*

RED CHERRY
PIE
1 cup sugar, ⅛ teaspoon salt, 2½ tablespoons cornstarch, 4 cups pitted sour cherries, 1 tablespoon butter, pastry.

Mix sugar, salt and cornstarch, add cherries, mix well and set aside until juicy and well blended. Cook slowly until thickened, add butter and cool. Pour into pastry lined pie pan, top with strips of pastry, lattice fashion. Moisten ends of strips and press to bottom crust. Turn edge under and press with floured fork. Bake in hot oven, 450°, for 15 minutes; then reduce heat to 400° and bake about 15 minutes longer or until crust is golden brown.

Mrs. W. J. Mott's receipt, revised
Emily Stone Barton's Book, 1850   *Baltimore*

3 eggs, separated; ¾ cup sugar, ¼ cup flour, ½ teaspoon salt, 1½ cups milk, ¼ cup butter, 1 teaspoon vanilla, 1 cup grated cocoanut, 1 baked pastry shell.

COCOANUT CUSTARD PIE

Beat egg yolks, add sugar, flour and salt; beat well. Add a little of the cold milk to thin slightly. Scald remaining milk, pour egg yolk mixture into it and cook slowly until it thickens. Fold hot custard into stiffly beaten egg whites, then add butter and stir until melted. Chill thoroughly, add vanilla and cocoanut, about half of which has been toasted. Pour into baked pastry shell, sprinkling top with a little of the toasted cocoanut.

Mrs. Francis E. Engle
Southwood Avenue   *Annapolis*

½ cup butter, ½ cup brown sugar, 1½ cups damson preserves, 3 eggs, 1 teaspoon vanilla, 1 tablespoon cornstarch.

DAMSON PIE

Cream butter and sugar; add preserves (no pits). Beat 1 whole egg and 2 egg yolks until light and lemon colored, reserving 2 egg whites for a meringue. Add beaten eggs to damson mixture; stir in vanilla and beat all together well. Cook over low heat until slightly thickened. To insure a firm pie filling, mix cornstarch with a little damson juice and add gradually to hot mixture; stir constantly until thick. Pour into a baked pie crust; cover with meringue made of the egg whites beaten stiff with 2 tablespoons powdered sugar and ¼ teaspoon vanilla. Return to a slow oven, 300°, and bake about 15 minutes, or until meringue is lightly browned.

Mrs. Decatur's receipt, revised
Miss Ann Chase's Book, 1811   *Annapolis*

---

2 cups sugar, 2 lemons, 3 eggs, 3½ tablespoons cornstarch, 2 cups boiling water, 1 heaping tablespoon powdered sugar.

LEMON MERINGUE PIE

To sugar, add juice and grated rind of lemons. Beat yolks of eggs until light and stir into sugar mixture. Make a paste of cornstarch with a little cold water, add to mixture, then the boiling water. Place on low heat and stir briskly until it boils clear. Have pie shell ready. Pour in custard and cover with stiffly beaten egg whites to which has been added the powdered sugar. Brown quickly in hot oven.

Pie shell: 1 cup flour, pinch of salt, baking powder on tip of teaspoon, 1 teaspoon sugar, 2 or more heaping tablespoons shortening.

Work all ingredients together until the mixture resembles coarse grains of sand. Add enough cold water to hold together. Roll thin and fit into pie pan. Sprinkle with a little sugar and bake in hot oven.

Elizabeth W. Bond
Plymouth Road   *Baltimore*

CHESS PIE
OR
CHEESE CAKE

4 eggs, ½ cup sugar, ¼ teaspoon salt, 1 cup creamed cottage cheese, ½ cup cream, ¼ teaspoon grated nutmeg, pinch of cinnamon, ½ cup sherry wine, ¼ cup brandy, 1 cup stale cake crumbs, pastry for a deep one-crust pie.

Separate eggs and beat yolks with sugar and salt. Mix cheese with cream; combine with egg yolks. Add nutmeg and cinnamon, then stir in wine, brandy and cake crumbs. Fold stiffly beaten egg whites into the mixture and pour into the pastry lined deep pie plate. Bake in hot (450°) oven for 10 minutes, then lower heat to 375° and bake about 20 minutes longer or until filling is set. Cool before serving.

Miss Susan Hacker
Cumberstone   *Anne Arundel*

MINCE MEAT,
SOUTHERN
MARYLAND

4 pounds lean beef, thoroughly cooked; 2 pounds beef suet, uncooked; 4 pounds raisins (2 pounds seeded raisins and 2 pounds seedless), 2 pounds currants, 1 pound citron, ½ pound candied lemon peel, ¼ pound finely chopped apples, peeled; juice and grated rind of 2 oranges, juice and grated rind of 2 lemons, 2 grated nutmegs, ¼ ounce cloves, ½ ounce cinnamon, 1 teaspoon salt, 2 pounds sugar, 1 quart wine, 1 quart brandy.

Chop beef and suet fine. Mix all ingredients thoroughly and then add wine and brandy. Makes about 2 gallons.

Mary Somerville Tongue
Solomons   *Calvert*

3 eggs, 2 tablespoons melted butter, 2 tablespoons flour, ½ teaspoon vanilla, ¼ teaspoon salt, ½ cup sugar, 1 cup dark corn syrup, 1 cup broken pecan meats, 1 unbaked 9″ pastry shell. **PECAN PIE**

Beat eggs and blend in butter, flour, vanilla, salt, sugar and syrup; beat together. Sprinkle pecans over bottom of pastry shell and pour syrup mixture carefully over the nuts. Bake in a hot oven (425°) for 10 minutes, then reduce heat to 325° and bake about 40 minutes longer. Serve cold with whipped cream if desired.

Mrs. Frank Hines
Chestertown

Kent

---

1 pound Irish potatoes, ⅔ cup country butter, ¾ cup sugar (good measure), salt to taste, ½ cup heavy country cream, ½ cup milk, ½ tea- spoon baking powder, juice and grated rind of 1 lemon, seasoning to taste with grated nutmeg, vanilla or ¼ cup sherry wine; 4 eggs. **WHITE POTATO PIE**

Cook potatoes, mashing them through a ricer when done. Add butter to hot potatoes and mix well; stir in sugar, salt, cream and milk, then baking powder, lemon juice and rind, nutmeg and vanilla or sherry. Beat eggs well and stir into potato mixture. Line a pie pan with thin pastry and fill with the mixture. Bake in a moderate oven until firm and brown. This pie has been a favorite for many years at All Hallows Thanksgiving Dinner.

Mrs. John Owens, Sr.
Harwood

Anne Arundel

1½ cups milk, ½ cup flour, 4 cups mashed pumpkin, ½ nutmeg, grated; 1 rounded tea- spoon ground cinnamon, ½ teaspoon ground mace, ½ teaspoon ground cloves, 1 teaspoon ground ginger, ½ teaspoon salt, 1½ cups sugar (more if your taste dictates), 1 large tablespoon butter, grated rind and juice of 1 lemon, ½ cup sherry, 3 eggs. **PUMPKIN PIE**

Bring milk to boil; blend flour with a little cold water and stir it into the boiling milk. Stir until thickened. Mix in bowl with pumpkin. Add spices and other ingredients. Lastly add eggs beaten light. Pour into pie shell and bake in a moderate oven until pumpkin is set and glazed.

Aunt Sally Murray's Choice Receipts
Ivy Neck, Rhode River

Anne Arundel

DEEP DISH PEACH PIE   Arrange whole, peeled peaches in deep baking dish. They must be a sweet variety and very ripe and mellow. Sprinkle liberally with sugar. Cover with a pastry crust, prick with a fork and bake in 450° oven for 10 minutes. Reduce heat to 350° and bake 30 or 40 minutes longer. Serve with rich cream.

Mrs. Henry C. Edgar
Evergreen   *Anne Arundel*

LARKIN'S HUNDRED RHUBARB PIE   3 cups rhubarb, plain pastry, 1 cup sugar, 2 tablespoons flour, ⅛ teaspoon salt, 2 eggs.

Peel rhubarb and cut in ½ inch pieces before measuring. Line a pie pan with plain pastry. Mix sugar, flour, salt and beaten eggs. Add to the rhubarb and pour into pastry-lined pie pan. Moisten edge of pastry with water. Cover with a top crust, trim and press edges together. Prick top with a fork. Bake in a quick oven (425°) 10 minutes. Reduce heat to a moderate oven (325°) and bake 25 to 30 minutes.

Mrs. Walter Hardisty
Larkin's Hundred   *Anne Arundel*

STRAWBERRY AND RHUBARB PIE   2 cups strawberries, 1½ cups sugar, pie paste (for 9″ pie with top crust), 2 tablespoons cornstarch, 2 cups diced rhubarb, 2 tablespoons flour, 1 tablespoon butter, powdered sugar.

Cap and clean berries and mix with ½ cup sugar, mashing slightly to extract juice. Set aside. Mix pie paste and line 9″ pan. Stir cornstarch into a little cold water until smooth. Mix with berry juice and pour over berries in a saucepan. Cook gently until clear and juice is thickened. Spread rhubarb over paste in pan, sprinkle with flour and 1 cup of sugar. Dot with butter. When berry mixture is slightly cooled, pour it over the rhubarb. Cover with pie paste; press edges together to seal, and slit top in a few places for steam to escape. Place pie in 450° oven for 10 minutes. Reduce heat to 350° and bake for 30 minutes more or until crust is golden brown. Remove from oven and sift powdered sugar over the crust.

Mary Gilmore's Farmlands receipt
Elizabeth R. Lloyd's Book, 1889   *Annapolis*

A. Aubrey Bodine

Eastern Shore Strawberries

1 cooled 9-inch baked pie shell, 1 package cream cheese (3 ounces), 1 quart fresh strawberries, 1 cup granulated sugar, 2 tablespoons cornstarch, 1 cup whipping cream.

FRESH STRAWBERRY PIE

Spread cream cheese, blended with sufficient cream to soften it, over bottom of cooled, baked pie shell. Wash berries, hull them, and drain well. Place half of the berries (the choicest ones) in the cheese-coated pie shell. Mash and strain remaining berries until juice is well extracted. Bring juice to boiling point, and slowly stir in sugar and cornstarch which have been mixed together. Cook slowly for about 10 minutes, stirring occasionally. Cool and pour over fresh berries in pie shell. Place pie in refrigerator until very cold. Decorate with sweetened whipped cream before serving.

Charlotte G. Marbury   *Prince George's*

Tarts

BANBURY TARTS   1 cup seeded and chopped raisins, 1 cup sugar, 3 tablespoons cracker crumbs, 1 egg, 1 tablespoon butter, ⅛ teaspoon salt, juice and rind of 1 lemon, pastry for tarts.

Roll pastry ⅛ inch thick and cut in 3 inch squares. Mix ingredients and put a generous teaspoon of the Banbury mixture in the center of one corner, wet edges of pastry and fold to form triangle. Press down the open sides with prongs of a fork. Prick several times and bake in brisk oven.

Aunt Sally Murray's Choice Receipts
Ivy Neck, Rhode River   *Anne Arundel*

BLACKBERRY TURNOVERS   1½ cupfuls pastry flour, ¼ teaspoonful salt, ¼ cupful butter, ¼ cupful lard, ice water, 1 pint blackberry jam.

Sift salt with flour. Work the shortening in carefully. Add enough ice water to make the dough manageable. Roll on floured board. Turn and fold, and break off pieces large enough to be rolled into circles 7 inches in diameter, and slightly thicker than pie crust. Put sufficient jam in center of circles for a well-filled turnover, and fold over. Turn back edges, press them down, and mark with a fork. Bake in a moderate oven, 350°, for about 30 minutes, or until pastry is lightly browned.

Margaret Thornton Marchand
Prince George Street   *Annapolis*

1 cup sugar, ¼ cup water, 1 quart gooseberries, 2 tablespoons currant jelly, 1 tablespoon arrow-root, 6 tart shells (baked).

GOOSEBERRY TARTS WITH DEVONSHIRE CREAM

Mix sugar and water in a saucepan and bring to a boil slowly. Add gooseberries and boil quickly until berries are clear (about 10 minutes). Strain juice and put berries aside to cool. Add currant jelly to juice, and arrowroot mixed to a paste with very little cold water. Boil slowly, stirring until clear and thickened. Divide gooseberries into tart shells and, when juice is cooled, pour over berries, filling the shells. When glaze has set, top with Devonshire Cream (see Sauces for Desserts).

Mrs. Truxtun Beale's Book, 1903
Decatur House

Washington

---

1 cup sugar, 1 heaping tablespoon cornstarch, 3 eggs, 1 tablespoon melted butter, juice and grated rind of 1 lemon, pinch of salt, 1 cup water, 3 tablespoons powdered sugar.

BEST LEMON TARTS

Mix sugar, cornstarch and egg yolks together. Then add butter, lemon juice and rind, salt and water. Cook in a double-boiler until thick and smooth. Pour into baked tart shells which have cooled. Beat egg whites until they stand in peaks and add very slowly the powdered sugar. Place meringue on tarts and put in oven to let meringue set and brown.

Mrs. Carroll Alden
Taney Avenue

Annapolis

---

1 cup butter, 2 cups sugar, 6 eggs, 4 lemons.

'RECEIT' TO MAKE LEMON CURD FOR TARTS

Melt and dissolve together butter and sugar. Beat eggs until foamy, and add to them the grated rind and juice of the lemons. Add eggs to the butter-sugar mixture, beating and stirring over slow fire until thick. When cool, pour into tart shells.

For the lovely Mrs. Chase
Miss Ann Chase's Book, 1811

Annapolis

FRESH PEACH TART
1 cup sugar, ½ cup water, 3 pounds ripe, mellow peaches (about 12 or 14); 2 tablespoons cornstarch, ¼ teaspoon almond extract. Pastry for tarts baked as individual shells or large tart.

Make a syrup of sugar and water, stirring until sugar dissolves. Pare and slice half a dozen peaches; add them to syrup and cook until soft. Mix cornstarch to a paste in a little water and add to peach syrup, stirring until thickened. Set aside to cool, then add almond flavoring. Near serving time, peel and halve remaining peaches, placing one un-cooked half in each individual tart shell (or arrange in large tart shell if preferred). Spoon syrup with peach slices over the peach halves until shells are nicely filled.

Alice's way
Tulip Hill, West River   *Anne Arundel*

GLAZED STRAWBERRY TARTS
1 cup sugar, 3 tablespoons cornstarch, ¼ cup cold water, ¾ cup crushed strawberries, 1 teaspoon lemon juice, 3 cups whole strawberries, 6 baked tart shells, heavy cream.

Mix sugar and cornstarch, stir in cold water until smooth. Add crushed berries and lemon juice. Cook slowly until clear, about 8 minutes. Let thicken and cool thoroughly. Place whole berries in tart shells. Pour cooked mixture over berries, filling the shells. Top with whipped cream.

Mrs. E. Mackall Childs
Tudor Hall   *Anne Arundel*

TO PRESERVE GREEN TOMATOES FOR TARTS
Take green tomatoes, skin them and cut them in four parts. To every pound of tomatoes put ½ pound of sugar, lemon peel and ginger to your taste, cinnamon if you choose. Stew them until done. Make a tart paste at the bottom of the dish and put the tomato preserve in without a top crust and bake them. Eat cold.

Receipt addressed to H. A. Harwood,
from Miss Chase, 1850   *Annapolis*

Cobblers and Dumplings

6 medium sized tart cooking apples, pared and **BAKED APPLE**
cored. Pastry for a 2-crust pie, ½ cup sugar, 1½ **DUMPLINGS**
teaspoons cinnamon, 1 tablespoon butter.

Roll out pastry slightly thicker than for pie, and cut in squares large
enough to wrap an apple. Place an apple in each square and fill cores
with the mixed sugar and cinnamon. Dot all with butter. Bring pastry
up over apples, moistening and sealing edges. Place dumplings, not
touching, in a baking dish.

The syrup: 1 cup sugar, 2 cups water, 3 tablespoons butter, ¼ teaspoon cinnamon; boil together for 3 minutes and pour around dumplings. Bake in a hot (425°) oven for about 45 minutes until crust is
browned and apples soft. Serve warm with cream.

Mrs. McBlair, Walnut Grove,
Maria T. Allison's Book, 1860

Baltimore

Peel enough apples, cut in eighths, to cover the **CRUSTY APPLES**
bottom of a baking dish (8″ by 12″) to depth of
about 2 inches. To these sliced apples add about ½ cup sugar (adjust
for tartness of apples), 2 teaspoons cinnamon, ¼ teaspoon nutmeg.

Topping: 1 cup flour, 1 cup sugar, ½ teaspoon baking powder, ¾ teaspoon salt, 1 egg (a little additional sprinkling of cinnamon and
nutmeg is good in topping also). Mix to a crumbly texture with fork,
then spread over apples in baking dish. Pour over this topping ¼ cup
melted butter. Bake at 350° for about 45 minutes. Serve warm, or cold;
good with vanilla ice cream.

Mrs. Oliver Haywood
Southwood Avenue

Annapolis

BERRY ROLY-POLY

3 cups flour, 2 tablespoons sugar, 1 teaspoon salt, ½ cup butter, ½ cup shortening, about 4 to 6 tablespoons ice water, 1 quart blackberries, 1 pint raspberries, 1½ cups sugar, ½ teaspoon nutmeg, 1 tablespoon butter.

Mix flour, sugar and salt. Work in butter and shortening until crumbly as coarse cornmeal. Add ice water slowly until dough can be gathered into a ball. Roll out on floured bread cloth into large circle. Spread thickly with blackberries and raspberries, mixed together; sprinkle sugar and nutmeg over them and dot with butter. Roll with aid of bread cloth into long roly-poly. Place in oblong baking dish and bake in a 400° oven for about 20 minutes. Reduce heat to 350° and bake about half an hour longer. The juice will be plentiful and syrupy. Cut across in thick slices and serve warm with rich cream.

Old Howard County receipt,
Mrs. Frederick G. Richards
Ridout House   *Annapolis*

The Ridout House

234

Cobblers

½ cup sugar, 1 tablespoon butter, 1 cup flour, 1 teaspoon baking powder, ½ teaspoon salt, ½ cup milk, 1 quart berries, sugar and butter, 1½ cups boiling water (use juice if you can, which is preferable). **BERRY COBBLER**

Cream sugar and butter. Sift flour, measure and sift again with baking powder and salt. Add to sugar mixture and then add milk. Spread dough in a well buttered baking dish, cover with berries, sprinkle with sugar and dot with butter. Pour boiling water or juice over the dish. Bake for an hour in a 375° oven.

Mrs. Frank Jack Fletcher
Araby

Charles

---

3 cups pitted red cherries, ½ cup sugar, 1 teaspoon almond extract, 1 tablespoon lemon juice, **CHERRY DOUCI** 1½ cups flour, ½ teaspoon salt, 3 teaspoons baking powder, ½ cup sugar, ⅓ cup shortening, ½ cup milk, 1 egg, 2 tablespoons sugar.

Spread cherries on buttered 8 by 12 inch baking pan, sprinkle with sugar, almond extract and lemon juice. Put in oven to warm. Sift flour, salt, baking powder and sugar, then cut in the shortening. Add the milk with beaten egg and beat all together well. Spread over cherries and sprinkle the 2 tablespoons of sugar over the top. Bake in 375° oven for about 40 minutes or until brown. Serve with Cherry Wine Sauce. (See Sauces for Puddings.)

Alice Key's receipt, revised
Maria T. Allison's Book, 1860

Baltimore

Puddings

Baked Puddings

APPLE PUDDING

4 eggs, 1½ cups sugar, 2 tablespoons flour, 2 tablespoons butter, 4 tablespoons brandy, 4 cups chopped or grated apples, nutmeg and cinnamon.

Beat yolks of eggs in a large bowl, add the sugar, flour, butter and brandy. Beat all together well, then add the finely chopped or coarsely grated apples. Lastly, fold in stiffly beaten egg whites. Pour into a buttered oven dish, sprinkle liberally with nutmeg and cinnamon and bake in a moderate oven (350°). Serve warm with Hard Sauce (see Sauces for Puddings) or rich cream.

Mrs. Moone's receipt, revised
Miss Ann Chase's Book, 1811   *Annapolis*

BERRY PUDDING

⅓ cup butter, 1 cup sugar, 2 eggs, 1¾ cups flour, ½ teaspoon salt, 2 teaspoons baking powder, ½ cup milk, ½ teaspoon vanilla, 1 pint huckleberries or blackberries.

Cream butter, adding slowly half the sugar, and beat until light and fluffy. Beat eggs well and add remaining sugar to them. Combine butter and egg mixtures. Save out ¼ cup flour for dredging berries. Mix and sift dry ingredients and add alternately with milk to batter. Beat well and add vanilla. Spread layer of batter in greased and floured pan. Dredge berries with reserved flour; strew berries over layer of batter in pan; repeat until batter and berries are used. Bake in a moderately hot, 375°, oven until straw tests done, about 30 minutes. Serve warm with Foaming Sauce. (See Sauces for Puddings.)

"For Mrs. William Harwood, from dear Fanny C.", adapted
The 1814 Account Book, Harwood Papers   *Annapolis*

½ cup butter, 1 cup sugar, 2 eggs, ½ cup sour **HUCKLEBERRY**
cream, ½ teaspoon soda, 2 cups flour, ½ teaspoon **PUDDING**
cream of tartar, 2 cups berries.

Cream butter and sugar; add beaten eggs, then sour cream in which
soda has been dissolved. Stir in one cup of flour mixed with cream of
tartar. Lastly, add berries which have been dusted with second cup of
flour. Bake in greased pan in moderate oven for one hour. Serve with
any desired sauce. Hard Sauce flavored with sherry wine is good.

Celeste Hull's way
Mrs. Charles McCurdy Mathias
Court Square
                                                        Frederick

---

8 medium sized apples, ½ cup sugar, ½ teaspoon **BIRD'S NEST**
ground cinnamon, ½ teaspoon grated nutmeg, ½ **PUDDING**
cup water.

Batter: 1 generous tablespoon butter, ½ cup sugar, 1 egg, 1 cup flour,
1 teaspoon baking powder, pinch of salt, ½ cup of milk.

Pare and core apples. Place in pudding dish and sprinkle in the holes
the mixed sugar and spices. Add water, cover and bake until apples
are almost tender. For batter, cream the butter and sugar well. Add egg
and beat until light. Sift dry ingredients and add to butter mixture
alternately with milk. Blend thoroughly and pour over apples. Bake
20 to 25 minutes in a 350° oven. Serve warm with Vanilla Sauce
(see Sauces for Puddings). Serves 8.

Mrs. Y. Kirkpatrick-Howat
Contee, Rhode River
                                                        Anne Arundel

---

4 squares of bitter chocolate, 2 cups of grated **CHILDREN'S**
bread crumbs, 4 cups milk, 3 eggs, 1 cup sugar. **CHOCOLATE**
                                              PUDDING

Melt chocolate, add bread crumbs, then milk
which must be boiling hot. Let mixture cool, then add eggs, well-
beaten, with the sugar. Pour into a well-buttered dish and bake 1 hour
in 375° oven. Serve hot with Hard Sauce. (See Sauces for Puddings.)

Mrs. Frank Hines
Chestertown
                                                        Kent

237

Baked Puddings

MAXWELTON BREAD PUDDING 4 cups milk, 2 cups bread crumbs, 1 tablespoon butter, 1 cup sugar, 4 eggs, rind and juice of 2 lemons, currant jelly, 4 tablespoons powdered sugar.

Heat milk and pour over bread crumbs; add butter, cover and set aside to cool. Beat sugar and egg yolks together and add grated lemon rind. Add to first mixture and pour all into a buttered pudding dish. Bake until firm and slightly browned—about ½ hour in 375° oven. Remove from oven and spread lightly with currant jelly (or any acid jelly). Spread with a meringue made with the egg whites whipped to a froth, to which have been added the powdered sugar and lemon juice. Brown in a slow oven to a light straw color. Serve warm with Lemon Pudding Sauce (see Sauces for Puddings) or cream. Also good very cold.

Mrs. R. Laurie Mitchell
Maxwelton   *Charles*

TO MAKE A CHARLOTTE Fit thin slices of bread, dipped in clarified butter, with great exactness into a small, deep Charlotte mould or pudding dish, lining bottom and sides.

When this is done, fill it up to the top with tart apples which you have peeled, cored and quartered and then stewed with about 2 table-spoons of butter, sugar (according to tartness of the apples), and lemon juice to your taste. The apples should be soft and thick but not watery. Cover the top with slices of bread dipped in butter, and on this place a plate with a weight upon it. If the bread is not put well together, the juice will come between the spaces and ruin the appearance of the Charlotte. Bake in moderate oven until Charlotte shell is crisp and golden brown. Loosen edges with a knife and turn out Charlotte care-fully on china dish. Serve warm with pitchers of maple syrup and thick cream.

Mrs. James Cheston's Everyday Book, 1857
West River   *Anne Arundel*

1¾ cups sugar, 1 cup butter, 4 eggs, 3 cups flour, **CHESTERTOWN**
3 teaspoons baking powder, ¾ of a nutmeg, **PUDDING**
grated; ⅔ cup milk, ⅓ cup sherry, 1 pound
raisins, or fewer.

Beat sugar and butter together, stir into this the beaten eggs; sift flour
with baking powder and nutmeg and add it gradually to egg mixture,
alternating with the milk. Add wine and blend all thoroughly. The
old receipt said "put in as many raisins as you please". To prevent fruit
from sinking to bottom, heat them in the oven and mix them with a
little flour (taken out of the 3 cups), before folding them into batter.
Pour into a pudding mold or fluted cake pan (Turk's head) well greased.
Bake in moderate oven (375°) for an hour. Serve warm with Maryland
Wine Sauce (see Sauces for Puddings). This is really a delicious cake
and can be eaten cold with equal relish.

Edith Willing's Old Waverly receipt *Queen Anne's*

---

1 grated cocoanut (about ½ pound), ½ cup **'ONE GRATED**
stale sponge cake, crumbled fine; ½ cup butter, **COCOANUT'**
1 cup sugar, a coffeecupful (about ½ cup) of rich
milk or cream, 6 eggs, 2 teaspoons vanilla, or brandy or rose-water to
your taste.

Toss cocoanut and cake crumbs together. Cream butter and sugar
well, and add the milk or cream. Beat eggs very light and stir them
gradually into butter cream mixture, in turn with cocoanut and crumbs.
Stir very hard, and add vanilla or flavoring of your choice. Stir again,
and put into a buttered dish and bake until set, ½ to ¾ hour in a
moderate oven. Three of the whites of eggs could be left out for a
handsome meringue on top of the pudding, sprinkled with a little
grated cocoanut to give the appearance of snowflake. Most excellent.

Mrs. Jacob Loockerman
Loockerman Book, 1835
Annapolis

PRISCILLA'S COTTAGE PUDDING   ½ cup butter, 1 cup sugar, 2 eggs, ½ cup milk, 1½ cups flour, 1½ teaspoons baking powder, ½ teaspoon vanilla.

Cream butter and sugar until well mixed. Add eggs, one at a time; beat and mix well. Stir in milk, then flour and baking powder, sifted together. Add vanilla. Bake in oven 350° until done.

Sauce: Blend ¼ cup butter with 2 cups brown sugar. Add sherry and nutmeg to taste.

Mrs. John Harrison Colhoun
Windsor   *Anne Arundel*

DELICATE INDIAN PUDDING   4 cups milk, 3 tablespoons cornmeal, ¼ teaspoon salt, ½ cup molasses, 3 eggs, ½ cup cold water, ¼ teaspoon ground cloves, 1 tablespoon cinnamon, ¼ teaspoon nutmeg.

Scald milk in top of a double-boiler. Stir in cornmeal gradually, then salt and molasses and cook for ½ hour. Remove from fire and pour into pudding dish. When nearly cold, stir in well beaten eggs and cold water, then the spices. Bake slowly for 2 hours in 275° oven. Serve warm or cold with vanilla ice cream.

Cousin H. Ridout's receipt, revised
Loockerman Book, 1835   *Annapolis*

PRUNE PUDDING   ½ pound prunes, scant cup powdered sugar, whites of 6 eggs, vanilla flavoring, whipped cream, wine, lemon peel.

Boil prunes, pit and pass through a sieve. Add sugar, egg whites which have been beaten to a stiff froth, and vanilla to taste. Bake in a moderate oven for 15 minutes. When cold, serve with whipped cream over the top. Put a little sugar and wine in cream before whipping it. A little lemon peel in the wine gives a nice flavor (of course, take it out). A pudding for 6 persons.

Elizabeth R. Lloyd's Book, 1889   *Annapolis*

2 eggs, 1 cup sugar, 2 rounded tablespoons flour, **LEMON**
¼ cup lemon juice, grated rind of 1 lemon, 1 **PUDDING**
tablespoon melted butter, 1 cup milk.

To beaten egg yolks, add sugar and flour, mixed; then stir in lemon
juice, grated rind, butter and milk. Lastly, fold in lightly beaten egg
whites. Pour into buttered oven dish (1 quart size) and place it in a
shallow pan of hot water. Bake for 50 minutes in 350° oven. Serves four.

Louise Kemp Hammond
Thompson Street
Annapolis

½ cup rice, 1 quart rich milk, 2 eggs, ¾ cup **OLD-FASHIONED**
sugar, pinch of salt, 1 lemon, ½ cup raisins, nut- **RICE PUDDING**
meg.

Boil rice slowly in milk until soft and creamy. Mix beaten yolks of
eggs with sugar, salt, juice and grated rind of the lemon. Add to rice;
stir in raisins and stiffly beaten whites of eggs. Pour into a pudding
dish; sprinkle with nutmeg and bake in 350° oven for 45 minutes.

Miss Fanny's Receipt Book
West River
Anne Arundel

Ripe peaches, ½ cup nut meats, cinnamon, 2 **PEACH**
eggs, 1 cup milk, ½ cup sugar, 1 cup cooked **RICE PUDDING**
rice.

Peel and halve fresh, ripe peaches and place with cavities up in a
baking dish and fill with nut meats. Sprinkle with a little cinnamon or
nutmeg. Beat eggs light and mix with the milk, sugar and cooked rice.
Pour rice custard over fruit and bake in a moderate oven for thirty
minutes. Serve with cream or Peach Sauce. (See Sauces for Puddings.)

Aunt Sally Murray's Choice Receipts
Ivy Neck, Rhode River
Anne Arundel

SWEET POTATO PUDDING Boil 4 Maryland goldskin sweet potatoes. Skin and mash with ¼ pound of butter and 1 cup sugar, but sweeten to taste if 1 cup not sufficient. Add juice and finely grated rind of 1 lemon, also 1 teaspoon vanilla. Beat 4 eggs separately; add first the yolks, then fold in the stiff whites. Grease pie plates, and if mixture is too stiff, thin with cream. Bake at 350° until light golden brown. This was an old Talbot receipt of my mother's, which some people cut down because they think it too extravagant with butter. Don't do it!

Miss Nellie Shackelford
The Anchorage, Miles River   *Talbot*

Steamed Puddings

NANNIE PINKNEY'S COMICAL FUDDING 3 cups flour, 1 teaspoon salt, 1 teaspoon cinnamon, ½ teaspoon each of ginger, nutmeg and cloves, 1 cup finely chopped suet, 1 cup molasses, 1 cup milk, 1 teaspoon soda, 1 cup seeded raisins.

Sift flour and mix with it the salt and spices; add the suet and blend well. Mix the molasses and milk; add the soda and then as much of the flour mixture as will make a stiff batter (not dough), then add the raisins, floured, and fill a covered pudding mold half full; steam for three hours. Serve with Foaming or Elegant Brandy Sauce (see Sauces for Puddings).

Miss Ann Chase's Book, 1811   *Annapolis*

FIG PUDDING 1 cup suet, finely chopped; 1 pound dried figs, 1 cup brown sugar, 2 cups light, dry bread crumbs; ½ teaspoon cinnamon, ½ teaspoon nutmeg, ½ teaspoon salt, 1 teaspoon soda, 1 cup sour milk, 3 eggs.

Mix together lightly the suet, figs, cut in small pieces; brown sugar, crumbs, cinnamon, nutmeg and salt. Stir soda into sour milk and add to well beaten eggs. Gradually add the liquid mixture to dry ingredients and blend. Fill one pound greased pudding tins two-thirds full, cover tightly and steam for 3 hours. Serve with Hard Sauce. (See Sauces for Puddings.)

Mrs. Lew Garrison Coit
The Lord's Bounty

Anne Arundel

½ cup butter, ½ cup granulated sugar, 1 egg, **GINGER**
2 cups sifted flour, 2 teaspoons baking powder, **PUDDING**
4 teaspoons ground ginger, ½ teaspoon soda,
pinch of salt, ½ cup milk, ½ cup golden syrup (Lyle's Golden, if you can find it), crystallized ginger.

Cream butter and add sugar gradually, then the well beaten egg. Beat until very light. Mix and sift flour, baking powder, ginger, soda and salt and add alternately with milk and golden syrup to creamed mixture. Mix thoroughly. Turn into a pudding basin, greased with butter, cover tightly and steam for 2 hours. Turn out on serving dish and sprinkle top with bits of crystallized ginger. Serve warm with Foaming Sauce. (See Sauces for Puddings.)

Carroll McTavish Elder
Tred Avon River

Talbot

¼ pound suet, chopped very fine; 1¼ cups sugar, **ONE PLUM**
10 ounces grated stale bread crumbs, ½ pound **PUDDING**
stoned raisins, ½ pound currants or seedless
raisins, 1 cup milk, ¼ cup brandy, 1 grated nutmeg, ½ teaspoon cinnamon, ½ teaspoon mace, rind and juice of ½ lemon, 5 eggs, 1 teaspoon salt.

Mix all ingredients except eggs. Add lightly beaten eggs last. Butter a two quart melon mould. Steam pudding four hours. When ready to serve, steam one hour. Serve with Foamy Sauce for Plum Pudding. (See Sauces for Puddings.)

Mrs. Gordon Fisher, Jr.
Wye Town Farm

Talbot

ARABY PLUM PUDDING   1 pound brown sugar, 1 pound bread crumbs, ½ cup molasses, 1 glass tart jelly, 8 lightly beaten eggs, 1 cup flour, ¾ pound beef suet, chopped fine; 1 large apple, finely chopped.

Mix the above ingredients, then add: 1 pound seeded raisins, 1 pound currants or seedless raisins, ½ pound cut-up citron, ¼ pound each orange and lemon peel, ½ teaspoon each nutmeg, cloves and cinnamon; 1 teaspoon salt, 1 cup chopped pecans.

Stir all ingredients together thoroughly so that fruit and spices are well distributed. Steam smaller puddings for 3 hours in greased, covered molds; a large pudding must be steamed at least 5 hours. Serve with Hard Sauce or Foamy Sauce for Plum Pudding. (See Sauces for Puddings.)

Mrs. Frank Jack Fletcher
Araby   *Charles*

CHRISTMAS PLUM PUDDING   1 pound kidney suet, ½ pound lemon peel, ½ pound orange peel, ½ pound citron peel, 1⅛ pounds raisins, seeded; 1 pound currants, 1 nutmeg, or 1 tablespoon, ground; 1⅛ pounds bread crumbs, ½ pound brown sugar, ½ teaspoon salt, 6 eggs, 2 teaspoons lemon extract, 1 cup brandy (8 ounces).

Suet must be white and fine and very cold; make into tiny bits. Cut citrus fruits into small bits; measure each exactly after preparing. Flour raisins and currants slightly. Grate nutmeg fresh. Make very tiny crumbs of stale bread, no crusts. In large bowl, mix suet and bread crumbs well, sugar, salt, nutmeg and fruits. Beat eggs light and add to dry mixture. Add lemon extract and brandy last. Place in buttered bowls, protect for boiling, and boil slowly 3 hours. Taste, as more sugar or nutmeg may be needed. Steam 2 hours before using. Mixture enough for three 3-pound bowls.

For the Christmas table, decorate pudding with a sprig of holly; pour lighted brandy around the dish, and baste pudding until flame dies. Serve with Christmas Hard Sauce (see Sauces for Puddings).

Mrs. John C. Plews   *Anne Arundel*

Desserts

Fruit Desserts

Wash and core, but do not peel, as many apples as you need. Put them in a baking pan and fill center of each apple with 1 tablespoon chopped Canton ginger mixed with enough brown sugar to fill hole. Add a little water to pan as needed while cooking. Bake in a moderate oven (350°) until tender. Cool and serve with heavy cream.

BAKED GINGER APPLES

Miss Fanny's Receipt Book
West River

Anne Arundel

A. Aubrey Bodine

Above the Fruited Plain

BLACKBERRY FLUMMERY 1 quart blackberries, 1 heaping cup sugar, 2 tablespoons cornstarch.

Stew blackberries and sugar together for 15 minutes. Strain out seeds, if preferred. Mix cornstarch with a little cold water and stir into berries. Cook until thickened and smooth. Pour into a cut glass bowl or individual stemmed glasses. Chill, and serve with whipped cream on top.

Mrs. Charles W. Williams
Welcome Here, Glyndon   *Baltimore*

CHERRIES IN CLARET 1 quart fine red cherries, 2 cups claret wine, 1 small stick cinnamon, 1 cup sugar, 1 tablespoon currant jelly.

Cut stems from cherries half way down. Put them in an enamel pan with the wine, cinnamon and sugar. Put on a low fire and cook for 10 minutes. Remove from fire and cool in their juice. Place in a dish one by one with the stems up. Put juice back on stove and reduce until thick and add currant jelly. When jelly is melted, pour over cherries and serve very cold with lady fingers.

Receipts from Araby   *Charles*

BAKED PRESERVED FIGS 1 quart jar Southern Maryland Preserved Figs, ½ cup chopped black walnuts, rind of 2 oranges, 3 tablespoons brandy.

Place figs in an oven dish with syrup, except ½ cup. Sprinkle nuts over the figs. Cut orange rind in very thin strips (just the outside yellow part) and cook in ½ cup fig syrup for 15 minutes. Remove from stove and add brandy. Pour it over figs and bake in a hot oven (400°) for about 15 minutes. Serve warm.

Mrs. F. T. Loockerman's receipt, revised, 1835
Hammond-Harwood House   *Annapolis*

Drain cooked fruits and reserve juices. Choice of **BAKED FRUIT**
fruits and amounts may vary with the season
and number to be served. Whole fruits look best.

Suggested fruits: 1 cup black cherries, 1 cup peaches, 1 cup apricots, 1
cup pears, 1 cup purple plums, juice of one orange, juice of one lemon,
the grated rind and fine slivers of both lemon and orange, ½ cup
brown sugar, 2 or 3 tablespoons Cherry Brandy.

Combine ½ cup cherry juice, ¼ cup apricot juice, and ¼ cup plum
juice (remaining juice useful for jellied desserts). Add juice of orange
and lemon and the slivers of rind. Heat and add sugar, stirring until
dissolved. Cook until syrup is reduced and thickened. Arrange fruit
attractively in baking dish. Spoon over it half the syrup. Place in moderate oven to poach and heat through, basting occasionally with remaining syrup. Before serving, spoon Cherry Brandy over all.

Mrs. Lewis R. Andrews
Tulip Hill, West River

Anne Arundel

½ cup water, 1 cup sugar, juice of ½ lemon, 2 **PEACH BLOOM**
quarts strawberries, 12 peaches, almonds.

Boil water, sugar and lemon juice until it spins a thread, then add
mashed strawberries. Stand on back of stove (or in warm place) for 1
hour, keeping covered. Blanch peaches in boiling water and skin. Two
hours before serving, pour strawberry sauce over whole blanched
peaches. Chill and serve garnished with blanched, sliced almonds.

Mrs. Truxtun Beale's Book, 1903
Decatur House

Washington

---

6 to 8 pears, Port wine, orange and lemon peel, **PEARS IN PORT**
cinnamon.

Peel pears, leaving them whole with stems attached, or cored and
halved as desired. Put in a deep saucepan and cover with Port wine.
Add a peel of orange, a peel of lemon and a pinch of cinnamon to
taste. Stew gently until the Port is thick and syrupy. Add a little sugar
if the Port is thin. Serve very cold.

Receipts from Araby

Charles

GREEN GAGE PLUMS IN SAUTERNE JELLY 2 dozen green gage plums, cooked whole and unpeeled; 2 tablespoons gelatine, softened in a little cold water; 1½ cups plum juice, 1 cup sugar, or to taste; 1½ cups Sauterne, 3 tablespoons lemon juice.

Dissolve gelatine in boiling plum juice. Add sugar to taste, Sauterne and lemon juice. Strain and pour over drained green gage plums arranged in a mold. Chill, and turn out on serving dish.

Mrs. George Maurice Morris
The Lindens   *Washington*

PURPLE PLUMS IN CLARET JELLY 2 dozen purple plums cooked, whole and unpeeled; 2 tablespoons gelatine, softened in a little cold water; 1½ cups plum juice, 1 cup sugar, or to taste; 1 cup Claret, ⅓ cup orange juice, 3 tablespoons lemon juice.

Make in same way as Green Gage Plums in Sauterne Jelly. A very pretty dessert if the two molds are used together, dishing a Purple Plum and a Green Gage for each serving.

Mrs. George Maurice Morris
The Lindens   *Washington*

RASPBERRY FOOL 2 cups raspberries, ½ cup sugar, ½ pint whipping cream.

Clean raspberries; add sugar to fruit and let stand to extract juice. Mash berries slightly, and bring slowly to the boil. Cook until soft, and pass through a sieve. After it is cold, whip the cream and add the fruit to it. Put on ice for 2 hours. Any other fruit may be used for a Fool. Serve with wafers or sweet biscuits.

Mrs. F. T. Loockerman's Book, 1835
Hammond-Harwood House   *Annapolis*

An Eighteenth Century Dinner
for
Twentieth Century Enjoyment

Sorrel Soup   Sippets

Scalloped Crabs
Baked Ham

Pilau of Rice   Asparagus with Boiled Dressing
Sally Lunn
Green Tomato Soy

Green Gage Plums in Sauterne Jelly
Purple Plums in Claret Jelly

Shrewsbury Cakes

The dishes were all prepared from receipts found in 18th century cook books. The Wines and Liqueurs served were all from distillers who were selling their wares to our Colonial forefathers.

Dinner given by Mrs. George Maurice Morris at
The Lindens   *Washington*

Dining Room, The Hammond-Harwood House

M. E. Warren

Dessert Cakes

CREAM ALMOND CAKE   4 eggs, 2 cups sugar, 1 teaspoon almond flavoring, 1 cup hot milk, 2 cups flour, 2 teaspoons baking powder.

Beat eggs until thick and creamy, add sugar gradually, then flavoring. Add hot milk alternately with flour to which baking powder has been added. Bake in three layers in 9-inch cake pans in moderate oven.

Filling and frosting: 1½ pounds almonds, 2 cups heavy cream, 2 tablespoons granulated sugar, 1 teaspoon almond flavoring.

Shell and blanch almonds, dry thoroughly and grind. Whip cream, add sugar and flavoring. Add almonds and spread between layers and over cake.

This famous cake, particular to Shady Side, is served at the traditional holiday gathering of the Leatherbury brothers and sisters on Christmas morning at the old homestead.

Miss A. Matilda Leatherbury
Shady Side   *Anne Arundel*

COMMODORE'S CREAM CAKE   4 eggs, 1 cup sugar, 1 lemon, 1 cup flour, 1 teaspoon baking powder, ¼ teaspoon salt.

Separate yolks and whites of the eggs; beat whites to a froth gradually adding 4 tablespoons of the sugar until meringue is stiff. Beat yolks until light; add remaining sugar and beat to a cream. Add grated rind of the lemon and a tablespoonful of the juice. Stir together until thick and creamy. Sift flour, baking powder and salt. Quickly and lightly, without beating, mix a third of the flour with the yolks, then a third of the whites, then more flour and whites until all are used. The mode of mixing must be very light, rather cutting down through the cake batter than beating it. Beating the eggs makes them light, but beating the batter makes the cake tough. Bake immediately in an ungreased square cake pan (9" x 9") in a 350° oven until a straw run into it can be withdrawn clean, about 30 minutes. When cool, split cake with a sharp broad-bladed knife and spread cream filling thickly between layers. Ripe peaches or strawberries may be sliced over the filling. Sprinkle top of cake with powdered sugar. Cut in squares to serve.

Cream filling: 1 pint milk, 2 eggs, 1 cup sugar, ½ cup flour, 1 tablespoon butter, 1 tablespoon lemon juice.

Put milk on to boil. Beat eggs, and add sugar and flour previously mixed. After beating well, stir into milk just as it comes to boiling point. Add butter and keep stirring one way until it thickens. Flavor with lemon juice.

Commodore John Bonnet Marchand's Book, 1862   *Annapolis*

⅓ cup orange juice, grated rind of 1 orange, ⅓ cup lemon juice, grated rind of 1 lemon, 1 cup granulated sugar, 2 eggs, 2 cups whipping cream, 2 sponge cake layers.

ORANGE DESSERT CAKE

Mix together the juices, grated rinds, sugar and lightly beaten eggs. Stir constantly over low heat until thick—about 15 minutes. Let stand in refrigerator until cold. Beat 1 cup of cream until stiff and fold into orange mixture. Spread between the cake layers, which have been split in two, making 4 layers. Let stand in ice-box 8 or more hours and spread with additional whipped cream before serving.

Mrs. M. Rea Shafer
Pourtney's Oversight   *St. Mary's*

The first refrigerator, a simple affair, was patented in 1803 by Thomas Moore, a Maryland farmer.

KOSSUTH CAKES   ½ cup butter, 1 cup sugar, 2 eggs, 1¾ cups pastry flour, 2½ teaspoons baking powder, ½ teaspoon salt, ½ cup milk, ½ teaspoon vanilla. Have everything at room temperature.

Cream butter and sugar well, add beaten eggs, and fold in flour, baking powder and salt (sifted together), alternately with the milk. Add vanilla. Bake at 350° in muffin pans. When done, cool, cut almost in half, fill with sweetened whipped cream and ice top of cakes.

Chocolate Icing: 2½ squares of chocolate, ¼ cup butter, ½ pound confectioners sugar, 2 egg yolks, salt, vanilla.

Melt chocolate and butter, add sugar and a little hot water until just soft enough to spread, then beat in egg yolks and add a pinch of salt and a little vanilla. Makes a soft icing.

Mrs. George Ray Hyde
Evesham   *Baltimore*

Strawberry Icing: 10 ripe strawberries, ½ teaspoon lemon juice, 2 cups confectioner's sugar.

Mash berries with a fork, add lemon juice. Gradually add sugar until stiff enough to spread, yet soft enough to run over top of cream-filled cakes which have been placed in low compotes or on individual dessert plates, ready to serve.

Elsie Melvin Kemp
Franklin Street   *Annapolis*

Kossuth Cake, that luscious dessert of sponge cake filled with whipped cream and topped with rich icing, was named for the Hungarian patriot, General Louis Kossuth, who visited Baltimore City more than a hundred years ago. The reception given him was said to have been exceeded in hospitality only by that accorded General Lafayette in 1824. However, in spite of Baltimore's enthusiasm to assist General Kossuth's struggle against tyranny, its monetary contribution amounted to only $25.00. It would seem that Baltimore got the best of the bargain. For, most important to its gastronomic tradition, was the creation by an unknown pastry cook of that delectable concoction, which to this day is enjoyed by Baltimoreans, known as Kossuth Cake.

1½ tablespoons cornstarch, 3 tablespoons granulated sugar, 2 cups milk, 6 eggs, 1 teaspoon vanilla, candied cherries, pineapple, orange rind, lemon peel, 1 cup brandy, 2 thin sponge cakes, rum, 6 egg whites, 12 heaping tablespoons powdered sugar, 1 teaspoon vanilla.

ARABY MERINGUE RUM CAKE

Mix cornstarch with sugar and a little cold milk until smooth. Add remainder of milk and make a custard by cooking in a double-boiler until thick and rawness has disappeared. Beat yolks of eggs and stir into custard, then cook another minute or two. Beat egg whites until they are stiff. Add vanilla to custard and pour into a large bowl, then fold in egg whites very carefully and, when cool, put in ice-box to chill. Cut up candied fruits and soak in brandy. Split cakes so that you have 4 thin layers. Sprinkle these liberally with rum. Place 1 layer, brown side down, on a baking dish and spread with a thin layer of candied fruit, then a generous layer of custard. Place on top another layer of cake with cut surface up. Continue until all cake, fruit and custard are used. Make a meringue with additional egg whites by beating until stiff and folding in powdered sugar. Flavor with vanilla and cover top and sides of cake with a thick layer of meringue. Pop into a moderate oven to brown, but watch carefully.

Mrs. Frank Jack Fletcher
Araby

Charles

Araby

Delectable Desserts

BOILED CUSTARD Boiled custard is the basis of many desserts. It requires care in cooking as too little cooking leaves it thin and a moment too long is apt to curdle and spoil it. It should have the consistency of thick cream and be perfectly smooth. Boiled or Soft Custard is used as a sauce for fruits and puddings; also, in trifles and frozen desserts.

1 quart of rich milk, 6 eggs, ½ cup sugar, ⅛ teaspoon salt, vanilla bean or 1 teaspoon vanilla extract.

Scald milk with vanilla bean, if you have one, in a double-boiler. The eggs may be beaten all together for a plain custard or separately for a fluffy one. The eggs, slightly beaten (or the yolks, if you prefer) are added to the sugar and salt. Pour scalded milk over beaten eggs and return to double-boiler, stirring all the time. Cook until custard thickens (having removed vanilla bean) and when it coats a silver spoon, it should immediately be removed from the fire. If only the yolks have been used, fold in stiffly beaten whites and vanilla (if the bean was not used). The plain custard may be eaten with cream. To make a floating island, top each serving of custard with a spoonful of well-beaten and sweetened egg white. A dab of jelly may be added to each, or a spoonful beaten into the egg white.

Miss Ann Chase's way, 1811   *Annapolis*

COLD SHERRY SOUFFLÉ 2 tablespoons gelatin, ½ cup cold water, 1½ cups sweet sherry, 6 eggs, ¾ cup sugar, 1 tablespoon lemon juice, 1 cup heavy cream, 12 lady fingers.

Soften gelatin in cold water, then dissolve over boiling water; add sherry and chill until mixture begins to thicken. Separate eggs and beat yolks with ¼ cup sugar. Beat into gelatin mixture. Beat egg whites until foamy and continue beating while gradually adding ¼ cup sugar. Add lemon juice and beat until stiff but not dry. Fold into gelatin mixture. Whip cream while slowly adding remaining ¼ cup sugar. When stiff, gently fold into mixture. Pour into deep dish lined with lady fingers divided into halves. Chill at least three hours or overnight. Serves 12.

Mrs. Robert Bond Welch   *Baltimore*

2 cups rich milk, 1 tablespoon gelatine, pinch of
salt, 3 eggs, 1 cup sugar, 1 teaspoon vanilla, 1 cup
sherry wine (or more), 2 cups heavy cream, 2
dozen lady fingers.

**CHARLOTTE
RUSSE**

Put milk, gelatine and salt in top of double boiler and scald. Beat egg
yolks with sugar; add to milk mixture, stirring constantly over low heat
until mixture coats the spoon. Remove from fire and allow to cool
(really cold). Beat egg whites until stiff; fold them into custard, add
vanilla. Beat all with egg beater until light. Now fold in 3 tablespoons
of sherry and the cream, whipped. Line a large dish with split lady
fingers; spoon some sherry over them. Have some extra lady fingers
split and cut into pieces. Dip these in sherry. Put a layer of custard
in dish, then a layer of lady fingers, then a layer of custard until dish
is filled. Put in a cold place until it sets. Turn out on platter. Save 2
or 3 spoonfuls of the whipped cream to decorate. This can be made
the day before using and serves 8 to 10 people.

Mrs. Frederick G. Boyce, Jr.
Greenway

Baltimore

---

4 egg yolks, ⅔ cup sugar, 2 tablespoons gelatin,
¼ cup rum or sherry, 1 cup ground (or puréed)
chestnuts; 1 cup heavy cream, 4 egg whites.

**CHESTNUT
MOUSSE WITH
CHOCOLATE
SAUCE**

Beat egg yolks with sugar until light and lemony. Soften gelatin in
rum or sherry and dissolve over hot water. When cool, add to egg mixture and stir in the chestnuts. Mix well. Fold in whipped cream, then
well-beaten egg whites. Pour into mold and chill. Serve with Chocolate
Sauce. Chestnuts will freeze either cooked or in the shells.

Chocolate Sauce: 1 cup water, 4 tablespoons cocoa, 2 squares chocolate,
1 cup sugar, 1 teaspoon vanilla, sherry.

Put water, cocoa, chocolate and sugar in saucepan and bring to boil,
stirring constantly. It will quickly cook up into smooth, thick sauce.
Remove from stove and stir in vanilla and enough sherry to thin to
desired consistency. May be served hot or cold.

Mrs. H. K. Rigg
Replica, Holly Beach Farm

Anne Arundel

LEMON CREAM　5 eggs, 2 lemons, 1 cup of sifted sugar. Beat the egg yolks with the juice and grated rind of the lemons, and the sugar. Cook in a double-boiler, stirring constantly, until it thickens like a custard. Remove from fire, and hastily fold in the whites of eggs beaten stiff. When blended, pile in glasses. In making this, always use a double-boiler.

Mrs. Gough's way
Mrs. F. T. Loockerman's Book, 1835　　　　　　　　　　*Annapolis*

WINE JELLY　3 tablespoons gelatin, 2 cups cold water, 3 lemons (juice and rind), 4 sticks cinnamon, 2 cups sugar, 3 cups boiling water, 2 cups sherry wine.

Combine gelatin, cold water, juice and rinds (cut very thin) of lemons and cinnamon. Let stand until thoroughly dissolved. Then add sugar and boiling water. When sugar is dissolved, add wine, strain and set away in a cool place to harden. The traditional way to serve is with boiled custard and pound cake.

Mrs. Carroll Alden
Taney Avenue　　　　　　　　　　*Annapolis*

CREAM PUFFS　½ cup butter, 1 cup boiling water, 1 cup sifted flour, ½ teaspoon salt, 4 eggs.

Melt butter in boiling water in saucepan. Place over medium heat; add flour and salt, stirring constantly until mixture leaves sides of saucepan. Remove from heat; cool slightly and add eggs, one at a time. Beat thoroughly after each addition until mixture is smooth and glossy. Drop about 2 tablespoonfuls for each puff onto buttered tins allowing plenty of space between mounds. Bake for 20 to 30 minutes in 425° oven until golden brown and well puffed. When cool, split and fill with custard filling. Makes 10-12 puffs.

Filling for Cream Puffs: 1 cup flour (scant), ½ cup sugar, yolks of 3 eggs, beaten; 1¾ cups warm milk, vanilla or almond to taste.

Mix flour, sugar and egg yolks until well blended. Gradually stir in milk. Place over gentle heat and beat constantly until cream is thick. Remove from heat and continue beating for 1 minute, adding desired flavoring.

Mrs. Blanchard Randall
Kenmore Road　　　　　　　　　　*Baltimore*

2 cups milk, 3 eggs, 1 cup sugar, 1 tablespoon **MACAROON**
gelatin, ¼ cup water, 1 teaspoon vanilla or 2 **BAVARIAN**
tablespoons sherry, 1 dozen almond macaroons, **MOLD**
1 cup heavy cream, nutmeg.

Scald the milk. Mix together beaten yolks of eggs and sugar, then gradually add scalded milk. Cook in top of a double boiler, stirring constantly until mixture coats the spoon. Soften gelatin in cold water five minutes and then dissolve in hot custard. Remove from heat, fold in stiffly beaten egg whites and vanilla or sherry wine. Line a pudding mold with macaroons and pour hot mixture over them. Chill overnight. When ready to serve, unmold, top with whipped cream and add a sprinkle of nutmeg. It makes a very pretty dish. Serves 8.

Miss Fanny's Receipt Book
West River
Anne Arundel

---

4 egg whites, 4 tablespoons sugar, 4 tablespoons **MARMALADE**
orange marmalade. **MERINGUE**

Beat egg whites stiff. Add sugar and beat well again. Add marmalade. Grease sides of top of double-boiler well with butter. Pour in mixture and cook 1 hour. Do not lift lid while cooking. Turn out carefully on serving dish.

Sauce: 1 cup powdered suger, 4 egg yolks, 4 tablespoons sherry. Add sugar to well beaten egg yolks. Beat thoroughly and add sherry. Chill in refrigerator, then beat again before serving. Serves 6.

Mrs. Sloan Doak
Hilversum, Ruxton
Baltimore

½ cup sugar, 2 cups peach pulp, 1 tablespoon **MARGARET'S**
gelatin, ½ cup tepid water, 1 cup heavy cream, **PEACH BAVARIA**
sponge cake, sherry.

Mix sugar with peach pulp. Soften gelatine in water, then dissolve over hot water. Mix with peach pulp and put in cold place to harden. As it begins to harden, beat it up well and fold in whipped cream. Pour into mold lined with strips of sponge cake dipped in sherry.

Mrs. Truxtun Beale's Book, 1903
Decatur House
Washington

SNOW BALLS   1½ tablespoons gelatin, ¼ cup cold water, 1 cup light cream, 1 cup sugar, 2 cups grated cocoanut, 1½ cups heavy cream, 2 egg whites, 1 teaspoon almond extract.

Sprinkle gelatin over water to soften. Scald cream, remove from heat and stir in gelatin and ½ cup of sugar to dissolve. Cool and chill the mixture until it begins to thicken. Fold in cocoanut, cream which has been whipped, and egg whites beaten with ½ cup sugar until stiff. Add almond extract and pour into individual round molds, such as custard cups or punch cups. Chill until firm. Unmold snow balls and serve with strawberry sauce. Makes eight snow balls or one large mold to serve 8-10.

Mrs. J. Marsh Matthews
Eagle's Nest   *Baltimore*

LEMON   3 egg yolks, 1 cup sugar, grated rind of 1 lemon,
MOUSSE   1 tablespoon gelatin, ½ cup water, ½ cup lemon juice, 1 teaspoon vanilla, 4 egg whites, 1 pint whipping cream.

Beat egg yolks and sugar until thick and lemon colored. Add grated rind to gelatin and water and set over pan of hot water to dissolve gelatin; add to egg yolk and sugar mixture. Add lemon juice and vanilla, stirring well. Beat egg whites until peaks form; whip cream stiff and add both to above mixture in order given. Pour mousse into bowl from which it is to be served and refrigerate several hours. Will serve 8 to 10. Strawberries or raspberries served with this add color and taste, but it is delicious alone.

Mrs. J. Dorsey Brown   *Owings Mills*

SPANISH CREAM   1 tablespoon gelatin, ½ cup cold water, 4 cups rich milk, 4 eggs, ¾ cup sugar, 1 tablespoon sherry wine (almond or vanilla extract may be substituted).

Dissolve gelatin in cold water. Combine milk, beaten yolks of eggs and sugar and cook in a double-boiler until custard thickens and coats the spoon. Remove from stove, add gelatin and stir until dissolved. Beat egg whites until very stiff. Add flavoring to custard and fold in egg whites. Pour into mold and chill. Serve with sweetened whipped cream. Serves 6-8.

Mrs. John C. Robertson
Shipwright Street   *Annapolis*

Macaroons, sherry wine, rich custard, raspberry   **A TRIFLE WITH**
jam, syllabub.   **SYLLABUB**

Lay macaroons over the bottom of a deep dish or glass bowl and pour over them as much sherry as they will absorb, then pour on them a rich, cold custard—it should stand two or three inches thick—on that put a layer of raspberry jam and cover the whole with whipped syllabub heaped up high.

Receipts from Waverly   *Queen Anne's*

Soak the peel of 1 'Lemmon' in a pint of sweet   **'LEMMON'**
wine (1 cup sherry and 1 cup Madeira is best).   **SYLLABUB**
Whip a quart of heavy cream until it begins to
hold its shape, then gradually add the wine, from which the peel has been removed, the juice of 2 'Lemmons' and 1 cup of sugar, beating it up as fast as you can till thick. Pile in glasses and sprinkle nutmeg on top.

Mrs. Snowden
Miss Ann Chase's Book, 1811   *Annapolis*

A sponge cake, currant jelly, ½ to 1 pint wine, a   **CARDINAL**
rich custard, blanched almonds, citron.   **PUDDING,**
                                                     AN ELEGANT
Slice a sponge cake cross-ways in 2 pieces. Spread   **TRIFLE**
it with currant jelly, and put the pieces together.
Pour over the cake from ½ to 1 pint wine, according to its size. Let it stand for several hours and then pour over it a rich custard, having first stuck blanched almonds and citron cut in strips all over the top of the cake. "This is an elegant trifle, and if served in glass, makes a very ornamental dish."

Winder family receipt
Presqu'ile-on-Wye   *Talbot*

259

Delectable Desserts

WYE TOWN STRAWBERRY MERINGUE
6 egg whites, ½ teaspoon cream of tartar, ¼ teaspoon salt, 1½ cups sugar, 1 teaspoon vanilla, ¼ cup slivered blanched almonds, 2 cups strawberries or more, 1 cup cream for whipping.

Turn on oven to 400°. Beat egg whites with cream of tartar and salt until foamy white (and almost level volume) in large bowl. Beat in sugar, 1 tablespoon at a time, beating well after each, until meringue stands in firm peaks. Sugar should be completely dissolved before adding more. Fold in vanilla. Spoon meringue into buttered 8-inch springform pan; make a slight hollow in middle with a spoon; sprinkle slivered almonds over. Place in hot oven, close oven door and turn heat off immediately. Leave meringue to slow-bake, without peeking even once, overnight, or at least 12 hours.

Remove meringue from oven, loosen around edge with knife, release spring and carefully lift off side of pan. Slide meringue off pan onto serving plate. About 1 hour before serving, hull and slice enough strawberries to make 1 cup, spoon over meringue. Beat cream until stiff in small bowl. Spoon over strawberries and chill. Garnish with remaining whole or sliced berries. Slice in wedges with a sharp knife.

Mrs. Gordon Fisher, Jr.
Wye Town Farm   *Talbot*

STRAWBERRY SHORTCAKE
1 quart strawberries, ½ cup sugar, 2 cups flour, 1 tablespoon sugar, 4 teaspoons baking powder, ½ teaspoon salt, 4 tablespoons butter, ½ cup milk, or enough to make a soft dough, powdered sugar, cream.

Crush berries slightly (leaving out some to use on top of shortcake) and mix with sugar. Sift flour, sugar, baking powder and salt together. Cut in butter or work in with fingers to crumble. Add milk and mix with fork into flour mixture. Roll ½ inch thick and bake in 3-inch rounds as biscuits or in square pan to cut in squares after baking. Bake in 400° oven for 30 minutes. Split at once and butter generously. Cover lower half of shortcake with crushed, sweetened berries. Place crust on top and cover with whole berries, sprinkled with powdered sugar. Serve with thick cream.

Frankie's way
Mrs. Amos Hutchins   *Annapolis*

Francis E. Engle

Ridout House

4 teaspoons gelatine, ⅓ cup cold water, ⅓ cup boiling water, ¾ cup sugar, 2 tablespoons lemon juice, 1 cup orange juice and pulp, ½ teaspoon grated orange peel, 4 egg whites.

**AUNT PRUE'S
ORANGE
CHARLOTTE**

Soften gelatine in cold water. Add boiling water and sugar, and stir over low heat until dissolved. Stir in the juices and peel, then set aside to congeal, but do not let it get as stiff as jelly. Beat whites of eggs very stiff, then beat in smoothly the congealed gelatine mixture, a spoonful at a time. Pour into a mold and set in a cold place to harden. To serve, unmold, and leave at room temperature for about fifteen minutes to ripen. Serve with a thin boiled custard, delicately flavored.

Prudence Gough Ridout Dugan's Way
Mrs. James N. Galloway

Annapolis

Frozen Desserts

VANDALUSIA BISQUE

1 cup sugar, ½ cup cold water, 2 egg whites, 2 cups whipping cream, 6 macaroons, ½ teaspoon almond or vanilla extract.

Boil sugar and water until it spins a thread, about 2 minutes, Do not overcook or it will crystallize. Pour slowly onto stiffly beaten egg whites, beating all the time. Continue beating until mixture is cold; then fold in cream which has been whipped stiff. Fold in finely crumbled macaroons and flavoring. Chill. This dessert will freeze nicely in a refrigerator tray and tastes even more delectable. Serves 4-6.

Mrs. George S. Radford
Carvel Hall   *Annapolis*

FROZEN ORANGE SOUFFLÉ

2 tablespoons gelatine, ½ cup cold water, ½ cup hot water, 1 pint orange juice, 2 cups sugar, 6 egg yolks, 1 quart whipping cream.

Soak gelatine in cold water, then dissolve in hot water. Mix orange juice and sugar to form a syrup. Beat egg yolks and mix with syrup. Add gelatine and stir carefully until it begins to thicken, then stir in quickly the cream which has been whipped. Freeze. It should not be as hard as ice-cream. Makes 10 servings.

Miss Bertha Trail   *Frederick*

MRS. HENSHAW'S MACAROON MOUSSE

1 cup sugar, ¼ cup water, yolks of 6 eggs, 2 tablespoons sherry, 1 tablespoon vanilla, 1 teacup broken macaroons, 1 pint heavy cream.

Boil sugar and water for 5 minutes. Pour slowly over the beaten egg yolks. Cook in double-boiler until it coats the spoon. Beat until cold. (This may be done the day before using.) Pour sherry and vanilla over macaroons. Whip cream and beat into the egg mixture. Fold in macaroons and freeze.

Mrs. Henshaw
Moreland   *Frederick*

262

2 tablespoons flour, ¼ cup sugar, ¼ teaspoon **BASIC CUSTARD**
salt, 2 cups milk, 1 egg, 1 teaspoon vanilla. **FOR ICE**
CREAM

Mix flour, sugar and salt. Add scalded milk; return to heat and cook ten
minutes, stirring constantly. Add to slightly beaten egg and cook three
minutes more. Add vanilla. This is the basic custard for several kinds
of ice cream and may be made the day before it is to be used.

---

1 cup sugar, ½ cup water, basic custard, 2 cups **CARAMEL**
heavy cream. **ICE CREAM**

Caramelize the sugar by putting it in a pan on the stove to brown until
quite dark. Add the water and stir together. Add the mixture to the
basic custard and freeze until very stiff. Remove from freezer, beat hard
and return to freeze again. When frozen the second time, beat it in
with the cream which has been whipped. Work very fast as it freezes
slowly but melts fast.

---

1 portion of basic custard, ⅔ cup preserved ginger **GINGER**
chopped with syrup, 2 cups heavy cream. Pro- **ICE CREAM**
ceed as above.

---

1 portion of basic custard, 12 crushed macaroons, **MACAROON**
2 cups heavy cream. Proceed as above. **ICE CREAM**

Miss Grace Kelly
Duke of Gloucester Street

Annapolis

FROZEN CUSTARD 2 cups milk, 4 egg yolks, 1 cup sugar, pinch of salt, 2 cups double cream, 2 tablespoons rum, 3 tablespoons brandy, 2 egg whites.

Scald the milk. In the meantime beat egg yolks with the sugar and salt. Pour in scalded milk gradually, stirring constantly and cook until smooth and thick. Let it cool. Whip cream, then fold it into custard. Pour into the freezer tray and freeze to a stiff mush. Take out into a bowl and beat in the rum and brandy. Fold in stiffly beaten egg whites and return to freezer.

Miss Fanny's Receipt Book
West River   *Anne Arundel*

HAMPTON FROZEN PUDDING 1 quart cream, ⅔ cup sugar, 1 tablespoon rum, 3 tablespoons sherry, 1⅓ cups preserved cherries, 1 dozen macaroons.

Stir sugar gradually into cream. Stir in rum and sherry taking care that it does not curdle; then cherries, drained from their juice, and last the macaroons broken into 3 or 4 pieces. Freeze and serve.

Ridgely Family receipt from Hampton
Society for the Preservation of Maryland Antiquities   *Baltimore*

Spring House at Hampton   Maryland House and Garden Pilgrimage

1 cup sugar, ¾ cup water, ¼ cup lemon juice, **LEMON**
1 teaspoon grated rind, 1 egg, 1 cup whipping **ICE CREAM**
cream.

Make a syrup with the sugar and water, cooking (not hard) about 10 minutes. Let it cool a bit and when lukewarm add lemon juice and grated rind. Beat egg well and then add to syrup and beat all together. Fold in stiffly beaten cream. Pour into a refrigerator tray and freeze until of a mushy consistency. Remove from tray into a bowl and beat hard until light and fluffy. Return to freeze. Serves 4-6.

Adapted from
Miss Ann Chase's Book, 1811 *Annapolis*

½ teaspoon gelatin, 1 teaspoon cold water, 2 cups **LEMON**
boiling water, 1 cup sugar, ¼ cup lemon juice, **SHERBET**
grated rind of ½ lemon, 1 egg white.

Soak gelatin in cold water for 5 minutes. Cook boiling water and sugar together for 5 minutes. Add gelatin and dissolve. Add juice and grated rind. Freeze to a mush. Turn out into a bowl and beat well. Fold in stiffly beaten egg white and return to ice-box to freeze, stirring once.

Receipts from Araby *Charles*

1¼ cups pure Garrett County maple syrup, 4 egg **AUNT HARRIET'S**
yolks, 1 tablespoon gelatine, 3 tablespoons cold **MAPLE MOUSSE**
water, 1 cup heavy cream, whipped; 1 teaspoon
vanilla.

Bring syrup to a boil in heavy saucepan, and boil for 1 minute. Beat egg yolks until thick and fluffy and slowly pour hot syrup into yolks, beating constantly. Cook mixture over hot water, stirring constantly, until custard coats a metal spoon. Soften gelatine in water and add to hot custard, stirring to dissolve. Cool custard until syrupy. Fold in whipped cream and vanilla. Pour mousse into crystal bowl or individual glasses and chill. Decorate with sweetened whipped cream sprinkled with chocolate shavings.

Mrs. Lew Garrison Coit
The Lord's Bounty *Anne Arundel*

PEACH ICE   4 cups sliced, mellow peaches; 1½ cups sugar, 2 cups water, ¼ cup lemon juice, ½ cup orange juice.

Make a purée by rubbing peaches through a colander. Boil sugar and water together for five minutes, then cool. To this syrup add peach pulp and lemon and orange juice. Turn into freezer tray and freeze until firm. Turn out into chilled bowl and beat well; return immediately to tray and finish freezing.

Aunt Sally Murray's Choice Receipts
Ivy Neck, Rhode River   *Anne Arundel*

Journal of William Black, 1744

'Dined with Governor Bladen at Annapolis, after which came a Dessert no less curious. Among the Rarities of which it was compos'd, was some fine Ice Cream which with the Strawberries and Milk, eat most Deliciously.'

WAVERLY   Sprinkle sugar over strawberries, mash well and
STRAWBERRY rub through a sieve. To a pint of the juice, add
CREAM   ½ pint of cream—make it very sweet. Freeze and when beginning to set, add a pint of whipped cream and, lastly, strawberries, sweetened.

Mrs. Morgan B. Schiller
Wye House, Wye River   *Talbot*

STRAWBERRY   1 quart fresh strawberries (frozen may be used out
ICE MOULD   of season). Wash and hull berries, and sweeten with about ½ cup of sugar, or to your taste. The old-fashioned way was to mash the berries and put them through a sieve, but now-a-days a blender is much better. Add juice of 1 lemon and if you like, ½ teaspoon of gelatine dissolved in warm water.

Line a mould heavily with whipped cream (1 pint cream whipped with 2 tablespoons powdered sugar and flavored with vanilla). Freeze, and when stiff and set pour in the strawberry mixture and freeze again. Turn out to serve. Raspberries may be used in the same way.

J. Harrison Colhoun
Windsor   *Anne Arundel*

The Campbell House   Merriweather

1 pint strawberries, 1¼ cups sugar, ½ tablespoon **STRAWBERRY**
gelatin, ¼ cup cold water, ¼ cup hot water, ½ **ICE CREAM**
lemon, 2 cups heavy cream.

Mash berries, add sugar and let stand 1 hour. Purée them through a
sieve (or in electric beater). Soften gelatin in cold water, then add hot
water to dissolve. Add to berry mixture with the lemon juice. Freeze
to a stiff mush, then beat until double in quantity. Freeze again to a
block. Remove from freezer and add to whipped cream, beating until
it doubles, but do not let it melt. Refreeze. It will take 6 to 8 hours
to freeze.

Mrs. Levin Campbell
Duke of Gloucester Street   *Annapolis*

---

2 quarts ripe strawberries, granulated sugar, 2 **STRAWBERRIES**
quarts vanilla ice cream, Cherry Heering liqueur. **ROEDOWN**

Wash and hull strawberries. Drain well, then mash or slice thin and
sprinkle with sugar to taste. Soften ice cream (do not melt). Stir in
strawberries and Cherry Heering to taste. Put back in freezer for 1 hour
or until ready to serve.

Mrs. John Murray Begg
Roedown   *Anne Arundel*

Sauces
for Puddings and Desserts

BERRY SAUCE 2 cups berries (raspberries, blackberries, or straw-berries), 1 tablespoon granulated sugar, 1 table-spoon butter, 1½ cups powdered sugar, 1 egg white.

Place berries in a bowl; add granulated sugar and mash slightly to draw out the juices. Soften butter in a warm place, beat in powdered sugar, then add stiffly beaten egg white. Add mashed berries just before serving.

Mrs. Spencer Watkins, 1897   *Montgomery*

ELEGANT 1 cup sugar, ½ cup butter, yolks of 4 eggs, 1 wine-
BRANDY SAUCE glass brandy or wine, pinch of salt, 1 cup hot cream or rich milk.

Cream together sugar and butter; when very creamy add well-beaten yolks of eggs. Stir in brandy or wine, salt and cream or milk. Beat well; put in saucepan over low heat, stir constantly until it thickens. Do not let it boil.

Maryland Cook Book, 1892
Mrs. Franklin B. Spriggs   *Anne Arundel*

CHRISTMAS 1 cup sugar, 1 cup butter, 3 tablespoons heavy
HARD SAUCE cream, 3 tablespoons brandy, 1 teaspoon vanilla.

Mix butter and sugar to a creamy consistency, very thoroughly. Then add heavy cream, brandy, and vanilla. Pile lightly in a pretty dish and serve promptly with a Fruit or Plum Pudding.

Mrs. John C. Plews   *Anne Arundel*

MARYLAND ½ pound butter, ½ pound brown sugar, 1 egg
WINE SAUCE yolk, large wine glass of wine or more if you like, nutmeg.

Beat together butter, sugar and egg until very light. Set over boiling water on the fire and add the wine by degrees. Add grated nutmeg. Heat without boiling, stirring until as thick and smooth as rich cream.

Waring family receipt, Bald Eagle
Elizabeth W. Bond   *Baltimore*

½ cup sugar, 2 tablespoons cornstarch, 1 cup cherry juice and ½ cup sweet red wine; ⅛ teaspoon almond extract. **CHERRY WINE SAUCE**

Cook together until thickened. Serve warm over cobbler or pudding.

Miss Fanny's Receipt Book
West River   Anne Arundel

---

3 ounces chocolate, not sweet; sweet butter size of a walnut (about 2 tablespoons); ¾ cup boiling water, 1¼ cups sugar, pinch of salt, 1 teaspoon vanilla or rum. **CHOCOLATE SAUCE**

Melt chocolate over hot water; add butter and gradually stir in boiling water. Bring to a boil over direct heat, stirring constantly. Add sugar a little at a time, and salt. Boil for about 5 minutes, watching carefully, then take from fire, add flavoring and beat until creamy. If to be served hot, reheat in double-boiler, but do not cook.

Miss Sally Hall
Lothian   Anne Arundel

Put 1 quart of absolutely fresh, very rich milk into a deep pan and do not disturb for a day and night. Then place on top of stove and let it come **DEVONSHIRE CREAM** to the boiling point. Quickly and carefully remove from the fire, put in a cool spot for a day. After that skim off the clotted cream in layers.

Mrs. Truxtun Beale's Book, 1903
Decatur House   Washington

---

1 cup sugar, ½ cup water, juice and rind of 2 lemons, 3 egg yolks. **LEMON PUDDING SAUCE**

Beat together the sugar, water, lemon juice and rind and place in double-boiler. Beat the yolks until light and add to syrup; beat rapidly over boiling water for 3 minutes. Take off fire and beat until thick and light.

Miss Sally Hall
Lothian   Anne Arundel

FAVORITE PUDDING SAUCE

Yolks of 2 large fresh eggs, white of 1 egg, 2 tablespoons confectioners sugar, 1 cup cream, whipped; vanilla or rum.

Beat the yolks until quite thick, add the beaten white and sugar. Place in a double-boiler and cook, stirring the while until thick. Pour into a cool china or earthenware bowl. Beat with a silver or wooden spoon until it is cold, then mix into this the whipped cream. Flavor with vanilla or rum to taste, as preferred. To be used with Cottage Pudding or Gingerbread when hot.

Mrs. William F. Fullam's receipt
Elizabeth R. Lloyd's Book, 1889   *Annapolis*

FIG SAUCE FOR VANILLA ICE CREAM

2 cups cut-up fresh figs, 1½ cups sugar, 1 cup seeded raisins, juice and grated rind of 1 small lemon and 1 small orange, ⅓ cup chopped nut meats.

Soak fresh figs in water containing a little baking soda for 1 hour. Wash thoroughly and cut into small pieces. Measure into a saucepan; add sugar, raisins, lemon and orange juice and rind. Cook until of syrup consistency and clear, stirring occasionally. Add nuts and cool.

Adapted from Kate Brice's Book, 1850   *Annapolis*

FOAMING SAUCE

4 tablespoons butter, 1 cup powdered sugar, 2 egg whites, ¼ cup sherry or 1 tablespoon vanilla.

Beat butter to a cream and gradually add sugar, then well-beaten whites of the eggs and finally the flavoring. Beat well and, when mixture is perfectly smooth, set bowl containing it in a pan of boiling water and stir until you have a frothy, foaming sauce. Serve when hot.

Mrs. R. d'Earle
Receipts from Waverly   *Queen Anne's*

1 cup butter, 3 cups brown sugar, 2 cups wine,   **PLUM PUDDING**
grated peel and juice of 1 lemon, grated nutmeg.   **SAUCE**

Cream butter and sugar; boil wine. Stir together while boiling. Add peel and juice of the lemon and season with a generous grating of nutmeg. Gently stew together until seasonings are well blended.

Mrs. R. T. Waters, 1897   *Montgomery*

---

1 cup confectioners sugar, ½ cup butter, 4 table-   **FOAMY SAUCE**
spoons sherry wine, 1 cup cream, whipped.   **FOR PLUM**
                                            PUDDING

Cream sugar and butter and slowly add the sherry wine. Set the bowl in boiling water and stir until the sauce is like cream. Remove from water, let cool and beat in 1 cup whipped cream.

Mrs. Gordon Fisher, Jr.
Wye Town Farm
                                         Talbot

½ cup sweet butter, 1 cup brown or powdered   **HARD SAUCE**
sugar, 2 tablespoons whiskey or brandy.

Cream butter and sugar together, adding sugar gradually. Add the liquor and beat until very light. Put in a small mold in cool place to harden. Unmold and dust with cinnamon.

Mrs. Dick
Emily Stone Barton's Book, 1850   *Baltimore*

2½ cups sweetened, mashed raspberries with their   **RASPBERRY**
juice, ¼ cup granulated sugar, juice of ½ lemon,   **SAUCE**
2 tablespoons cornstarch.

Cook raspberries with sugar and lemon juice until soft. Mash through a sieve and add the cornstarch mixed with ¼ cup cold water. Bring slowly to a boil, and stir until clear and thickened.

Sue Cheston Hacker's Book, 1897
The Cottage   *Anne Arundel*

PEACH SAUCE   1 cup sliced peaches, sugar, 1 teaspoon cornstarch, ½ teaspoon almond flavoring or 1 tablespoon peach brandy, ½ cup powdered sugar.

To sliced peaches add sugar to lightly sweeten and extract juice. Set aside for a while, then mash with a fork. Strain and to the juice (about ¼ cup) add cornstarch mixed with a little cold water. Simmer until clear and slightly thickened. Remove from heat and add flavoring or brandy. Mix powdered sugar with mashed peaches, then blend in the cooked sauce. Serve hot or cold on puddings, cake or custard.

Miss Fanny's Receipt Book
West River   *Anne Arundel*

STRAWBERRY   1 quart strawberries, powdered sugar, grated rind
SAUCE   of 1 orange, a little lemon or lime juice, a small glass of currant jelly.

Slice stemmed and washed strawberries and strew with powdered sugar to taste. Sprinkle grated orange rind and a few drops of lemon or lime juice over berries. Beat currant jelly with a fork to soften and stir into berries.

Mrs. Harry R. Slack's Book
Bishop's Road   *Baltimore*

VANILLA SAUCE   1 tablespoon butter, 1 tablespoon flour, 1 cup scalded milk, ½ cup sugar, 1 egg, well beaten; 2 tablespoons cold water, salt, 1 teaspoon vanilla.

Melt butter, blend in flour; add gradually the hot milk and sugar, stirring constantly until the boiling point is reached. Remove from stove and add well-beaten egg, diluted with the cold water. Beat vigorously, adding a pinch of salt and vanilla.

Mrs. Y. Kirkpatrick-Howat
Contee, Rhode River   *Anne Arundel*

La Grange

Cakes

10 egg whites, 2 teaspoons cream of tartar, 1¼ cups sugar, 1 cup sifted flour, 8 egg yolks, 1 teaspoon almond extract, 1 teaspoon vanilla.

BIRTHDAY CAKE

Beat egg whites until foamy. Add cream of tartar and beat until stiff. Gradually add ¼ cup sugar which has been sifted. Sift together remaining cup sugar and all flour 5 times. Beat egg yolks until thick and light. Add flavorings. Fold all into egg white mixture. Bake in an ungreased tube pan in moderate oven (325°) for 1 hour and 15 minutes. Invert pan and cool. Remove and slice in 2 layers. Fill with Mocha Filling and cover outside with White Icing of your choice.

Mocha Filling: 2 tablespoons butter, 2 cups sifted powdered sugar, ¼ cup strong coffee, ¾ cup lightly toasted almonds. Cream butter; gradually add sugar and coffee. Beat until creamy, then add almonds, broken or grated.

Mrs. John M. Lorimer
La Grange

Charles

AMBROSIA CAKE   1 cup butter (scant), 2½ cups powdered sugar, 5 eggs, 1 cup milk, 3 cups flour, 3 heaping teaspoons baking powder, 1 teaspoon fresh orange juice. Mix as any other layer cake and bake in moderate oven for about ½ hour.

Filling: ¾ cup sweet cream, whipped stiff; 2 cups powdered sugar, 1 grated cocoanut, 1 grated orange rind, juice of a medium orange. Mix these ingredients to spreading consistency. Put some of the cocoanut in the filling and sprinkle the rest over the cake.

Mrs. Bradley Worthington   *Washington*

APPLESAUCE   1 cup butter, 2 cups sugar, 2 eggs, ½ teaspoon
CAKE   salt, 3 cups flour, 1 tablespoon cinnamon, 1 tablespoon soda, 1½ teaspoons nutmeg, 1 teaspoon cloves, 2½ cups applesauce, 2 tablespoons corn syrup, 1 cup chopped walnuts, 1 cup raisins, 1 teaspoon vanilla.

Cream butter, add sugar gradually. Add unbeaten eggs, one at a time, and beat well after each addition. Sift all dry ingredients and add alternately with applesauce to which syrup has been added. Add nuts, raisins and vanilla. Bake in a 300° oven for 1½ hours. Makes two loaves.

Mrs. Everard Briscoe   *Calvert*

MISS SUE   ½ cup butter, 2 cups sugar, ½ cake chocolate (4
MUMFORD'S   ounces), 1½ cups milk, yolks of 3 eggs, 2 cups
BLACK   flour, 2 scant teaspoons baking powder, ¼ tea-
CHOCOLATE   spoon baking soda, 1 teaspoon vanilla.
CAKE

Cream butter and 1 cup of sugar together. Put the other cup of sugar, chocolate and ½ cup of milk on the stove and let melt; then add to butter and sugar mixture. Beat in egg yolks. Add flour, sifted with baking powder, alternately with other cup of milk in which soda has been dissolved. Flavor with vanilla and bake in 3 buttered layer cake pans for about 30 minutes in a 350° oven.

Icing: Boil 1 cup cold water with 2 cups granulated sugar until it spins a thread; do not overcook. Beat whites of 2 eggs stiff. Cut ½ cake chocolate in pieces and add to boiling syrup. When melted, pour syrup over egg whites and beat until stiff enough to spread.

Helen Cassin Kinkaid's Book   *Annapolis*

Amish Children Cracking Nuts

A. Aubrey Bodine

Cakes

1 cup butter, 2 cups sugar, 3 cups flour, 2 tea- **BLACK WALNUT**
spoons baking powder, 1 cup milk, 1 cup black **CAKE**
walnut meats, 5 egg whites.

Cream the butter and sugar. Add gradually, alternating with milk, the
flour and baking powder which have been thoroughly sifted together.
Then add the floured nut meats and egg whites, which have been beaten
to a stiff froth. Beat vigorously. Use a funneled cake pan and bake in
a slow oven (325°) for 45-60 minutes. When cool, cover with white
frosting.

Frosting: Moisten powdered sugar with a few drops of almond flavoring.
When smooth, spread over the entire cake. Place the cake in a hot oven
for a few seconds to glace.

Miss Ruby R. Duval
Southgate Avenue   *Annapolis*

Cakes

FRESH COCOANUT CAKE

1 cup butter, 2 cups sugar, 1 teaspoon vanilla, ½ teaspoon almond extract, sprinkle of nutmeg, 5 eggs, 3 cups sifted flour, 2 teaspoons baking powder, ½ teaspoon salt; milk from 1 fresh cocoanut, adding plain milk to make 1 cup.

Cream butter with sugar until very smooth, add vanilla, almond flavoring and nutmeg. Add 3 whole eggs and 2 yolks, one at a time, and beat well (reserving 2 egg whites for icing). Sift flour with baking powder and salt, then add alternately with milk. Mix thoroughly. Pour into 2 greased cake pans. Bake at 350° for about 35 minutes. Remove from pans and cool on racks.

White Boiled Icing: 2 egg whites, pinch of salt, 2 cups granulated sugar, ½ cup hot water, pinch of cream of tartar, ½ teaspoon vanilla, ¼ teaspoon almond extract, grated cocoanut.

Beat egg whites with salt until stiff. Place sugar, hot water and cream of tartar in saucepan and stir well. Boil until mixture forms a thread when dripped from spoon. Pour into egg whites, beating while pouring. Add vanilla and almond flavoring and beat well. Spread icing between layers and sprinkle with cocoanut. Ice top and sides of cake and cover generously with cocoanut.

Mrs. Frank O. Spriggs
Magothy River   *Anne Arundel*

CHRISTMAS GIFT FRUIT CAKE

½ pound chopped citron, ¼ pound lemon peel, ¼ pound orange peel, 1 pound pitted dates, 1 pound dried figs, 1 pound raisins, 1 pound currants, ¼ pound walnut meats, 1 glass strawberry preserves, 1 pound butter, 1 pound sugar, 1 dozen eggs, 1 pound flour, 3 tablespoons molasses, 1 teaspoon soda, Brandy.

Chop citron, lemon and orange peels; halve dates and cut up figs. Flour all fruits and nuts. Cream butter and sugar and beat in eggs. Mix all ingredients; use Brandy with discretion until mixture is right consistency. Bake in buttered pans of desired size for 2 to 3 hours at 275°. Makes about 8 pounds of cake. The receipt may be halved or quartered.

The Commodore's grand-daughters, Katharine del Valle and Valentine Welch, still use this receipt for Christmas gift cakes.

Commodore John Bonnet Marchand's Book, 1862   *Annapolis*

276

John Moll

The Anchorage

Cakes

½ cup butter, 1 cup sugar, 3 eggs, 1½ cups flour, ½ cup milk or water, 1 cup grated fresh cocoanut, ½ pound almonds (shell and blanch), ½ pound citron, ¼ pound conserved pineapple, 1 teaspoon almond extract.

CHRISTMAS NIGHT FRUIT CAKE

Cream butter and add sugar slowly. When thoroughly creamed together, beat in well-beaten egg yolks, then the sifted flour and milk (or water) alternately until well mixed. Stir into batter the cocoanut, almonds (cut into slivers), citron (cut in tiny strips) and cut-up pineapple. Flavor with almond extract, then carefully fold in stiffly beaten egg whites. Bake in three greased and floured layer cake pans in a moderate oven. When cool, put together and ice with white boiled icing.

"You see we always had a party on Christmas night. Our big table was set for fourteen. We had chicken salad, beaten biscuit, hot chocolate, cake and egg-nog. The same people always came and it was really a love feast."

Miss Nellie Shackelford
The Anchorage, Miles River

Talbot

GREAT-GRANDMOTHER CALVERT'S FRUIT CAKE

1 pound seeded raisins, 1 pound currants, ½ pound citron, sliced thin; ½ pound each of candied cherries and pineapple, cut nicely as you please; ½ pound dates—you must cut them fine.

1 pound whole pecan meats, 1 pound ground almonds, 1 pound Brazil nuts, cut thin; 1 pint good Brandy, or ½ Brandy and ½ Sherry Wine; 1 cup dark molasses or 1 pint preserved figs, 1 pound butter, 1 pound brown sugar, 1 dozen eggs, 1 pound sifted flour, pinch of salt, ½ teaspoon soda, 1 teaspoon allspice, slightly rounded; 1 teaspoon each of cinnamon and nutmeg, ¾ teaspoon cloves. (Not an over-spiced cake.)

Prepare fruit and nuts and soak overnight in half the brandy or wine in a tightly covered container. (Keep cut-up dates separate, as they tend to stick together.) The soaking keeps fruit and nuts well apart, makes cake moist and pleasantly aromatic.

The next day, beat butter to a rich cream, then add sugar slowly and beat until fluffy and light. Add molasses and mix well. Beat yolks of eggs until lemon colored, then add to butter mixture and beat very light. Sift flour, salt and soda, mix in spices, and add to mixture, alternating with remaining brandy or sherry. Stir in soaked fruit and nuts. (Only the cut-up dates need be floured lightly.) Beat whites of eggs until stiff and fold them into cake. Bake in a slow oven in greased, paper-lined pans for 3 or 4 hours, according to size. Quantity makes 1 large cake or 2 medium sized ones. When cool wrap in an old napkin moistened with brandy, make airtight and put away in a cool, dark place to mellow.

Mrs. Ford K. Brown
King George Street *Annapolis*

KATE BRICE'S BLACK FRUIT CAKE

1 cup butter, 1 cup sugar, 5 eggs, 2 cups flour, 1 small nutmeg, grated; ½ heaped teaspoon each of mace, cinnamon and allspice, 1 wine glass brandy, juice of ½ lemon, ½ teaspoon soda, 2 pounds stoned raisins, 1½ pounds currants, 1 pound citron, ½ pound blanched almonds.

Cream butter and sugar together. Add eggs, one at a time, beating after each addition. Add flour, sifted with spices, alternately with brandy, which should be added a little at a time, and the lemon juice.

Add soda which has been dissolved in a little warm water. Divide batter into three parts. Put a third of the batter in greased and paper-lined pan, then a layer of raisins, one of currants, one of almonds and one of citron, all lightly floured; then another third of batter with layers of fruit and nuts as before, and cover with remaining third of batter. Let it bake in a slow oven until a straw tests done.

Kate Brice's Book, 1850   *Annapolis*

---

2 cups butter, 2 cups fine sugar, 10 eggs, 1 nut-   **OLD ENGLISH**
meg, grated; 1 teaspoon soda, 1 teaspoon baking   **WHITE**
powder, 4½ cups flour, 1 wine glass rum, 2   **FRUIT CAKE**
oranges, grated peel and juice; 1 teaspoon vanilla,
½ pound citron, 1 pound currants, 2 pounds seeded raisins, 1 pound blanched almonds, flour for dredging fruit.

Cream butter, sugar and eggs in one bowl until very light; sift dry ingredients together in another bowl; dredge fruit and nuts lightly in flour in a third. Then blend dry ingredients into creamed mixture with the rum, orange juice and peel, and vanilla; stir in the floured fruits. Put batter in buttered deep pans, and bake in a moderately slow oven. Small cakes should take 1½ hours, large one 2 hours, but test with a straw. When cool, wrap in a piece of linen moistened with rum, and keep in an air-tight container.

Mrs. Bradley Worthington
Hagerstown   *Washington*

---

1 cup butter, 1 cup sugar, 3 eggs, separated; 1½   **CHERRY NUT**
cups cake flour, 6 ounces marachino cherries, 2   **TEA CAKE**
ounces candied pineapple, 2½ cups pecans, 1
tablespoon lemon extract.

Cream butter and gradually work in sugar until mixture is smooth and light. Blend in well beaten egg yolks. Sift flour over cherries, well drained; pineapple, coarsely chopped; and nuts broken into pieces. Toss mixture with the hands until fruit and nuts are well coated with flour. Stir flour mixture into creamed mixture, and add lemon extract. Beat egg whites stiff but not dry and fold gently into batter until thoroughly mixed. Pour into well oiled loaf pan and bake cake in a slow oven, 300°, for about 1 hour or until it tests done. Let cake cool on rack for 10 minutes, remove from pan, and let cool completely before slicing.

Cmdr. Harrison Colhoun
Old receipt from Windsor   *Anne Arundel*

one of citron, all lightly floured; then another third of batter with layers of fruit and nuts as before, and cover with remaining third of batter. Let it bake in a slow oven until a straw tests done.

Kate Brice's Book, 1850 *Annapolis*

---

2 cups butter, 2 cups fine sugar, 10 eggs, 1 nutmeg, grated; 1 teaspoon soda, 1 teaspoon baking powder, 4½ cups flour, 1 wine glass rum, 2 oranges, grated peel and juice; 1 teaspoon vanilla, ½ pound citron, 1 pound currants, 2 pounds seeded raisins, 1 pound blanched almonds, flour for dredging fruit. **OLD ENGLISH WHITE FRUIT CAKE**

Cream butter, sugar and eggs in one bowl until very light; sift dry ingredients together in another bowl; dredge fruit and nuts lightly in flour in a third. Then blend dry ingredients into creamed mixture with the rum, orange juice and peel, and vanilla; stir in the floured fruits. Put batter in buttered deep pans, and bake in a moderately slow oven. Small cakes should take 1½ hours, large one 2 hours, but test with a straw. When cool, wrap in a piece of linen moistened with rum, and keep in an air-tight container.

Mrs. Bradley Worthington
Hagerstown *Washington*

---

1 cup butter, 1 cup sugar, 3 eggs, separated; 1½ cups cake flour, 6 ounces marachino cherries, 2 ounces candied pineapple, 2½ cups pecans, 1 tablespoon lemon extract. **CHERRY NUT TEA CAKE**

Cream butter and gradually work in sugar until mixture is smooth and light. Blend in well beaten egg yolks. Sift flour over cherries, well drained; pineapple, coarsely chopped; and nuts broken into pieces. Toss mixture with the hands until fruit and nuts are well coated with flour. Stir flour mixture into creamed mixture, and add lemon extract. Beat egg whites stiff but not dry and fold gently into batter until thoroughly mixed. Pour into well oiled loaf pan and bake cake in a slow oven, 300°, for about 1 hour or until it tests done. Let cake cool on rack for 10 minutes, remove from pan, and let cool completely before slicing.

Cmdr. Harrison Colhoun
Old receipt from Windsor *Anne Arundel*

279

The Maryland Scene

Maryland Hunt Cup
A Picnic Hamper

Mint Juleps

Maryland Fried Chicken   Deviled Eggs

For Sandwich Making
Thin sliced home-made bread, buttered   Sliced Maryland Ham
A chilled Garden Bowl containing a bunch of watercress
cucumbers   lettuce   tomatoes

Bread and Butter Pickle

Nut and Raisin Spice Cake   Maryland Fudge Cake

½ cup butter, 1 cup sugar, 2 squares bitter choco-   **MARYLAND**
late, ½ cup flour, ½ teaspoon salt, 2 eggs, 1 tea-   **FUDGE CAKE**
spoon vanilla, 1 cup black walnut meats.

Cream butter and sugar. Melt chocolate over hot water. Sift flour and
salt. Beat eggs very light. Combine ingredients, adding vanilla and
walnut meats. Mix well, and spread on paraffin paper in a shallow
pan. Bake 10 minutes in a hot oven at 400°. Ice and cut in squares.

Icing: 2 teaspoons butter, 1 cup powdered sugar, 2 tablespoons cocoa,
3 tablespoons or less boiling coffee. Cream butter and sugar, add cocoa,
then coffee gradually until of spreading consistency.

Miss L. C. Claude
State Circle   *Annapolis*

½ cup butter, 2 cups sifted flour, 1½ cups granu-   **NUT AND**
lated sugar, 3 teaspoons baking powder, ¼ tea-   **RAISIN**
spoon salt, 1 teaspoon nutmeg, 1 teaspoon cinna-   **SPICE CAKE**
mon, ¼ teaspoon cloves, 1 cup milk, 2 large eggs.

Place butter in mixing bowl, add all dry ingredients, sifted together;
cut in the shortening as you would for pie crust. Add the sweet milk
and eggs, and beat well. Bake in 2 layer pans at 350° for 30 minutes.

Icing: 2½ tablespoons flour, ½ cup granulated sugar, pinch of salt, 1
teaspoon cinnamon, 1 teaspoon nutmeg, ½ cup milk, 1 heaping tablespoon butter, 1 cup raisins, ¾ cup chopped nuts, about 1½ cups confectioners sugar.

Blend dry ingredients in a small saucepan, then stir milk in gradually;
add butter and cook slowly, stirring constantly, until it begins to
thicken a little. Add raisins (which have been plumped in hot water
a few minutes) and continue to cook until it thickens. Remove from
heat and add nuts. Cool slightly, then add enough confectioners sugar
to make the right consistency for spreading between and on top of
layers.

Miss Daisy Magruder
Rockville   *Montgomery*

MRS. BENJAMIN CHEW HOWARD

"Fifty Years in a Maryland Kitchen" by Mrs. B. C. Howard, was published in Baltimore in 1873. Mrs. Howard was 72 years of age when she made this collection of her famous receipts which have been treasured and followed by Marylanders for almost a century. They were representative, in their lavish luxury and skillful use of native Maryland foods, of the high standard of cookery in which Baltimore took a just pride.

Mrs. Howard was born in 1801, and died in the 90th year of her age. She was married in 1818 to Gen. Benjamin Chew Howard when she was but 17 years of age, and began to raise a family which numbered twelve children. In 1827 her husband inherited Belvidere from his father, John Eager Howard, and his accomplished wife became its hostess. Until 1842, when Belvidere was sold, Mrs. Howard received within its hospitable walls many of the leading public figures of the country and fully maintained the high reputation which Belvidere had enjoyed for so long as one of the "foremost seats of elegant hospitality" in the country.

Mrs. Howard undertook the task of compiling her book and was persuaded to acknowledge its authorship "solely for the purpose of aiding certain benevolent undertakings." During her long life she was actively engaged in charitable work, and in 1865 was made president of the Great Southern Relief Association which held a fair in Baltimore city at which nearly $200,000 was raised for the benefit of those who lost their all in the Civil War. She was identified with almost every charitable enterprise which the ladies of Baltimore undertook, and her life was one long career of good works.

A friend wrote of her— "she possessed great earnestness of purpose, a strong and resolute mind, and unfailing energy. Her character was adorned with womanly tenderness, unaffected and simple courtesy, rare charm and uncommon beauty. She was a delightful conversationalist."

It is not to be wondered that Mrs. Howard was a universally beloved figure in her place and time, Baltimore of the 19th century, or that her warm and competent image remains bright in the twentieth.

BELVIDERE

Ground was broken for Belvidere in 1786, but it was eight years before the rambling mansion was completed. Col. John Eager Howard, who built the house, has been described as Maryland's most prominent citizen. Revolutionary War hero, Governor and United States Senator, his three names, John, Eager and Howard are memorialized in Baltimore street names.

The estate came to be known as Howard's Park, dominating the city of Baltimore, the entire area buried in a deep wood. In a day of dueling, more than one supposedly besmirched honor was washed out in blood in obscure, shady corners of the vast estate. Before the Revolution, races were run over John Eager Howard's grounds, between the present Liberty and Greene streets, Baltimore city.

Howard's Park was made freely available to the people of Baltimore for picnics, meetings and community entertainments, and as the growing city began to encroach upon the stately mansion, portions of the grounds were given up as sites for Lexington Market and for Washington Monument and Mount Vernon Place.

Belvidere   Maryland Historical Society

Cakes

JELLY CAKE
ROLLED UP

4 eggs, separated; ¼ teaspoon cream of tartar, ¾ cup sugar, ½ teaspoon vanilla, ½ cup sifted flour, ¼ teaspoon salt, ½ teaspoon baking powder, 1 glass currant or other tart jelly.

Beat egg whites and cream of tartar until stiff but not dry. Gradually beat in half the sugar to form a stiff meringue. Add remaining sugar to the egg yolks and beat well. Add vanilla and combine the two mixtures, then carefully fold in sifted dry ingredients. Pour into a greased jelly roll pan (10½ by 15 inches) which has been lined with waxed paper. Bake in a 350° oven from 15 to 18 minutes. Loosen sides and turn out on towel sprinkled with powdered sugar. Remove waxed paper, trim crusts, spread with jelly and roll up.

Mrs. Benjamin Chew Howard
from original family copy of
Fifty Years in a Maryland Kitchen, 1873
Whitehall Creek   Anne Arundel

HARD
JELLY CAKE

1 cup shortening, 1 cup sugar, 1 egg, 3½ cups flour, 2½ teaspoons baking powder, ½ teaspoon salt, ½ teaspoon nutmeg, ½ cup milk, 1½ glasses red currant jelly.

Cream together the shortening, sugar and egg. Sift dry ingredients and add alternately with milk to creamed mixture. Chill dough. Take a small piece of chilled dough and roll until thin. Select the top of a cooking pot or a small plate of the size desired and, after dough is rolled, place it on top and, using a pie crimper or knife, cut a circle of dough the shape of guide. Using two spatulas, slip one under each side of circle and carefully lift it onto greased cookie sheet. A large cookie sheet holds three 7" circles. Bake at 350° for 8 to 10 minutes.

When browned slightly, remove from oven, place one layer on cake plate, spread with jelly, put another warm layer on top, spread with jelly, and continue in this manner until you have a jelly layer cake with about 10 to 14 layers. To make a pretty cake, before baking the last layer, sprinkle it with red colored sugar crystals. Also, it may be sprinkled with powdered sugar after baking. Makes 2 cakes, 7" in diameter of 10 to 12 layers. This is an old southern Maryland receipt, popular at Christmas time. A Shady Side speciality, it keeps very well and looks festive when sliced thin.

Mrs. Edgar Linton
Shady Side   Anne Arundel

1 cup butter, 2 cups sugar, 4 eggs, 1 cup milk, **LADY**
3 cups flour, 4 teaspoons baking powder, ½ tea- **BALTIMORE**
spoon salt, 1 teaspoon vanilla or almond extract. **CAKE**

Cream butter and sugar together. Add beaten egg yolks, then the milk, alternately with sifted dry ingredients. Add extract and fold in beaten egg whites. Bake in two 9-inch greased cake pans in 350° oven for 35 to 40 minutes.

Filling and icing: 1½ cups sugar, ¼ teaspoon cream of tartar, ¼ teaspoon salt, ⅓ cup cold water, 2 beaten egg whites, one cup chopped raisins, one cup chopped walnuts, 12 figs, finely cut; ½ teaspoon almond or vanilla flavoring.

Mix the first four ingredients and stir until sugar dissolves. Cook on low heat until syrup dropped from a spoon will spin a thread. Keep covered and do not stir while cooking. Pour syrup gradually on beaten egg whites, beating all the while until mixture stands in peaks. Add chopped fruits and nuts and spread on layers as filling and icing.

Mrs. Millard Tydings
Oakington, Susquehanna River *Harford*

½ cup butter, 1 cup brown sugar, 1 cup molasses, **RINGGOLD**
2½ cups flour, 2 teaspoons baking powder, 1 **SOFT**
tablespoon ground ginger, 1 cup cold water. **GINGERBREAD**

Cream butter and sugar, then add molasses. Sift flour with baking powder and ginger and add, alternately with water, to butter mixture. Beat all together well, and pour into greased pan which has been lightly dusted with flour (10″ x 14″), and bake in 350° oven for about half an hour. For a dessert, serve warm with Favorite Pudding Sauce (see Sauces for Puddings).

Adapted from an 18th century receipt
Old Mrs. Ringgold's way, of Chester Towne, about 1795 *Kent*

JONAS
GREEN HOUSE
ORANGE CAKE

2 cups sugar, 4 eggs, 1 orange, 2 cups flour, 2 teaspoons baking powder, ½ cup boiling water.

Add sugar to 4 yolks and 2 whites of eggs (saving 2 whites for icing) and beat full of bubbles. Add grated rind and juice of orange, then flour and baking powder, sifted. Mix, add water and beat very hard. Bake in moderate oven (350°) in ungreased tube pan.

Icing: 2 egg whites, powdered sugar, 1 orange. Beat whites of eggs until stiff. Add enough sugar and the orange juice and rind to consistency for spreading.

Evelyn Green Bowers
Jonas Green House   *Annapolis*

MRS. CHEW'S
POUND CAKE

1 pound butter (2 cups), ½ to 1 teaspoon mace, 1 pound sugar (2¼ cups), 10 eggs, separated; 1 pound fine flour, sifted (4 cups); ½ teaspoon salt, 1 teaspoon vanilla, 2 tablespoons brandy or 8 drops of rose water.

While butter is softening, sprinkle over it the mace, so that the flavor may be absorbed. Cream butter; add sugar and cream together until very light and fluffy. Beat in egg yolks, one at a time; beat thoroughly. Fold in the sifted dry ingredients, the vanilla, brandy or rose water, and at the last, the stiffly beaten egg whites. Pour batter into greased loaf pans, or large tube pan. Bake at 300° for an hour and a quarter to an hour and a half, until cake is golden brown and slightly shrunken from sides of pan.

Revised from the 1814 Account Book
Harwood Papers   *Annapolis*

CHESTON'S
SPONGE CAKE

8 large eggs, 2 cups sugar, juice and grated rind of 1 large lemon, 1 cup sifted flour.

Beat egg yolks with sugar. Add lemon juice and rind, then mix in flour. Lastly, fold in stiffly beaten whites of eggs. Bake in ungreased tube pan at 325° for about 1 hour, or straw test. Turn upside down and cool before removing cake from pan. Makes 26 cup cakes or 1 large cake in tube pan.

Mrs. Robert S. Burwell
West River   *Anne Arundel*

Jonas Green House

Francis E. Engle

Cakes

¾ cup butter, 2 cups sugar, 4 eggs, 3 cups sifted flour, 1 tablespoon cinnamon, 1 tablespoon cloves, 1 teaspoon nutmeg, 1 cup sour milk, 4 tablespoons molasses, 2 teaspoons soda, 1 cup chopped raisins.

PRINCE OF WALES CAKE

Cream butter and sugar, and add well-beaten eggs. Sift dry ingredients (except soda), and add them to butter mixture alternately with sour milk. Warm molasses slightly, and stir into it the soda which has been dissolved in a little warm water. Add it to cake batter with the chopped raisins. Bake in deep buttered cake tin in a moderate oven (350°) until cake tests done.

Icing: 1½ cups brown sugar, 1 cup milk, 2 tablespoons butter. Boil all together until a drop hardens in water. Cool and add vanilla.

Mrs. James Waring
Southampton

St. Mary's

287

SEVEN SEAS
CAKE
2 eggs, 1 cup sugar, 1 cup flour, 1 teaspoon baking powder, ½ cup milk, 1 tablespoon butter, 1 teaspoon vanilla.

Beat the eggs until thick and lemon colored. Add sugar, very little at a time, beating constantly. Gradually add flour, sifted with baking powder. Then, slowly add milk and butter, which have been heated just to the boiling point; add vanilla. Bake at 350° for 30 to 35 minutes in an ungreased pan.

Icing: 3 tablespoons butter, 2 tablespoons cream, 5 tablespoons brown sugar, ½ cup cocoanut. Make these measurements generous. Heat butter, cream and sugar just until sugar is melted. Add cocoanut, mix well; spread on hot cake as it comes from the oven. Put under broiler until it bubbles and is brown. This cake freezes wonderfully. It also keeps fresh for days on end. Use fresh or prepared cocoanut.

Mrs. Paul Heineman
Weems Creek   *Annapolis*

———————

WHIPPED
CREAM CAKE
1 cup heavy cream, 1 cup sugar, 2 eggs, 1 teaspoon vanilla, 1½ cups cake flour, 2 teaspoons baking powder, ¼ teaspoon salt.

Whip cream until very thick but not too stiff; fold in sugar gradually, then the beaten eggs. Add vanilla and gently fold in the flour, baking powder and salt, which have been sifted together. Mix only until smooth. Fill two 9-inch cake tins or 1 dozen cup cake tins, greased and floured, and bake in a moderate oven (350°) about 30 minutes. This is an easy cake to mix, the cream taking the place of shortening and milk. It makes a soft, moist cake. Double the ingredients for a four layer cake. Use any desired filling and icing.

Miss Fanny's Receipt Book
West River   *Anne Arundel*

Ridout House Silver, 1770

Francis E. Engle

Little Cakes and Cookies

6 cups flour, 2 cups brown sugar, 1 cup butter, **ALBANY CAKES**
2 ounces cinnamon, 1 tablespoon soda, 1 cup
milk, 1 egg.

Mix flour and sugar first, then work in butter; add cinnamon. Dissolve
soda in milk, mix egg with the milk and work in dough. Roll out a
snake by hand (a round roll about 5 inches long), then roll this in
sugar, being careful that the sugar sticks on the outside and does not
get worked into the dough. Twist around in small cakes like a snail
shell, or tie like a pretzel, and bake about 10 minutes in a hot oven,
watching carefully.

Receipts from The Anchorage, Miles River
Mrs. Levin Campbell
Annapolis

½ cup butter, 1 cup powdered sugar, ½ cup milk, **SPREAD**
pinch of salt, 1 cup flour, ¼ teaspoon almond **ALMOND**
extract, ¾ cup or more chopped almonds. **FANCIES**

Cream butter and sugar, add milk and salt, then flour and almond
extract. Spread as thin as possible on buttered cookie sheet and sprinkle
on the nuts. Bake in slow oven. Take from oven, cut in small squares.

Mrs. Page Bowie
Bay Ridge Farm
Anne Arundel

Little Cakes and Cookies

**DAINTY
CUP CAKES**

1 cup butter, 2 cups sugar, 4 eggs, 3 cups flour, 2 teaspoons baking powder, ¼ teaspoon nutmeg, 1 cup milk, 1 teaspoon lemon or vanilla extract.

Cream butter, gradually adding sugar; add beaten egg yolks, then flour, sifted with baking powder and nutmeg, alternately with milk. Blend in flavoring and beat well. Lastly, fold in stiffly beaten egg whites. Bake in buttered cup cake tins 20-25 minutes in 325° oven. Cool and cover with icing of your choice—chocolate, orange or lemon.

Sarah Gill's way
Waverly Receipts

Queen Anne's

KISSES

3 egg whites, pinch of salt, 1 cup superfine sugar, 1 teaspoon vanilla.

Beat egg whites with salt until stiff. Add sugar very gradually and continue beating until mixture stands in peaks and sugar is dissolved. Fold in vanilla. Grease a large baking sheet and drop small spoonfuls of the meringue, shaping in spiral cones, or put through a pastry bag. Bake in slow oven, 250°, for 30 to 40 minutes. They should be dry but not browned. Do not overbake. Will make about 3 dozen Kisses, or 10 Meringue Shells.

Mrs. Murray's Bride's Book, 1858
Ivy Neck, Rhode River

Anne Arundel

LADY FINGERS

7 eggs, 1 cup sugar, 1 teaspoon baking powder, 1 saltspoon salt, 1 teaspoon vanilla, 1 cup sifted flour.

Beat egg whites stiff and add sugar gradually. Fold in beaten egg yolks with baking powder and salt. Add vanilla. Sift in flour, stirring gently all the while. Press dough through pastry tube into lady finger shapes of desired size. Place them on brown paper, sprinkle with powdered sugar and bake slightly less than 10 minutes in a 350° oven.

Gertrude Allison Brewster
Olney Inn

Montgomery

1 pound shelled almonds, rose water or almond **MACAROONS**
extract, whites of 3 eggs, 2 cups sugar.

Blanch almonds with boiling water, then throw them into cold water
and skin them. Dry with a cloth, pound in a mortar—not too fine.
Moisten while beating with a little rose water (or almond extract).
Beat whites of eggs very light and fold in sifted sugar, then the almonds.
Drop them on unglazed paper on a cookie sheet and bake in a 300°
oven for 30 minutes. Dampen back of paper to remove.

Mrs. Henry Ogle's way
Ivy Neck Book, 1858
Anne Arundel

---

1 cup butter, ½ cup sugar, 3 eggs, 3 cups flour, **MAIDS OF**
½ teaspoon salt, 3 teaspoons baking powder, 2 **HONOUR**
cups strawberry jam, ½ cup walnuts or pecans
(chopped), whipped cream.

Cream butter and sugar, add eggs and beat very light. Stir in flour,
salt and baking powder (sift first together). Form into small balls
the size of walnuts. Place in little greased muffin tins or gem pans.
Dip the bottom of a glass (slightly smaller in diameter than the muffin
tins) lightly in flour and press down in center of dough to form a cup.
Fill center with jam and nuts mixed. Bake in quick oven, 400°, for
15 minutes. Take from pans while warm, and when cool, decorate tops
with whipped cream. Makes about 3 dozen.

Mrs. Charles dePeyster Valk
Duke of Gloucester Street
Annapolis

---

1 cup butter, 1½ cups brown sugar, 3 eggs, 1 tea- **ROCKS**
spoon cinnamon, 1 teaspoon soda, 2½ cups flour,
1 pound English walnuts (shelled and chopped), 1 pound raisins
(seeded), 1 pound citron (cut fine).

Cream butter and sugar, add well-beaten eggs and beat well; add sifted
dry ingredients, using some of the flour mixture to lightly coat the
nuts and fruit. Drop by teaspoonfuls on greased cookie pan. Bake at
350° for about 15 minutes. Keep in stone crock.

Mrs. Frank W. Mish, Jr.
Washington

Georgian Silver Kettle
Hammond-Harwood House

Little Cakes and Cookies

NUT AND RAISIN TEA CAKES ½ cup butter, ½ cup brown sugar, ½ cup white sugar, 2 eggs, 6 tablespoons milk, 1 teaspoon vanilla, ½ cup pecan meats, ½ cup raisins, 1½ cups flour, 1½ teaspoons baking powder, pinch of salt.

Cream butter with brown sugar, then gradually add white sugar and continue creaming until mixture is light. Stir in beaten egg yolks. Sift flour, baking powder and salt and add to creamed mixture alternately with milk. Add vanilla and stir in nuts and raisins. At the last, fold in stiffly beaten egg whites. Bake in little buttered muffin tins in a moderate oven, 350°. If icing is desired, Caramel is the most delicious choice.

Mrs. Charles Parrish
Helen Cassin Kinkaid's Book *Annapolis*

PECAN CRESCENTS 1 cup ground pecans, 1 cup real butter (no substitute), ¾ cup sugar, 2½ cups sifted flour, 1½ teaspoons vanilla, confectioners sugar.

Combine the ground nuts, softened butter, and sugar. Mix well; stir in flour, then vanilla. Knead to a smooth dough. Break off small pieces (about a teaspoonful) and shape into crescents by rolling a piece an inch and a half long and turning ends to form a crescent. Place on ungreased cookie sheet and bake in moderate oven (350°) until slightly browned (about 15 minutes). Have some vanilla sugar handy in which to roll the crescents while still warm. After they have cooled, roll again in the sugar. This is confectioners sugar which has been tightly closed in a jar with a vanilla bean for several days or longer.

Miss Fanny's Receipt Book
West River *Anne Arundel*

3 eggs, 1 cup sugar, juice of ½ lemon, grated   **LITTLE**
rind of 1 lemon, ½ cup flour.   **SPONGE CAKES**

Separate eggs and beat yolks very light. Add sugar, lemon juice and rind and beat some more (about 3 minutes in electric mixer), then add flour. Be sure to use only ½ cup flour. Beat whites until stiff and add last. Spoon into cup cake molds or muffin tins, unbuttered, and bake about 30 minutes in a slow oven.

Mrs. W. A. Boykin, Jr.
Ruxton
    Baltimore

½ cup molasses, ½ cup butter, ⅔ cup sugar, 1   **BRANDY SNAPS**
cup flour, 3 teaspoons ginger, ¼ teaspoon salt.

Boil molasses, add butter, and sift all other ingredients together into this, beating and mixing well until all are incorporated. Drop batter from a small spoon onto a buttered cookie sheet, about 2 inches apart. Bake in a slow oven for 12 to 15 minutes. They burn easily, so do not let them get dark. Scrape them off immediately and roll around a wooden spoon handle. Fill with whipped cream and serve cold. These rolls keep well when protected from the air, to be used when wanted for tea or dessert.

J. Harrison Colhoun
Windsor
    Anne Arundel

---

1 cup butter, 2 cups dark brown sugar, 2 eggs,   **BROWN SUGAR**
3 cups flour, 1 teaspoon baking powder, ¼ tea-   **COOKIES**
spoon baking soda, 1 well-rounded tablespoon
cinnamon, grated rind of 1 orange.

Cream butter and sugar; when well creamed, add eggs, beaten light. Sift dry ingredients together, and stir into creamed mixture with grated orange rind. When well mixed, shape into roll and place in icebox for several hours. Cut off small amount at a time, roll out thin and cut with cookie cutter. (Use as little flour as possible.) Sprinkle with cinnamon sugar before baking. Bake in oven at 250°, or faster if desired, but watch out so they will not burn.

Mrs. Carroll Alden
Taney Avenue
    Annapolis

CHOCOLATE THINS   1 square (1 ounce) unsweetened chocolate, ¼ cup butter, ½ cup sugar, 1 egg, ¼ cup sifted flour, ⅛ teaspoon salt, ¼ cup finely chopped walnuts, pecans or Brazil nuts.

Melt chocolate and butter over low heat. Remove from stove and add sugar, stirring well. Beat in egg, add flour and salt; mix well. Turn batter into two buttered 8-inch square pans and spread evenly and thinly with spatula. Sprinkle with nut meats. Bake 12 to 15 minutes in 375° oven, watching carefully. While warm mark into 2-inch squares. Cut and break into crisp squares.

Mrs. Robert Mackey   *Cecil*

CEDAR PARK GINGER CAKES   ½ cup butter, 1 cup granulated sugar, 1 cup black molasses, 2 cups flour, ½ teaspoon soda, 2 tablespoons ground ginger, 1 teaspoon cinnamon.

Cream butter and sugar together. Mix with molasses, then sift in flour, with soda, ginger and cinnamon. Add enough more flour slowly to prevent stickiness. Chill dough in refrigerator for easier handling. Roll thin, cut out cookies and bake in 400° oven.

Mrs. Eveleth W. Bridgman, Jr.
Cedar Park, West River   *Anne Arundel*

SOFT GINGER CAKES   1½ cups dark brown sugar, 1 cup butter, 1 cup dark molasses, 2 eggs, 1 cup sour cream, 3½ cups flour, 2 teaspoons soda (scant), 2 teaspoons ginger, 2 teaspoons cinnamon.

Combine sugar, butter and molasses; then beat in eggs, then sour cream. Sift flour with soda, ginger and cinnamon and add to mixture, making a soft dough. Drop from teaspoon onto greased baking sheets and bake in moderate oven.

Mrs. A. Calvert
Maryland Cook Book, 1892   *Annapolis*

1 cup butter, 2 cups sugar, 2 eggs, 4 cups flour, **MRS. LLOYD'S**
2 teaspoons baking powder, ½ teaspoon ground **JUMBLES**
mace, ⅓ cup sweet cream, 1 teaspoon vanilla.

Cream butter and sugar, beat in eggs, then stir in flour with baking powder and mace. Blend in cream and flavor with vanilla. Make up overnight, chill, and next morning roll out very thin. Cut into shapes and place jumbles on a greased baking sheet. Bake in 350° oven until light brown. This is a splendid receipt. It improves the appearance to have a few whole raisins and half nuts to lay on top of the cakes.

Mrs. Lloyd's way, of the Eastern Shore
Wye House
                                                    Talbot

Maryland House and Garden Pilgrimage   *Wye House*

Little Cakes and Cookies

OLD AUNTIE'S WHISKEY JUMBLES — 1 cup butter, 1¼ cups light brown sugar (firmly packed), 1 egg, 2½ cups flour, 1½ teaspoons ground nutmeg, pinch of salt, ½ cup rye whiskey.

Cream butter and sugar, add egg and beat well. Sift flour with nutmeg and salt. Pour whiskey very gradually on creamed mixture, beating all the while. Add sifted flour, mix well, and put in refrigerator to stiffen. When ready to make, take a small piece of dough and roll with the hand on a board and shape into rings about the size of a hen's egg. Place on a greased baking sheet, and bake for about 15 minutes in a 400° oven. Remove from oven, put on waxed paper and do not pile until cold. When shaping the jumbles, use flour if necessary to prevent sticking to the hands. Makes about 2 dozen jumbles. This is one half of old receipt.

Mrs. Charles Greenwell
Foxes Point   *St. Mary's*

JANE'S LEMON COOKIES — 1 cup butter, 1 cup sugar, 2 tablespoons lemon juice, 1 egg, 1 teaspoon grated lemon rind, 2½ cups sifted flour, ¼ teaspoon salt, ¼ teaspoon soda.

Cream butter, sugar and lemon juice well. Add beaten egg and lemon rind. Sift flour, salt and soda and add a little at a time. Roll dough thin, cut out cookies and bake at 400° to start, then lower heat.

Mrs. Truxtun Beale's Book, 1903
Decatur House   *Washington*

OATMEAL TEA COOKIES — 1 cup butter, 1 cup sugar, ½ cup sour milk, 1 teaspoon soda, 2½ cups flour, 1 cup quick oatmeal, rolled fine; ¼ teaspoon salt.

Cream shortening and sugar together; add milk and soda. Add flour, oatmeal and salt to make a soft dough. Chill, roll thin and cut out. Bake at 400° until light brown. A delicious cookie with tea as it is not too sweet. It is crisp, delicate and quite unlike the usual oatmeal cookie.

Mrs. William Erwin Lee
Bethesda   *Montgomery*

SAND TARTS

1 cup butter, 2 cups sugar, 4 cups well sifted flour, 3 eggs, leaving out one white, cinnamon sugar, almond halves.

Cream butter and sugar, then add flour and well beaten eggs, alternately, kneading well. Set on ice overnight or longer. Then roll out very thin and cut out. Wash each cookie with white of egg, sprinkle with cinnamon sugar and stick an almond on each. Bake on greased cookie sheet about 8 minutes at 375°. Watch, as they burn easily. (Quantity of old receipt has been reduced and modern measures used.)

Mrs. Harold Knapp
Bowieville

Prince George's

SHREWSBURY CAKES

1 cup butter, 1½ cups sugar, 3 cups flour, ½ nutmeg, grated; ⅓ cup dried currants, 2 eggs, 1 or more tablespoons brandy.

Beat butter to a cream; add sugar gradually, beating until light, then add flour, nutmeg, and currants, washed and dried. Now moisten with the eggs, well beaten; brandy to flavor well. If batter is too dry, you may add another egg. Knead well, roll the paste out thin; cut with a round cutter of a fair size with a scalloped edge. Bake in a moderate oven until a nice brown.

Mrs. Snowden's way
Miss Ann Chase's Book, 1811

Annapolis

SPICE COOKIES

½ cup butter, ½ cup shortening, 3 cups sugar, 3 eggs, 4 cups flour, 5 tablespoons each cinnamon and cloves, ½ teaspoon salt, 3 tablespoons milk.

Cream shortening, add sugar and mix well; add beaten eggs, then flour —one cupful at a time (sifted with spices and salt) alternately with milk. Roll out to ⅛ inch thickness on well floured board. Cut out and bake on greased baking sheet in 400° oven for 12-15 minutes. Makes about 100 very spicy cookies. Good with punch or egg nog.

Anna Ridout McFadden
Rousby Hall, Patuxent River

Calvert

SUGAR CAKES　　1 cup granulated sugar, ½ cup butter, 1 egg, 2¼ cups sifted flour, ⅓ teaspoon ground mace, 1 teaspoon baking powder, 3 tablespoons sweet cream.

Cream sugar and butter; add unbeaten egg and mix well. Sift flour, mace and baking powder; then mix in, with cream, to butter mixture and stir well. Drop dough by teaspoonfuls onto greased cookie sheet. Pat each one thin. Bake in a 350° oven until light brown, 12 to 15 minutes. Take off sheet while hot.

Mrs. James M. Hemphill
Elkridge　　　　　　　　　　　　　　　　　　　　　　　　*Howard*

WALNUT　　　　1 cup brown sugar, 2 eggs, 2½ tablespoons sifted
WAFERS　　　　flour, pinch of salt, 1 cup shelled walnuts, broken, not chopped; ½ teaspoon vanilla.

Stir brown sugar and unbeaten eggs together until sugar dissolves, but do not beat thin; then add flour, salt, nuts and vanilla. Drop half teaspoon of mixture on well-buttered pans and cook in moderate oven (325°) not too quickly. Slide sharp flat knife under each wafer while still a little warm, then they will not break. Also good with hazel nuts. Makes 2½ dozen.

Mrs. James M. Petty, Jr.
Shelburne House　　　　　　　　　　　　　　　　　　*Anne Arundel*

WHISKEY　　　　1 cup butter, ¾ cup sugar, 2 eggs (small), 2 cups
NUT COOKIES　　flour (or enough to make a dough stiff enough to roll), ½ pound pecans, ground; ½ cup whiskey, powdered sugar, cinnamon.

Put butter in mixing bowl and work soft with hands. Add sugar and cream smooth; add eggs, working in with hands; add part whiskey and part flour. Mix about half of flour with pecans. Alternately add the flour, pecans and whiskey until dough is stiff enough to roll out. Then roll thin and cut in strips. Bake in slow oven (325°)—do not brown. When cold, dip in mixture of powdered sugar and cinnamon. These will keep indefinitely. (This is one-half quantity of old receipt.)

Augusta Tucker Townsend
Pendennis Mount, Severn River　　　　　　　　　　*Anne Arundel*

The Maryland Scene

Christmas Greens Day
at
The Hammond-Harwood House

Wassail

Cookies

Albany Cakes	Shrewsbury Cakes
Jumbles	Sand Tarts
Brown Sugar Cookies	Cedar Park Ginger Cakes
Oatmeal Tea Cookies	Jane's Lemon Cookies
Sugar Cakes	Spice Cookies

Pecan Crescents

Ready for Winter   A. Aubrey Bodine

Pickles, Relishes and Preserves

Pickles

HOMEWOOD   2 pecks fully ripe tomatoes, 1 quart cider vinegar,
SWEET   4 pounds brown sugar, 1 ounce whole cloves, 1
TOMATO PICKLE   ounce whole allspice.

Scald and skin tomatoes, cutting only the very large ones in half and
leaving the rest whole. Place in kettle with the vinegar, brown sugar
and spices (which have been sewn in a cheesecloth bag for later
removal). Place on fire and boil furiously for 30 minutes. Then simmer
for 2¼ to 2¾ hours. Stir only to prevent boiling. Result should be
quite stiff, but not as stiff as jam. Do not drive all vinegar off, but jar
whole lot. Tomatoes should be as whole as possible. Turn jars upside
down until cool. Some time can be saved by pouring off the juice after
first half hour of boiling. Set tomatoes aside, boil juice down, and join
it again with tomatoes. Heat and jar.

Richard Randall   *Baltimore*

16 to 20 cups sliced cucumbers (not peeled), 6 or 7 onions, sliced; ½ cup salt. Arrange cucumbers and onions in layers in a large container, sprinkling each layer with salt. Cover this mixture with ice and let chill for 3 hours.

BREAD AND BUTTER PICKLES

Mix and bring to a boil: 4 cups sugar, 2 tablespoons mustard seed, 1 teaspoon celery seed, ½ teaspoon ground cloves, ½ teaspoon turmeric, 4 cups vinegar, 1 cup water. Drain cucumbers, pour the above hot mixture over them and bring to a boil. Pack in hot sterilized jars and seal.

Mrs. Harold Butler
Southwood Avenue

Annapolis

---

1 quart each of small snapbeans, green tomatoes (cut), cauliflower, in small flowerettes; large cucumbers (cut in pieces), small cucumbers, whole; small onions, whole; 3 small red peppers, 3 green peppers, cut in rings.

MUSTARD PICKLE

Put all in strong brine made of 6 pints water and 1½ pints salt. Let stand 24 hours, then scald in brine and drain. Make a paste of 9 heaping tablespoons of ground mustard, 1½ heaping tablespoons of turmeric, 1½ cups of flour and 1½ pints of vinegar. Mix mustard, turmeric and flour together, moisten with a little vinegar until smooth, then add remaining vinegar slowly until the consistency of cream. Boil 3 quarts of vinegar, stir in the paste and cook until it thickens. Take off fire and add 1½ cups sugar. Pour whole over pickle. Makes 1 gallon, 1 pint. This is a great deal of trouble in the making but very rewarding. I assure you it is a very fine pickle.

Given by Admiral George Dewey's wife to
Mrs. Dennis Claude Handy

Annapolis

---

1 peck green tomatoes, 8 large onions (I use Spanish), 6 green peppers, 2 red peppers (optional, nice for color), 10 tablespoons salt, 1 cup vinegar (for vinegar water), 2 quarts vinegar, 4 pounds brown sugar, 4 ounces mustard seed, 2 ounces celery seed, 2 ounces cinnamon, 2 ounces cloves (whole), 1 ounce allspice (whole), 1 ounce allspice (ground), 2 ounces whole ginger, 1 tablespoon Coleman's mustard.

GREEN TOMATO PICKLE

Slice tomatoes and onions thin. Cut green peppers in small pieces. Sprinkle salt over vegetables and let stand 10 to 12 hours. Drain and wash well. Add 1 cup vinegar to 1 gallon water; pour over tomatoes and boil 25 minutes. Drain and discard water. Mix vinegar and brown sugar and stir to make a syrup. Tie spices, except mustard, in a muslin bag; add tomatoes, red peppers (if used), and spices to syrup, then add mustard. Cook slowly until a good dark green and syrup not too runny, usually about two hours. Use enamel pot, never aluminum. Put up in sterilized glass jars.

Mrs. E. H. Richardson
Naylor   *Prince George's*

SWEET CUCUMBER RINGS

Take 10 pounds brown sugar and cover with 3 pints of cider vinegar. Put in 1 cup whole black peppers and 1 cup whole allspice.

While this is heating, cut 50 large, sour cucumber pickles into a jar or crock. Sprinkle through as you cut, ½ dozen onions, cut up fine. Pour over them 1 cup olive oil. When vinegar and sugar, etc., have come to a boil, add 2 cups of Tarragon vinegar and pour all over the pickle. Tie up, and in 2 or 3 days turn out and mix well before putting into jars.

This receipt was handed down from the daughter of Maury the Great Navigator.

Miss Nellie Shackelford
The Anchorage, Miles River   *Talbot*

SOUTHAMPTON PICKLED FIGS

5 pounds fresh figs, 8 cups white sugar, 2 cups vinegar, 2 tablespoons mustard seed, 2 tablespoons whole cloves, 4 pieces stick cinnamon, 2 tablespoons whole allspice.

Wash figs in a solution of soda and water but do not peel. Make a syrup of the vinegar, sugar and spices and boil 8 to 10 minutes. Add figs, bring to a boil and boil 10 minutes. Allow to stand until next morning, then bring to full rolling boil. Do this 3 times. Cool and pack in jars.

Ethel K. Waring
Southampton   *St. Mary's*

Pare rind and cut in pieces. Place in sauce pan **CITRON OR**
with layer of rind and layer of grape leaves. Cover **WATERMELON**
with boiling water, adding 1 teaspoon alum to **PICKLE**
sauce pan full. Cook until clear. Drain and put
in stone bowl or crock and pour over it a syrup made of 1 pound of
white sugar to 1 pound rind, and ½ pint white vinegar to each pound
of sugar. Spices for 6 or 7 pounds of rind are: 1 tablespoon whole cloves,
1 tablespoon cinnamon sticks, ½ nutmeg, grated. Drain off syrup each
day, bring to the boil and pour over rind. Do this for 6 days, then bottle.
The grape leaves give a nice green color, the alum crispness to the pickle.

Gizelle Bowdoin's receipt
Mrs. W. T. Murray

Anne Arundel

Rind of large watermelon peeled, pink fruit cut **GINGERED**
out. Cut in 1-inch pieces. Cover fruit with water, **WATERMELON**
add 1 ounce of ground ginger and boil until rind **PICKLE**
is tender and pricked easily with a fork. Drain.

Mix 1 ounce whole cloves, 1 ounce stick cinnamon, and sew in small
cheese-cloth bags, 4 to 6 bags. Put fruit, 10 pounds of granulated sugar
and spice bags into a kettle and cover with vinegar, about 3 quarts.
Boil 10 minutes. Remove rind when transparent and put in stone
crock. Boil syrup and bags until syrup thickens, then pour over fruit
in crock with spice bags. Cover, put away and do not use for a year
preferably.

Mrs. Robert E. Lee George
Ruxton

Baltimore

---

7 pounds small peaches, 3 pounds sugar, 1½ **PICKLED**
cups vinegar, ½ cup water, whole cloves. **PEACHES**

Peel peaches and stick a clove in each. Mix sugar, vinegar and water
and bring to a boil. Add enough peaches to be covered by syrup. Cook
until straw pushes easily to seed. Pack in hot sterilized jars. Fill with
hot syrup and seal jars.

Mrs. Donald E. Jefferson

Caroline

PICKLED Wash fruit; cook unpeeled. Remove stems of
PEACHES pears. Allow 2 quarts vinegar to ½ kettle of
OR PEARS water, using enough liquid to cover fruit. Add
enough sugar for heavy syrup. Add at least ½ box
of stick cinnamon (break up sticks); add ⅓ box of whole cloves. Boil
hard; cook until soft, but do not break skins. Remove fruit carefully.
Place in crock, covering with syrup. Cool and cover with cloth.

Mrs. Frank W. Mish, Jr.   *Washington*

TO PICKLE The walnuts should be gathered when the nut is
ENGLISH so young you can run a pin into it easily; about
WALNUTS June is the usual time. Pour boiling salt and
water on, and let them be covered with it nine
days, changing it every third day. Take them out and spread on dishes
and expose to the air for a short time when you change the water;
this makes them black much sooner. To a two gallon pot strew over
them one ounce of whole black peppers, half an ounce of cloves, an
ounce of mace, an ounce of allspice, a piece or so of garlic, a pint
of mustard seed, a pint of horseradish, scraped and dried, and two
pounds of brown sugar. Cover the whole with boiling vinegar.

Mrs. George Tabb's receipt
Mrs. Frederick W. Brune's Book, 1860   *Baltimore*

TO PICKLE Wash the fruit and stick in several places with
DAMSONS a fork. To 3 pounds of fruit add 2 pounds of
sugar and 1 pint of vinegar. Scald the vinegar
and sugar for 9 successive days and pour it on the fruit, taking care the
first day to have it merely warm, to avoid splitting the damsons.
Tie your spices up in a muslin bag and put them in the jar the first
day. To a 2 gallon jar of fruit put 2 tablespoons of mace and 1 of cloves
not pounded.

Mrs. George Tabb's receipt
Mrs. Frederick W. Brune's Book, 1860   *Baltimore*

Relishes

1 peck of peeled ripe tomatoes, 6 large onions, **SANDY SPRING**
4 bunches of celery, 5 green peppers, 4 ounces **QUAKER RELISH**
salt, 1 ounce celery seed, 1 ounce mustard seed,
2½ pints vinegar, 2 pounds brown sugar.

This relish does not have to be cooked. Chop vegetables and sprinkle
them with salt; drain in a sugar sack over night. Dissolve sugar in the
vinegar and mix in celery and mustard seeds. Mix well and seal in
air-tight containers. Yields about 4 quarts.

Gertrude Allison Brewster
Olney Inn
Montgomery

---

24 red peppers, 24 green peppers, 12 medium **PEPPER RELISH**
onions, 3 cups sugar, 5 cups vinegar, 3 teaspoons
salt.

Cut up peppers and onions and put through a chopper. Cover with
boiling water and let stand for 15 minutes. Strain; add sugar, salt and
vinegar. Bring to a boil and simmer for 35 to 40 minutes. Pack in hot,
sterile jars and seal.

Mrs. Compton Swann
St. Mary's

---

7 pounds red peppers, 4 pounds sugar, 1 pint **RED PEPPER**
vinegar. **RELISH, ARABY**

Cut off stems, remove seeds and put in weak salt water over night.
In the morning, drain, cut in thin strips, add 1 cup water and put on
to boil with the sugar until syrup is thick. Let simmer until peppers
are nearly transparent, then add vinegar and cook until peppers are
transparent and limp. Put in jars and seal. Very good with ham.

Mrs. Frank Jack Fletcher
Araby
Charles

305

CORN RELISH   12 ears fresh, green corn; 4 large ripe tomatoes, 6 green sweet peppers, 6 tablespoons salt, 1⅓ cups sugar, 1 small head cabbage, 2 hot red peppers, 6 onions, 3 teaspoons ground mustard, 2 pints vinegar.

Cut corn from cob, scoring kernels down each row. Scald tomatoes, skin them and cut into small pieces. Dice other vegetables very fine; mix all ingredients together, boil for 30 minutes and seal.

Mrs. Harry R. Slack's Book
Bishop's Road   *Baltimore*

SPICED   5 pounds Dolgo crabapples, whole cloves, 7 cups
CRABAPPLES   sugar, 2 cups cider vinegar, 2 cups water, 2—4-inch sticks cinnamon.

Choose apples which are colored but just ripened, not mellow. Rinse well, leaving stems on. Stick a whole clove in blossom end of each apple. Bring to a boil in a large kettle the sugar, vinegar, water and cinnamon. Add apples and boil gently, turning apples in syrup until they are tender when pricked. Pack into clean, hot quart jars. Cover with boiling syrup and seal.

Mrs. Crain's Way
Miss Ann Chase's Book, 1811   *Annapolis*

PEACH   4 pounds peaches, 2 medium onions, 1 clove
CHUTNEY   garlic, 1 cup raisins, 2 tablespoons mustard seed, ¼ pound chopped candied ginger, 2 tablespoons chili powder, 1¼ pounds brown sugar, 1 quart vinegar.

Peel peaches, cut in pieces and chop fine. Chop onions, garlic and raisins fine, or put through food grinder. Mix together in a large heavy saucepan, add mustard seed, ginger, chili powder and sugar. Pour in vinegar and stir well over fire until it begins to boil. Boil until mixture thickens, stirring occasionally; then lower heat and simmer until quite thick, stirring frequently or it will scorch. Pour into hot jars and seal.

Miss Fanny's Receipt Book
West River   *Anne Arundel*

4 apples, chopped fine; 4 peppers (2 of them red, **APPLE**
2 green); 6 tomatoes, peeled; 4 large onions, **CHUTNEY**
chopped; ¼ cup salt, ½ pound brown sugar, ½
pound raisins, chopped; 1 quart vinegar, ½ ounce ginger. Chop all
ingredients fine and boil them together until thick. This makes 6 pints.

Rodgers' Papers
Sion Hill
                                                    Harford

---

3 quarts gooseberries (washed, headed and **SPICED**
tailed), 1 pint vinegar, 4 pounds sugar, 2 table- **GOOSEBERRIES**
spoons cinnamon, 1 tablespoon ground cloves,
1 tablespoon ground allspice.

Cook all together until thick, stirring often. It will take about 2 hours.
Pour into sterilized glasses and seal. Makes about 14 glasses.

Mrs. Lew Garrison Coit
The Lord's Bounty
                                                Anne Arundel

---

5 pounds Concord grapes, 4 pounds sugar, 2 tea- **SPICED GRAPES**
spoons cinnamon, 2 teaspoons allspice, ½ tea-
spoon cloves, ½ teaspoon mace, 1 cup vinegar. Spice more highly if
you please.

Pulp grapes and reserve skins. Cook pulp until soft and juicy, then put
through sieve to remove seeds. Return to kettle, add skins, sugar,
spices and vinegar. Boil thoroughly until thickened. Place in jars and
seal. Skins may be ground if preferred.

Tulip Hill Receipts
West River
                                                Anne Arundel

---

3 pounds rhubarb, 3 pounds granulated sugar, 2 **RHUBARB**
pounds seedless white raisins, ½ pound English **CONSERVE**
walnut meats, 2 whole oranges, ½ lemon.

Wash and cut up rhubarb. Slice oranges and lemon fine, leaving the
rind on. Combine all ingredients and boil slowly for 1 hour. Use no
water. Put in glass jars while hot and seal with paraffin. Exceptional
with cold meats, fowl or game.

Olney Inn
                                                Montgomery

Juices, Catsups and Seasonings

SAVORY
TOMATO JUICE
2 cups tomato juice, ½ teaspoon each of marjoram, basil, tarragon, thyme, savory, salt, 1 tablespoon chopped chives, 1 teaspoon sugar, juice of 1 orange, juice of 1 lemon.

Mix all ingredients except orange and lemon juice to infuse overnight. Strain and add juices before serving ice-cold.

Mrs. Coleman Rogers
Belvoir
Anne Arundel

TOMATO JUICE
½ bushel ripe tomatoes, 6 large onions, 4 green peppers, 4 stalks celery with tops, bunch parsley.

Scald tomatoes in hot water, remove skin and stem end, and cut in quarters; cut up onions, peppers, celery and parsley. Bring to a boil and cook until well done, then strain. Pour juice into large preserving kettle (there should be about 11 quarts) and add to it 1 cup sugar, 1 teaspoon salt for each quart of juice, plus 1 tablespoon extra to whole quantity; ½ teaspoon cayenne pepper, 1 teaspoon black pepper, 2 tablespoons Worcestershire sauce, 2 teaspoons Tabasco sauce. Bring to a boil, then fill sterilized jars with juice; process in hot water bath for just 5 minutes. Makes 10 quarts of delicious juice.

Mrs. Francis E. Engle
Southwood Avenue
Annapolis

CHILI SAUCE
24 ripe tomatoes, 8 onions, 5 green peppers, 8 tablespoons sugar, 4 tablespoons salt, 4 teaspoons ground cloves, 4 teaspoons ginger, 4 teaspoons cinnamon, 4 teaspoons mustard seed, 6 teacups cider vinegar.

Peel and mash tomatoes, chop fine onions and green peppers. Combine with other ingredients. Boil 2 hours and stir constantly.

Rodgers' Papers
Sion Hill
Harford

308

Take 1 gallon of skinned tomatoes, 4 tablespoons **TOMATO**
salt, 4 of black pepper, 1 of allspice, 3 of mustard **CATSUP**
seed, and 8 pods of red pepper. Grind them fine
and add a quart of vinegar. Simmer the whole 4 hours, strain through a
wire sifter and bottle for use.

Mrs. Perrin
Emily Stone Barton's Book, 1850 *Baltimore*

Use larger mushrooms known as umbrellas or **MUSHROOM**
flaps, very fresh and not gathered in wet weather. **CATSUP**
Wash, cut in quarters and place in wide, flat crock
in layers, sprinkling each layer with salt. Let stand 24 hours; then take
out mushrooms and press out juice, which must be bottled and corked.
Put mushrooms back in crock, and in another 24 hours press them
again, bottling and corking the juice. Repeat this for third time, then
mix together all juice extracted, add to it pepper, allspice and 1 or more
cloves pounded together, the spices according to taste and quantity of
juice. Boil the whole, skim as long as any scum rises, bottle when cool;
put in each bottle 2 cloves and 1 peppercorn. Cork and seal, put in a
dry place, and it will keep for years. An excellent seasoning.

Mrs. Decatur's way
Miss Ann Chase's Book, 1811 *Annapolis*

1 bushel tomatoes, 1 peck okra, 6 onions, 10 green **VEGETABLE**
peppers, 2 dozen ears of corn, 1 teacup salt. **SOUP STOCK**

Scald, peel and cut tomatoes in eighths; cut okra in small pieces; chop
onions fine; take seeds from green peppers and chop fine; scrape
kernels from ears of freshly picked corn. Put tomatoes, onions, peppers
and salt in large soup kettle and cook all together until a little reduced
and hot through. Add the corn, and last of all the okra. Cook until
like jam, 1½ to 3 hours. Bottle for use.

Judy Tabb's receipt
Mrs. Frederick W. Brune's Book, 1860 *Baltimore*

GREEN TOMATO SOY   4 quarts sliced, green tomatoes; salt, 6 large white onions, sliced; 2 tablespoons white mustard, 1 ounce ground cloves, 1 tablespoon black pepper, 1 tablespoon ginger, 1 tablespoon allspice, 1 pound brown sugar, cider vinegar.

Wash firm green tomatoes and cut in slices without peeling. Arrange layers in a large crock or bowl, sprinkling each layer with 1 tablespoon salt. Let stand overnight, then drain off the juice that has formed. Cut onions in thin slices and mix with spices and brown sugar. Arrange layers of tomatoes and the onion mixture in a large saucepan and add enough vinegar to just cover. Simmer for an hour or until onions look clear and tomatoes are very tender. Put in glass jars and seal.

Mrs. Charles dePeyster Valk's Book
Duke of Gloucester Street   *Annapolis*

MA COMP'S SOUP SEASONING   1 peck red-ripe tomatoes, ¾ peck okra, 8 large onions, 1 pound brown sugar, 2 tablespoons black pepper, ½ cup salt, 1 tablespoon ground allspice, 1 tablespoon ground cloves, ½ cup celery seed.

Scald tomatoes, peel and cut up. Cut okra into small pieces. Chop onion, leaving no long pieces. Add sugar and spices to vegetables. Cook very slowly, stirring frequently, until the mixture is of marmalade consistency. On an old-fashioned stove, it sat at the back of the stove all day; on a modern stove it cooks perfectly on a controlled unit set very low. The cooking time is from 6 to 12 hours, depending on heat control. Put in jars and seal.

The Seasoning is used generously (2 or 3 tablespoons in a bouillon cup) with a very hot clear meat broth such as consomme poured over it. It is also good used as a condiment, or as seasoning for a meat dish.

Mrs. Beverley C. Compton
Ruxton   *Baltimore*

Little Miss Proctor
by Charles Willson Peale 1785

The Portrait Doll
Hammond-Harwood House

Preserves and Jellies

1 large grassy field, ½ dozen children, 2 or 3 small dogs, a pinch of brook, some pebbles, flowers.

HOW TO PRESERVE CHILDREN

Mix the children and dogs well together, stirring constantly. Pour the brook over the pebbles. Sprinkle the field with flowers. Spread a deep blue sky over all and bake in a hot sun. When brown, remove and set away to cool in a bath tub.

Ellen Ligon Galloway
Howard's Inheritance

Anne Arundel

Take different fruits; stone plums and slice pears and apples. Put them in alternate layers in a jar, and set them in an oven until quite soft. Then pass the pulp through a coarse sieve. To every pound of fruit add one pound of moist sugar. Set over a slow fire and stir until very thick. Then put in a wide shallow pot and cut in slices for use.

ALMACK'S PRESERVE

Rodgers' Papers
Sion Hill

Harford

CRABAPPLE JELLY   Stem and wash apples and put on stove in water not quite to cover. Boil until very soft. Put in cheesecloth bags and drain overnight. Measure syrup in pints and boil between 15 to 20 minutes. Add 1 pound of sugar to every pint of syrup which has been measured. Strain juice of 2 lemons and add to each batch you are cooking. Stir well while adding sugar. Let come to a boil and when drops congeal from spoon, fill glasses. When cool cover with paraffin.

Belle Hayden
Helen Cassin Kinkaid's Book   *Annapolis*

MINT JELLY   To make a splendid jelly prepare apple juice by cutting into pieces and stewing apples in water to cover until soft. Let drip through cheese-cloth or jelly bag. Add 5 cups sugar to 8 cups juice and a handful of fresh mint leaves on the stalks. Let boil and, when ready to jell, lift out the mint stalks and leaves.

Aunt Sally Murray's Choice Receipts
Ivy Neck, Rhode River   *Anne Arundel*

ROSE GERANIUM JELLY   Wash apples (not too ripe), cut in pieces without paring or coring. Barely cover with water and boil until very soft. Pour all into a bag of coarse material, such as a sugar bag; hang it over a container and allow to drip overnight. Do not squeeze or apple juice will be cloudy. To 2 cups juice add 2 cups sugar and the juice of ½ lemon. Boil until syrup will jell. Place a rose geranium leaf in the bottom of each jelly glass. Pour in hot jelly and cover with paraffin. Store in a cool place.

Miss Fanny's Receipt Book
West River   *Anne Arundel*

JAPONICA JELLY   Gather fruit from the Japanese Quince bush just before frost. Wash them and cut in quarters. Cook in enough water to cover until soft. Allow to drip through cheese cloth bag; do not squeeze or jelly will be cloudy. Measure equal amounts of sugar and juice and boil rapidly until syrup will jell when cooled. Pour into glasses and cover with paraffin. Makes a delicate, amber jelly.

Miss Fanny's Receipt Book
West River   *Anne Arundel*

312

½ pound sugar to 1 pound fruit. This makes a **DAMSON**
juicy preserve, tart to taste; good for pancakes or **PRESERVES**
biscuits.

Wash damsons and place in saucepan with water to nearly cover fruit.
Add sugar and cook slowly, stirring occasionally, until damsons are
tender. Pour into sterilized jars and seal immediately.

Katherine's way
Mrs. Henry M. Murray   *Anne Arundel*

Southern Maryland brown, fresh figs, 5 pounds; **SOUTHERN**
1 gallon cold water, ½ cup salt, 5 pounds sugar, **MARYLAND**
2½ cups water, 1 lemon, thinly sliced. **PRESERVED**
FIGS
Wash figs and weigh. Cover with brine made with
cold water and salt and let stand 4 hours. Remove figs from brine, wash
in cold water and drain. Place sugar and water in preserving kettle.
Bring to a boil, stirring until sugar is dissolved, then add figs and
lemon. Bring to a boil and boil gently 20 minutes. Let stand 12 to 24
hours. Bring to a boil and boil gently 20 minutes. Repeat on third day.
Pack in hot sterilized jars and seal immediately. Makes approximately
5 pints.

Mrs. Maynard Barnes
St. Richard's Manor, Patuxent River   *St. Mary's*

Pick over, wash, drain and hull large, selected, **SUN COOKED**
ripe berries. For each pound of berries, use an **STRAWBERRIES**
equal weight of sugar. Put alternate layers of
berries and sugar in a granite pan, cover, and let stand in cool place
overnight. In the morning, heat gradually to boiling point, and let
simmer five minutes. Lift out berries, lay on platters, and boil syrup
five minutes longer. Skim, and pour over berries. Cover platters with
panes of glass, put in sun and leave for three days, when syrup should
be thick as honey. Heat to boiling point, fill jars to overflowing and seal.

Aunt Sally Murray's Choice Receipts
Ivy Neck, Rhode River   *Anne Arundel*

Preserves

STRAWBERRY PRESERVES Wash and cap strawberries, discarding soft or green berries. Measure 1 quart of berries to 1 quart of sugar. It is important to cook only 1 quart at a time. Put over a low flame (no water) and dissolve sugar slowly. When it begins to boil cook for 20 minutes. Stir gently now and then so as not to mash berries. They should remain whole. Skim off foam and, as each quart is cooked, pour into a large bowl and let stand overnight. Next morning stir well and put away cold in sterilized jars.

Mrs. Robert S. G. Welch
State Circle *Annapolis*

TOMATO PRESERVES 3 pounds firm red, yellow or green tomatoes; 2 lemons, ½ pound conserved ginger, 3 pounds granulated sugar.

Scald tomatoes 1 minute, dip in cold water and remove skins. Cut tomatoes in pieces and put with sliced lemons and ginger through grinder. Boil with juice 1 hour without stirring. Then add sugar and boil gently, frequently stirring, until thick, bright and clear, about 1 hour longer. Pack in hot jars and seal.

Mrs. Washington Claude
Helen Cassin Kinkaid's Book *Annapolis*

SEEDLESS BLACKBERRY JAM 4 quarts blackberries, 4 cups water, sugar.

Wash and pick over fruit. Place berries in preserving kettle, crush well, add water and heat slowly until juice flows freely. Boil hard until half the juice has evaporated. Strain through sieve to remove seeds. Measure and add ⅔ cup sugar for each cup of juice. Boil until thick (not very long). Pour into sterilized jars and seal with paraffin.

Mrs. Lew Garrison Coit
The Lord's Bounty *Anne Arundel*

PEACH 'JAMB' To every pound of peeled, whole peaches, 1 pound of Sugar spread over them. Let them stand till the Sugar is dissolved. Boil them very brisk till all broke, then take them up and break them smaller. Put them again in the syrup leaving out stones, all save a few. Boil them altogether over the fire till like a marmalade.

Mrs. Snowden's way
Miss Ann Chase's Book, 1811 *Annapolis*

To every 6 oranges (sour), take 1 lemon; slice **ORANGE**
them very thin and take out all seeds. To every **MARMALADE**
pound of fruit, put 3 pints of cold water and let
stand 24 hours. Then boil until fruit is very tender and set away till
next day. Dip it out, mixing well to get fruit and water equal, and to
each pint add 1¼ pounds sugar. Boil until fruit is transparent, and
syrup jellies. Instead of cooking it all in one kettle it is better to use
two small ones. The syrup does not get so dark if quietly cooked. Use
only 1 pound of sugar to a pint unless the oranges are very, very sour.

Mrs. Davison's receipt
Mrs. Frederick W. Brune's Book, 1860 *Baltimore*

Pare, core and quarter fruit; weigh it, and allow **QUINCE**
an equal quantity of white sugar. Put parings **MARMALADE**
and cores in preserving kettle, cover with water
and boil for ½ hour. Strain through fine sieve and put juice back into
kettle. Boil quinces in it, not too many at once, until tender. Lift out
with a drainer; add water to kettle if liquid seems scarce. When all are
cooked, add sugar to juice and boil 10 minutes before putting in
quinces; you may cut them smaller if you like. Cook for an hour or
more on a slow fire until they change color to a pretty rosy red.
Watch that they do not burn, but on no account stir them. Have 2
fresh lemons cut in thin slices, and when fruit is being put in jars, lay
a slice or two in each.

Hester Ann Harwood's Book, 1848
Hammond-Harwood House *Annapolis*

---

9 pounds Kiefer pears, 7 pounds sugar, ¼ pound **GINGER PEARS**
ginger root, 4 lemons.

Remove skins from pears and slice thinly, discarding cores. To prepared
fruit add sugar, scraped ginger root and grated peels of 2 lemons. Add
a little water to dissolve sugar. Cook over a low heat, stirring until
syrup is boiling gently. Add lemon juice and cook slowly until pears
are transparent and thick. Pour into hot, sterilized jars. Good with
vanilla ice-cream.

Mrs. James N. Galloway
Howard's Inheritance *Anne Arundel*

GREEN SWEETMEATS Scrape rind of citron or watermelon until it is about ½ inch thick; cut it into whatever shapes fancy dictates, dropping them in water until all are finished. Put a layer of grape leaves and one of rind alternately, sprinkling on them a little alum. Cover them with water and boil until pieces are sufficiently green. Lay them in water for three days, changing it night and morning to soak out alum. To one pound of rind put 2 pounds of sugar. Make syrup by putting half a pint of water to every pound of sugar. Add whites of a few eggs whipped to a froth to clarify, stew it a little, strain it, and put in the rind. Stew it gently until pieces are perfectly clear.

Sue McCandlish's way
Emily Stone Barton's Book, 1850   *Baltimore*

MARRONS Shell large chestnuts until you have a pint (see Chestnuts under Vegetables). Make a heavy syrup with 2 cups sugar and 1 cup water, and add the whole chestnuts. Allow them to cook until tender. Season with vanilla or brandy, and bottle. In the fall when chestnuts are plentiful and cheap, these marrons may be prepared to use with winter desserts. They are delicious as a sauce for ice-cream.

Katherine del Valle's Book
Cornhill Street   *Annapolis*

Brandied Fruits

MRS. TALIAFERRO'S BRANDY PEACHES To 3 pounds of peaches, put 1 of sugar. Dissolve sugar in as much brandy as will cover your peaches. Put peaches, pared but whole, in a stone pot or crock, pour the sugar and brandy over them, and set pot in a larger pot of water. Heat it up, and let it remain on fire until peaches are soft enough to run a straw in them.

Mrs. Agnes Taliaferro's way
Emily Stone Barton's Book, 1850   *Baltimore*

Put peaches in boiling water, then throw in cold water to remove skins. Take half the weight of peaches in sugar and put on stove with enough water to make a syrup. Drop the peaches into **PEACH BRANDY PRESERVES** syrup, a few at a time, and let them cook until you can run a straw through them. Take out the peaches but let syrup boil until sufficiently rich, then add brandy to your taste and a few cloves; mace and all-spice.

Old Stonestreet family receipt, La Grange
Elizabeth W. Bond   *Baltimore*

---

4 cups prepared fruit, 4 cups sugar, 1 cup brandy, **TUTTI-FRUTTI** additional fruits and sugar.

Tutti-Frutti is a mélange of spring and summer fruits; its preparation begins in the spring with strawberries.

Place the fruit and sugar in a stone crock. Add the brandy and stir. As fruits come into season, add to the mixture with an equal amount of sugar and stir well. To each additional quart of fruit and sugar add a cup of brandy. Peel and slice peaches, stem and pit cherries, wash and cap berries, before adding them. Serve as a Pudding Sauce or with Ice Cream.

Mrs. James Madison Doyle
Cornhill Street   *Annapolis*

The Doyle House
M. E. Warren

Fragrances and Seasonings

Herbs

"The housewife must have knowledge of all sorts of herbs belonging unto the kitchen; whether they be for the pot, for sallets, for sauces, for servings, or for any other seasoning or adorning, which skill of knowledge of herbs she must get by her own labour and experience."

From "English Housewife," 1615

Basil

An annual sweet herb, indispensable for tomato dishes, green salads, cooked vegetables, stews and soups.

Chives

Slender tube-like leaves have delicate onion taste. Used, chopped fine, in cottage cheese, egg and fish dishes, salads, meats and sauces, and to garnish cold soups.

Dill

Soft feathery leaves used fresh or dried for flavoring fish dishes and sauces, vegetables and salads; seeds for pickling and for vinegar.

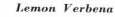

Lavender

Gray-green narrow leaves, fragrant lavender flower spikes. Used in perfume, sachets and sweet bags for linens.

Lemon Verbena

Crisp light green leaves, when dried, keep fragrance well. Used in potpourri and sachets. Fresh sprigs give delicious flavor to iced tea and other drinks.

Marjoram

Fragrant soft green leaves used in salad, soup and stew. Especially good with lamb. Wild marjoram, or oregano, used in tomato dishes.

Mint

For flavoring beverages, lamb, peas, sauces and jelly.

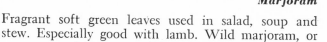

Parsley

Dark green curly leaves used as a garnish for many dishes; chopped fine in eggs, soups and sauces.

Fragrances and Seasonings

Rose Geranium

An old-fashioned favorite for sachets, scented pillows and perfume. The fresh leaves give a rose-like flavor to jellies, custards and cakes.

Rosemary

Narrow, fragrant gray-green leaves used to flavor chicken, fish, lamb and pork; also good chopped fine in biscuits.

Sage

Coarse gray-green leaves are strong seasoning for sausage, pork dishes and poultry stuffing. May be used in moderation for cheese dishes and fish.

Savory

One of the best culinary herbs, combines well with marjoram and thyme to add aroma and piquant flavor to soups, omelets, meats, salads and vegetables.

Tarragon

Pungent green leaves used for flavoring vinegar, in egg dishes, salads and fish sauces.

Thyme

Very aromatic, tiny leaves of many uses to flavor fish, soups, stews, chicken, meats, eggs and vegetables.

Take lavender, rosemary, sage, rue and mint, of **HERBS IN**
each a large handful, put them in a pot of earth- **VINEGAR**
enware, pour on them 4 quarts of very strong vin-
egar, cover the pot closely, and put a board on the top. Keep it in the
hottest sun for 2 weeks, then strain and bottle it, putting in each bottle
a clove of garlic. When it has settled in the bottle and become clear,
pour it off gently; do this until you get it free from sediment. The proper
time to make it is in June, when the herbs are in full vigor. This vinegar
is very refreshing in a sick room, or in crowded rooms.

Mrs. C. H. Steele's Book
14th June, 1870 *Annapolis*

Make a faggot of the stalks of celery, parsley, **A FAGGOT**
thyme and bay leaf and other sweet herbs such as **OF HERBS**
marjoram, fennel or tarragon, should the pot call
for them. Tie them up, so that they may leave their seasoning within the
pot, and be easily removed therefrom.

Mrs. F. T. Loockerman's Book, 1835
Hammond-Harwood House *Annapolis*

Tarragon should be gathered on a dry day just **TARRAGON**
before it blooms. Pick the leaves off the stalks **VINEGAR**
and dry them a little before the fire. Put them
then into wide mouthed bottles and cover with the best cold vinegar
and let it stand for two weeks then strain and bottle for use. Another
portion of vinegar may be added to the same leaves which is very fine
to flavor pickled cucumbers.

Mrs. Murray's Bride's Book, 1858
Ivy Neck, Rhode River *Anne Arundel*

"In the Spring are several sorts of Herbs, a corn-sallet, violets, sorrel,
purslaine—all of which are very good and wholesome and by the Eng-
lish used for sallets and in broth."

Leonard Calvert, Governor of Maryland, in a letter to
his brother, Lord Baltimore in England—circa 1636.

M.E. Warren

Dooryard Herb Garden of the Slicer-Shiplap House on Pinkney Street in Annapolis. Project of the Four Rivers Garden Club.

HERBS FOR WINTER To prepare herbs for winter use, such as sage, summer savory, thyme, mint or any of the sweet herbs, they should be gathered fresh in their season. Examine them well, throwing out all poor sprigs; then wash and shake them, tie into small bundles, and tie over the bundles a piece of netting or old lace (to keep off the dust). Hang up in a warm, dry place, the leaves downward. In a few days the herb will be thoroughly dry and brittle. Pick off all leaves and tender tops of the stems; put them in a clean, large mouthed bottle that is perfectly dry. When wanted for use, rub fine and sift through a sieve. It is much better to put them in bottles as soon as dried, as long exposure to the air causes them to lose strength and flavor.

White House Cook Book, 1887
Contee, Rhode River   Anne Arundel

"We cannot make so much as a little good pottage without Herbes, which give admirable relish and make them wholesome for our Bodies."

W. Cole, The Art of Simpling—1656.

322

Perfumes

Dry and blend leaves of lavender, lemon verbena, **SWEET BAGS**
rose geranium, rosemary and southernwood. Pro- **FOR LINENS**
portions may be to your taste, letting one scent
predominate; or use one alone. Fill, lightly, small silk or muslin bags.
Sew up and tie prettily with ribbons and laces. These will scent your
linens and clothes and lend sweet scent to your rooms.

Hester Ann Harwood's Book, 1848
Hammond-Harwood House *Annapolis*

---

1 quart alcohol 90%, 1 drachm each of oil of **THE POPE'S**
violet, lemon verbena, orange, lemon, lavender, **COLOGNE**
clove and 1 drachm of orange flowers. If you wish
this stronger, add 1 drachm of tube rose and 1 drop of attar of roses.

My grandmother's sister, Miss Antoinette Polk, daughter of Bishop
Leonidas Polk, married General Charette, Pope Pius IX's direct contact
with the Roman Catholic Church in France, about 1870 to 1878.
Tradition has it that General Charette was, before his marriage, a
member of the Papal Guard, and at this time was given the receipt for
the Pope's Cologne.

Adair Skipwith Alden
Taney Avenue *Annapolis*

For each pomander ball,— 1 orange, whole cloves, **POMANDER**
powdered orris root, ground cinnamon. **BALLS, A**
CHRISTMAS
Stick whole cloves firmly into skin of orange, **FRAGRANCE**
covering entire surface. You may leave some space
between cloves, as the ball shrinks. Combine orris root and cinnamon,
roll orange in mixture, patting in as much as it will hold. Wrap ball in
several thicknesses of tissue paper. Store in a cool, dry place several
weeks to dry and develop fragrance. When ready to use, put pomander
in china holder made for the purpose, and place it where you wish to
scent the air.

Miss Anne Cheston Murray
Ivy Neck, Rhode River *Anne Arundel*

The Rose

CRYSTALLIZED VIOLETS OR ROSES
About 4 cups fresh violets, or 2 cups fresh, small rose buds; 1 cup hot water, 2 cups granulated sugar.

Stem violets, wash and drain them, being careful not to bruise petals; stem rose buds, wash and drain. Dissolve sugar thoroughly in hot water. Add flowers, either violets or roses, and let syrup simmer until it reaches the soft-ball stage in cold water. Stir flowers gently with wooden spoon. Remove from flame and continue to stir until syrup begins to granulate and reaches consistency of coarse meal. Empty over wire rack or colander and shake off extra sugar. Cool, pack in jars and seal. The flowers will keep indefinitely and are a pretty decoration for cakes or tea plates.

Mrs. William Wootton   *Baltimore*

ROSE BRANDY
Gather the leaves of roses as soon as they open and while the dew is on them. Put them into a wide-mouthed bottle, and when the bottle is full, pour in the best of fourth proof French brandy. It will be fit for use in 3 or 4 weeks and may be frequently replenished. It is sometimes preferable to wine as a flavoring to pastries and pudding sauces.

Mrs. James Cheston's Everyday Book, 1857
West River
                                                      Anne Arundel

Take the leaves of the common rose, place them **TINCTURE OF** in a bottle, pressing them. Pour some good spirits **ROSES** of wine on them, close the bottle and let it stand for use. This tincture will keep for years and yield a perfume little inferior to 'Otto' of roses. A few drops of it will suffice to impregnate the atmosphere of a room with a delicious odour. Common vinegar is greatly improved by a very small quantity being added to it.

Kate Brice's Book, 1850 *Annapolis*

Use the old fashioned roses, Provence, Damask, **MYRTLE** etc. Dry the petals where the air can circulate **GROVE** (I use a wire screen in attic covered with tissue **POTPOURRI** paper, and have it raised so there is air). When thoroughly dry, sprinkle with powdered orris root and use a few drops of certain oils:—oil of lemon, cinnamon, cloves, lavender. As I have lavender in garden I use the blossom instead of the oil. I find red roses make the prettiest. The pink ones, (hundred leaf, cabbage, etc.) are brown when dry. Almost any blue flower will look nice in the mixture, though they add no fragrance.

Mrs. Robert Goldsborough Henry
Myrtle Grove, Miles River *Talbot*

Myrtle Grove Don Swann

Governor Sharpe's Punch Bowl, Chase Lloyd House   M. E. Warren

The Festive Bowl

On Entertaining

"From the signs of the times there is great reason to hope that the period is fast approaching when large, crowded, and extravagantly luxurious parties will become obsolete; at least in those classes of American society that are or ought to be the most distinguished for good taste and refinement. Surely the most rational, agreeable, and in every respect the most eligible manner of keeping up social intercourse, is to see your friends frequently, but in small numbers, instead of once or twice in the season giving what is called a squeeze, asking every one you may happen to know, (and consequently many whom you do not care for), and incurring a great and sometimes very inconvenient expense, and a vast deal of fatigue, for a purpose that, after all, affords no real pleasure, either to the family or their guests.

We are glad to find that, in the most really genteel circles, it is now becoming very customary to have only small parties, inviting but twenty or thirty persons at a time, till, in the course of the season, you get round all your friends; and selecting, on each occasion, those that are likely to be most agreeable and best suited to each other. And, as at these assemblages, nothing is provided that is entirely for show, and the style of dress is comparatively simple, the expense and trouble of receiving company, or of going into it, is greatly and properly diminished, and the enjoyment proportionably increased."

From Miss Leslie's House Book, 1841
Mrs. John F. Meigs' copy   *Annapolis*

326

To every 5 quarts of blackberries put 1 quart of **BLACKBERRY**
good brandy. Boil 1 quart of water 5 minutes **CORDIAL**
with 4 pounds of sugar and pour boiling hot on
the berries. Let it stand all night, add 2 quarts more of brandy, and
place all in a stone jar. Let stand for 1 month, then bottle it.

Sarah B. Henriques, July 20th, 1892
Wilton   *Harford*

---

7 pounds of wild cherries (or morellos). Best **CHERRY**
alcohol, 2 quarts. Put in a gallon jug and shake **BOUNCE**
thoroughly every day for a month. At the end of
3 months make a syrup of 4 pounds white sugar and 4 quarts water.
Boil these together and strain into the jug. Let this stand 4 months,
strain and bottle. This should make 6 quarts of bounce.

*I make mine with morello cherries and I also put in a little whiskey
and Jamaica rum. The latter idea was told me by Miss Ridgley of
Baltimore and they were famous for their Bounce.*

Sarah Perry Rodgers, daughter of Commodore Perry
Sion Hill   *Harford*

There are, no doubt, a hundred and one receipts **MILK EGG-NOG**
for Egg-Nog; most suffer from being too sweet
or too rich. Egg-Nog has been served on New Year's Day in my
family for at least four generations, and it has always been made in the
same way, in the same bowl. It has been made to drink, not to taste
ritually. The passing years seem to have confirmed the judgment of
older generations.

Our bowl is about 12" across the top and 8" deep, and this will about
half fill it: ¾ pint of the best Jamaica Rum, 1½ pints of the best
Bourbon Whiskey, 2 quarts milk, yolks of 8 eggs, beaten; ⅓ cup granulated sugar.

Stir these together in the bowl and float on top the whites of the eggs,
beaten until stiff, and sprinkle freshly grated nutmeg over the whole.
Do not heat or chill it, do not compromise with the quality of liquors
used, and do not use cream.

Jack Peacock-Green
Dogwood Mooring, Whitehall Creek   *Anne Arundel*

HOWARD COUNTY EGG-NOG

6 eggs, 1 full quart brandy or if scant, 1 gill peach brandy (this makes it better), ½ cup sugar or less, 1 quart thin cream, nutmeg.

Beat yolks and sugar together until very light, add brandy little by little, beating all the time. Then add ⅔ of the egg whites beaten very stiff; add cream and flavor with nutmeg. Put a little of the sugar in rest of egg whites and put on top. Dust with nutmeg.

Old Howard County receipt of
Charles Worthington Dorsey Ligon   *Howard*

COMMODORE MAHAN'S EGG-NOG

To every egg a wine glass of brandy, a tablespoon of granulated sugar and a tumbler of cream. To every 12 yolks, 3 whites beaten up very light, separately. Mix them. Beat again as if for pudding, then add sugar and beat again. Add brandy, stirring all the time, then stir in by degrees the cream. Flavor, if you choose, with rum or peach brandy. Put other whites on top. On New Year's Day at 'Sion Hill' old Mrs. Rodgers and I make it. We beat in all the whites and add 4 wine glasses of rum to 8 wine glasses of brandy. Delicious and potent.

Mrs. John A. Rodgers
From Sion Hill Papers   *Harford*

MAGRUDER FAMILY EGG-NOG

1 quart rich cream, 1 quart milk, 1 quart Brandy (or Whiskey), ½ pint Rum, 12 eggs, sugar to taste. Beat egg yolks until very light, add liquor very slowly, beating all the time. This cooks the eggs, so to speak. Add sugar, then spices judiciously, nutmeg, cloves and allspice. Stir in carefully the whites of eggs, beaten very stiff. Keep in refrigerator 3 days to mellow before serving. This is a traditional Maryland receipt.

Rev. Daniel Randall Magruder, great-great grandson of
Eleanor Calvert of Mount Airy   *Prince George's*

Covered Cup
Gov. Sharpe's Crest, 1751

1 bottle claret, 1 bottle soda **CLARET CUP**
water, 1½ cups crushed ice,
4 tablespoons powdered sugar, ¼ teaspoon grated
nutmeg, 1 liqueur glass maraschino, a sprig of
green borage.

Put all the ingredients into a silver cup, regulating
the proportion of ice by the state of the weather. Hand the cup around
with a clean napkin passed through one of the handles, that the edge of
the cup may be wiped after each guest has partaken of the contents
thereof. This is an old family receipt.

Mrs. James Neville Galloway
Howard's Inheritance   *Anne Arundel*

---

2 quarts tea, 1 pound sugar, juice of 6 lemons, **VALENTINE'S**
juice of 6 oranges, ½ pint Jamaica Rum, 2 quarts **CLARET PUNCH**
Claret, 1 gill Maraschino.

Strain all through cheese cloth and serve with block of ice. Liquors
can be increased.

Helen Cassin Kinkaid's Book
Hanover Street   *Annapolis*

---

18 lemons, 4 pounds white sugar, 2½ quarts **ADMIRAL**
Jamaica rum, 2½ quarts good brandy, 2 quarts **BUCHANAN'S**
boiled milk, 5 quarts boiled water, 2 whole nut- **FAMOUS**
megs, grated. **EGYPTIAN**
PUNCH

Peel lemons and steep peels in 1 quart rum for
24 hours, covering closely. Next day, squeeze lemon juice over sugar.
Pour boiling water over rinds. Let stand until cool then squeeze and
remove rinds. Add grated nutmeg, water and scalded milk. Stir all ingredients together for at least 10 minutes. Add brandy and rum. Stir.
Strain through cheese cloth into jar or crock, then clear through filter
paper. It will drip through as a clear amber color. Serve chilled or over
cracked ice. If kept in a warm place, while filtering, it will drip faster.
This makes about 14 quarts. Treasured family receipt.

Amelia Pinkney D. Lurman   *Harford*

Fort George Meade, Md.
March 30, 1937

'THE QUINTESSENCE OF GENTLEMANLY BEVERAGES'   My dear General:

Your letter requesting my formula for mixing Mint Juleps leaves me in the same position in which Captain Barber found himself when asked how he was able to carve the image of an elephant from a block of wood. He replied that it was a simple process consisting merely in whittling off the part that didn't look like an elephant.

The preparation of the quintessence of gentlemanly beverages can be described only in like terms. A mint julep is not the product of a formula. It is a ceremony and must be performed by a gentleman possessing a true sense of the artistic, a deep reverence for the ingredients and a proper appreciation of the occasion. It is a rite that must not be entrusted to a novice, a statistician nor a Yankee. It is a heritage of the old South, an emblem of hospitality and a vehicle in which noble minds can travel together upon the flower-strewn paths of happy and congenial thought.

So far as the mere mechanics of the operation are concerned, the procedure, stripped of its ceremonial embellishments, can be described as follows:

Go to a spring where cool, crystal-clear water bubbles from under a bank of dew-washed ferns. In a consecrated vessel, dip up a little water at the source. Follow the stream through its banks of green moss and wild flowers until it broadens and trickles through beds of mint growing in aromatic profusion and waving softly in the summer breeze. Gather the sweetest and tenderest shoots and gently carry them home. Go to the sideboard and select a decanter of finest Bourbon, distilled by a master hand, mellow with age yet still vigorous and inspiring, an ancestral sugar bowl, a row of silver goblets, some spoons and some ice and you are ready to start.

330

In a canvas bag, pound twice as much ice as you think you will need, make it fine as snow, keep it dry and do not allow it to degenerate into slush.

In each globlet, put a slightly heaping teaspoonful of granulated sugar, barely cover this with spring water and slightly bruise one mint leaf into this, leaving a spoon in the goblet. Then pour elixir from the decanter until the goblets are about one-fourth full. Fill the goblets with snowy ice, sprinkling in a small amount of sugar as you fill. Wipe the outside of the goblets dry and embellish copiously with mint.

Then comes the important and delicate operation of frosting. By proper manipulation of the spoon, the ingredients are circulated and blended until Nature, wishing to take a further hand and add another of its beautiful phenomena, encrusts the whole in a glistening coat of white frost. Thus harmoniously blended by the deft touches of a skilled hand, you have a beverage appropriate for honorable men and beautiful women.

When all is ready, assemble your guests on the porch or in the garden, where the aroma of the juleps will rise Heavenward and make the birds sing. Propose a worthy toast, bury your nose in the mint, inhale a deep breath of its fragrance and sip the nectar of the gods.

Being overcome by thirst, I can write no further.

Sincerely,
S. B. Buckner, Jr.

JULEP LORE

Sir: . . . I can accept General Buckner's directions with one exception. He says "—go to the sideboard and select a decanter of the finest Bourbon—." Now really a law should be passed or at least a commission appointed to prevent such heresy. Envision the damage to the image of the Maryland Gentleman, who, shuddering at the thought of drinking corn whisky, always drank rye. Sound drinking advice is to drink the *vin du pays*. So let Kentuckians drink their corn, Georgians their peach brandy, and Marylanders their rye.

Janon Fisher, Jr.
Glyndon, Oct. 28, 1963 (From the *Baltimore Sun*)

Peggy Stewart House

PEGGY STEWART TEA PUNCH — 3 pints cold water, 8 teaspoonfuls best tea, thin rind and juice of 8 lemons, 1½ pounds cut sugar, 1 quart rum, ½ pint whiskey.

Let tea boil, leaving lemon rind in. While on the fire throw in pulp of lemons (having squeezed out juice). When boiled sufficiently pour off into a bowl. Put in sugar, juice of the lemons and add rum, and whiskey if you like. Pour over ice to serve.

Mrs. J. Pierre Bernard
Peggy Stewart House   *Annapolis*

THE PEGGY STEWART TEA PARTY

In Annapolis harbor, October 19, 1774, Anthony Stewart, merchant, was forced to apply the torch to his Brig The Peggy Stewart, with its cargo of hated taxed tea. Thus ended a fierce controversy between the Patriots and the Tories that had raged in the city and nearby counties for many days. Because of this historic event, his residence, overlooking the harbor and from which the spectacular burning could be seen, has come to be known as the Peggy Stewart House. Crowds on the waterfront witnessed the dramatic defiance of the authority of the King of England, inspired and directed by zealous patriots as proof of their determination to become free and independent. The Peggy Stewart Tea Party occurred ten months after the historic Boston precedent of December 16, 1773.

6 oranges, whole cloves, 1 quart apple brandy, ½
gallon sweet cider, sugar and spices to taste.   **FARMER'S
BISHOP, A
CHRISTMAS
PUNCH**

Cut oranges in half and stick skins full of whole
cloves. Bake in oven until juice begins to run.
Remove to bowl that can be kept hot. Add sugar to taste and pour over
them 1 quart apple brandy. Light brandy and after it has burned a
few seconds, extinguish by pouring over the cider. Place bowl over a
low flame or at back of stove. Add pinch of cinnamon, whole allspice
and nutmeg (go easy on spices). Stir mixture until hot. It should be
kept hot while being served but must never reach boiling. Serves about
24. This punch was served in the countryside when the Bishop was
expected. The receipt said, "Add brandy to the amount of the capacity
of the Bishop."

Amelia Pinkney D. Lurman   *Harford*

---

1 bottle rum, 1 bottle brandy, 1 bottle Port wine,   **A FINE-BODIED
PUNCH**
1 bottle strong tea (but white wine is better), the
juice of 10 lemons, ½ pint curacao, 3 cups pul-
verized white sugar.

Take rind of squeezed lemons and add them to stock. Stir well. Let
stand for a couple of hours, strain and bottle stock. (Should you use
tea, it should not draw long enough to become bitter.)

By a bottle, it is understood an ordinary wine bottle, 4½ to a gallon.
When punch is needed take 8 bottles of soda to 4 bottles of stock
with plenty of ice. Stir well and serve. Will serve 25 to 30 persons. The
stock may be allowed to settle and then filtered. This gives a good
color but ordinarily is unnecessary.

Commodore Rodgers' receipt
Sion Hill Papers   *Harford*

Reflection on sharing one's treasured receipts.

*"I will be glad to let you have my receipts as you request although no
one to whom I have ever given them has taken the trouble to follow
them."*   Commodore Rodgers

The Festive Bowl

Great Neck   John Moll

GREAT NECK   2 fifths light rum, 2 fifths dark rum, 1 cup sherry
PUNCH   wine, dry; 1 tablespoon grenadine, 2 frozen
                    lemonade, small size; 2 frozen lemon juice, small;
1 quart frozen peaches, 1 quart frozen strawberries, 1 large can diced
pineapple, 1 bottle cocktail cherries.

This quantity is for a large punch bowl. If ingredients are added in
frozen state and punch used about ½ hour later, no additional chilling
is necessary. If it stands too long, add ice cubes. This is seldom necessary. A bottle of sparkling water may be added if a weaker punch is
desired. This is a very popular and exhilarating drink.

Mrs. Reginald Truitt
Great Neck   *Kent Island*

AMBER   1 quart cold tea, juice of 4 lemons, 4 cups orange
FRUIT PUNCH   juice, 4 seedless oranges, 2 cups sugar, 3 quarts
                    gingerale, 1 quart charged water, 1 gallon cracked
ice, large bunch fresh mint.

Combine tea, fruit juices, thinly sliced oranges and sugar, stirring until
sugar dissolves. Chill and just before serving add gingerale, charged
water and ice. Garnish with mint.

Mrs. Washington Claude
Helen Cassin Kinkaid's Book   *Annapolis*

DECATUR   Juice of 8 lemons, ¾ pound sugar, ½ pint brandy,
HOUSE PUNCH   ¼ pint peach brandy, ¼ pint Jamaica rum, 2
                    pints aerated water or champagne. Mix 4 or 5
hours before using. Serves 6 people. Very strong.

Mrs. Truxtun Beale's Book, 1903
Decatur House   *Washington*

334

Take 1 quart of vinegar and pour over 2 quarts of **MARYLAND**
mashed raspberries. Let it stand for 24 hours, **RASPBERRY**
then strain and pour over 2 quarts more mashed **SHRUB**
raspberries. Strain this after 24 hours. Measure
1 pound of sugar to each pint of juice and boil 20 minutes, then bottle.

To serve, fill tall glasses with crushed ice, pour in equal amounts of
Shrub and soda water. Blackberries or strawberries may also be used
to make Shrub.

Miss Sarah Berry's receipt
Mrs. Charles dePeyster Valk's Book *Annapolis*

---

15 Stayman or Winesap apples. Stick a clove in 8 **APPLE TODDY**
of them and bake all until just ready to burst.

4 quarts Whiskey, 1 quart Brandy, 1 quart Peach Brandy, 1 quart
Jamaica Rum, 1 pound sugar dissolved in as little water as will do the
trick; say a little over 1 pint.

Put the baked apples in a stone jar, well glazed. Pour the liquors on
them, tie a close-fitting air-tight cover on the jar and set aside. Add 6
quarts of cold water when ready to serve, plus a lump of ice. (Should
be made in January for use the following Christmas.)

Dorsey Gassaway's receipt
Church Circle *Annapolis*

Bake 6 large apples, cored but not peeled. Place **HOT**
in bottom of 3 gallon stone crock on hearth be- **APPLE TODDY**
fore a hot fire. Add ½ gallon boiling water, ½
pound sugar and let simmer for ½ hour, turning crock occasionally.
Then add 1 gallon apple juice slowly, 1 gallon Maryland Rye whiskey
and 1 quart Jamaica rum. Keep turning over with ladle and turning
crock so as not to heat too much on one side. When it has simmered
for 1 hour add skins of 6 lemons cut in long spirals, ¼ ounce whole
cloves, ¼ ounce stick cinnamon, ¼ ounce ground nutmeg. Allow to
simmer for a couple of hours. Serve in cups which are first dipped in
hot water. This toddy is made at the South River Club for the winter
breakfasts. It should serve about 25 moderate drinkers.

Forbes Colhoun
Ivy Neck, Rhode River *Anne Arundel*

WHITE WINE PUNCH Rub ½ pound loaf sugar over peel of 3 lemons until all oil is extracted. Put sugar in punch bowl and add strained juice of the lemons. Heat 1 quart white wine until just at boiling point, then take from fire and add 1 pint of strong green tea. Pour mixture on sugar and lemon juice. Stir until sugar is dissolved, and add 1 pint good rum. Serve with crushed ice.

From the Rodgers' Papers
Commander John F. Meigs *Annapolis*

MULLED WINE 2 bottles Port wine, 1 bottle Claret, 1 cup sugar, 4 ounces dried apricots, 3 ounces raisins, 3 ounces split prunes, 2 ounces shelled almonds, 1 ounce shelled cardemon, 1 ounce whole cloves, 1 ounce cinnamon sticks.

Mix fruit, nuts and spices and tie them in a cheese cloth bag. Heat the Port wine, Claret and sugar slowly until sugar is dissolved, add bag of fruits and spices, and simmer gently until liquid is boiled down to 2½ bottles. When cool, pour into a large glass jar or bottle and leave bag of spices in wine for 24 hours. To serve, remove bag of spices, add 1 part brandy to 1 part wine and heat slowly to warm. Do not allow to boil. Serve in punch glasses with 2 almonds and 3 raisins in each glass. Add some cloves to the wine while re-heating.

John Murray Begg
Roedown *Anne Arundel*

WASSAIL 1 gallon apple cider, 48 whole cloves, 4 teaspoons whole allspice, 12 pieces stick cinnamon, 2 cups sugar, or to taste, 1 cup orange juice, 6 tablespoons lemon juice.

Combine ingredients and bring to a slow boil. Simmer 10 minutes. Strain and serve hot. 4 cups apple brandy may be added after boiling, if desired.

Served on Christmas Greens Day at
The Hammond-Harwood House *Annapolis*

Bay Schooner in Port of Annapolis

The Festive Bowl

Port, a popular wine in the 18th century, is mulled in the same manner as was customary in the old seaport of Annapolis.

PORT OF ANNAPOLIS PUNCH

1 quart bottle of Port, juice of 1 lemon, 2 tablespoons of sugar, 1 cinnamon stick, rind of 1 lemon, 1 orange, peeled spirally; grated nutmeg.

Dissolve sugar in 1 cup of boiling water. Combine this with the lemon juice and Port in a lined pot over an open fire. Add cinnamon stick and the rinds. Serve hot with a dusting of nutmeg.

Historic Annapolis, Inc.   *Annapolis*

Account of an Entertainment given by the General Assembly of Maryland to his Excellency, General Washington.

December 23, 1783

Entertainment for General Washington, 1783

At noon, on December 23, 1783, George Washington appeared before the Congress assembled in the Old Senate Chamber of the State House at Annapolis. Here he resigned his commission as Commander-in-Chief of the Continental Armies. On January 14, 1784, in this handsome and historic room, the treaty of peace with England was ratified by the Congress.

M. E. Warren

Gentlemen's Entertainments

GENTLEMEN'S SUPPER PARTIES, 1841-1961

"For a gentlemen's supper party, it is usual to have terrapin, canvasback ducks, or game; and sometimes French dishes. On some occasions, all the articles for a gentlemen's supper party are cold. The table is set out nearly the same as for dinner, first seeing that the room is well lighted and well warmed. It is not usual at suppers to have either wine-coolers or finger-glasses, or to hand round coffee at the close. There is sometimes chocolate and rusk. Pastry is rarely seen on a supper table. The dessert is of ice-creams, oranges, grapes, etc. Decanters of wine are on the table."

From Miss Leslie's House Book, 1841
Comdr. John F. Meigs' copy   Annapolis

Maryland Food and Wine Society Supper, 1961

Chincoteague Oysters on the Half Shell	Chablis
Diamond Back Terrapin Maryland Beaten Biscuits	Sherry
Wild Duck or Broiled Squab (according to season) Compote of Apples Peas	Chateauneuf du Pape
Maryland Ham Salad	
Kossuth Cake	Tokaji Aszu

Coffee

Henry Powell Hopkins   Baltimore

THE ANCIENT SOUTH RIVER CLUB, CIRCA 1700

On a winding country road near All Hallows Church and old London-towne stands a quaint one-room building which, since 1742, has been "The House in which the Society or Company commonly called The South River Club meets". The original deed to this one-half acre of ground was dated July 3, 1740. For over 200 years it has been a meeting place for "the gentlemen of the neighborhood, where comradeship and good fellowship have reigned supreme".

The exact, or even approximate date of the founding of the Club is unknown, as a fire destroyed the Club House in 1740 or '41, the minute books and all records. In any case, it is thought to be the first social organization of its kind among the English settlements in America and is, so far as is known, the oldest social club with continuous life in the Western Hemisphere.

The old Club House is a one room, severely plain, clapboarded building, barely of sufficient size to accommodate the twenty-five members and the few guests of the serving member. In a separate building, behind the Club House, is the kitchen, with its old wood stove on which many a tasty meal has been cooked by Gertrude and her predecessors. One such dinner was described in a letter from General George H. Steuart of Baltimore to his son, William J. Steuart at Londontowne in May, 1852.

"You must remember that I am to serve at the Club on Thursday, the 2nd of June and you must have the cart ready at the Ferry on arriving of the boat at 10. . . . A fine lamb to be killed on Wednesday, the forequarter roasted and the hindquarter boiled, the other two quarters can be put in ice in a cloth and sent to Baltimore the next day, Thursday, in a large basket, with strawberries, etc., etc.

"Several dozen crabs must be caught and immediately boiled, picked and partially baked so that they can be warmed up the next day, to be seasoned with salt, pepper and butter. You must have some asparagus ready to be boiled and I will bring potatoes and peas. . . . Of course I shall bring bread, sugar, lemons, brandy, whiskey, pepper, mustard, salt, etc. . . . Let the ice be sent down by Mr. Purdy early in the morning and also the fresh butter. . . . Instead of pone, Lucy may prepare two or three nice Johnny cakes. I forgot to mention that I shall bring a boiled ham, and a fine piece of beef."

It is more than a hundred years since General Steuart made preparations for serving this dinner, but today the same care is observed by the "serving member" to provide a typical Maryland repast and, to quote from the 10th Rule of the Club, drawn up in 1793, "The Steward appear . . . provided with two and a half gallons of spirit, with ingredients for toddy, by one o'clock and a sufficient dinner with clean pipes and tobacco. . . ."

Maryland House and Garden Pilgrimage   *The Ancient South River Club*

Dinner Served by a Member in May

South River Club Crab Soup

Fried Chicken with Cream Gravy

Soft Shell Crabs   Maryland Ham

Hominy   Asparagus

Hot Biscuits

Strawberry Short Cake

South River Club Punch

Cigars   Maryland Rye Whiskey

A December Saturday Noon Breakfast

Hot Apple Toddy

Sausage   Scrambled Eggs

Buckwheat Cakes   Maple Syrup

Coffee

Ceiling Detail, Whitehall

GOVERNOR SHARPE ENTERTAINS
GOVERNOR EDEN
AT WHITEHALL, 1769

M. E. Warren

Governor Sharpe built Whitehall about 1760 on an estate of 1000 acres overlooking the Chesapeake Bay, and set about creating there "the most desirable situation in this, or in any of the neighboring provinces".

When Lord Baltimore's brother-in-law, Robert Eden, came out from England to succeed Governor Sharpe in 1769, it was doubtless the occasion for one of the great entertainments for which Whitehall was famous.

One can but imagine the pride with which His Excellency acquainted the distinguished new arrival in the province with his splendid house and adjacent grounds "so judiciously disposed, that utility and taste were everywhere happily united".

A harmonious composition of lawns, walks and gardens stretched to meet the blue water of the Bay, and on the land side a curious and intricate pattern of earth works lent character to the design, and afforded the great manor a measure of protection from the menacing wilderness.

For the delectation of his guests, the hospitable bachelor Governor was limited only by the seasons in the choice of provisions for his abundant table. The waters of the Bay teemed with a variety of shell and finny fish. Diamond Back Terrapin burrowed in the tide-washed shores. Pasture and farmyard produced domesticated animals and fowl. From espaliered fruit trees and orchards came luscious fruits; from the gardens, all the herbs and vegetables known to this remarkable gentleman horticulturist. Game abounded in the forests, and at certain seasons, the sky was darkened by the passage of untold numbers of wild duck, geese and swan.

It is not surprising that Governor Sharpe, on his retirement, chose not to return to his home in England, but tarried at Whitehall until 1773. Here he continued the cultivation of his vast land holding, the importation and breeding of great horses such as Othello and the satisfaction of bringing his creative and extensive plan to fruition.

A. Aubrey Bodine   *Whitehall*

Dinner for Governor Eden

Diamond Back Terrapin   Stewed Oysters   Fish Dressed with Sauce

Peacock   Wild Goose   Broiled Quail
Veal Collops with Oyster Forcemeat   Maryland Ham
Savoury Fried Rabbit

Tomato Pie   Cymlings   Broccoli
Sally Lunn   Rusk

Green Sweetmeats   Tomato Soy   Spiced Figs
Lemon Cheese Cakes   Ginger Pudding   Brandy Peaches
Pound Cake   Fruit Cake

Nogs, Cordials and Punches

PRESIDENT MONROE AND HIS CABINET AT
CEDAR PARK, 1818

In June of 1818 Miss Margaret Mercer of Cedar Park, West River, wrote to a cousin in Virginia, "The President and Cabinet spent two days with us last week." The President was James Monroe and the time, according to an item in the Maryland Gazette, was May 30 and 31, 1818. When the President of the United States visited his old friend Col. John Francis Mercer, 10th Governor of Maryland, Cedar Park had reached its height of beauty and elegance. Built in the 17th century by Richard Galloway, the estate passed by inheritance through several generations to the wife of Col. Mercer. At the time of President Monroe's visit the house and the surrounding park must have looked very much as it did a few years later when Mr. William Wirt, United States Attorney General and native Marylander, wrote the following description of a visit there to his daughter.

Washington 7/17/22

"The approach to the house is through a park, composed of open, sunny, green hills and vales. . . . Now in that same beautiful park there are several hundred of the finest fallow deer I ever beheld . . . they played all around our carriage as we passed, as if to welcome us, and show this beautiful place to advantage. Such is the scene at one side. Then you come to the house which is a fine, grand old fashioned mansion; having a grand entree like the President's house, opening into four large rooms, and, besides this, to the south a grand summer saloon, into which we were invited; and here the whole Chesapeake Bay, covered with vessels of all sizes and forms—from the ship of the ocean, to the lightest river craft, and moving with different velocities in all directions—burst suddenly upon the eye. Some of them were moored within the mouth of West River and were lying at anchor within two or three hundred yards of the house—a rich cultivated field of grass between. Thus, on one side is the beautiful park animated with deer, on the other the broad bay animated with vessels in full sail, and when you add to this the noble old mansion filled with fine paintings, and the elegant and hospitable mistress of the whole establishment, was it not worth seeing?"

Some years later, 1825-1834, Cedar Park was the site of "Miss Mercer's School" for young ladies. Many present day Marylanders may find the name of an ancestress among the list of pupils from the Southern States as well as Baltimore, Washington and Philadelphia. Mellow with time, the old house is still the home of descendants of the builder.

Francis E. Engle   *Cedar Park*

Dinner for the President

Clam Soup

Soft Crabs   Shad Roe Croquettes
Chicken with Maryland Ham

Asparagus
Artichokes à la Palestine

Southern Spoon Bread   Beaten Biscuit

Charlotte Russe   Cherries in Claret
Cedar Park Ginger Cakes

White Wine Punch

345

Parkhurst Francis E. Engle

SOIRÉE AT PARKHURST, 1857

The pleasure of Mr. G. Cheston, Jr. and Lady's Company is respectfully requested at PARKHURST, on Tuesday, 11th inst., at 5 p.m.; the Dancing will commence at 8 p.m.
West River, August 3rd, 1857.

W. C. Mercer	Geo. B. Steuart
Arthur Brogden	R. J. Estep
John B. Steuart	Chas. Contee
Fenwick Hall	Thomas T. Hall, Jr.

Supper

Crab Flake Maryland   Augustine's Chicken Croquettes
Veal and Ham Pie, Jellied   Goose in Aspic

Dressed Cucumbers   Chilled Sliced Tomatoes

Hot Rolls

A Trifle with Syllabub

Peach Ice   Lemon Ice Cream
Little Sponge Cakes   Maids of Honour

Queen's Punch   Claret Cup   Cherry Bounce

THE TUESDAY CLUB, 1745-1755

Gentlemen's Clubs in the English tradition flourished in Annapolis during the eighteenth century. The most celebrated and unique was The Tuesday Club, whose members "seem to have been serious only about not being serious." The unbridled fun, after the fashion of the period, was actually based upon most difficult forms of wit, ridicule and caricature. Songs and poems were an important part of the entertainment, but "discussions that level at party matters or the administration of the government of this province, or any matter disagreeable to this Club shall be silenced by vociferous and roaring laughter."

Mr. Charles Cole was elected perpetual president "for his good singing and elegant entertainment." Mr. William Thornton, Protomusicus, was ordered never to address the club except by singing his motion or speech. The popular publisher of the Maryland Gazette, Mr. Jonas Green, was the Club's poet laureate, and was found ineligible for other office because he already had five P's behind his name, Poet, Printer, Punster, Purveyor, and Punch-Maker.

The convivial company of friends gathered each Tuesday at the house of a member. "The candles being lit, the punch made and the pipes fairly set going, after 2 or 3 rounds of the punch bowl, they applied themselves to make and to pass some wholesome laws for the good government and regulation of the Society. Having passed these laws with great wisdom and sagacity, they betook themselves again to their punch and pipes and then, the gammon, according to rule, appeared on a sideboard—"

A gallant rule of the Club was that "immediately after supper, the ladies shall be toasted, before any other toasts or healths shall go round;" and a provident rule provided that "no fresh liquor shall be made, prepared or produced after 11 o'clock at night."

The Tuesday Club provided the inspiration and pattern for many that were to follow. The Homony Club, founded in 1770, counted among its distinguished members such famous Marylanders as William Paca, Anthony Steuart, Reverend Jonathan Boucher, Denis Dulaney, and Charles Willson Peale.

The Supper

Gammon	Wild Duck
Steak and Kidney Pie	Pan Roast Oysters
Cheese	Fruit

Punch

THE AGRICULTURAL SOCIETY, 1805

The Agricultural Society was first organized in 1805, with William Hayward as Chairman, and Robert Henry Goldsborough of Myrtle Grove as Secretary. A "Society for the Promotion of Agriculture and Rural Economy" was its ponderous title. In 1818 the same group met and organized the Maryland Agricultural Society. There were to be 6 Curators for both the Eastern and Western Shores. Meetings were held at irregular intervals in both Baltimore and Easton.

In 1824 at a meeting at the Court House in Easton, it was resolved that 12 Trustees be elected for the Eastern Shore. In 1825 the 12 elected were: Edward Lloyd, Samuel Stevens, Nicholas Hammond, Daniel Martin, Thomas Hayward, Robert Henry Goldsborough, Henry Hollyday, Robert Bauning, Perry Benson, Nicholas Goldsborough, Tench Tilghman, Samuel Kennard.

Col. Edward Lloyd of Wye House was President of the Society for 45 years, until his death in 1904. Except for a lapse of several years during the Civil War, the meetings have continued without interruption until the present day.

In reviewing the history of this unique organization of great land-owners and practical farmers, the question arises as to which was nearest the heart of its members, husbandry, or the "Sumptuous Repasts" which climaxed each meeting day.

Before Dinner there would be a viewing of the host's gardens, green-house, orangery, orchards, fields, stables and smokehouse which led to a lively exchange of ideas on agricultural methods and breeding. It was the host's pride to present the most succulent meats and fowl, accompanied by four or five native vegetables according to the season, and an array of orchard or hot-house fruits.

An Agricultural Society Dinner at Wye House, Home of Colonel Edward Lloyd

Crab Gumbo Soup

Saddle of Mutton   Panned Squab   Baked Ham

Tomatoes, Corn, Cymlings, Beans, Potatoes

Rolls   Mint Jelly

Vanilla Ice Cream with Preserved Figs

Fruits

Maryland Rye Whiskey   Wines

A DINNER OF THE GOURMET SOCIETY, 1950

Almond Soup

Boned Broiled Shad   Small Cull Soft Shell Crabs

Maryland Beaten Biscuit

Boned Squab Chicken

Native Asparagus

Plain Salad with Paté and Ham Flakes in Aspic

Strawberries

Liqueurs   Cigars   Coffee

Fine Vintage Wines served with each course

The Soup, the receipt for which was given by Henry James' niece to tonight's impresario, is made from veal shank and/or neck base to which is added the usual ingredients to form a tasty broth, plus pounded almonds and mace. There is no clear record that Henry James ever made or heard of this soup, or that he even liked soup.

The Boned Broiled Shad is edged with smallest 'small cull soft crabs' from our host's lower district, Crisfield in Somerset County.

The Famed Maryland Beaten Biscuits were made here in Easton this morning.

The Plain Salad is accompanied by an aspic, at the bottom of which lies a paté and through which are found flakes of Talbot County raised and cured ham.

The Strawberries are served with either clotted cream or powdered sugar.

To Our Guests

Members of the Gourmet Society do not smoke immediately before or during the dinner. One who smokes while dining is not a gourmet.

The Society must not be used for business contacts. During "Meetings" no reference is to be made by members or guests to religious beliefs or politics.

Hon. Edward T. Miller, Host
Carroll McTavish Elder and Donald Ross, Impresarios
Saturday, May 13th, 1950
The Chesapeake Bay Yacht Club, Easton—Talbot

Bringing in the Oysters   M. E. Warren

OYSTER ROASTS, 1841–1961

"At an oyster supper, it is usual to have all the various preparations of oysters, fried, stewed, broiled, roasted, raw and in patties. Potatoes mashed, and browned, are generally added. The roasted oysters are served in the shell, on very large dishes, and brought in "hot and hot", all the time, as they are generally eaten much faster than they can be cooked. Small buckets (usually of maple or stained wood, with brass hoops) are placed on the floor, for the purpose of receiving the shells, beside the chairs of the gentlemen; as the business of opening the oysters mostly devolves on them. At the right hand of each plate is placed a thick folded towel and an oyster knife, which is used only to open the shell; at the other side of the napkin, fork, bread, tumbler, wine-glasses, etc. On the side-table let there be plenty of plates, knives and forks to change with; a basket of bread or light rolls; pitchers of water; bottles of port and cider; decanters of wine being on the table. Several butter plates, with a butter knife to each, should be set along the table. Sometimes the butter is made up into the shape of a pineapple or basket of flowers.

From Miss Leslie's House Book, 1841
Comdr. John F. Meigs' copy   *Annapolis*

SOCIETY OF COLONIAL WARS IN THE STATE OF MARYLAND
1634   **1961**

Oysters will be available in all forms; roasted, fritters, fried, panned. on the half-shell, and in oyster stew. The Dinner Committee has provided a sufficiently broad menu so that those who cannot live on oysters alone will be well provided for.

Oyster Roast at the Maryland Club.   Baltimore

THE RING TOURNAMENT

A sport pageant known as Riding at the Ring or Ring Tilting was introduced in America in 1840. From the first elaborate and elegant tournament which took place at The Vineyard, an estate near Baltimore, in that year this form of jousting spread into almost every county of Maryland and has been proclaimed the official Maryland sport. In an area of fine horses and excellent horsemanship it became a popular form of entertainment at country fairs and church sociables. Briefly, Ring Tilting consisted of a rider "taking" rings, suspended 9 feet from the ground, on a lance, while riding a given distance at full speed. Each rider or "knight" had three trials at the ring and the champion was proclaimed by herald, bugle and fanfare. His was the honor of crowning the lady of his choice "Queen of Love and Beauty."

Excerpts from a Letter from Miss Mary Thomas of Lebanon

West River, July 28, 1870.

My dear Sally,

I put off writing till today to tell you all about the tournament. The heat was terrible. It began to be lively as we came in sight of the ground. The first we saw was Beauregard running away with Nevell. It was a long way before he could stop him. The knights were practicing and they did look so well and imposing—Dr. Murray in a black coat and white pants, green plume and baton was followed by his little son and Jimmie Cheston as pages, in red and white and blue. Then came his son, Dan, in red and black, as marshal. Then came the knights, George Stewart and A. Murray first, then John and Robbie and so on— 20 knights. Stewart was the prettiest dressed, with green scarf and trimmings and plume. Alex was the handsomest knight of all there, dressed in purple plume and scarf. Nevell looked so well and Beauregard was much admired. John Steele was gorgeous in scarlet and white. Jim Cheston and Johnie Hopkins were the heralds and much bedecked with ribbons.

When the Steam Boats arrived Dr. Murray formed his procession and went in order to the Boat to meet the Band. The procession looked beautiful as it came up, preceded by band playing. A speech was made by a Mr. Tucker, no one heard it. Then the riding began. By that time there were long lines of carriages—4 or 500 persons assembled. Each knight that was successful—the band struck up and Jim C. and J. Hopkins galloped after him and escorted him along the line—the knight bowing and the people cheering. G. Stewart, the first rider, took the ring. Robbie took it twice—John Steele twice, Morris Cheston and many others took it once. My John missed every time. As soon as he had had his ride I and the Johns party went to the cake table and after each knight had ridden 3 times, every one came down and drank lemonade and ate ice-cream and had dinner. There was a nice breeze and it was very pleasant.

Church Dinner at A Ring Tournament

Cold Fried Chicken	Deviled Crabs
Maryland Ham	
Sliced Tomatoes	Cold Slaw
Corn Relish	Beaten Biscuits
Fresh Peach Ice-Cream	
Chocolate Cake	Cocoanut Cake
Lemonade	Iced Tea

Start for a Race, at Pimlico, about 1875

Colors represented are those of Oden Bowie, G. L. Lorillard, Pierre Lorillard, Joseph Donohue, John F. Chamberlin, etc.

Annals of the Turf in Colonial Maryland

The period from the middle of the eighteenth century to the beginning of the American Revolution was remarkable for fine horses in Maryland, and the matching of thoroughbreds on the turf became the vogue throughout the Province.

During the years 1745 to 1775, racing was established at almost every convenient town and public place in Maryland,—"where the inhabitants almost to a man, were fond of horses, especially those of the race breed; when gentlemen of fortune expended large sums on their studs, sparing no pains or trouble in importing the finest strains of English and Arabian thoroughbreds and improving the breed by judicious crossing." Governors, councillors, legislators and gentlemen either imported, bred or matched thoroughbred horses, and their keenness and zeal for the sport resulted here, as in neighboring Virginia, in founding the thoroughbred industry on this side of the Atlantic.

Regular matched races between pedigreed horses in the English style are said to have been introduced by Governor Ogle about 1745. The first announcement of public horse-racing at Annapolis appeared in the Maryland Gazette of May 17th of that year. At about this time the Maryland Jockey Club was first founded. After this, purse-racing and racing for cups became a regular amusement at every county town during Court.

The harassments and troubles along the frontiers from 1755 to 1764 due to the French and Indian War make the records of the turf during this period either extremely scant, or significantly silent. In 1774, out of deference to a recommendation of the Continental Congress, the Fall races at Annapolis were postponed due to the political state of the country and racing was not revived in Maryland until after the war. When peace was established in 1783, the Maryland Jockey Club was placed on its former respected footing, and it was considered a distinguished honor to be a member. At the close of the Revolutionary War, it was composed of such gentlemen as Gov. Paca (signer), and Richard Sprigg, Esq. (stewards); Hon. Col. Edward Lloyd (father of the Gov.), Hon. Benj. C. Stoddert (first Secretary of the Navy), Hon. Col. Stone (afterwards Gov.), Hon. Charles Carroll of Carrollton (signer), Col. John Eager Howard (afterward Gov.), Benj. Ogle, Esq. (afterward Gov.), Hon. Col. Plater (afterward Gov.), Gen. Cadwallader, Dr. Wm. Murray, and Messrs. Tilghman, Steuart, Galloway, Brogden, Pearce, Courcy, Davidson, and others. The Maryland Jockey Club as it exists to-day was revived and incorporated by an act of the Maryland Legislature on March 1, 1872.

COLONIAL MARYLAND'S FOREMOST TURF PATRONS AND THEIR THOROUGHBREDS

Gov. Samuel Ogle returned in 1747 with his family after a five year's sojourn in England to resume for the second time, the office of Governor of Maryland. He brought over the celebrated "Spark," presented to him by Lord Baltimore, and also the English brood mare," Queen Mab." From that time on, horse-racing became the king of sport in Maryland.

Col. Benjamin Tasker soon emulated his brother-in-law, Gov. Ogle, and imported "Selima," daughter of the Godolphin Arabian. She was invincible on the turf and became equally distinguished as a breeder. As with her sire in England, her blood flows in the veins of almost every racehorse of distinction that has run in this country from that day to the present.

Samuel Galloway, Esq. of Tulip Hill in Anne Arundel County was a noted devotee of the turf in Maryland,—"as true a sportsman as any the olden times of 1750 to 1784 could furnish." He owned the Maryland-bred "Selim," the record-getter of the turf before the Revolution. In November, 1766, the gentlemen of Chestertown, Kent County, raised a purse of 100 pistoles, with a view of bringing together the two most celebrated horses on the continent, "Selim" of Maryland, and "Yorick" of Virginia. The Maryland horse came in winner.

Dr. Thomas Hamilton, of Mount Calvert Manor in Prince George's County, imported in 1765 the great horse "Figure," of whom it was said,—"he never lost a race." Dr. Hamilton also imported the famous "Dove."

Gov. Horatio Sharpe, whose seat was Whitehall, encouraged racing in Maryland by giving small purses and running his horses in matches as long ago as the French and Indian War. About the year 1757, he imported the famous stallion "Othello."

These names of first importance in Maryland turf annals were soon followed in celebrity by the names of Mr. Calvert, owner of "Regulus," Mr. Hall, owner of "Fearnaught," Col. Lloyd, owner of "Traveller" and "Nancy Bywell," Mr. MacGill, owner of "Nonpareil," Col. Sim, owner of "Wildair," and by Gov. Eden, owner of "Why Not."

Material by courtesy of Francis Barnum Culver's, "Blooded Horses of Colonial Days"

Grand Sweepstake at Pimlico, October 24th, 1877

P. Lorillard's Parole—4 years, 105 pounds (Barrett) 1
F. B. Harper's Ten Broeck—5 years, 114 pounds (Walker) 2
G. L. Lorillard's Tom Ochiltree—5 years, 114 pounds (Barbee) 3
Distance, 2½ miles; Time, 4:37¾
Congress, for the first time in its history, adjourned for this Race

Belair—Prince George's   Don Swann

> *BELAIR was built by Gov. Samuel Ogle after his marriage to Anne, daughter of Benjamin Tasker. Here the Ogles lived in splendid plantation state, their town house at Annapolis claiming their presence only during the social season. Gov. Ogle had a renowned stud of racehorses, his private race course, kennels of hunting dogs, and a deer park of six hundred acres.*

Under the patronage of Governor Robert Eden, the turf in Maryland became more fashionable than at any other period, and the racing season in Annapolis during September and October was the gayest period of the year in the provincial capital. George Washington, a great admirer of fine horses, came up regularly from Mount Vernon during the early 'seventies' to enjoy the races. He attended the theatre and balls given on these occasions, and was hospitably entertained by the social leaders of the town. The days were spent at the track, where the priveleged saw the races and laid their wagers from the tops of coaches, fifty being counted at a single meet. Toward evening the teas were followed by dinner and supper parties, the theatrical performances, and the dances.

Washington's Diary

1771—Sept. 21 "Set out—for the Annapolis Races.—"

24 "Dined with the Govr. and went to the Play and Ball afterwards."

1772—Oct. 5 "Dined at the Coffee House with the Jockey Club and Lodged at the Govrs. after going to the Play."

7 "Dined at the Govrs. and went to the Play afterwards."

1773—Sept. 26 "I set off for the Annapolis Races.—Got into Annapolis between five and six o'clock. Spent the Evening and lodged at the Governor's."

27 "Dined at the Govr's and went to the Play in the Evening."

28 "Again Dined at the Govr's and went to the Play and Ball in the Evening."

Dining at the Govr's.

Mr. Paca's Way to Dress Crabs

Sippets   Thin Wafer Biscuits

A Brown Fricassee   Broiled Partridges

Spiced Ham   Veal and Oyster Pie

Roast on a Spit

Sally Lunn

Walnut Catsup   Green Tomato Soy

Jerusalem Artichokes   Broccoli   Summer Squash

Ice Creams   Brandied Fruits   Syllabubs   Trifles

Green Sweetmeats   Almack's Preserve

Nogs, Cordials and Punches

COCK-FIGHTING

"The pittens entered a circle formed of plank staked up, the spectators ranged themselves around outside. The cocks were held up together to see if they were ready for the combat. They answered yes by pecking fiercely at each other's eyes. The protagonists then retired to opposite limits of the circle, and set their principals on the ground. These strutted about for a moment, eyeing each other askance, and then, flapping their wings, poured forth clarion notes of mutual defiance.

This was the signal for the onset. They advanced, squared themselves, and incontinently pitched into each other. For a moment they struck rapidly, hitting and dodging like practiced boxers, but becoming entangled, they tumbled over together, the Black above. "Hung!" exclaimed Woodpecker, "handle 'em." "Stand back!" shouted Greencoat, "He's in the feathers!" "You're in my wing," replied Woodpecker, and took up his bird. They examined the birds and set them down again.

There was no preliminary strutting this time. As soon as they touched the ground, they rushed to the combat. After some smart rapping without apparent result, the cocks seemed to be getting a little blown. The Spangle got his head under the Black's wing, and they both stood panting for some minutes in this position.

The Spangle appeared to be seriously revolving something in his mind, and it was perceived that blood was dripping from his neck. At the third round the Spangle, instead of meeting the Black's advance, took to his heels. The Black pursued him to the barrier, giving him a rap behind which helped him over. Away he went, pursued by half a dozen boys with mingled shouts of derision and merriment. "Kill him! Cut his head off!" Used up were the ribald expressions which followed the ignominious bird.

The victor behaved himself much like a gentleman. Leaping upon the barrier, he saw his recreant adversary in full flight. Disdaining to pursue, for the truly brave is never truculent, he hopped back into the pit, proclaimed his victory as it was his bounden duty to do, and then quietly suffered himself to be taken and disarmed."

Found in the 1814 Account Book, several pages of which had been neatly and discreetly cut out. Could Spangle and other 'ignominious' birds have been responsible for an adverse balance?

Cock-Fighting

TOBACCO IN MARYLAND

Tobacco has been grown in Maryland since the founding year, 1634. Corn was already under cultivation by the Indians, but notwithstanding bountious supplies of food, the Maryland General Assembly soon passed a law compelling the planting of two acres of corn for each acre of tobacco. Experience had shown that too much emphasis on tobacco, the money crop, and not enough on basic food might prove disastrous. Thus Maryland was the only one of the three first permanent English settlements to survive its formative years without partial devastation by starvation, fire or massacre.

During the 17th and into the 18th centuries tobacco was used as a medium of exchange. Towns and villages were slow to develop in this tobacco colony as vessels, loading for export, anchored in the many creeks and rivers near the source of supply. Maryland's first roads were ways cleared for rolling tobacco hogsheads from the drying sheds to the ship landings. These were called "rolling roads".

Besides the business of growing, shipping and trading in tobacco, the "noxious weed" was in great demand for smoking in taverns and gentlemen's clubs alike. One of the original rules for entertaining at the Ancient South River Club was that the steward provide pipes and tobacco as well as food and drink. When the popular Jonas Green, publisher of the Maryland Gazette, was admitted into the Tuesday Club, he responded to the toast with, "May good fellowship dispel every cloud that may threaten us, excepting on that of Tobacco, the dear specific condensator of political conceptions." When Mr. William Thornton proposed that the use of long clay pipes be dispensed with, the President's excepted, he was voted down.

Most of Maryland's early fortunes can be attributed either directly or indirectly to the growing of tobacco. Many planters were also merchants, and receipts from exported tobacco were invested in various goods and commodities which were, in turn, sold at great profit. This made possible the gracious plantation living of the Colonial period and the building of so many fine 17th and 18th century houses in and about the tidal regions. It was not, however, until the mid-18th century that early tobacco fortunes were reflected in the building of fine town houses, as in Annapolis. There the noted hospitality of the Maryland manor was the pattern for the more sophisticated social life of the Town.

Today, more than three centuries later, tobacco is still the money crop in most of Maryland's southern counties.

M. E. Warren

Cutting Tobacco, Southern Maryland

A. Aubrey Bodine

Air-Curing Tobacco

Seal of Maryland

Postscript

THE ACT OF TOLERATION

The Act of Toleration, passed by the General Assembly in 1649 with the hearty concurrence of Lord Baltimore, provided for the unrestricted freedom of conscience in Maryland.

By virtue of this Act (liberally interpreted), the users of this book are encouraged to employ such utensils, materials, methods and devices as may be designed to save them time and patience. It is understood, however, that such usage should in no way interfere with the preparation of a dish to perfection, or otherwise injure or impair the three hundred year old tradition of open door and abundant table to which the Marylander is somewhat consciously devoted.

To the prodigality of Nature in this "Land of Sanctuary", may be added the inventiveness of Man.

Some Articles and Devices Subject to the Unrestricted Freedom of Conscience

The New

Controlled-heat Stoves	Rotisseries
Refrigerators	Mixers
Deep Freezes	Blenders
Thermometers	Pressure Cookers
Frozen Foods	Canned Foods
Accurate Measures	Aluminum Foil

The Old

Soap Stone Griddles	Muffin Rings
Iron Skillets	Turks Head Pans
Nutmeg Graters	Patty Pans
The Punch Bowl	The Tureen
The Herb Garden	The Preserve Shelf
The Oaken Plank	Water-Ground Meal

Acknowledgments

The editors wish to express sincere thanks to the Marylanders who kindly shared their treasured family receipts to provide the basis for this collection; and to the Maryland House and Garden Pilgrimage, Historic Annapolis, Inc., the Department of Tidewater Fisheries and the editors of "Maryland Conservationist" and "The Skipper Magazine" for assistance generously offered.

For skillfully depicting the Maryland scene, we are grateful to photographers and artists A. Aubrey Bodine, Francis E. Engle, Marion E. Warren, Fred Thomas, Marina Hiatt, Claire Leighton, John W. Taylor, John Moll and Don Swann.

Mrs. Beverly C. Compton and Mrs. J. Dorsey Brown, as original committee chairman and treasurer, undertook the first printing of "Maryland's Way" with the enthusiastic guidance of Mr. Willard E. Brown of Judd and Detweiler, and gave unstintingly of their time and efforts to ensure the success of early editions.

Our printers, Victor Graphics, Inc. of Baltimore, have continued to maintain the high standards established originally by Washington press Judd and Detweiler.

Through the years the Hammond-Harwood House Association has given cooperative support to the small group of volunteers responsible for the book's distribution, promotion and reprinting.

Old Annapolis Town 1858

The Port of Annapolis

For 300 years entertainment of the traveler has been a tradition in Annapolis, Maryland's principal pre-revolutionary seaport. The first inn was established in the 1600's, and within the century visitors who came to town by ship, sailing ferry, and stagecoach ecstatically referred to Annapolis as "the most genteel city in the colonies". They enjoyed an atmosphere compounded of splendid new State House, Georgian mansions, "justly famous taverns", such as "Harp and Crown" and "King of France", and the salty air of a busy tobacco port. Along the old streets running from water's edge to towngate were shops of perukemakers, silversmiths, cabinetmakers, sailmakers and tobacconists. At night there were pleasant diversions of theatres, balls and good company at the inns and taverns.

Often the visitor enjoying the pleasant living of Maryland's capital city was here on business of Crown and Colony and thus concerned with the noted events of historic interest that took place in Annapolis. Today, Historic Annapolis, Inc., is working to save the ancient buildings of the Port of Annapolis that they may ever remind us of the period that saw the birth of our nation.

Index

BEVERAGES

Blackberry Cordial, 327
Cherry Bounce, 327
Claret Cup, 329
Egg-Nog
   Commodore Mahan's, 328
   Howard County, 328
   Magruder Family, 328
   Milk, 327
"on Entertaining", 326
Mint Julep—"The Quintessence of
   Gentlemanly Beverages", 330
Mulled Wine, 336
Punch
   Admiral Buchanan's Famous
      Egyptian, 329
   Amber Fruit, 334
   Claret, Valentine's, 329
   Decatur House, 334
   Farmer's Bishop, A Christmas
      Punch, 333
   a Fine Bodied, 333
   Great Neck, 334
   Peggy Stewart Tea, 332
   Port of Annapolis, 337
   White Wine, 336
Raspberry Shrub, Maryland, 335
Toddy, Apple 335
   Hot Apple, 335
Wassail, 336

BREADS

Biscuits

Beaten, Miss Julia's, 27
Buttermilk, 25
Hot, 25
Maryland, 27
Moonshines, 28
Rosemary, 25
Thin Wafer, 28
Vandalusia, 27

Corn Breads

Batter Bread, Riverside Farm, 32
Cakes, Corn, 34
Corn Bread, Elizabeth, 29
   Spider, 31
Hoe Cake, 30
Johnny Cake, 30
Muffins, 22
Mush, Fried, 29
Scratch Backs, 29

Spoon Bread, Auntie's, 32
   Southern, 32
Sticks, Cornmeal, 31
   Atholl Corn, 31
Wafers, Corn, 30

Griddle Cakes and Pancakes

Buckwheat, Old-Fashioned, 33
   South River Club, 33
Buttermilk, 34
Corn, 34
French Pancakes, 35
'Panne' Cakes, Shrove Tuesday, 34

Light Bread and Rolls

Fried Bread, 20
Generals, 19
Ivy Neck Light Bread, 19
Rolls, Hot, 20
   Jubilee, 20
   Potato, 21
Salt Sticks, 21
Sippets, 19

Muffins

Berry, 23
Buttermilk, 22
Cornmeal, 22
Crumpets, 24
Good-Morning, 23
Laplanders, 24
Popovers, 24
Sally Lunn, 39

Sweet Buns

Amish Bun, Garrett County, 37
Cinnamon Rolls, 37
Coffee Cake, 39
   Raisin, 39
Rusk, Mr. Paca's, 38

Waffles

Confederate, 36
Liza's, 36
Rice, Superior, 36
West River, 35

CAKES

Ambrosia, 274
Applesauce, 274
Birthday, 273
Black Walnut, 275
Chocolate, Black, Miss Sue Mumford's,
   274
Cocoanut, Fresh, 276

367

Maryland's Way

THE *Hammond-Harwood House* COOK BOOK
19 Maryland Avenue, Annapolis, Md. 21401

Name _____

Street _____

City _____ **State** _____ **Zip** _____

Please send _____ copies of Maryland's Way at $15.95 per copy. (Maryland residents include sales tax.)

Mailing charges: U.S.A., $1.50; Canada and Foreign Countries, $1.55

Enclosed is my check or money order for $ _____

---

cut along this line

Maryland's Way

THE *Hammond-Harwood House* COOK BOOK
19 Maryland Avenue, Annapolis, Md. 21401

Name _____

Street _____

City _____ **State** _____ **Zip** _____

Please send _____ copies of Maryland's Way at $15.95 per copy. (Maryland residents include sales tax.)

Mailing charges: U.S.A., $1.50; Canada and Foreign Countries, $1.55

Enclosed is my check or money order for $ _____

---

cut along this line

Maryland's Way

THE *Hammond-Harwood House* COOK BOOK
19 Maryland Avenue, Annapolis, Md. 21401

Name _____

Street _____

City _____ **State** _____ **Zip** _____

Please send _____ copies of Maryland's Way at $15.95 per copy. (Maryland residents include sales tax.)

Mailing charges: U.S.A., $1.50; Canada and Foreign Countries, $1.55

Enclosed is my check or money order for $ _____

... Crumbs or ... a half of ...
half a pint of milk 3 or 6 spoonsful
and let it boil three hours

Soda — 2 Scruples
—— 2 Do
—— 2 Do
... 1/2 ounce
boiling water to be ...
... ingredients ...
... taken every ...

J. Lockerman
the North East
Castle

... with a little ...
Mrs Hester Chase

the best except that
over was
... of the round
... a gallon of water
... add a little
... toasted and ...
... any fat more ...
throw, a softer a ...
... for Such people
Mrs Chase
... Make Yeast
... of hops boiled in
strain it and Buckwheat
... thick as fritters

24

Black Cake
Butter one pound
Sugar one pound
Flour one pound
Currents Two pounds
Raisins Two pounds
Citron 1/4 pound
Nutmegs 2. Mace one
... to your taste
Brandy & Rose w...
... Rose w...

... Calfs head with the ...
which must be cut into pieces ...
Clean these well, dry them in a
... with four quarts of ... bro...
... take six or seven pounds of b...
... two Carrots, a turnip, a shank ...
and whole pepper a bunch of sw...
Truffles, and eight quarts of ...
broth be reduced to four qua...
... above directed Then ...
..., a little savory, thyme
... Then add some ...
cayan pepper som...
... mushrooms
... together gen...
... that a ...
...

them. Season with pepper,
and mace; Just before yo...
them up add a half a pin...
Cream.

To Dress ...
Take out the meat and ...
from the Skin put it in ...
Stew pan with half a pin...
white wine, a little ...
... and Salt, over a slow ...
throw in a few crumbs of ...
heat up one Yolk of an ...
with one spoonful of vi...
then shake the Sauce ...
round a minute, and ...
... upon a plate.